PUB QUIZ BOOK

PAUL DREW

STOPWATCH

This edition published by
Stopwatch Publishing Limited
1-7 Shand Street
London SE1 2ES

for
Bookmart Limited
Desford Road
Enderby
Leicester
LE9 5AD

This edition published 2000

Printed and bound in Finland

Written and compiled by Paul Drew

© Stopwatch Publishing Limited

ISBN 1 900032 14 7

FOREWORD

Welcome to the Carling Pub Quiz Book.

To my mind there are three types of pub quizzer. The first is the punter who usually goes down to his or her local each week to do battle with the three blokes in the corner who win every time, usually getting 19 out of 20 into the bargain. There is the joiner-in who gamely tries to impress their partner or chip in with the odd nugget on their specialist area of knowledge - be it knowing the title of every episode of Star Trek, the natural habitat of the Dartford Warbler (heaths, as it happens), or the name of the lead singer with Oi!Zone, a skinhead boy band. (I'm hoping there isn't such a band, but you get the idea.) The third member of our trio is the drinker who steadfastly refuses at the beginning of the evening to take any part in the proceedings, then realises that he knows more than he thought he would and goes to the bar after eight questions to try and organize a quiz sheet and a pen.

The questions in this book will satisfy all of these people, containing as it does general knowledge that everyone should know, questions that can be dug out of the dark recesses of the mind after a bit of deep thought or another pint, and some that will turn also-rans into legends on the strength of one right answer.

Whether you're a film buff, a sports fanatic or just happen to know the year of the American Declaration of Independence because that was the afternoon you turned up for history class and it somehow stuck, this is the one for you.

Impress your friends!

Increase your knowledge!

Enjoy!

GENERAL KNOWLEDGE

ENTERTAINMENT

SPORT

POP MUSIC

ART AND LITERATURE

GEOGRAPHY

WORDS

SCIENCE

PEOPLE

HISTORY

GENERAL KNOWLEDGE

1. Josip Broz was the original name of which world leader?

2. What are the two main ingredients of the West Indian dish cou-cou?

3. A farrow is a litter of which farmyard animals?

4. Where on the body would you wear a heitiki?

5. Approximately how many million people visited Edinburgh Castle in 1990 - 1, 2 or 3?

6. Approximately how many million people spoke the Hungarian language in 1993?

7. What type of bird is a gadwall - a duck or a swan?

8. What is the German equivalent of the English surname Taylor?

9. There were 127 centres for the Samaritans in the U.K. in 1971. How many were there in 1981?

10. What is the young of a goose called?

11. What is the French name of the German city Aachen?

12. Which Russian word meaning 'restructuring' became popular in the 1980s?

13. In which year was Oliver Cromwell born?

14. What is the standard monetary unit of Bangladesh?

15. What was the most popular breed of pedigree cats registered in 1992?

ENTERTAINMENT

1. Which Hollywood actor narrated the 1981 series *Big Jim and the Figaro Club*?

2. In which year was the singer Placido Domingo born?

3. Which film was voted 1948 Best Motion Picture in the New York Film Critics Awards?

4. In which year was *Abba - the Movie* released?

5. Which writing duo penned the 1982 sitcom *The Further Adventures of Lucky Jim*?

6. Who played Tommy Devon in the 1974 series *The Zoo Gang*?

7. Who played Clark Gable in the 1976 film *Gable and Lombard*?

8. Who composed the music for the ballet *The Wooden Prince*?

9. Which duo from *Whose Line is it Anyway* starred in the 1992 sitcom *The Big One*?

10. In which year was comedian Jimmy Jewel born?

11. Who choreographed the 1951 ballet *Pineapple Poll*?

12. Who directed the 1997 film *The Game*?

13. Who was television's *The Gaffer*?

14. Who played Heinrich Himmler in the film *The Eagle Has Landed*?

15. Who did Liza Minnelli play in the 1972 film *Cabaret*?

SPORT

1. Who won the women's marathon title at the 1983 IAAF World Championships?

2. Who became the first president of the French Professional Footballers' Union in 1963?

3. Who was the 1993 world women's singles badminton champion?

4. Which cyclist won the 1998 Tour de France?

5. Who was the 1998 USPGA golf champion?

6. Which men's team won the European Club Champions Cup in hockey from 1988-95?

7. Which horse won the 1998 Grand National?

8. Who was men's open judo champion 1987-91?

9. Which country won the Thomas Cup in badminton in 1986, '88 & '90?

10. Which politician is the life president of the Raith Rovers Supporters Club?

11. Who was the 1988 Superbikes world champion in motor cycling?

12. Of which country was Imre Földi the greatest weightlifter?

13. In which year did Hank Aaron hit his 715th home run, breaking Babe Ruth's record of 714?

14. To what did basketball player Lew Alcindor change his name after embracing the Muslim faith?

15. In which year did leg-spin bowler Abdul Qadir make his Test debut for Pakistan?

ANSWERS 1. Grete Waitz **2.** Just Fontaine **3.** Susi Susanti **4.** Marco Pantani **5.** Vijay Singh **6.** Uhlenhorst Mülheim **7.** Earth Summit **8.** Naoya Ogawa **9.** China **10.** Gordon Brown **11.** Carl Fogarty **12.** Hungary **13.** 1973 **14.** Kareem Abdul-Jabbar **15.** 1977.

POP MUSIC

1. Who had a hit single with *Wordy Rappinghood*?

2. Which instrumental group charted with *The Ice Cream Man* in 1963?

3. Who recorded the 1999 album *Rides*?

4. What was the title of Echo and the Bunnymen's early 1999 album release?

5. What nationality was 1980's pop artist Nash the Slash?

6. Which Jamaican vocalist had a 1969 hit single with *Red Red Wine*?

7. On which label did Tracie chart in 1983 with *The House That Jack Built*?

8. Who produced the A.B.C. album *The Lexicon of Love*?

9. Which U.S. glam band recorded the album *Too Much Too Soon*?

10. On which 1982 studio L.P. did Van Morrison record *Cleaning Windows*?

11. What was Morrissey's first solo album called?

12. Which author is quoted on the back of Mott the Hoople's L.P. *Mott*?

13. What was T'Pau's follow-up single to the No. 1 *China in your Hand*?

14. Which T.Rex song did Bauhaus release as a single in late 1980?

15. Which group charted with *John Kettley (is a Weatherman)*?

ANSWERS 1. Tom Tom Club 2. The Tornados 3. Reef 4. What Are You Going To Do With Your Life 5. Canadian 6. Tony Tribe 7. Respond 8. Trevor Horn 9. New York Dolls 10. Beautiful Vision 11. Viva Hate 12. D.H. Lawrence 13. Valentine 14. Telegram Sam 15. Tribe of Toffs.

ART AND LITERATURE

1. Painter James Tissot's London house was near which cricket ground?

2. What was painter Augustus John's elder sister called?

3. On which island was bird illustrator John James Audubon born?

4. Whose novels include *Rabbit Run* and *Rabbit at Rest*?

5. In which 1947 novel did the character Geoffrey Firmin appear?

6. What are the names of Shakespeare's *Two Gentlemen of Verona*?

7. Who painted 1859's *Absinthe Drinker*?

8. Whose fables include 'Asleep with one eye open' and 'Crying wolf too often'?

9. Which German Expressionist painter was killed in the Battle of Verdun in 1916?

10. Whose books include *Vox* and *The Mezzanine*?

11. In which year did artist Henri Matisse die?

12. Which Scottish author wrote *The Wasp Factory*?

13. Who was the painter of 1878's *Snow at Louveciennes*?

14. Who wrote the poem *The Twa Dogs*?

15. What nationality was the painter Ando Hiroshige?

GENERAL KNOWLEDGE

1. Which size of paper is larger - A4 or A5?

2. The king, queen and jack in a pack of cards are known as court cards. What are they known as in the U.S.?

3. In sport, what is fartlek also called?

4. What is the approximate population of Algiers in millions - 1.2, 1.7 or 2.2?

5. Who preceded Claudius I as Roman emperor?

6. In which city is the University of Surrey?

7. Who succeeded Binyamin Netanyahu as Israeli prime minister in 1999?

8. In which year did cosmonaut Yuri Gagarin die?

9. Which Labour cabinet minister died suddenly in May, 1999?

10. What does the French phrase 'raison d'être' mean?

11. Which birthstone is associated with the month of January?

12. In which year was athlete Harold Abrahams born?

13. In house purchasing what does MIRAS stand for?

14. In World War II what did the German phrase 'Drang nach Osten' mean?

15. Which famous fictional character's mother was Aase?

ANSWERS 1. A4 **2.** Face cards **3.** Interval training **4.** 1.7 million **5.** Caligula (Gaius Caesar) **6.** Guildford **7.** Ehud Barak **8.** 1968 **9.** Derek Fatchett **10.** Reason for being **11.** Garnet **12.** 1899 **13.** Mortgage interest relief at source **14.** Drive to the East **15.** Peer Gynt.

ENTERTAINMENT

1. Who played Billy Liar in a 1970's sitcom?

2. Who was voted 1949 Best Actor in the New York Film Critics Awards?

3. In which year did librettist Oscar Hammerstein II die?

4. Who played Det. Sgt. Tom Stone in the police drama *Z Cars*?

5. What was the character name of Samantha Janus in *Game On*?

6. Who directed the 1981 film *Gallipoli*?

7. Who played *The Abominable Doctor Phibes*?

8. Who composed music for the ballet *Romeo and Juliet,* which was first performed in 1938?

9. In which city was comedian Jimmy Logan born?

10. What was Sharon's surname in T.V.'s *Birds of a Feather*?

11. Who directed the 1970 film *The Games*?

12. Which composer's operas include 1772's *Ottone*?

13. Who directed the 1988 film *Earth Girls Are Easy*?

14. Who played *The Cable Guy* in the 1996 film?

15. Which Verdi opera was premiered in Florence in May, 1847?

ANSWERS 1. Jeff Rawle **2.** Broderick Crawford **3.** 1960 **4.** John Slater **5.** Mandy Wilkins **6.** Peter Weir **7.** Vincent Price **8.** Prokofiev **9.** Glasgow **10.** Theodopolopoudous **11.** Michael Winner **12.** Handel **13.** Julian Temple **14.** Jim Carrey **15.** Macbeth.

THE ULTIMATE PUB QUIZ BOOK

SPORT

1. Who was runner-up in the 1994 Formula 1 motor racing world championship?

2. Which team were Scottish football league champions from 1905-1910?

3. Who is the only Yorkshire wicket-keeper to have made 1000 runs in a season three times?

4. Which boxer lost to Tommy Morrison in a WBO world heavyweight title fight in June 1993?

5. Who won the women's marathon at the 1987 IAAF World Championships?

6. How many times was Arsenal player Ray Bowden capped for England?

7. Who did Manchester United defeat in the semi-final of the 1998/9 European Champions League?

8. What height in metres did Dick Fosbury jump to win the 1968 Olympic gold?

9. Where were the 1987 IAAF World Championships held?

10. Which country won the Uber Cup in badminton five times from 1984-92?

11. At what sport did Canadian Sid Abel excel?

12. Who was the 1924 Olympic mens 100m champion?

13. Rosemarie Ackermann won a 1976 Olympic gold at which field event?

14. What is the name of Philadelphia's American Football team?

15. Which Division One football league team were once known as St. Judes?

ANSWERS 1. Damon Hill 2. Celtic 3. David Bairstow 4. George Foreman 5. Rosa Mota 6. Six 7. Juventus 8. 2.24m 9. Rome 10. China 11. Ice hockey 12. Harold Abrahams 13. High jump 14. Philadelphia Eagles 15. Q.P.R.

POP MUSIC

1. Which female singer's surname is Gudmundsdottir?

2. Which female singer recorded the 1982 hit *Ieya*?

3. Who is lead singer with the group *Gay Dad*?

4. Under what name do Paul and Phil Hartnoll usually record?

5. What name did Frank Tovey record under in the 1980s?

6. 'Two fat persons, click, click, click...' - which Ian Dury song?

7. Which German group had a hit in 1982 with *Da da da*?

8. Who recorded the album *Quit Dreaming And Get On The Beam*?

9. Which group had hit singles in 1973 with *Crazy*, *Hypnosis* and *Dynamite*?

10. Who played lead guitar on *Champagne Supernova* by Oasis?

11. Which U.S. group recorded the 1978 album *The Modern Dance*?

12. What was Toto's highest placed U.K. single?

13. On which label did Ultrasound record their L.P. *Everything Picture*?

14. Which group recorded the album *Gentlemen Take Polaroids*?

15. Who recorded the 1999 album *The Marshall Suite*?

GEOGRAPHY

1. In which European country is the cathedral city of Breda?

2. Caen is the capital of which French department?

3. In which English county are the Clee Hills?

4. In which European country is the village of Fatima, a centre of Roman Catholic pilgrimage?

5. Drammen is a seaport in which European country?

6. Which village in West Yorkshire was the home of the Brontë sisters?

7. Des Moines is the capital of which U.S. state?

8. Mount Kosciusko is the highest peak in which continent?

9. In which ocean is the volcanic Lord Howe Island?

10. Off which English county do the Manacle Rocks, a dangerous reef, lie?

11. The Mosquito Coast is an area of which Central American country?

12. What is the capital of the Czech Republic?

13. On which bay is the Spanish seaside resort of Santander?

14. Which is larger, the Sudan or Chile?

15. Ujpest is an industrial suburb of which eastern European country?

GENERAL KNOWLEDGE

1. Which book did Miles Coverdale famously translate into English in 1535?

2. Which playing card is known as the Curse of Scotland?

3. Who wrote the 1901 play *Dance of Death*?

4. In which year did comedian Lenny Bruce die?

5. In Norse mythology from what type of tree was the first man created?

6. In Greek mythology, how many fates were there?

7. What nationality was the comic film actor Fernandel?

8. What would you do with a helicon - play it or dance it?

9. For what would you use Benesh notation?

10. Who was commander-in-chief of British forces at Bunker Hill in 1775?

11. In which year was the Chinese Cultural Revolution?

12. Which Jules Verne character is associated with the submarine *Nautilus*?

13. Where are the resort beaches of Meadfoot, Oddicombe, and Redgate?

14. Who was the beaten Wimbledon men's singles tennis finalist in 1974?

15. Which gulf separates the Red Sea from the Arabian Sea?

ANSWERS 1. The Bible **2.** Nine of Diamonds **3.** August Strindberg **4.** 1966 **5.** Ash **6.** Three **7.** French **8.** Play it - it's a musical instrument **9.** Recording the movements of a ballet **10.** Thomas Gage **11.** 1966 **12.** Captain Nemo **13.** Torquay **14.** Ken Rosewall **15.** Gulf of Aden.

ENTERTAINMENT

1. Which stand up comedian hosted the 1997 comedy show *Gas*?

2. Who was voted 1950 Best Actress in the New York Film Critics Awards?

3. What nationality is conductor and composer Okko Kamu?

4. Who played *Abraham Lincoln* in a 1930 film?

5. Who directed the 1980 comedy film *Caddyshack*?

6. Who played Mrs. Miggins in *Blackadder the Third*?

7. Who played Wilbur Post in the T.V. comedy *Mr. Ed*?

8. Who won the 1951 Best Direction accolade in the New York Film Critics Awards?

9. Which comic actress plays bubbly Gayle Tuesday?

10. Who starred as *Gandhi* in a 1982 film?

11. Which composer's operas include 1782's *Orlando Paladino*?

12. 'The Slave of Duty' is the subtitle of which operetta by Gilbert & Sullivan?

13. Which entertainer was born in Rothwell, Northamptonshire, in 1935?

14. Who directed the 1987 film *Gardens of Stone*?

15. Who was awarded a Best Supporting Actress Oscar for her role in *East of Eden*?

ANSWERS 1. Lee Mack **2.** Bette Davis **3.** Finnish **4.** Walter Huston **5.** Harold Ramis **6.** Helen Atkinson Wood **7.** Alan Young **8.** Elia Kazan **9.** Brenda Gilhooly **10.** Ben Kingsley **11.** Haydn **12.** The Pirates of Penzance **13.** Jim Dale **14.** Francis Coppola **15.** Jo Van Fleet.

SPORT

1. For which rugby league club did Neil Fox make his debut in 1956?

2. Who trained Aldaniti to win the 1981 Grand National?

3. Which team won Superbowl XV in 1981, beating Philadelphia 27-10?

4. Which two Italian teams contested the 1991 UEFA Cup Final?

5. Who was European men's singles badminton champion from 1992-96?

6. Which cyclist won the 1997 Tour de France?

7. Which football team does Alastair Campbell, chief press secretary to Tony Blair, support?

8. What job did bowls player Janet Ackland do prior to turning professional in 1980?

9. In which city was tennis player Andre Agassi born?

10. What nationality was motor cyclist Giacomo Agostini?

11. Who was Spencer Oliver fighting in 1998 when a punch left him brain damaged?

12. Who was Pakistan's top scorer in their 1999 cricket World Cup Group B game against Scotland?

13. Who won the women's 100m hurdles at the 1993 & '95 IAAF World Championships?

14. Wigan rugby league player Wes Davies is the grandson of which rugby league star?

15. Which football team were Scottish League runners-up from 1923-26?

POP MUSIC

1. Which male singer recorded the 1982 album *Killer on the Rampage*?

2. Which Manchester group recorded the early 1980s L.P. *Pindrop*?

3. What was Gilbert O'Sullivan's debut L.P. called?

4. What was Roy Orbison's middle name?

5. Peter Perrett was singer/songwriter for which late 1970s punk band?

6. Which make of guitar is Wreckless Eric holding on the cover of his debut L.P.?

7. Whose 1979 live album was called *Live Rust*?

8. Which group recorded the song *There's no lights on the Christmas tree, mother, they're burning Big Louie tonight* on the album *Framed*?

9. Which punk band recorded the 1978 album *The Scream*?

10. What was Slade's first No. 1 single?

11. Ron and Russell Mael form the basis of which group?

12. Which duo comprised the group Soft Cell?

13. Which actor features on the cover of *The Queen is Dead* by The Smiths?

14. Which member of the Velvet Underground produced Patti Smith's L.P. *Horses*?

15. Which songwriting duo wrote the song *Itchycoo Park*?

ANSWERS 1. Eddy Grant 2. The Passage 3. Himself 4. Kelton 5. The Only Ones 6. Rickenbacker 7. Neil Young & Crazy Horse 8. The Sensational Alex Harvey Band 9. Siouxsie & the Banshees 10. Cos I Luv You 11. Sparks 12. Marc Almond and David Ball 13. Alain Delon 14. John Cale 15. Steve Marriott and Ronnie Lane.

HISTORY

1. Who was Israeli prime minister from 1948-53?

2. In which year was Malta awarded the George Cross?

3. In which year did Martin Luther nail his 95 Theses to the Wittenberg Church door?

4. In which year was the Croix de Guerre instituted in France?

5. Which London institution moved from Throgmorton St. to Old Broad St. in 1972?

6. In which year was Desmond Tutu made archbishop of Cape Town?

7. What was the official residence of the N. Ireland prime minister until 1972?

8. Who succeeded Indira Gandhi in 1977 as prime minister of India?

9. In which year was Joan of Arc burnt at the stake?

10. Which famous diamond was presented to Edward VII in 1907?

11. Who succeeded François Mitterand as French president in 1995?

12. In which year was Sir Thomas More executed?

13. In which year did the Shakespeare Memorial Theatre at Stratford-on-Avon burn down?

14. Where in Pennsylvania was there a major nuclear accident in 1979?

15. In which year did Ivan the Terrible become Tsar of Russia?

ANSWERS 1. David Ben Gurion 2. 1942 3. 1517 4. 1915 5. London Stock Exchange 6. 1986 7. Stormont 8. Morarji Desai 9. 1431 10. Cullinan diamond 11. Jacques Chirac 12. 1535 13. 1926 14. Three Mile Island 15. 1547.

GENERAL KNOWLEDGE

1. What is the marsh plant water hemlock also called?

2. In Russia what is a feldsher?

3. Which horse won the 1977 Grand National?

4. What creature is also called an ant bear?

5. Who wrote the novel *Smiley's People*?

6. Who was the companion of Don Quixote?

7. Which actor played the Joker in the television show *Batman*?

8. What is the name of the private eye in the novel *The Maltese Falcon*?

9. Which racecourse hosts the Irish Derby?

10. Who wrote the novels *Clarissa* and *Pamela*?

11. In Australia, what sort of animal is a brumby?

12. Which treaty ended the War of Spanish Succession?

13. Which prison was demolished following the death of Rudolf Hess?

14. Who became Secretary of State for War in 1960?

15. In which year did the collection of monies to fund the BBC first begin?

ENTERTAINMENT

1. What was Stephen Fry's character name in T.V.'s *Blackadder Goes Forth*?

2. Who played *The Absent-Minded Professor* in a 1961 film?

3. Who played Cleopatra in the 1946 film *Caesar and Cleopatra*?

4. In which city was choreographer Sir Kenneth Macmillan born?

5. Who originally hosted the T.V. game show *You Bet!*?

6. Who directed the 1976 film *Gator*?

7. Which music-hall entertainers were known as Gert and Daisy?

8. Who composed the opera *Cosi Fan Tutte*?

9. Which film won the Best Motion Picture accolade in the 1952 New York Film Critics Awards?

10. What was the character name of Jan Francis in *Just Good Friends*?

11. Who did Bonnie Langford play in the 1970's T.V. show *Just William*?

12. Which actor starred as Martin Sweet in the 1992 sitcom *Get Back*?

13. Who played Jerome Morrow in the 1997 film *Gattaca*?

14. Which singer played an underwater demolitions expert in the film *Easy Come, Easy Go*?

15. Who won the Best Actress accolade at the 1948 Golden Globe Awards?

ANSWERS 1. General Hogmanay Melchett **2.** Fred MacMurray **3.** Vivien Leigh **4.** Dunfermline **5.** Bruce Forsyth **6.** Burt Reynolds **7.** Elsie & Doris Waters **8.** Mozart **9.** High Noon **10.** Penny Warrender **11.** Violet Elizabeth Bott **12.** Ray Winstone **13.** Jude Law **14.** Elvis Presley **15.** Jane Wyman.

SPORT

1. Which golfer won the Algarve Open in April, 1999?

2. Who was the first man to win the Indianapolis 500 race four times?

3. Who was European women's singles badminton champion in 1990 & '92?

4. Who scored the only goal in the 1995 F.A. Cup Final?

5. Who won the women's 400m hurdles at the 1993 IAAF World Championships?

6. Who won the women's long jump in 1987 & '91 at the IAAF World Championships?

7. Who was the 1996 US Masters golf champion?

8. Which Toulouse Olympique rugby league player captained the French national side from 1969-70?

9. Which Ugandan won the 1972 Olympic men's 400m hurdles title?

10. Which Hungarian was 1967 European Footballer of the Year?

11. In which sport is the Henry Leaf Cup played for?

12. Where were the 1984 Summer Olympics held?

13. Which sport are Tian Bingye and Li Yongbo linked with?

14. At what racecourse are the 1,000 Guineas and 2,000 Guineas held?

15. At which golf course were the 1985 & '89 Ryder Cups held?

POP MUSIC

1. Which U.S. group recorded the 1985 L.P. *No Free Lunch*?

2. Who produced Gary Glitter's 1972 L.P. *Glitter*?

3. Who was the lead singer of the U.S. group *The Gun Club*?

4. Who is lead singer with the group James?

5. On which 1979 studio album did The Jam's song *The Eton Rifles* appear?

6. Joanne Catherall and Susanne Sulley are singers with which group?

7. What is the name of Courtney Love's group?

8. Which group's debut L.P. featured the song *Lemon Firebrigade*?

9. Who recorded the 1989 album *New York*?

10. Which blues artist wrote the song *Take Out Some Insurance*?

11. Which U.S. punk group had a hit with *Sheena is a Punk Rocker*?

12. Keith Reid and Gary Brooker were the songwriting force behind which group?

13. Charlie Reid and Craig Reid comprise which singing duo?

14. Who wrote the song *Simon Smith and the Amazing Dancing Bear*?

15. Which singer worked for the Crown Electric Company in 1953 as a truck driver?

ANSWERS 1. Green on Red 2. Mike Leander 3. Jeffrey Lee Pierce 4. Tim Booth 5. Setting Sons 6. The Human League 7. Hole 8. Haircut One Hundred 9. Lou Reed 10. Jimmy Reed 11. The Ramones 12. Procol Harum 13. The Proclaimers 14. Randy Newman 15. Elvis Presley.

WORDS

1. Which foodstuff is named after the French word for 'crescent'?

2. What is the name given to one of the 10 black-belt grades of proficiency in judo?

3. In anatomy, what is the dorsum better known as?

4. If something were falcate, what would it be shaped like?

5. What in heraldry is a 'fesse point'?

6. What method of transport in the U.S. is a jitney?

7. What is the card dealer at a gaming table called?

8. Which plant is named after the French phrase 'tooth of a lion'?

9. What is the name for a male duck?

10. What is the U.S. term for autumn?

11. What is a 'hug-me-tight'?

12. What animal is known in West Africa as a jocko?

13. The Curragh is an Irish racecourse. What is a curragh?

14. For what title is D.B.E. an abbreviation?

15. What is the name given to light rain whose droplets are less than 0.5mm in diameter?

ANSWERS 1. Croissant **2.** Dan **3.** The back **4.** A sickle **5.** The midpoint of a shield **6.** A small passenger-carrying bus **7.** Croupier **8.** Dandelion **9.** Drake **10.** Fall **11.** A woman's knitted jacket **12.** Chimpanzee **13.** Coracle **14.** Dame Commander of the Order of the British Empire **15.** Drizzle.

GENERAL KNOWLEDGE

1. Of what is Gaillard Cut a part?

2. Who wrote the play *The Night of the Iguana*?

3. For which 1979 film did Peter Sellers receive an Oscar nomination?

4. On which sea does the town of Morecambe stand?

5. Which mountain range contains the volcano Cotopaxi?

6. Who wrote the play *Noises Off*?

7. Which Verdi opera was first performed in Venice in 1853?

8. Who was England cricket captain in the 1986/7 Ashes series?

9. Who was German chancellor from 1930-32?

10. How much did it cost to post a standard first class letter in 1977?

11. What does the Latin phrase 'crambe repetita', meaning an old story, translate as?

12. Which of the Ten Commandments is 'Thou shalt not kill'?

13. What is the standard monetary unit of Albania?

14. In which year was actor Spencer Tracy born?

15. What is the approximate population of Cairo in millions - 7, 10 or 13?

ANSWERS 1. The Panama Canal **2.** Tennessee Williams **3.** Being There **4.** Irish Sea **5.** Andes **6.** Michael Frayn **7.** La Traviata **8.** Mike Gatting **9.** Heinrich Brüning **10.** 9p **11.** Cabbage repeated **12.** Sixth **13.** Lek **14.** 1900 **15.** 13 million.

ENTERTAINMENT

1. What was Maxwell Smart's agent number in *Get Smart*?

2. Who directed the 1989 film *The Abyss*?

3. Who composed the four act opera *The Maid of Orleans*?

4. Who won the Best Actress award at the 1959 Golden Globe Awards?

5. Who played Wild Bill Hickok in the 1953 film *Calamity Jane*?

6. Who voiced *Yogi Bear*?

7. About whom was the 1998 film *The General*?

8. Who composed the 1831 opera *Norma*?

9. Who played Kate in the sitcom *Kate & Allie*?

10. The 1988 film *The Accidental Tourist* was based on whose bestseller?

11. Who played Corporal Marsh in the 1970s sitcom *Get Some In!*?

12. Which comedian's characters include Dennis Pennis?

13. Who directed the 1953 film *Genevieve*?

14. Who directed the 1969 film *Easy Rider*?

15. Who played *Caligula* in the 1979 film of the same name?

ANSWERS 1. Agent 86 2. James Cameron 3. Tchaikovsky 4. Gloria Swanson 5. Howard Keel 6. Daws Butler 7. Martin Cahill 8. Bellini 9. Susan Saint James 10. Anne Tyler 11. Tony Selby 12. Paul Kaye 13. Henry Cornelius 14. Dennis Hopper 15. Malcolm McDowall.

SPORT

1. Who scored for Sunderland in their 1998/99 league fixture at Bradford City?

2. In which year was athlete Brendan Foster born?

3. Which former batsman coached the 1999 Bangladesh World Cup cricket side?

4. Which country did Astrid Kumbernuss represent in winning women's shot at the 1995 and '97 IAAF World Championships?

5. Which horse won the 1995 St. Leger?

6. Who was men's heavyweight judo champion 1979-83?

7. Which former world professional snooker champion was born in Wishaw?

8. In which year did rally driver Roger Clark die?

9. Which cricketer scored the earliest century in the history of the county championship on April 15, 1999?

10. Which former Sheffield United player managed Benfica, winning them three Portuguese league titles?

11. What was the nickname of baseball star Jimmy Foxx?

12. Where were the 1991 IAAF World Championships held?

13. Who scored the fourth goal for Brazil in the 1970 World Cup Final?

14. Which millionaire woman golfer won the U.S. girls' Junior Amateur title in 1973?

15. Which Australian bowler exceeded 40 wickets twice in a series against England, in 1981 & '89?

ANSWERS 1. Niall Quinn 2. 1948 3. Gordon Greenidge 4. Germany 5. Classic Cliché 6. Yasuhiro Yamashita 7. John Higgins 8. 1998 9. Dougie Brown 10. Jimmy Hagan 11. Double X 12. Tokyo 13. Carlos Alberto 14. Amy Alcott 15. Terry Alderman.

POP MUSIC

1. Which U.K. group's only Top Ten single was 1970s *Love Like a Man*?

2. On which label did Terrorvision record their hits *Oblivion* and *My House*?

3. Which singer recorded the hit albums *The Last Waltz* and *A Man without Love*?

4. Which group recorded the L.P. *Autoamerican*?

5. Which group recorded the album *Kings of the Wild Frontier*?

6. From which city did group Young Marble Giants hail?

7. On which studio album by Siouxsie and the Banshees did the single *Christine* appear?

8. What was Echo and the Bunnymen's debut single?

9. On what date did John Lennon die?

10. Which U.S. group featured the talents of Black Francis and Mrs. John Murphy?

11. What is the girl's name in Pulp's song *Disco 2000*?

12. The 1981 album *Talk Talk Talk* was recorded by the group Talk Talk - true or false?

13. What is unusual about the cover of the 1979 L.P. *The Return of the Durutti Column*?

14. Who recorded the album *New Boots and Panties*?

15. Who is the driving force behind the group *The The*?

ANSWERS 1. Ten Years After **2.** Total Vegas **3.** Engelbert Humperdinck **4.** Blondie **5.** Adam and the Ants **6.** Cardiff **7.** Kaleidoscope **8.** Pictures on my Wall **9.** December 8, 1980 **10.** The Pixies **11.** Deborah **12.** False, it is by the Psychedelic Furs **13.** It is covered in sandpaper **14.** Ian Dury **15.** Matt Johnson.

SCIENCE

1. Which is the thinnest of the earth's three crustal types - transitional, oceanic or continental?

2. During which era was the Jurassic period of geological time?

3. What is an aquifer?

4. On the Mohs scale of hardness what is No. 8?

5. What do the letters AC stand for in electrical appliances?

6. Which Hungarian-born Nobel prize winner is credited with the invention of holography?

7. What in physical geography is an erg?

8. What is the melting point in °C of carbon?

9. What is the symbol for the element actinium?

10. What is the name given to an angle of less than 90° in mathematics?

11. What in geological terms is creep?

12. Who discovered the element thorium?

13. In which year did English chemist Henry Cavendish die?

14. What is the mass of partially decomposed organic matter in soil called?

15. Which German bacteriologist, born in 1854, pioneered the science of chemotherapy?

GENERAL KNOWLEDGE

1. In which country was architect Le Corbusier born?

2. Who replaced John Reid as transport minister in May 1999?

3. What does A&R stand for in the music industry?

4. Which poet is associated with Dove Cottage in Grasmere?

5. Abbotsford was the home of which Scottish author?

6. What are usually kept in an earthenware pot called a gallipot?

7. In what card game might you use the Culbertson system?

8. Who wrote the 1932 play *Dangerous Corner*?

9. What type of art form is Hans Henze's *The Tedious Way to the Place of Natasha Ungeheuer*?

10. Who wrote the novel *Caravan to Vaccares*?

11. Who was the Roman god of wine?

12. On what island is the volcano Askja?

13. In which year was Queen Elizabeth II born?

14. What was the original name of entertainer Tommy Steele?

15. In which ocean are the Marquesas Islands?

ANSWERS 1. Switzerland **2.** Helen Liddell **3.** Artists and Repertoire **4.** William Wordsworth **5.** Sir Walter Scott **6.** Ointments **7.** Bridge **8.** J.B. Priestley **9.** An opera **10.** Alistair Maclean **11.** Bacchus **12.** Iceland **13.** 1926 **14.** Thomas Hicks **15.** Pacific Ocean.

ENTERTAINMENT

1. What was the name of the family in the sitcom *Bless This House*?

2. Which film was voted Best Motion Picture (Drama) at the 1952 Golden Globe Awards?

3. Who directed the 1951 film *Ace in the Hole*?

4. Who starred as Peter Mayle in the unpopular T.V. drama *A Year In Province*?

5. What was Dudley Rush's profession in the 1980's sitcom *Keep It In The Family*?

6. Who composed the 1775 opera *The Shepherd King*?

7. Who played Mrs. Muir in the U.S. sitcom version of the film *The Ghost and Mrs. Muir*?

8. What was Patricia Routledge's character called in *Keeping Up Appearances*?

9. What was the name of Hank's wife in the cartoon series *King of the Hill*?

10. What nationality is composer R. Murray Shafer?

11. Which comedian created the character Kevin Turvey?

12. Who directed the 1970 film *Claire's Knee*?

13. What animal was *Ed* in a 1996 film starring Matt LeBlanc?

14. Which comedian starred in the 1963 film *Call Me Bwana*?

15. What does Schubert's song-cycle *Die Schöne Müllerin* translate as?

ANSWERS 1. The Abbotts **2.** The Greatest Show on Earth **3.** Billy Wilder **4.** John Thaw **5.** Cartoonist **6.** Mozart **7.** Hope Lange **8.** Hyacinth Bucket **9.** Peggy **10.** Canadian **11.** Rik Mayall **12.** Eric Rohmer **13.** Chimpanzee **14.** Bob Hope **15.** The Fair Maid of the Mill.

SPORT

1. Who was European women's singles badminton champion in 1996 & '98?

2. Which Premier League football team does Chief Secretary to the Treasury Alan Milburn support?

3. At which sport does Graham Garden play for Great Britain?

4. In which year did Adi Dassler make his first pair of running shoes?

5. Who rode Midnight Court to win the Cheltenham Gold Cup in 1978?

6. Which Scottish football team were League Champions from 1928-31?

7. Who was runner-up in the 1995 world Formula 1 motor racing championship?

8. Which woman won the 1980 Boston marathon but was later discovered to have run only the last two miles of it?

9. In which year did Grant Fox make his All Black debut in rugby union?

10. Which team won the 1995 world series in baseball?

11. Which Finn won the 1000 Lakes Rally from 1978-80?

12. In which year did Muhammad Ali regain the world heavyweight title from George Foreman?

13. At what sport did American Elizabeth Allan-Shetter excel?

14. Who finished third in the 1993 Belgian Grand Prix?

15. Who was the Australian Open men's singles title winner in 1989 & '90?

ANSWERS 1. Camilla Martin 2. Newcastle United 3. Ice hockey 4. 1920 5. John Francombe 6. Rangers 7. Damon Hill 8. Rosie Ruiz 9. 1985 10. Atlanta Braves 11. Markku Alen 12. 1974 13. Water skiing 14. Alain Prost 15. Ivan Lendl.

POP MUSIC

1. Who had a No. 2 single in 1977 with *Ain't Gonna Bump No More (With No Big Fat Woman)*?

2. Which artist recorded the albums *Rebel Yell* and *Whiplash Smile*?

3. Who was lead singer with the group Amen Corner?

4. Which songwriting duo penned *Sittin' on a Fence* for 1960s act Twice As Much?

5. Which group recorded the album *Thirty Thousand Feet Over China*?

6. Which singer formed the group Doll By Doll in 1977?

7. Brian Eno's song *King's Lead Hat* was intentionally an anagram of which group?

8. Whose hit singles included *Metal Guru* and *Truck On (Tyke)*?

9. Which vocal group's hits included *Psychedelic Shack* and *My Girl*?

10. Which U.S. band had a 1977 hit album with *Marquee Moon*?

11. Who was lead singer with The Undertones?

12. Which 1960's icon recorded the 1983 album *Climate of Hunter*?

13. John Foxx was lead singer with which latterly successful punk band?

14. Who recorded the 1981 L.P. *The Flowers of Romance*?

15. On which label did Them record the 1965 hit *Here Comes the Night*?

ANSWERS 1. Joe Tex **2.** Billy Idol **3.** Andy Fairweather Low **4.** Jagger/Richard **5.** The Passions **6.** Jackie Leven **7.** Talking Heads **8.** T.Rex **9.** Temptations **10.** Television **11.** Feargal Sharkey **12.** Scott Walker **13.** Ultravox **14.** Public Image Limited **15.** Decca.

PEOPLE

1. Which Cuban dictator was overthrown by Castro in 1959?

2. Who became King of Belgium in 1951?

3. Who became Queen of the Netherlands in 1980?

4. Which model is married to Bon Jovi drummer Tico Torres?

5. Which Radio 2 presenter was suspended in April 1999 following allegations of drug use?

6. What is the home town of actress Gena Lee Nolin?

7. Who was Chairman of the British Railways Board from 1963-65?

8. Who was prime minister of Algeria from 1962-65?

9. Which American physical fitness expert developed the dynamic tension method of bodybuilding?

10. In which country was actress Isla Fisher, of T.V. show *Home and Away*, born?

11. Which former *EastEnders* actress sang in the pop group Milan?

12. Who is the female singer in the pop group No Doubt?

13. Which French actress was born in the tiny village of Gassin?

14. What is the surname of former Gossard model Caprice?

15. What is the name of the singer Baby Spice?

ANSWERS 1. Batista 2. Baudouin 3. Beatrix 4. Eva Herzigova 5. Johnnie Walker 6. Duluth, Minnesota 7. Richard Beeching 8. Ahmed Ben Bella 9. Charles Atlas 10. Saudi Arabia 11. Martine McCutcheon 12. Gwen Stefani 13. Emmanuelle Béart 14. Bourret 15. Emma Bunton.

GENERAL KNOWLEDGE

1. Bucephalus was the favourite horse of which historical figure?

2. Approximately how many people visited Shakespeare's birthplace in Stratford in 1991 - 300,000, 500,000 or 700,000?

3. In which city is the University of Strathclyde?

4. In which year did author Laurie Lee die?

5. Who in May 1999 became professor of poetry at Oxford?

6. What is the art of cutting hedges into ornamental shapes?

7. What was the middle name of Dame Ngaio Marsh?

8. Who was the biblical sister of Mary and Lazarus?

9. In which year was the Battle of the Falaise Gap in World War II?

10. Who wrote the 1925 play *Fallen Angels*?

11. What is the name given to the opening move in chess in which a chessman is sacrificed to secure an advantageous position?

12. What is the name of the fat knight in the play Henry IV?

13. What colour is the liqueur crème de menthe?

14. What is the Finnish name for Finland?

15. On which ship did Napoleon formally surrender after defeat at Waterloo?

ANSWERS 1. Alexander the Great 2. 500,000 3. Glasgow 4. 1997 5. Paul Muldoon 6. Topiary 7. Edith 8. Martha 9. 1944 10. Noël Coward 11. Gambit 12. Sir John Falstaff 13. Green 14. Suomi 15. HMS Bellerophon.

ENTERTAINMENT

1. In which year was Mike Yarwood born?

2. Who was voted Best Actor at the 1954 Golden Globe Awards?

3. What was the subtitle of 1995's *Ace Ventura* film?

4. Who played Blott in the 1985 T.V. comedy serial *Blott on the Landscape*?

5. Who played Geronimo in a 1962 film?

6. Who starred as Kit Curran in the T.V. comedy *The Kit Curran Radio Show*?

7. Who composed the 1812 opera Tancredi?

8. Who played Gilligan in the comedy series *Gilligan's Island*?

9. Which singer played the Goblin King in the 1986 film *Labyrinth*?

10. Who directed the 1997 film *L.A. Confidential*?

11. Which film was based on the Ted Lewis novel *Jack's Return Home*?

12. Who directed the 1957 film *Campbell's Kingdom*?

13. What nationality is composer Mikis Theodorakis?

14. Who scripted the 1997 film *The Edge*?

15. What nationality is conductor Karl Rickenbacher?

ANSWERS 1. 1941 2. Marlon Brando 3. When Nature Calls 4. David Suchet 5. Chuck Connors 6. Denis Lawson 7. Rossini 8. Bob Denver 9. David Bowie 10. Curtis Hanson 11. Get Carter 12. Ralph Thomas 13. Greek 14. David Mamet 15. Swiss.

SPORT

1. Who defeated Chelsea in the semi-final of the 1998/9 European Cup Winners' Cup?

2. Which boxer won a gold medal as a heavyweight at the 1964 Olympics?

3. What was the middle name of cricketer W.G. Grace?

4. Which swimmer was named Australian of the Year in 1967?

5. Who was 1964 Olympic men's 100m champion?

6. For which county side did cricketer Tom Graveney play from 1948-60?

7. Which team won Superbowl V in 1971 in American Football?

8. With which side did basketball star Walt Frazier end his playing career?

9. Who won the women's shot at the 1991 & '93 IAAF World Championships?

10. What was the winning boat in the 1995 America's Cup?

11. Which English Test cricketer was chairman of the Test selectors from 1955-61?

12. Who won the inaugural world men's triathlon championship in 1989?

13. Which team did Phog Allen coach in winning the 1952 Olympic basketball title?

14. What is the nationality of snooker player Doug Mountjoy?

15. In cycling, who won the 1993 World Road Race?

ANSWERS 1. Real Mallorca 2. Joe Frazier 3. Gilbert 4. Dawn Fraser 5. Bob Hayes 6. Gloucestershire 7. Baltimore Colts 8. Cleveland Cavaliers 9. Zhihong Huang 10. Black Magic I 11. Gubby Allen 12. Mark Allen 13. The U.S. 14. Welsh 15. Lance Armstrong.

POP MUSIC

1. On which label did Frankie Goes to Hollywood record their 1984 L.P. *Welcome to the Pleasuredome*?

2. Why did Peter Gabriel's 1986 studio album *So* differ from its four predecessors?

3. Which group's albums include *Heartbreaker* and *Fire and Water*?

4. Which Irish guitarist's albums included *Deuce* and *Tattoo*?

5. Who recorded 1978's *Well, well, said the Rocking Chair* L.P.?

6. Which groups albums included 1979's *The Adventures of the Hersham Boys*?

7. Which group had a No. 1 single with *Ebeneezer Goode*?

8. Which group had a No. 1 single in Thailand with the song *Ocean Pie*?

9. What is Texas-born singer Karen Johnson better known as?

10. Which duo recorded the 1966 album *Parsley, Sage, Rosemary and Thyme*?

11. Which group's debut album in 1979 was *Life in a Day*?

12. What was the first single of the band Simply Red?

13. Which U.S. singer's first single, in 1961, was *Cufflinks and a Tie Clip*?

14. Sahm, Kagan, Perez, Meyer and Morin - which 1960's band?

15. Which group were formed in Leeds in 1980 by Andrew Eldritch and Gary Marx?

ART AND LITERATURE

1. Who painted the *Garden of Earthly Delights*?

2. In which century did French painter Francois Boucher live?

3. Who was Poet Laureate from 1968-72?

4. Which French author wrote the novel *Germinal*?

5. Who painted *Sunday Afternoon on the Island of the Grande Jatte*?

6. In which city was artist Egon Schiele born?

7. Which British writer and illustrator wrote the 1946 manual *The Craft of the Lead Pencil*?

8. In which European city did the Phalanx group of artists form in 1901?

9. Which famous artist was born at Caprese, Italy, in 1475?

10. Which 19c English artist painted 1850's *Christ in the House of His Parents*?

11. Which Spanish artist designed the ballet *Jeux d'enfants* in 1932?

12. Which Irish author wrote the novellas *First Love* and *The Expelled*?

13. Which Russian author's books include *The Idiot* and *The Devils*?

14. Which U.S. author's children's books include *Superfudge*?

15. What was the controversial 1991 book by Bret Easton Ellis?

GENERAL KNOWLEDGE

1. What drink is the legendary Flemish king Gambrinus said to have invented?

2. Who wrote the novel *Cry, the Beloved Country*?

3. Which king of England was known as Farmer George?

4. From which football club did Coventry City sign Liam Daish?

5. Farringford was the home of which poet?

6. Argent is the poetic name for which metal?

7. On which bay is the town of Aberystwyth?

8. FIDE is the world federation of which sport?

9. As what is 'herpes labialis' better known?

10. What is the capital of the Netherlands?

11. Who wrote the book *Uncle Silas*?

12. What is the name given to the red ring on an archery target?

13. Who was the 1978 British Open golf champion?

14. Who wrote the play *The Zoo Story*?

15. Which farmyard animal suffers from the disease gapes?

ANSWERS 1. Beer **2.** Alan Paton **3.** George III **4.** Birmingham City **5.** Lord Tennyson **6.** Silver **7.** Cardigan Bay **8.** Chess **9.** A cold sore **10.** Amsterdam **11.** Sheridan Le Fanu **12.** Inner **13.** Jack Nicklaus **14.** Edward Albee **15.** Domestic fowl.

ENTERTAINMENT

1. Who directed the 1952 film *Actors and Sin*?

2. Which actor was born Cyril Louis Goldbert?

3. Which comedian wrote and starred in the 1994 comedy series *My Blue Heaven*?

4. Who directed the 1995 film *Get Shorty*?

5. Which actor won the Cecil B. DeMille Award at the 1966 Golden Globe Awards?

6. Who composed the opera *Gianni Schicchi*?

7. Who co-wrote and directed 1995's *The Glam Metal Detectives*?

8. Who directed the 1961 comedy film *The Ladies' Man*?

9. What was Angus Deayton's character name in the sketch show *KYTV*?

10. Who directed the 1994 film *Ladybird Ladybird*?

11. Which comedian was known as 'The Little Waster'?

12. Which private eye did Frank Sinatra play in the film *Lady in Cement*?

13. What nationality is harpsichordist and organist Kenneth Gilbert?

14. Who directed the 1990 film *Ghost*?

15. Who played *The Candidate* in a 1972 film?

ANSWERS 1. Ben Hecht **2.** Peter Wyngarde **3.** Frank Skinner **4.** Barry Sonnenfeld **5.** Charlton Heston **6.** Puccini **7.** Peter Richardson **8.** Jerry Lewis **9.** Mike Channel **10.** Ken Loach **11.** Bobby Thompson **12.** Tony Rome **13.** Canadian **14.** Jerry Zucker **15.** Robert Redford.

SPORT

1. What nationality is synchronized swimming champion Sylvie Fréchette?

2. Who was the 1997 US Masters golf champion?

3. What age was Steffi Graf when she won her first Grand Slam title in 1987?

4. In which make of car did Jones, Reuter and Wurtz win the 1996 Le Mans race?

5. How many century opening partnerships did Gordon Greenidge and Desmond Haynes record for the West Indies?

6. Following Liverpool's 2-1 defeat in the 1971 F.A. Cup Final, which was the next defeated team to register a goal in the final?

7. Which Scottish football team were runners-up in the League in 1933 & '34?

8. Which two Italian teams met in the 1990 UEFA Cup Final?

9. Which American Football star was known as 'the Galloping Ghost'?

10. Which boxer was born Thomas Rocca Barbella?

11. Who won the women's javelin title at the 1987 IAAF World Championships?

12. Who scored the only goal in the 1985 F.A. Cup Final?

13. Jose Altafini played for Brazil in the 1958 World Cup. Which country did he play for in the 1962 World Cup?

14. Which Briton won the 1952 Olympic women's figure skating title?

15. Which Texas-born American Football star of the 1960s was known as 'Bambi'?

ANSWERS 1. Canadian 2. Tiger Woods 3. 17 4. Porsche 5. 16 6. Liverpool, in 1977 7. Motherwell 8. Juventus and Fiorentina 9. Red Grange 10. Rocky Graziano 11. Fatima Whitbread 12. Norman Whiteside 13. Italy 14. Jeanette Altwegg 15. Lance Alworth.

POP MUSIC

1. What was the identity of Miss X, who had a hit single in 1963 with *Christine*?

2. Which girl singer recorded the 1998 album *Honey to the B*?

3. Who recorded the 1998 album *Decksandrumsandrockandroll*?

4. What was the title of Ringo Starr's 1998 solo album?

5. Which female singer recorded the 1999 album *Central Reservation*?

6. Which trio recorded the 1994 hit single *All For Love*?

7. Who had a 1981 hit single with *Swords of a Thousand Men*?

8. What was the title of Whitney Houston's 1987 No. 1 album?

9. Perrin, Wright, Finney, Nicholls, Sidebottom - which 1980s Manchester group?

10. Which member of the Police recorded under the name of Klark Kent?

11. Which group's albums included Fickle Heart and *The Game's Up*?

12. Who was lead guitarist with the band Roxy Music?

13. What was the name of The Beat's elderly Jamaican saxophone player?

14. Which punk group recorded the album *Kiss Me Deadly*?

15. Who produced the 1979 debut L.P. by The Specials?

GEOGRAPHY

1. What is the capital of Uzbekistan?

2. In which country of the Americas is the state of Tabasco?

3. In which European country is the town of Schiedam, which is associated with the gin industry?

4. In which African country is Ujiji, meeting place of Stanley and Livingstone?

5. In which European country is the resort town of Spa?

6. Sandbach is a market town in which English county?

7. In which U.S. state is the tourist town of Redondo Beach?

8. On which river is the motor car manufacturing town of Pontiac?

9. Which Italian city lies at the foot of Mount Vesuvius opposite ancient Pompeii?

10. In which South American country is the oil refining town of Moron?

11. Which is larger - Massachusetts or Maine?

12. Which strait separates Chile and Tierra del Fuego?

13. On which river is Louisville, Kentucky?

14. In which English county is the holiday resort of Looe?

15. In which island group is Ibiza?

GENERAL KNOWLEDGE

1. What is the nickname of Sheffield Wednesday F.C.?

2. Who is Conservative M.P. for Billericay?

3. What would you do with Atholl brose - drink it or plant it?

4. Who composed the opera *Porgy and Bess*?

5. In which book by Charles Dickens does the Fat Boy appear?

6. What location was the setting for the hotel-based soap opera *Crossroads*?

7. In which department is the French tourist resort St. Tropez?

8. In which year did dancer Martha Graham die?

9. What sort of animal is a bufflehead - a snake or a duck?

10. For what does the abbreviation HGV stand?

11. How many are in a gross?

12. What was the first book in the Father Brown series?

13. Who directed the 1993 film *Manhattan Murder Mystery*?

14. Which ancient Egyptian goddess is usually depicted as having cow's horns?

15. Which naval officer marries *Madame Butterfly* in Puccini's opera?

ANSWERS 1. The Owls 2. Teresa Gorman 3. Drink it - it's whisky and honey 4. George Gershwin 5. Pickwick Papers 6. King's Oak 7. Var 8. 1991 9. A duck 10. Heavy goods vehicle 11. 144 12. The Innocence of Father Brown 13. Woody Allen 14. Isis 15. Pinkerton.

ENTERTAINMENT

1. In which year did T.V. animal trainer Barbara Woodhouse die?

2. What was the subtitle of Mahler's Symphony No. 2 in C minor?

3. In which year was football commentator Kenneth Wolstenholme born?

4. Which comedian and pianist was born Borg Rosenbaum in Copenhagen in 1909?

5. Who directed the 1984 comedy *Ghostbusters*?

6. Who composed the 1840 comic opera *King for a Day*?

7. Who played Ron Glum in the 1978 sitcom *The Glums*?

8. Which film won the award for Best Original Score at the 1967 Golden Globes?

9. Who played the title role in the 1972 film *Lady Caroline Lamb*?

10. Who starred as *The Admirable Crichton* in a 1957 film?

11. Who played Ronnie Barker's son Raymond in the sitcom *Going Straight*?

12. Who starred as Lester in the 1982 sitcom *L for Lester*?

13. Who directed the 1956 film *Giant*?

14. Which musician played a Mexican gardener in the 1968 film *Candy*?

15. Who scripted the 1983 film *Educating Rita* from his own play?

ANSWERS 1. 1988 2. Resurrection Symphony 3. 1920 4. Victor Borge 5. Ivan Reitman 6. Verdi 7. Ian Lavender 8. Camelot 9. Sarah Miles 10. Kenneth More 11. Nicholas Lyndhurst 12. Brian Murphy 13. George Stevens 14. Ringo Starr 15. Willy Russell.

SPORT

1. In which year did Curtly Ambrose make his Test debut for the West Indies?

2. Which England Test wicket-keeper was manager and secretary of Kent from 1960-74?

3. French football defender Manuel Amoros won a record 82 international caps. How many goals did he score in those games?

4. Who, in 1999, became the second German to play in an F.A. Cup Final?

5. Which team won the 1996 world series in baseball?

6. Which cyclist won the 1996 Tour de France?

7. Which footballer scored for both sides in the 1981 F.A. Cup Final?

8. Which footballer scored for both sides in the 1987 F.A. Cup Final?

9. Who was world rally champion 1996-8?

10. Who was Wimbledon men's singles tennis champion in 1960?

11. Who was English flat racing champion in 1961, '62 & '63?

12. In which U.S. state was swimmer Mark Spitz born?

13. Which yacht deprived the USA of the America's Cup in 1983?

14. Which golfer won the 1993 Canon European Masters?

15. Which team were Scottish football league champions in 1951 & '52?

ANSWERS 1. 1988 2. Leslie Ames 3. One 4. Dietmar Hamann 5. New York Yankees 6. Bjarne Riis 7. Tommy Hutchison 8. Gary Mabbutt 9. Tommi Makinen 10. Neale Fraser 11. Scobie Breasley 12. California 13. Australia II 14. Barry Lane 15. Hibernian.

POP MUSIC

1. Which U.S. vocalist had a 1976 hit with *I Recall a Gypsy Woman*?

2. Who recorded the 1998 album *Songs from Ally McBeal*?

3. Which group recorded the album *Gran Turismo*?

4. Which singer recorded the 1979 album *The Pleasure Principle*?

5. Which group recorded the concept album *The Lamb Lies Down on Broadway*?

6. Which French songwriter recorded the 1971 album *Histoire De Melody Nelson*?

7. Which group recorded the 1999 album *Bury the Hatchet*?

8. Which member of the group Yes recorded the 1975 L.P. *Beginnings*?

9. Which reggae group recorded the album *Handsworth Revolution*?

10. Who recorded the album *Doc at the Radar Station*?

11. *Another Music in a Different Kitchen* was the debut album of which band?

12. Which songwriting team's hits include *Alfie* and *I Say a Little Prayer*?

13. Milton Reame-James was keyboard player in which 1970's band?

14. Who recorded the 1998 album *A Thousand Leaves*?

15. Which rap duo had a 1982 hit single with *Magic's Wand*?

ANSWERS 1. Don Williams 2. Vonda Shepard 3. The Cardigans 4. Gary Numan 5. Genesis 6. Serge Gainsbourg 7. The Cranberries 8. Steve Howe 9. Steel Pulse 10. Captain Beefheart and the Magic Band 11. Buzzcocks 12. Bacharach & David 13. Cockney Rebel 14. Sonic Youth 15. Whodini.

HISTORY

1. In which year was the Battle of Marston Moor?

2. Who was defeated by Franklin D. Roosevelt in the 1944 U.S. presidential election?

3. What was American philanthropist James Buchanan Brady known as?

4. In which year did William III become sole sovereign?

5. In which century did French mathematician Pierre de Fermat live?

6. Which Portuguese navigator was killed by chieftain Lapu-Lapu in 1521?

7. John Hopkins University was formed in which Maryland city in 1876?

8. In which year did Charles II of England sell Dunkirk to Louis XIV of France?

9. In which year was the Great Fire of London?

10. In which year did Ramsay MacDonald die?

11. In which year did Henry VIII marry Catherine of Aragon?

12. What did Edward I erect in 1291 in memory of his wife Elaine?

13. Which king of Scotland was killed at Alnwick in 1093?

14. In which year was Nelson Mandela released from prison at the age of 71?

15. In which year was the Chappaquidick incident in which Mary Jo Kopechne drowned?

GENERAL KNOWLEDGE

1. Who created the fictional private eye Matt Helm?

2. In Greek mythology who succeeded Oedipus as King of Thebes?

3. For what would you use a hibachi in Japan?

4. BD is the abbreviation for which postcode area?

5. Which pope succeeded John XXIII in 1963?

6. What is the standard monetary unit of Belarus?

7. What is the approximate population of Nairobi in millions - 1.4, 2.4 or 3.4?

8. The ABC chain of teashops first opened in 1884. What did ABC stand for?

9. What does the Latin phrase 'ab initio' mean?

10. During which war were the two Battles of the Bull Run?

11. What is the Italian name for the city Florence?

12. In which novel by Charles Dickens does Jerry Cruncher appear?

13. In which year was composer Aaron Copland born?

14. In which novel by Turgenev does the character Bazarov appear?

15. Which actor played Sigmund Freud in a 1962 film?

ENTERTAINMENT

1. Which actress won the Cecil B. DeMille Award at the 1969 Golden Globes?

2. Who did Barbara Bain play in the T.V. show *Space: 1999*?

3. What nationality is choreographer Antony Tudor?

4. Who played Dave Deacon in the 1980's sitcom *Bottle Boys*?

5. Which film won the Best Motion Picture (Drama) accolade at the 1972 Golden Globe Awards?

6. Who directed the 1997 film *G.I. Jane*?

7. What nationality is composer Louis Glass?

8. Which actress starred in the sitcom *The Labours of Erica*?

9. What was the sequel to the U.S. sitcom *The Golden Girls*?

10. Who played Lady Jane Grey in the 1986 film *Lady Jane*?

11. Who played the inventor in the 1940 film *Edison, the Man*?

12. Who composed the symphonic fairy-tale *Peter and the Wolf*?

13. What is the subtitle of the 1995 film sequel to *Candyman*?

14. Who directed the 1989 film *The Adventures of Baron Munchausen*?

15. Who composed the 1937 cantata *In Honour of the City of London*?

ANSWERS 1. Joan Crawford 2. Dr. Helena Russell 3. English 4. Robin Askwith 5. The Godfather 6. Ridley Scott 7. Danish 8. Brenda Blethyn 9. The Golden Palace 10. Helena Bonham Carter 11. Spencer Tracy 12. Prokofiev 13. Farewell to the Flesh 14. Terry Gilliam 15. William Walton.

SPORT

1. Where were the 1993 IAAF World Championships held?

2. Which 1970 England World Cup squad member died in June 1998?

3. Who did Lazio defeat in the semi-final of the 1998/9 European Cup Winners' Cup?

4. Which country did Trine Hattestad, winner of the 1993 & '97 women's javelin title at the IAAF World Championships, represent?

5. Which horse won the 1996 St. Leger?

6. Which Scottish football team were championship runners-up four times out of five from 1960-64?

7. Who was men's heavyweight judo champion 1993-97?

8. Who partnered John Lowe to win the first World Pairs title at darts in 1986?

9. Which successful baseball team of the 1970s were known as 'The Big Red Machine'?

10. Which boxing weight division is between Heavyweight and Light-heavyweight?

11. Where were the equestrian events for the Melbourne Olympics held?

12. In which year was Lester Piggott born?

13. Who was Olympic men's 5,000m and 10,000m champion in 1972 & '76?

14. What is a luge?

15. How many times in succession did Bjorn Borg win Wimbledon?

ANSWERS 1. Stuttgart 2. Keith Newton 3. Lokomotiv Moscow 4. Norway 5. Shantou 6. Kilmarnock 7. David Douillet 8. Bob Anderson 9. Cincinnati Reds 10. Cruiserweight 11. Stockholm 12. 1935 13. Lasse Viren 14. A light one-man toboggan 15. Five.

POP MUSIC

1. Which singer duetted with Elvis Costello on the song *The Only Flame in Town*?

2. What was the title of Fleetwood Mac's 1987 No. 1 album?

3. Which duo recorded the 1987 album *Seduced and Abandoned*?

4. Who recorded the 1980 album *Without Radar*?

5. What was the debut single from the group Magazine?

6. In which year did Joy Division singer Ian Curtis kill himself?

7. Which production company did Ian Marsh and Martyn Ware form after quitting The Human League?

8. Which group recorded the 1981 single *Is Vic there?*?

9. Who was the original manager of the group Spandau Ballet?

10. Which girl group recorded the 1980 album *The Story So Far*?

11. Which poet recorded the album *Snap, Crackle (&) Bop*?

12. Which poet recorded the album *Bass Culture*?

13. What was the title of Foreigner's 1984 No. 1 album?

14. Who recorded the 1994 album *Let Love In*?

15. Who wrote the 1972 hit *Sea Side Shuffle*?

ANSWERS 1. Daryl Hall 2. Tango in the Night 3. Hue and Cry 4. The Yachts 5. Shot by Both Sides 6. 1980 7. The British Electric Foundation 8. Department S 9. Steve Dagger 10. The Modettes 11. John Cooper Clarke 12. Linton Kwesi Johnson 13. Agent Provocateur 14. Nick Cave and the Bad Seeds 15. Jona Lewie.

WORDS

1. What is the name given to a person who makes cutlery?

2. What in Russia is a droshky?

3. Why might you display famille?

4. What in Australian rhyming slang is a 'Joe Blake'?

5. What is a young swan called?

6. In the American legal system, what does D.A. stand for?

7. What, in the military, is a D.S.C.?

8. What sort of garment is the Indian dupatta?

9. Fango is used in the treatment of rheumatic disease. What is it?

10. What is the two-piece cotton costume worn in judo?

11. What type of fish is a kelt?

12. What in the U.S. is one's fanny?

13. What vegetable is also known as jibbons?

14. In chess, what does the symbol KBP stand for?

15. Parts of which animal were formerly cooked and eaten in a humble pie?

ANSWERS 1. A cutler **2.** A four-wheeled horse-drawn carriage **3.** It is a type of porcelain **4.** A snake **5.** Cygnet **6.** District Attorney **7.** Distinguished Service Cross **8.** A scarf **9.** A type of mud **10.** A judogi **11.** A salmon **12.** The buttocks **13.** Spring onion **14.** King's Bishop's Pawn **15.** Deer.

GENERAL KNOWLEDGE

1. Harry A. Atkinson was the first prime minister of which country?

2. Which writer was also the 1st Baron Tweedsmuir?

3. How much did it cost to post a standard first class letter in 1990?

4. What is the former Leeds Polytechnic now known as?

5. Who was elected Labour M.P. for Exeter in 1997?

6. In which country was Indian politician Sonia Gandhi born?

7. What is 157 x 300?

8. In which year did Grace Darling and her father rescue the shipwrecked off the Farne Islands?

9. Which African river joins the River Zaïre at Irebu?

10. Who wrote the 1980 novel *How Far Can You Go?*?

11. What is the name given to the bottommost plank of a vessel's hull?

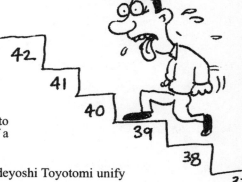

12. In which century did Hideyoshi Toyotomi unify Japan under one rule?

13. Who became archbishop of Canterbury in 1928?

14. In which city is the Robert Gordon University?

15. Which wine bottle holds the equivalent of 16 normal bottles?

ENTERTAINMENT

1. Who was voted Best Actress (In a Musical/Comedy) at the 1973 Golden Globes?

2. What is actor David Soul's real name?

3. Gimme Shelter was a 1970 documentary film about which pop group?

4. Who directed the 1955 film *The Ladykillers*?

5. Who played Angie in the sitcom *Lame Ducks*?

6. Which comic duo wrote and starred in T.V.'s *Bottom*?

7. Who composed the 1982 opera *The Photographer*?

8. Who did Diana Ross portray in the 1972 film *Lady Sings the Blues*?

9. Which comic actor played Mr. Kent in the 1982 sitcom *Goodbye Mr. Kent*?

10. Which comedian starred in the 1990 film *The Adventures of Ford Fairlane*?

11. On a story by whom was the 1998 film *The Gingerbread Man* based?

12. Who directed the film *Edward Scissorhands*?

13. In which year was the International Folk Music Council formed?

14. Who produced and directed the 1969 film *Can Hieronymus Merkin Ever Forget Mercy Humppe and Find True Happiness*?

15. Which movie won the Best Film accolade at the 1957 British Academy Awards?

SPORT

1. Which golfer won the U.S. Open from 1903-5 after having emigrated from Scotland?

2. French rugby union player and Olympic athlete Georges André was nicknamed after which animal?

3. Who was the 1978 World Formula 1 motor racing champion?

4. For which French rugby union side did Rob Andrew play from 1991-2?

5. Who scored 27 points for Scotland against Romania in a 1987 rugby union match?

6. Who was MVP in Superbowl XVI and XIX in American Football?

7. What nationality is six-times Olympic canoeing gold medal winner Gert Fredriksson?

8. Which Scottish team did IFK Gothenburg beat in the 1987 UEFA Cup Final?

9. Who became president of FIFA in 1974?

10. Which cyclist won the 1995 Tour de France?

11. Which baseball star was known as 'the Fordham Flash'?

12. In which city was U.S. basketball star Connie Hawkins born?

13. Which horse won the 1978 Grand National?

14. Which golfer won the British Open from 1954-56?

15. From which country were speedway stars Ivan Mauger and Barry Briggs?

ANSWERS 1. Willie Anderson **2.** The Bison **3.** Mario Andretti **4.** Toulouse **5.** Gavin Hastings **6.** Joe Montana **7.** Swedish **8.** Dundee United **9.** João Havelange **10.** Miguel Indurain **11.** Frank Frisch **12.** New York **13.** Lucius **14.** Peter Thomson **15.** New Zealand.

POP MUSIC

1. What was the name of the country music album by Elvis Costello and the Attractions?

2. Which group recorded the 1983 album *Strive to Survive Causing Least Suffering Possible*?

3. What was the title of the Human League's 1980 No. 1 album?

4. What was the debut album from Midlands group *The Beat*?

5. Which female singer's albums include 1980's *The Blue Meaning*?

6. Who was lead singer with the U.S. band Dead Kennedys?

7. What was the debut album of Echo and the Bunnymen?

8. Which studio album by Orchestral Manoeuvres in the Dark featured *Enola Gay*?

9. Which country singer wrote the song *Funny How Time Slips Away*?

10. What were the forenames of the Walker Brothers?

11. On which 1966 L.P. did the Supremes record *You Can't Hurry Love*?

12. Ralf Hütter and Florian Schneider are members of which group?

13. Which group recorded the L.P. *Zenyatta Mondatta*?

14. Who was lead singer with The Teardrop Explodes?

15. Which vocal group recorded the 1967 album *Reach Out*?

ANSWERS 1. Almost Blue **2.** A Flux of Pink Indians **3.** Dare **4.** I Just Can't Stop It **5.** Toyah **6.** Jello Biafra **7.** Crocodiles **8.** Organisation **9.** Willie Nelson **10.** Scott, John and Gary **11.** A' Go Go **12.** Kraftwerk **13.** The Police **14.** Julian Cope **15.** The Four Tops.

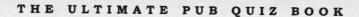

SCIENCE

1. Of what is diamond a crystalline form?

2. In which German city was Albert Einstein born?

3. In an equilateral triangle what does each of the angles measure in degrees?

4. What is the name given to a 12-sided polygon?

5. What is a collection of gas above an oil deposit called?

6. What in mechanics does the abbreviation KE stand for?

7. What is a collarbone also called?

8. How many grams of fat per 100 grams are there in butter?

9. For what did Donald Glaser win the 1960 Nobel prize for physics?

10. What is the boiling point in °C of aluminium?

11. What is one half of a sphere called?

12. In which century did the inventor Henry Bessemer live?

13. Which mineral is the main source of mercury?

14. What was the nationality of Jagadis Bose, known for his studies of electric waves?

15. What bone in the inner ear is also called the incus?

ANSWERS 1. Carbon 2. Ulm 3. 60° 4. Dodecagon 5. Gas cap 6. Kinetic energy 7. Clavicle 8. 82 9. Development of the bubble chamber 10. 251° 11. A hemisphere 12. 19th 13. Cinnabar 14. Indian 15. Anvil.

GENERAL KNOWLEDGE

1. What is the Greek name for the city of Nicosia?

2. What was the subtitle of the film *Star Wars Episode 1*?

3. In which year was the Haigh murder case trial?

4. In which county of the southwest is Dartington Hall?

5. What is a facsimile transmission system more commonly known as?

6. In which year did the Crimean War end?

7. In which city did the Belgrade Theatre open in 1958?

8. In which year did the First Fleet of convict ships arrive in Port Jackson, Australia?

9. Which cartoon cat famously 'kept on walking'?

10. Of what whole number is 7.74596 the square root?

11. In which novel by Charles Dickens does Vincent Crummles appear?

12. What was the first national anthem of the U.S.?

13. Which caddish character in *Tom Brown's Schooldays* reappeared in stories by George MacDonald Fraser?

14. John Nyren was the son of the founder of which cricket club?

15. What is bully beef?

ANSWERS 1. Lefkosia 2. The Phantom Menace 3. 1949 4. Devon 5. Fax 6. 1856 7. Coventry 8. 1788 9. Felix the Cat 10. 60 11. Nicholas Nickleby 12. Hail Columbia! 13. Flashman 14. Hambledon Club 15. Tinned corned beef.

ENTERTAINMENT

1. Who played Maid Marian in the 1938 film *The Adventures of Robin Hood*?

2. What was the alternative title to the 1968 film *The Girl on a Motorcycle*?

3. In which year was comedian Max Boyce born?

4. Who played Marsha Stubbs in the T.V. drama *Soldier, Soldier*?

5. Who played Alf Larkins in the 1950's sitcom *The Larkins*?

6. Which movie won the Best British Film accolade at the 1958 British Academy Awards?

7. What nationality is trumpeter Edward Tarr?

8. Who directed the 1962 film *Advise and Consent*?

9. What was the title of the 1973 Xmas Special by *The Goodies*?

10. In which year was current affairs presenter Peter Snow born?

11. Who did Jeffrey Tambor play in the T.V. comedy *The Larry Sanders Show*?

12. Who played the lead in the 1954 film *The Glenn Miller Story*?

13. Who directed the 1991 film *Edward II*?

14. Which comedienne started by billing herself *The Sea Monster*?

15. Who played *The Canterville Ghost* in a 1944 film?

ANSWERS 1. Olivia de Havilland 2. Naked under Leather 3. 1943 4. Denise Welch 5. David Kossoff 6. Room at the Top 7. American 8. Otto Preminger 9. The Goodies and the Beanstalk 10. 1938 11. Hank Kingsley 12. James Stewart 13. Derek Jarman 14. Jo Brand 15. Charles Laughton.

SPORT

1. By how many points did Mike Hawthorn beat Stirling Moss to win the 1958 World Formula 1 motor racing title?

2. Who was the 1998 U.S. Masters golf champion?

3. Which Danish badminton player lost in the final of the 1987 men's world championship?

4. Lily Gower beat R.C.J. Beaton in 1905 to win the Croquet Open Championships. What did they do together later that year?

5. Which Scottish football team were league champions from 1966-74?

6. Who won the Boston men's marathon from 1993-95?

7. Which country were men's world champions at quad sculls rowing from 1994-98?

8. Who skippered the America's Cup-winning boat *Stars and Stripes* in 1987 & '88?

9. What, in the Tour de France, is the 'maillot jaune'?

10. For prowess at which sport was American Earl Anthony known as 'The Doomsday Stroking Machine'?

11. Which golfer won the 1978 world matchplay championship?

12. Who in football was 'the Galloping Major'?

13. When was the last British Grand Prix in motor racing held at Aintree?

14. Who were the 1987 rugby union world cup winners?

15. With which sport do you associate Norbert Koof and Hartwig Steenken?

ANSWERS 1. One 2. Mark O'Meara 3. Morten Frost 4. Marry each other 5. Celtic 6. Cosmas N'Deti 7. Italy 8. Dennis Conner 9. Yellow jersey 10. Bowling 11. Isao Aoki 12. Ferenc Puskas 13. 1962 14. New Zealand 15. Showjumping.

POP MUSIC

1. Which female singer recorded the 1989 album *Electric Youth*?

2. Which male vocalist recorded the 1973 album *Touch Me*?

3. Which group recorded the 1980 album *Trance and Dance*?

4. Which wacky U.S. group recorded the single *Rock Lobster*?

5. What was the title of the second L.P. by The Specials?

6. What is reggae singer Winston Rodney better known as?

7. Who was Stevie Wonder's writing partner on the song *Do Yourself a Favour*?

8. Which American cult band's L.P.s include *The Tunes of Two Cities*?

9. Who was the lead singer of Dexy's Midnight Runners?

10. Which album proclaimed itself 'The Fourth Roxy Music album'?

11. Mark E. Smith is the lead singer with which Manchester group?

12. Which trio recorded the 1983 album *Waiting*?

13. Which reggae group recorded the album *Two Sevens Clash*?

14. Martin L. Gore is the keyboard player with which group?

15. Which duo recorded the albums *L* and *Ismism*?

ANSWERS 1. Debbie Gibson 2. Gary Glitter 3. Martha and the Muffins 4. The B-52's 5. More Specials 6. Burning Spear 7. Syreeta Wright 8. The Residents 9. Kevin Rowland 10. Country Life 11. The Fall 12. Fun Boy Three 13. Culture 14. Depeche Mode 15. Godley and Creme.

PEOPLE

1. Which female pop singer has a Venezuelan father and Irish mother?

2. Which ex-girlfriend of Ryan Giggs later played a part in the T.V. soap *Hollyoaks*?

3. Who is the actress wife of David Duchovny?

4. Which actress on *The Larry Sanders Show* appeared in the films *Reality Bites* and *The Truth About Cats and Dogs*?

5. Which magazine editor wrote the best-selling novel *Sex and the Single Girl*?

6. The brother of ex-president Carter died in 1988. What was his name?

7. Which husband of Princess Caroline of Monaco died in a boating accident in 1990?

8. In which year did French fashion designer Christian Dior die?

9. Nancy Hanks was the mother of which U.S. president?

10. Who was the wife of William Shakespeare?

11. What is the middle name of American publisher Hugh Hefner?

12. Which *Baywatch* actress is married to Mötley Crüe bass player Nikki Sixx?

13. Who plays Rachel in the T.V. comedy *Friends*?

14. Which former Miss USA contestant and actress married baseball star Dave Justice?

15. What is the name of Simon Le Bon's model wife?

GENERAL KNOWLEDGE

1. Which horse racecourse is 9 miles south-east of Glasgow?

2. Which country's police force is named after the phrase 'guard of the peace'?

3. Who created the fictional detective Mike Hammer?

4. In which U.S. city is the flatiron building?

5. Who was the third son of David in the Old Testament?

6. What is the nickname of West Ham F.C.?

7. In which year was the Battle of Bannockburn?

8. HKJ is the international car registration of which country?

9. For which constituency did entertainer Lenny Beige stand at the 1997 election?

10. Which Irish political party was formed by De Valera in 1923?

11. In which year did Robert Louis Stevenson die?

12. Which creature is also called a fitch?

13. What was poet W.H. Auden's first name?

14. In which year did musician Frank Zappa die?

15. Who composed the opera *Cavalleria Rusticana* ?

ANSWERS 1. Hamilton Park 2. Republic of Ireland 3. Mickey Spillane 4. New York 5. Absalom 6. The Hammers 7. 1314 8. Jordan 9. Putney 10. Fianna Fail 11. 1894 12. Polecat 13. Wystan 14. 1993 15. Pietro Mascagni.

ENTERTAINMENT

1. Which movie won Best Film at the 1959 British Academy Awards?

2. Who directed the 1953 film *Glen or Glenda*?

3. What, musically, is a 'tampon double'?

4. Who composed the opera *Ruslan and Lyudmila*?

5. Under what name did Sam Spiegel produce the 1951 film *The African Queen*?

6. Who directed the remake in 1979 of Hitchcock's *The Lady Vanishes*?

7. Who played Foggy Dewhurst in the T.V. comedy *Last of the Summer Wine*?

8. Which ex-*Coronation Street* actor played George Fairchild in the 1980's comedy series *Brass*?

9. Who played King Arthur in the 1963 film *Lancelot and Guinevere*?

10. Who played David Bliss in the 1960 sitcom *A Life of Bliss*?

11. Which writing duo created T.V.'s *Goodnight Sweetheart*?

12. In which year was comedian Mel Smith born?

13. In which year did composer Sir Edward German die?

14. Who directed the 1963 film *8 and a half*?

15. Who directed the 1962 film *Cape Fear*?

SPORT

1. Who retained the WBA featherweight boxing title in September 1993?

2. Where were the 1995 IAAF World Championships held?

3. Which team won the 1997 world series in baseball?

4. Which team won the 1993 AXA Life League in cricket?

5. Who was the men's light-heavyweight judo champion in 1995 & '97?

6. In which year did racehorse trainer Gordon Richards die?

7. Which England Test cricket captain played for Southampton in the 1902 F.A. Cup Final?

8. Which horse won the 1997 St. Leger?

9. Who was the losing finalist in the world professional snooker championship from 1952-54?

10. Celtic were runners-up to Rangers in the Scottish Premier League in the 1995/96 season. In which season had they last finished in the top two?

11. Who won the Boston women's marathon from 1994-96?

12. Which country were men's world champions at coxless four rowing in 1997 & '98?

13. Who won the 1984 Olympic men's 5000m title?

14. What nationality was baseball player Luis Aparicio?

15. What fruit gave Swedish table-tennis star Mikael Appelgren his nickname?

POP MUSIC

1. Which group recorded the 1988 album *Birth School Work Death*?

2. Jackie Hamilton, Gary McAndless, Austin Barnett - which Irish pop group?

3. Which mod revival band recorded the 1980 album *Behind Closed Doors*?

4. Webb, Baillie, Jobson, Adamson - which Scottish group?

5. Which artist recorded the 1980 album *Scary Monsters and Super Creeps*?

6. Dave Barbarossa and Leigh Gorman were members of which 1980's pop group?

7. Which group recorded the albums *Glory Road* and *Future Shock*?

8. Which group recorded the 1980 L.P. *Black Sea*?

9. Which member of Roxy Music recorded the 1973 album *These Foolish Things*?

10. Which punk band comprised the members Vanian, Scabies, James and Sensible?

11. Who was the lead singer of the group Magazine?

12. Who recorded the L.P. *Too-Rye-Ay*?

13. Which group recorded the 1980 L.P. *Get Happy*?

14. On which studio album does Van Morrison perform *Crazy Love*?

15. On which L.P. did the Mekons record the song *Charlie Cake Park*?

ANSWERS 1. The Godfathers 2. The Moondogs 3. Secret Affair 4. The Skids 5. David Bowie 6. Bow Wow Wow 7. Gillan 8. X.T.C. 9. Bryan Ferry 10. The Damned 11. Howard Devoto 12. Dexy's Midnight Runners 13. Elvis Costello and the Attractions 14. Moondance 15. Honky Tonkin'.

ART AND LITERATURE

1. What was Luke Rhinehart's 1971 cult novel called?

2. Who wrote the 1937 novel *Dead Man Leading*?

3. Who wrote the 1990 novel *L.A. Confidential*?

4. Which Russian author wrote the novel *The Master and Margarita*?

5. What nationality was painter Mary Cassatt?

6. In which year did artist Paul Cézanne die?

7. Which co-founder of the Pre-Raphaelite Brotherhood died in 1882 in Birchington-on-Sea?

8. Which American artist's *Death and Disaster* series featured train wrecks and electric chairs?

9. Tobias Tweeney and Ickey the Pig were the creations of which U.S. short story writer?

10. Who wrote *Gentlemen Prefer Blondes*?

11. Which Leghorn-born artist said 'I am going to drink myself dead'?

12. Which Dutch artist's paintings include *Boogie-Woogie*?

13. In which city was artist Paula Rego born?

14. Who was the king's jester in the play *Hamlet*?

15. Who created the character 'Berry' Pleydell?

GENERAL KNOWLEDGE

1. What was English novelist Elizabeth Cleghorn Stevenson better known as?

2. What sort of crop is burley, which is grown especially in Kentucky?

3. In which year was the Battle of the Boyne?

4. What stone is associated with a 45th wedding anniversary?

5. In what year was Walt Disney born?

6. Which country's international car registration is RCH?

7. In which year did playwright Ben Travers die?

8. Which vegetable has the varieties Nevada and Canberra?

9. What line is coloured green on a London underground map?

10. Which politician was Chancellor of the Exchequer from 1947-50?

11. On what date is Flag Day in the U.S.?

12. In which country was the Auschwitz concentration camp?

13. On which river is the Indian city of Gauhati?

14. For what does the abbreviation HMSO stand?

15. Who became archbishop of Canterbury in 1945?

ANSWERS 1. Mrs. Gaskell 2. Tobacco 3. 1690 4. Sapphire 5. 1901 6. Chile 7. 1980 8. Cauliflower 9. District 10. Stafford Cripps 11. June 14 12. Poland 13. Brahmaputra 14. His/Her Majesty's Stationery Office 15. Geoffrey Fisher.

ENTERTAINMENT

1. What was the belated follow-up, in 1992, to the show *Are You Being Served?*?

2. Who directed the 1985 film *After Hours*?

3. Who played Vincent in the 1990 film *The Godfather Part III*?

4. Who won Best British Actor at the 1962 British Academy Awards?

5. Whose opera *The Rape of Lucretia* reopened Glyndebourne after World War II?

6. In which city was composer George Gershwin born?

7. Who played *Lassiter* in a 1984 film?

8. Who directed the 1930 film *L'Age D'Or*?

9. Which comedian was born Cyril Mead in 1942?

10. Who directed the 1991 film *The Last Boy Scout*?

11. What nationality was composer William Billings?

12. Which movie was judged Best Film at the 1963 British Academy Awards?

13. Who scripted the 1965 film *The Agony and the Ecstasy*?

14. Who wrote the sitcom *Bread*?

15. Who played an ex-rodeo champion in the film *The Electric Horseman*?

SPORT

1. What age was Wentworth Gore when he won the 1908 Wimbledon singles title?

2. In which year did the UEFA Cup replace the Inter-Cities Fairs Cup?

3. Who was British Open men's squash champion from 1950-55?

4. Who was MVP in Superbowl XIII & XIV in American Football?

5. Who was the 1995 U.S. Open golf champion?

6. Who was the 1998 world professional snooker champion?

7. What was baseball star Leon Allen Goslin known as?

8. Who was All-England women's badminton champion from 1961-64?

9. Who beat Bastia 3-0 on aggregate in the 1978 UEFA Cup Final?

10. Which Olympic swimming champion announced her retirement in 1973 at the age of 16 years, 9 months?

11. What was the nickname of U.S. jockey Eddie Arcano?

12. Which Argentinian was appointed manager of Swindon Town in 1989?

13. Who was manager of Leeds United when they reached the 1975 European Cup Final?

14. Who won the Lancome Trophy in golf in 1993?

15. Which boxer retained his WBO Middleweight title in September 1993?

ANSWERS 1. 40 2. 1972 3. Hashim Khan 4. Terry Bradshaw 5. Corey Pavin 6. John Higgins 7. Goose 8. Judy Hashman 9. PSV Eindhoven 10. Shane Gould 11. Banana Nose 12. Ossie Ardiles 13. Jimmy Armfield 14. Ian Woosnam 15. Chris Pyatt.

POP MUSIC

1. On which label was the single *When Will I See You Again* by the Three Degrees?

2. Which group recorded the 1980 album *Mad About the Wrong Boy*?

3. Which 2-Tone group's first single was *Away*?

4. Which group recorded the 1980 album *Do A Runner*?

5. Who recorded the 1983 L.P. *Duck Rock*?

6. Which member of Roxy Music recorded the album *Diamond Head*?

7. Which member of the Pixies recorded the solo album *Teenager of the Year*?

8. Which reggae band recorded the songs *Plastic Smile* and *Shine Eye Gal*?

9. What was Rufus Thomas's only Top 20 hit single?

10. Who recorded the 1999 album *Post Orgasmic Chill*?

11. Which group recorded the 1980 album *Kilimanjaro*?

12. Who was the female singer with the punk group Penetration?

13. Which group had a 1961 hit with *The Lion Sleeps Tonight*?

14. Who recorded the 1980 album *Signing Off*?

15. In which country was ska singer Laurel Aitken born?

GEOGRAPHY

1. Antananarivo is the capital of which island?

2. Which mountain is also known as Monte Cervino and Mont Corvin?

3. Which is larger - Morocco or Mozambique?

4. In which country is Lake Nipissing?

5. In which European country is the copper-producing town of Rio Tinto?

6. In which ocean is the Rockall Deep submarine trench?

7. Which is the largest island of the Inner Hebrides in Scotland?

8. In which country is the ancient city of Tarsus?

9. Which African country is sandwiched between Benin and Ghana?

10. In which South American country is the port of Valparaiso?

11. In which U.S. state are the volcanoes Mauna Loa and Mauna Kea?

12. What is the capital of Mauritius?

13. Auckland is on North Island, New Zealand. True or false?

14. What is the name of the former island penal colony at the entrance of Table Bay, South Africa?

15. Which is larger - Poland or Sri Lanka?

ANSWERS 1. Madagascar 2. Matterhorn 3. Mozambique 4. Canada 5. Spain 6. Atlantic Ocean 7. Skye 8. Turkey 9. Togo 10. Chile 11. Hawaii 12. Port Louis 13. True 14. Robben Island 15. Poland.

GENERAL KNOWLEDGE

1. In which year was photographer David Bailey born?

2. What is the standard monetary unit of Botswana?

3. Which was founded first - Balliol College, Oxford or Magdalen College, Oxford?

4. What in Australia is a bundy?

5. Who was chief photographer of the magazine *Rolling Stone* from 1973-83?

6. Whose painting, *Woman Nude Before Garden*, was damaged in May 1999 by a Utrecht psychiatric patient?

7. What is the approximate population in millions of Cape Town - 2, 3 or 4?

8. What is Tintin's dog Snowy called in the original stories?

9. In which year was the Aberfan disaster?

10. Who wrote the absurdist play *The Cresta Run*?

11. What is the name given to the lowest temperature theoretically attainable?

12. In which county is the fishing port of Fleetwood?

13. What is the middle name of actor Dustin Hoffman?

14. In which novel by Charles Dickens does Miss Rosa Dartle appear?

15. In which year was the Battle of Flodden?

ENTERTAINMENT

1. In which year was comedian Tony Slattery born?

2. Who directed the 1998 film *Godzilla*?

3. Who played *Grandad* in the early 1980's children's T.V. series?

4. In which city was composer Berthold Goldschmidt born?

5. Who played gangster John Smith in the 1996 film *Last Man Standing*?

6. What nationality is composer Colin Brumby?

7. Who directed the 1980 film *The Elephant Man*?

8. Which duo produced the 1978 film *Lemon Popsicle*?

9. Who directed the 1944 film *Laura*?

10. Who directed the 1960 film *Let's Make Love*?

11. Who played *The Elusive Pimpernel* in a 1950 film?

12. Who was the male lead in the 1945 film *Objective, Burma!*?

13. In which city was Rory Bremner born?

14. Who directed the 1978 film *Goin' South*?

15. Who directed the 1997 film *Air Force One*?

SPORT

1. Which unfashionable team lost the 1935 Scottish F.A. Cup Final?

2. Who did John Spencer defeat in the 1969 World Professional Snooker Championship final?

3. Which country were women's quad sculls rowing world champions from 1994-98?

4. Which boxer published the autobiography *Gloves, Glory and God*?

5. At what sport was Frenchwoman Catherine Arnaud a world and European champion?

6. Which motor racing driver was killed testing a Ferrari at Monza in May, 1955?

7. Which team won the 1994 AXA Life League in cricket?

8. What is former cricketer David Gower's middle name?

9. Who did Ipswich Town defeat in the 1981 UEFA Cup Final?

10. What field event is Kate Staples associated with?

11. Who won the men's 200m at the 1976 Olympics?

12. The Jets and Giants represent which city in American Football?

13. In boxing, who was 'the Brown Bomber'?

14. Which England Test cricketer once shared the world record for the long jump?

15. Which horse won the 1967 Aintree Grand National?

POP MUSIC

1. How many Top Ten singles did the Thompson Twins have in the U.K.?

2. What is singer Buster Bloodvessel's real name?

3. Who recorded the 1999 album *Twisted Tenderness*?

4. In which year did trombone player Don Drummond die?

5. Which female vocalist had a 1988 No. 1 with *I Think We're Alone Now*?

6. Who was the original bass player in the group Killing Joke?

7. Who was the lead singer of Scottish group The Associates?

8. Which reggae group recorded the album *Live and Direct* at the 1983 Notting Hill Carnival?

9. Which band recorded the songs *Warlord of the Royal Crocodiles* and *Salamanda Palaganda*?

10. Which group recorded the album *See jungle! See jungle! Go join your gang yeah, city all over! Go ape crazy!*?

11. On which studio L.P. did David Bowie record *Sound and Vision*?

12. Fripp, Wetton and Bruford comprised which band in 1974?

13. Who recorded the L.P. *Fresh Fruit in Foreign Places*?

14. On which label did Joy Division's *Unknown Pleasures* L.P. appear?

15. Which Sting song appears on Grace Jones's album *Nightclubbing*?

ANSWERS 1. Five 2. Doug Trendle 3. Electronic 4. 1969 5. Tiffany 6. Youth 7. Billy Mackenzie 8. Aswad 9. Tyrannosaurus Rex 10. Bow Wow Wow 11. Low 12. King Crimson 13. Kid Creole and the Coconuts 14. Factory Records 15. Demolition Man.

HISTORY

1. In which century did Samuel de Champlain discover and name Lake Champlain, U.S.A.?

2. In which year did publishing company Simon and Schuster print the first book of crossword puzzles?

3. In which year did Oliver Cromwell become Lord Protector?

4. In which year was the Boston Tea Party?

5. Which king of France initiated the War of the Devolution in 1667?

6. In which year did the Crimean War end?

7. In which year was the South Sea Bubble financial crisis?

8. In which year was Queen Victoria proclaimed Empress of India?

9. In which year was Robert Devereux, 2nd Earl of Essex, beheaded?

10. Which French politician formed the National Front in 1972?

11. In which year was the 'Popish Plot'?

12. In which U.S. state was Abraham Lincoln born?

13. Which U.S. zoologist, author of *Gorillas in the Mist*, was found murdered in 1985?

14. Which queen of Henry VIII was imprisoned in the Tower of London in May 1536?

15. In which year did the War of the Spanish Succession begin?

GENERAL KNOWLEDGE

1. In which year was Prince Charles born?

2. Which actress was born Vivian Mary Hartley?

3. Who in May 1999 became the first Asian minister in the government?

4. Where is the World War II destroyer HMS Cavalier now housed?

5. Which secretary of state for Northern Ireland resigned in 1992 after singing on television?

6. Of what whole number is 5.4772255 the square root?

7. What is the name given to the holder of the chair of French at Oxford?

8. In which year was the Battle of Midway?

9. What is the name of the former slum area of Washington which is the site of the headquarters of the CIA?

10. In which year did comedian Willie Rushton die?

11. Who wrote the children's story *The Midnight Folk*?

12. In which year did scientist Alexander Fleming die?

13. What is the name of the dog in the film *The Wizard of Oz*?

14. Which is the 'Beaver State' of the U.S.?

15. In which year did author Stella Gibbons die?

ENTERTAINMENT

1. Which was Best British Film at the 1965 British Academy Awards?

2. Who directed the 1932 film 'Air Mail'?

3. Which comic actress played Cynthia Bright in the 1985 sitcom *The Bright Side*?

4. Who played Catherine of Aragon in the 1970 drama series *The Six Wives of Henry VIII*?

5. Who played Sinbad in the 1974 film 'The Golden Voyage of Sinbad'?

6. Who directed the 1976 film *Obsession*?

7. Who wrote the 1970 T.V. comedy drama *The Gravy Train*?

8. Which actor won the 'Most in Need of Retirement' title at the 1944 Harvard Lampoon Movie Worsts Awards?

9. What section of Mendelssohn's hymn 'Hear my prayer' is often performed separately?

10. Who starred in the 1980 action film *The Octagon*?

11. Which comedian was born Eddie McGinnis in 1942?

12. Who starred in and directed the 1942 film *The Gold Rush*?

13. Who played *Captain Kidd* in a 1945 film?

14. In which year was composer Harrison Birtwistle born?

15. Who played the Reverend Elton in the 1996 film *Emma*?

ANSWERS 1. The Ipcress File **2.** John Ford **3.** Paula Wilcox **4.** Annette Crosbie **5.** John Phillip Law **6.** Brian De Palma **7.** Malcolm Bradbury **8.** Paul Muni **9.** O for the wings of a dove **10.** Chuck Norris **11.** Eddie Large **12.** Charles Chaplin **13.** Charles Laughton **14.** 1934 **15.** Alan Cumming.

SPORT

1. By what score did Aberdeen defeat Celtic on penalties in the 1990 Scottish F.A. Cup Final?

2. Where were the 1997 IAAF World Championships held?

3. Which team won the 1998 world series in baseball?

4. Which horse won the 1998 St. Leger?

5. Who was men's world middleweight judo champion in 1987 & '89?

6. In tennis, who won the 1993 Romanian Open?

7. Who were 1988 men's Olympic basketball champions?

8. Which sportsman was ousted in 1997 as M.P. for Falmouth and Camborne?

9. Where were the 20th Summer Olympics held?

10. Who in snooker is known as 'the Grinder'?

11. Which Austrian motor racing driver was 1970 Formula 1 world champion?

12. What nationality was tennis player Maria Bueno?

13. In which year did tennis player Arthur Ashe die?

14. Who won the 1984 Olympic women's 100m title?

15. Which rugby league player was player-coach at Wigan from 1963-9?

ANSWERS 1. 9-8 2. Athens 3. New York Yankees 4. Nedawi 5. Fabien Canu 6. Goran Ivanisevic 7. USSR 8. Sebastian Coe 9. Munich 10. Cliff Thorburn 11. Jochen Rindt 12. Brazilian 13. 1993 14. Evelyn Ashford 15. Eric Ashton.

POP MUSIC

1. What was the name of Eagle-Eye Cherry's debut album?

2. Who duetted on the 1974 hit *Mockingbird*?

3. In which year did The Fall have a hit single with *There's a Ghost in my House*?

4. Which group's L.P.s include *Ma Kelly's Greasy Spoon*?

5. Which U.S. vocalist recorded the 1986 album *Three Hearts in the Happy Ending Machine*?

6. What was David Bowie's '70's album of cover versions called?

7. Which reggae artist recorded the 1979 album *Forces of Victory*?

8. Jilted John was the alter ego of which actor?

9. Cleo, Zainem and Yonah Higgins comprise which vocal group?

10. Who recorded the 1980 album *Songs the Lord Taught Us*?

11. Which group recorded the 1979 album *Replicas*?

12. Who recorded the 1999 album *Ffrr*?

13. William Reid and Jim Reid comprise which group?

14. On which record label did Led Zeppelin record *Physical Graffiti*?

15. Which electronic duo recorded the 1979 L.P. *The Bridge*?

WORDS

1. What in Russia is a kazachok?

2. What creatures live in an apiary?

3. What does the musical term 'da capo' mean?

4. What does the German word dachshund mean?

5. What, in the Caribbean, is a duppy?

6. What type of food is a fairing?

7. What, in Portugal, is a fado?

8. In printing, what is the narrowest rule in paper production?

9. What in law is a 'felo de se'?

10. Kaph is the 11th letter in which alphabet?

11. What would you do with a kanzu - fly it or wear it?

12. What type of garment is a 'Jacky Howe'?

13. What is an ICBM?

14. What sort of creature is a 'fer-de-lance'?

15. What, in Asia, is dacoity?

GENERAL KNOWLEDGE

1. What in New Zealand is hokonui?

2. Which author built Fonthill 'Abbey' in Wiltshire?

3. In which year was the Battle of Crécy?

4. Who wrote the historical novel *Musk and Amber*?

5. What was the name of the Prince of Wales's home near Sunningdale from 1929-36?

6. In which year was Mata Hari executed as a spy?

7. In which year was the French military decoration the Crois de Guerre established?

8. What was the name given to the feudal code of the Japanese samurai?

9. What type of wood is acajou, which is used by cabinet makers?

10. In which South American country is the city of Avellaneda?

11. What was the name of Oliver Cromwell's son, who was born in 1626?

12. In education, what did the initials CSE stand for?

13. Who in mythology was the first wife of Aegeus?

14. Who was the arch enemy of comic character Dan Dare?

15. In which year was the QEII launched?

ANSWERS 1. Illicit whisky **2.** William Beckford **3.** 1346 **4.** A.E.W. Mason **5.** Fort Belvedere **6.** 1917 **7.** 1915 **8.** Bushido **9.** Mahogany **10.** Argentina **11.** Richard **12.** Certificate of Secondary Education **13.** Meta **14.** The Mekon **15.** 1967.

ENTERTAINMENT

1. In which year did comedian Larry Grayson die?

2. Which actor in *Coronation Street* played Tippy the Tipster in the children's show *Bright's Boffins*?

3. In which city was composer Georges Bizet born?

4. How much in dollars was Julie Andrews paid for the film *Mary Poppins*?

5. Who directed the 1953 film *Albert R.N.*?

6. In which year was newsreader Peter Sissons born?

7. Who played Melanie in the film *Gone with the Wind*?

8. What was the name of the pet pig in the U.S. comedy *Green Acres*?

9. Who composed the song-cycle *The Heart's Assurance*?

10. Who directed the 1960 film *Ocean's Eleven*?

11. What was ITV's disastrous version of the sitcom *The Golden Girls* called?

12. Who scripted the 1977 film *The Goodbye Girl*?

13. Who directed the film *The Empire Strikes Back*?

14. Which member of The Grumbleweeds was Wilf 'Gasmask' Grimshaw?

15. What was the U.S. title of the 1952 film *The Card* which starred Alec Guinness?

ANSWERS 1. 1995 2. Johnny Briggs 3. Paris 4. $125,000 5. Lewis Gilbert 6. 1942 7. Olivia de Havilland 8. Arnold 9. Michael Tippett 10. Lewis Milestone 11. Brighton Belles 12. Neil Simon 13. Irvin Kershner 14. Carl Sutcliffe 15. The Promoter.

SPORT

1. For which country did Asif Iqbal play Test cricket from 1964-80?

2. To what did U.S. jockey Brian Asmussen legally change his name?

3. With what sport might you associate Reading-born Nigel Aspinall?

4. Which basketball team did Red Auerbach coach to eight consecutive NBA titles in the 1950s & '60s?

5. Who was men's world middleweight judo champion in 1995 & '97?

6. Who were rugby league world cup winners 1975-95?

7. Who was the 1998 men's world open squash champion?

8. What colour ball is worth two points in snooker?

9. Who were Olympic men's volleyball champions in 1984 & '88?

10. Who won the U.S. Open men's singles tennis championship from 1979-81?

11. Who won the 1988 Olympic men's 100m breaststroke swimming title?

12. In which country was orienteering invented?

13. Who was captain of the 1993 European Ryder Cup team?

14. In which city was Martina Navratilova born?

15. Which famous footballing brothers were born in Ashington, Northumberland?

ANSWERS 1. Pakistan **2.** Cash **3.** Croquet **4.** Boston Celtics **5.** Jeon Ki-Young **6.** Australia **7.** Jonathan Power **8.** Yellow **9.** United States **10.** John McEnroe **11.** Adrian Moorhouse **12.** Sweden **13.** Bernard Gallacher **14.** Prague **15.** Bobby and Jack Charlton.

POP MUSIC

1. Who was lead singer with the group American Music Club?

2. Which group recorded the 1980 album *Back in Black*?

3. Which singer's albums include *Reg Strikes Back* and *A Simple Man*?

4. Which female vocal duo had a 1978 hit with *Boogie Oogie Oogie*?

5. Who recorded the L.P. *Back in the D.H.S.S.*?

6. From which country did 1970's keyboard maestro Bo Hannson hail?

7. What was John Lennon's 1975 album of cover versions called?

8. Who wrote Jerry Lee Lewis's hit *Breathless*?

9. David Hidalgo and Louie Perez are the main songwriters in which group?

10. Which songwriter recorded the 1991 album *West of Rome*?

11. Who recorded the 1998 album *The Sky is Too High*?

12. Which children's choir had a 1981 hit with *My Mum is One in a Million*?

13. How many Top Ten U.K. singles did Tavares have?

14. What was the Teardrop Explodes' only Top Ten single?

15. What was the title of Cockney Rebel's 1974 chart album?

SCIENCE

1. What nationality was mathematician Leonhard Euler?

2. Which scientist became an assistant to Humphry Davy in 1813?

3. Which Italian-born physicist helped test the first atomic bomb in 1943?

4. After whom is the element nobelium named?

5. Which element has the atomic number 99?

6. What is the blue variety of the mineral corundum?

7. What is the symbol for the element platinum?

8. In which century did the scientist Robert Boyle live?

9. In which year did astronomer Galileo die?

10. What nationality was astronomer Anders Celsius?

11. In which century did German physicist Hermann von Helmholtz live?

12. Which 17c French lawyer is regarded as the creator of the modern theory of numbers?

13. Which English physicist, born in 1635, formulated the law of elasticity?

14. Which 18c Scottish chemist evolved the theory of latent heat?

15. What is the Moho discontinuity?

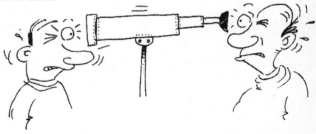

GENERAL KNOWLEDGE

1. What do you do to a whale if you flense it?

2. In which year was the Battle of Pearl Harbor?

3. Which Old Testament book comes between Joshua and Ruth?

4. What is the computing programming language Fortran a corruption of?

5. In which U.S. city is Logan airport?

6. What type of creature is a matamata?

7. TAP is the chief airline of which country?

8. What is Fletcherism?

9. What does ASLEF stand for?

10. In which South American country is the plateau region the Mato Grosso?

11. Who in history was 'the Bloody Butcher'?

12. In architecture, what is a camponile?

13. What was the pseudonym of the artist and editor of Punch magazine Kenneth Bird?

14. Which comedian's real name is Joseph Levitch?

15. What nationality is the composer Heinz Hollinger?

ANSWERS 1. Strip it of blubber or skin 2. 1941 3. Judges 4. Formula translation 5. Boston 6. A turtle 7. Portugal 8. The practice of chewing food thoroughly and sipping liquids to aid digestion 9. Associated Society of Locomotive Engineers and Firemen 10. Brazil 11. The Duke of Cumberland 12. A bell tower 13. Fougasse 14. Jerry Lewis 15. Swiss.

ENTERTAINMENT

1. How much in dollars was Marlon Brando paid for the 1951 film *A Streetcar Named Desire*?

2. Who starred as *Al Capone* in a 1959 film?

3. Who were actors Paul Barber and Philip Whitchurch in a 1980's sitcom?

4. In which country was comedy actress Carmen Silvera born?

5. Who directed the 1996 film *The English Patient*?

6. Which duo co-scripted and starred in the 1997 film *Good Will Hunting*?

7. Of which female political figure was Joyce Grenfell the niece?

8. Who composed the 1883 opera *Henry VIII*?

9. Which Australian comedian created the character Norman Gunston?

10. Who won Worst Single Performance - Male for his role in the film *The Stranger* at the 1946 Harvard Lampoon Movie Worsts Awards?

11. What musically are 'bleeding chunks'?

12. Which jazz artist wrote *At the Woodchoppers Ball*?

13. How much in dollars was Clint Eastwood paid for the 1964 film *A Fistful of Dollars*?

14. Who directed the 1955 film *Oklahoma!*?

15. What was the U.S. title of the 1964 film *The Caretaker*, based on Harold Pinter's play?

SPORT

1. Which team won the 1995 AXA Life League in cricket?

2. By what score did Rangers beat Hearts in the 1996 Scottish F.A. Cup Final?

3. Who was men's world light-middleweight judo champion in 1981?

4. What nationality is Nordic skier Berit Aunli?

5. What was the nickname of tennis player Henry Wilfred Austin?

6. In which year was U.S. tennis player Tracy Austin born?

7. Hashim Khan and Azam Khan contested the British Open squash final three times from 1953-59. How were they related?

8. Which horse won the 1989 Irish Derby?

9. At which sport do the Pittsburgh Penguins compete?

10. For which motor-racing team did Damon Hill drive in 1996?

11. With which sport do you associate Bob Pettit?

12. Which India cricketer made centuries in each of his first three Tests, beginning in 1984?

13. At what sport did Shirley Babashoff win eight Olympic medals?

14. Which Commonwealth Games javelin winner was born in Sidcup, Kent, in 1969?

15. Which heavyweight boxer was known as 'the Livermore Larruper'?

POP MUSIC

1. Who backed Yazz on her 1988 No. 1 single *The Only Way Is Up*?

2. On which record label did X.T.C. record their 1979 single *Making Plans for Nigel*?

3. Who recorded the 1998 album *Psyence Fiction*?

4. The composer of *Blue Suede Shoes* died in 1998. Who was he?

5. At which famous New York venue was Portishead's live album *PNYC* recorded?

6. In which year did the Sweet chart with the song *Love is like Oxygen*?

7. Which duo had the 1979 hit single *With You I'm Born Again*?

8. What was the only U.K. Top Ten single registered by Talking Heads?

9. Which group's only album chart entry was 1974's *Spyglass Guest*?

10. In which year did Haircut 100's Pelican West L.P. chart?

11. Who was the proprietor of Glasgow's Postcard Records?

12. Which singer fronted the group The 13th Floor Elevators?

13. Which punk group recorded the album *Fulham Fallout*?

14. Which member of Roxy Music recorded the solo album *In Search of Eddie Riff*?

15. Who recorded the 1998 album *Philophobia*?

PEOPLE

1. Which actress plays *Xena: Warrior Princess* on T.V.?

2. What is singer Sporty Spice's name?

3. Which Swedish model played Mrs. Freeze in the film *Batman and Robin*?

4. Which American stuntman was born in Butte, Montana, in 1938?

5. Who was executed for the kidnapping and murder of aviator Charles Lindbergh's son?

6. In which year was Marie Antoinette guillotined?

7. In which year was the spy Mata Hari executed?

8. By what name was American gambler Nicholas Andrea Dandolos known?

9. On which island was the Duke of Edinburgh born?

10. Who was the famous sister of writer Lee Radziwill?

11. In which country was fashion designer Yves St. Laurent born in 1936?

12. Which U.S. actress had a romance with Prince Andrew in 1982?

13. Which American T.V. evangelist was sentenced to a 45 year jail term in 1989 for defrauding his followers?

14. Which Dublin-born social reformer opened his 'Homes for Boys' in 1870?

15. By what name was U.S. murderer David Berkowitz known?

GENERAL KNOWLEDGE

1. What is the name given to a small hammer used by an auctioneer?

2. In which year did Constantine II of Greece abdicate?

3. What is the U.S. term for a pedestrian crossing?

4. What is the name givn to the broad flat limb of seals and penguins?

5. On what date was Easter Sunday in 1990?

6. What is the standard monetary unit of Ecuador?

7. What in ecology is the name given to the area in which an animal normally ranges?

8. In which province is the Irish county of Leitrim?

9. What is the approximate population of Buenos Aires in millions - 7, 10 or 13?

10. What do the initials of the organization ACAS stand for?

11. Who wrote the collection of essays *Abinger Harvest*?

12. In which year did broadcaster Brian Redhead die?

13. What is the home of Fulham F.C.?

14. Of what whole number is 9.9498743 the square root?

15. What is the more common name of the butterfly bush?

ANSWERS 1. Gavel 2. 1974 3. Crosswalk 4. Flipper 5. April 15 6. Sucre 7. Home range 8. Connaught 9. 10 million 10. Advisory Conciliation and Arbitration Service 11. E. M. Forster 12. 1994 13. Craven Cottage 14. 99 15. Buddleia.

ENTERTAINMENT

1. What was Karl Howman's character name in the T.V. comedy *Brush Strokes*?

2. Who composed the theatre piece *Blind Man's Buff*?

3. Who played *Shoestring* on television?

4. What nationality was composer Max Bruch?

5. How much, in dollars, was Dustin Hoffman paid for the film *The Graduate*?

6. Who scripted the 1966 film *Alfie* from his own play?

7. In which year was comedian George Burns born?

8. What is actress Jane Seymour's real name?

9. Who directed the 1979 film *Escape from Alcatraz*?

10. About whom was the 1988 film *Gorillas in the Mist*?

11. Who wrote the 1983 sitcom *Hallelujah!* which starred Thora Hird?

12. Who wrote the 1971 sitcom *Lollipop Loves Mr. Mole*?

13. In which year did pianist Dame Myra Hess die?

14. Who played Bill Sikes in the 1948 film *Oliver Twist*?

15. Who directed the 1996 film *Carla's Song*?

SPORT

1. Which snooker player beat Ronnie O'Sullivan in the Irish Open in December 1998?

2. What did Ian Woosnam score in the first round of the 1999 U.S. Masters?

3. Who was MVP in Superbowl I & II in American Football?

4. For which rugby league side did Andy Goodway sign in July 1985?

5. By what score did Everton beat Rapid Vienna in the 1985 European Cup Winners' Cup Final?

6. Who won the 1993 men's 100m title at the IAAF World Championships?

7. Against which international side did Gary McAllister play for Scotland in April, 1999 - his first such game for 16 months?

8. Who won the 1996 U.S. Open golf championship?

9. Which tennis player married Roger Cawley in 1975?

10. Who was 1998 British Open men's squash champion?

11. Which was the only horse to beat Brigadier Gerard, in the 1972 Benson & Hedges Gold Cup at York?

12. What was the nickname of Spanish cyclist Federico Bahamontes?

13. Which England Test cricketer captained Essex from 1961-6?

14. In which year did Virginia Wade win the Wimbledon singles title?

15. Where were the Summer Olympic Games held in 1900?

ANSWERS 1. Jimmy Michie **2.** 71 **3.** Bart Starr **4.** Wigan **5.** 3-1 **6.** Linford Christie **7.** Czech Republic **8.** Steve Jones **9.** Evonne Goolangong **10.** Peter Nicol **11.** Roberto **12.** Eagle of Toledo **13.** Trevor Bailey **14.** 1977 **15.** Paris.

POP MUSIC

1. With which standard did Mari Wilson have a Top 30 single in 1983?

2. In which year did Jackie Wilson first chart in the U.K. with *Reet Petite*?

3. Who recorded the 1998 album *Fin de Siècle*?

4. Which former drummer with Black Sabbath and Rainbow died in 1998?

5. What was the debut album of group Delakota?

6. Who recorded the 1998 album *Kingsize*?

7. On which record label did Sweet Sensation record their No. 1 single *Sad Sweet Dreamer*?

8. In which year did Taffy chart with *I Love My Radio (my dee jay's radio)*?

9. Which guitarist's albums include 1975's *Voyage of the Acolyte*?

10. Hadley, Norman, Keeble, Kemp and Kemp - which group?

11. Which U.S. electronic band comprises Alan Vega and Martin Rev?

12. Which poet recorded the 1979 mini-album *Walking Back to Happiness*?

13. What was Take That's first No. 1 single?

14. Which group recorded the 1998 album *Nu-clear Sounds*?

15. On which record label did Yazoo score five Top Twenty singles from 1982-90?

ANSWERS 1. Cry me a River **2.** 1957 **3.** The Divine Comedy **4.** Cozy Powell **5.** One Love **6.** The Boo Radleys **7.** Pye **8.** 1987 **9.** Steve Hackett **10.** Spandau Ballet **11.** Suicide **12.** John Cooper Clarke **13.** Pray **14.** Ash **15.** Mute.

ART AND LITERATURE

1. Who wrote the novel *The Kraken Wakes*?

2. Wamba is a jester in which novel by Walter Scott?

3. Which literary character was, eventually, '... withered, wrinkled, and loathsome of visage'?

4. Which controversial novel features the character Humbert Humbert?

5. What are the colours yellow, red and blue collectively known as?

6. In which city was artist Patrick Heron born?

7. Black-figure is one of the two major divisions of Greek vase painting. What is the other?

8. Who is the author of *Desert Crop* and *Bondage of Love*?

9. Who wrote the crime novel *Certain Justice*?

10. Which U.S. thriller writer authored *The Long Goodbye*?

11. In which year did sculptor Henry Moore die?

12. Which famous inventor and little-known artist was first president of the National Academy of Design at New York?

13. Which U.S. artist said 'What ethical consciousness, a painter is only a decorator'?

14. Which artist designed the first penny post envelope issued by Rowland Hill?

15. In which year did painter L.S. Lowry die?

GENERAL KNOWLEDGE

1. Which was founded first - Queen's College, Oxford or Keble College, Oxford?

2. In which sea is the Greek island of Lemnos?

3. In which year did the Shah of Iran abdicate?

4. Which Biblical character slew the giant Goliath?

5. In which year was Rudyard Kipling born?

6. How would you eat avgolemono - with a spoon or a knife and fork?

7. In which European country is the zinc-smelting town of Crotone?

8. In which year did comedian Michael Bentine die?

9. In which year was the Daylight Saving Act which first introduced British Summer Time?

10. Who was elected M.P. for Tatton in 1997?

11. What type of creature is a gelada - a gazelle or a baboon?

12. What colour are the flowers of the plant honesty?

13. What was the job of St. Matthew?

14. What is the name of the ruined abbey near Ripon, Yorkshire?

15. In which year was footballer Sir Stanley Matthews born?

ENTERTAINMENT

1. What nationality was composer Ole Bull?

2. Who played *Alfred the Great* in a 1969 historical film?

3. Who directed the 1983 film *Gorky Park*?

4. Which comic actor played Adam Parkinson in the sitcom *Butterflies*?

5. Who directed and starred in the 1961 film *One-Eyed Jacks*?

6. Who directed the 1983 film *Eureka*?

7. Which two comedians form the satirical partnership *The Long Johns*?

8. Who composed the 1926 opera *Cardillac*?

9. Who directed the 1959 film *Operation Petticoat*?

10. How much was Steve McQueen paid, in dollars, for the film *Bullitt*?

11. Who played Dan Conner in the sitcom *Roseanne*?

12. To which comedienne was comic Peter Butterworth married?

13. Who starred as Eddie Booth in the sitcom *Love Thy Neighbour*?

14. *Man in a Cocked Hat* was the U.S. title of which comedy starring Terry-Thomas?

15. Who directed the 1986 film *Gothic*?

ANSWERS 1. Norwegian **2.** David Hemmings **3.** Michael Apted **4.** Nicholas Lyndhurst **5.** Marlon Brando **6.** Nicolas Roeg **7.** John Fortune & John Bird **8.** Paul Hindemith **9.** Blake Edwards **10.** $1m **11.** John Goodman **12.** Janet Brown **13.** Jack Smethurst **14.** Carlton-Browne of the F.O. **15.** Ken Russell.

SPORT

1. Which Italian football team won the 1993 European Cup Winners' Cup?

2. Who won the Boston marathon for women in 1997 & '98?

3. Which unfashionable team won the 1997 Scottish League Cup Final?

4. Who were 1997 Super League champions in rugby league?

5. Which team won the AXA Life League in cricket?

6. What was the nickname of U.S. baseball player Frank Baker?

7. Which England cricketer made 113 against Australia on her Test debut in 1968?

8. At what field event did Iolanda Balas win 150 consecutive competitions between December 1956 & June 1967?

9. Who beat Linfield in the First Round of the 1993 European Cup?

10. With which sport do you associate the Dubai Duty Free Classic?

11. Which horse won the 1993 Prix de l'Arc de Triomphe?

12. Who, in 1973, played Billie Jean King in the 'Battle of the Sexes'?

13. Where will the Summer Olympics be held in 2000?

14. From which football team did Liverpool buy defender Julian Dicks?

15. Who were All-Ireland gaelic football champions in 1982?

ANSWERS 1. Parma 2. Fatuma Roba 3. Stranraer 4. Bradford Bulls 5. Surrey 6. Home Run 7. Enid Bakewell 8. High Jump 9. F.C. Copenhagen 10. Snooker 11. Urban Sea 12. Bobby Riggs 13. Sydney 14. West Ham United 15. Offaly.

POP MUSIC

1. Which group recorded the 1975 album *Rotters Club*?

2. Which female vocal group had a 1982 hit with *Dracula's Tango*?

3. Which group recorded the albums *Bandstand* and *It's only a Movie*?

4. On which label did the Tourists record their 1979 hit *I only want to be with you*?

5. What was the title of the 1989 No. 1 L.P. by Fine Young Cannibals?

6. Which group recorded 1977 album *Quark Strangeness and Charm*?

7. What is Pulp's lead singer called?

8. Which U.S. band recorded 1968 L.P. *Crown of Creation*?

9. *Long Live Love* and *Girl Don't Come* were hit singles for which 1960's singer?

10. Who recorded the 1998 album *One Head, Two Arms, Two Legs*?

11. Which bandleader wrote the song *A Swingin' Safari*?

12. Which U.S. guitar band's albums included *Where the Action is*?

13. Which German group had a surprise hit in 1976 with *I Want More*?

14. Which group's albums include 1997's *Dots and Loops*?

15. What did The Shadows change their name from in 1959?

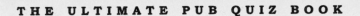

GEOGRAPHY

1. In which English county is the market town of Blandford Forum?

2. In which county of the Republic of Ireland is the seaside resort of Bray?

3. What is the capital of Brazil?

4. In which county of the Republic of Ireland is Blarney?

5. Which naval port in France is the base of the French Atlantic Fleet?

6. What is the name of the delta district at the mouth of the River Rhône famous for its colony of flamingos?

7. In which English county is the town of Burnham-on-Crouch?

8. In which European country is the cattle market town of Zwolle?

9. Which is the largest of the United Arab Emirates?

10. What became the capital of Nigeria in 1991?

11. In which South American country would you find that 153,170 square kilometres is an Acre?

12. Which river of Italy flows through Lake Como to the River Po?

13. What is the capital of Barbados?

14. Brisbane is the capital of which Australian state?

15. Which city in Massachusetts is the seat of Harvard University?

ANSWERS 1. Dorset 2. Wicklow 3. Brasilia 4. Cork 5. Brest 6. Camargue 7. Essex 8. The Netherlands 9. Abu Dhabi 10. Abuja 11. Brazil (Acre is a state) 12. River Adda 13. Bridgetown 14. Queensland 15. Cambridge.

GENERAL KNOWLEDGE

1. The avocado is named after which part of the body?

2. What sort of insect is a culex?

3. In which South American country is Florianopolis?

4. Which pop singer's forenames are Robert Frederick Zenon?

5. In which year did tennis player Ivan Lendl become a U.S. citizen?

6. In which year was the R-101 disaster?

7. What sort of creature is a houting - a fish or a bird?

8. In which year was the Battle of Britain?

9. Near which city is RAF college Cranwell?

10. What part of the body is also called the axilla?

11. Who was elected Labour M.P. for Tottenham in 1997?

12. What was the name of Edgar Wallace's first novel?

13. In which year did Louis B. Mayer receive an honorary award from the Academy of Motion Picture Arts and Sciences?

14. Who shot Mahatma Gandhi in 1948?

15. Which poet wrote *The Lake Isle of Innisfree*?

ENTERTAINMENT

1. In which city was comedian Tony Hancock born?

2. What nationality was conductor Hans von Bülow?

3. How much was Barbara Streisand paid, in dollars, for the 1969 film *Hello, Dolly!*?

4. Who played the title role in the 1972 film *Alice's Adventures in Wonderland*?

5. Who starred as Felix Cramer in the 1990 BBC T.V. drama series *A Sense of Guilt*?

6. Who directed the 1977 film *Grand Theft Auto*?

7. Who played *Carmen Jones* in a 1954 film?

8. Who was paid more for the 1967 film *Guess Who's Coming to Dinner* - Spencer Tracy or Katharine Hepburn?

9. Whose catchphrase is 'I wanna tell you a story'?

10. Who starred as Galen in the T.V. series *The Planet of the Apes*?

11. Who was photographer on the 1940 film *The Grapes of Wrath*?

12. What were comedians Rowan and Martin's forenames?

13. Near which city is the 25,000 seat Hollywood Bowl?

14. Who directed the 1964 film *The Carpetbaggers*?

15. In which year was the Chicago Symphony Orchestra founded?

ANSWERS 1. Birmingham **2.** German **3.** $750,000 **4.** Fiona Fullerton **5.** Trevor Eve **6.** Ron Howard **7.** Dorothy Dandridge **8.** Spencer Tracy **9.** Max Bygraves **10.** Roddy McDowall **11.** Gregg Toland **12.** Dan & Dick **13.** Los Angeles **14.** Edward Dmytryk **15.** 1891.

SPORT

1. At what sport was Balbir Singh a three-time Olympic gold medal winner?

2. What is football manager Alan Ball's middle name?

3. Which golfer became the first European winner of the U.S. Masters in 1980?

4. Who did Newcastle United defeat in the semi-final of the 1998/99 F.A. Cup?

5. Who became Britain's Davis Cup captain in 1995?

6. Who did Great Britain beat in their opening game of the 1999 World Championship Pool B ice hockey tournament in Denmark?

7. Which boxer died following a 1962 world title fight against Emile Griffith?

8. Which team were National Cup winners in basketball in 1995?

9. Who won the men's 100m at the 1995 IAAF World Championships?

10. Which woman won the London Marathon from 1992-94?

11. Who was men's world lightweight judo champion in 1989 & '91?

12. Which horse won the Oaks in 1995?

13. Which club won the inaugural world club championship in rugby league in 1997?

14. Who was women's world squash champion from 1996-98?

15. What did Colin Montgomerie score in the first round of the 1999 U.S. Masters?

POP MUSIC

1. Who recorded the 1999 album *Open All Night*?

2. Rene Dif is singer with which group?

3. Which group recorded the 1973 album *Ooh-La-La*?

4. Which group recorded the 1999 single *Mama Beat*?

5. Which country singer's albums include *Luxury Liner* and *Elite Hotel*?

6. *The Boy with the Arab Strap* was which group's 1998 album?

7. Which member of Velvet Underground recorded the album *Vintage Violence*?

8. Which group's second album is called *Only the Strongest will Survive*?

9. What is the opening track on *Gorilla* by Bonzo Dog Band?

10. Quentin Depieux recorded the single *Flat Beat* under what name?

11. Which singer recorded the 1999 album *Mule Variations*?

12. What was Abba's 2nd U.K. No.1 single?

13. Which comedian had a hit in 1982 with *A Day in the Life of Vince Prince*?

14. Who had a 1993 hit single with *All that she wants*?

15. Which group had a 1994 No.1 single with *Let me be your fantasy*?

ANSWERS 1. Marc Almond **2.** Aqua **3.** The Faces **4.** Cast **5.** Emmylou Harris **6.** Belle and Sebastian **7.** John Cale **8.** Hurricane # 1 **9.** Cool Britannia **10.** Mr. Oizo **11.** Tom Waits **12.** Mamma Mia **13.** Russ Abbot **14.** Ace of Base **15.** Baby D.

HISTORY

1. Who was Lord Chancellor prior to Lord Mackay's appointment in 1987?

2. In which year was Ferdinand Marcos first elected as president of the Philippines?

3. Which of France's kings was known as 'the Quarrelsome'?

4. Which two people officially opened the Channel Tunnel in 1994?

5. In which year was La Défense, an architectural development to the west of central Paris, begun?

6. In which country was Che Guevara killed in 1967?

7. Which country annexed the Galapagos Islands in 1832?

8. Who was Queen of the Netherlands from 1890-1948?

9. In which century did Sir Martin Frobisher discover and name Frobisher Bay in the Arctic Ocean?

10. In which year was the Battle of Dettingen in Bavaria?

11. Who has been king of Spain since 1975?

12. In which year did Jean Jacques Dessalines proclaim Haiti an independent republic?

13. The half-crown was demonetized on the last day of which year?

14. In which year was Gatwick officially opened by the Queen as London's second airport?

15. In which century did the volcano Mount Fujiyama last erupt?

ANSWERS 1. Lord Hailsham **2.** 1965 **3.** Louis X **4.** Queen Elizabeth II and François Mitterand **5.** 1958 **6.** Bolivia **7.** Ecuador **8.** Wilhelmina **9.** 16th **10.** 1743 **11.** Juan Carlos I **12.** 1804 **13.** 1969 **14.** 1958 **15.** 18th (in 1707).

GENERAL KNOWLEDGE

1. What type of fruit is a Cox's Orange Pippin?

2. What is acetylsalicylic acid better known as?

3. In which European country was prime minister Marcelo Caetano replaced by a military coup in 1974?

4. Of which country was John Curtin prime minister from 1941-45?

5. What would you do in New Zealand with a gem iron?

6. In which year was Amnesty International founded?

7. What is French leave?

8. Who won the 1990 Nobel prize for peace?

9. In which musical does the song *76 Trombones* feature?

10. The Folketing is the parliament of which country?

11. Genf is the German name of what city?

12. Which instrument did Glenn Miller play?

13. Which 18c French politician was nicknamed 'Friend of the People'?

14. Of which country was King Zog monarch?

15. In what year did Mbabane become capital of Swaziland?

ANSWERS 1. Apple 2. Aspirin 3. Portugal 4. Australia 5. Cook with it - it's an oven dish for baking cakes 6. 1961 7. Departure without permission or warning 8. Mikhail Gorbachev 9. The Music Man 10. Denmark 11. Geneva 12. Trombone 13. Jean Paul Marat 14. Albania 15. 1902.

THE ULTIMATE PUB QUIZ BOOK

ENTERTAINMENT

1. How much a day, in dollars, did Rudolph Valentino earn for the 1918 film *Alimony*?

2. Who directed the 1986 film *Aliens*?

3. Which singer does Dennis Quaid portray in the 1989 film *Great Balls of Fire*?

4. Which porcine puppet pairing were created by Jan and Vlasta Dalibor?

5. Which former pop star created 1983 children's sitcom *Luna*?

6. In which year did Marti Caine die?

7. In which year was the Chelsea Opera Group founded?

8. Which comic actress played Esmerelda Stavely-Smythe in 1967 sitcom *Hancock's*?

9. Who starred as Dr. Charles Sweet in Channel 4 sitcom *Rude Health*?

10. In which year did composer Gustav Holst die?

11. Who directed the 1963 film *The Great Escape*?

12. Which comedian's real name is Thomas Derbyshire?

13. Who directed the 1994 film *Even Cowgirls Get the Blues*?

14. Which Hollywood actress starred in the 1987 film *Allan Quatermain and the Lost City of Gold*?

15. Who starred as *Carrie* in a 1976 film?

SPORT

1. Which football team won the 1995 Scottish League Cup Final on penalties?

2. Who won the men's 200m title at the 1991 & '95 IAAF World Championships?

3. Which woman won the London Marathon four times out of five from 1984-88?

4. Which team won the 1997 AXA Life League in cricket?

5. Which football league team did Gordon Banks play for prior to Leicester City?

6. Roger Bannister ran a mile in 3:59.4 in May 1954. Who ran it in 3:57.9 in the same year?

7. Against who did Franco Baresi win his first international cap for Italy?

8. Which member of the U.S. Olympic basketball 'Dream Team' of 1992 is nicknamed 'The Round Mound of Rebound'?

9. What was the final score in the 1993 Ryder Cup?

10. Where was the 1993 Portuguese Grand Prix held?

11. Who was the 1976 Olympic men's 1500m champion?

12. At what sport is the Ranji Trophy competed for?

13. Which horse and rider won the British show jumping Derby from 1976-9?

14. Who won the 1993 Mercedes German Masters golf tournament?

15. Which horse won the 1999 Epsom Derby?

ANSWERS 1. Raith Rovers 2. Michael Johnson 3. Ingrid Kristiansen 4. Warwickshire 5. Chesterfield 6. John Landy 7. Romania 8. Charles Barkley 9. US -15, Europe -13 10. Estoril 11. John Walker 12. Cricket 13. Boomerang & Eddie Macken 14. Steve Richardson 15. Oath.

POP MUSIC

1. What is the name of Frank Black's backing band on the 1999 album *Pistolero*?

2. What was the title of Fairground Attraction's 1988 hit album?

3. Which female singer recorded the 1981 album *Koo Koo*?

4. The names of which four girls provided Top ten singles for the Bachelors between 1963-65?

5. 'Ne-ne na-na na-na nu-nu' was which group's first Top 30 single?

6. Who duetted with Phil Collins on the No.1 *Easy Lover*?

7. Whose singles in 1992 included *You're the one for me, Fatty*?

8. On which record label did Suede record the 1999 single *Electricity*?

9. Which female vocalist features on the single *What's it gonna be?* by Busta Rhymes?

10. Which disc jockey records under the name *Fatboy Slim*?

11. Which group's second album is called *Come on Die Young*?

12. Which country provided a 1968 single hit for Long John Baldry?

13. Who recorded the 1985 hit single *Tarzan Boy*?

14. What was the only U.K. No. 1 hit single for the Bangles?

15. Which disc jockey wrote the autobiography *Wicked Speed*?

ANSWERS 1. The Catholics **2.** The First of a Million Kisses **3.** Debbie Harry **4.** Charmaine, Diane, Ramona and Marie **5.** Bad Manners **6.** Philip Bailey **7.** Morrissey **8.** Nude **9.** Janet Jackson **10.** Norman Cook **11.** Mogwai **12.** Mexico **13.** Baltimora **14.** Eternal Flame **15.** Annie Nightingale.

THE ULTIMATE PUB QUIZ BOOK

WORDS

1. What is the lower part of an interior wall called?

2. Where would you hear the phrase 'faites vos jeux'?

3. What in law is a feme sole?

4. What would you do with a humpty - cook it or sit on it?

5. What is the insecticide dichlorodiphenyltrichloroethane better known as?

6. What is the Australian name for a duvet?

7. What is the game spillikins also known as?

8. What in New Zealand is a huntaway?

9. What is the German term for a ghostly duplicate of a living person?

10. What does DMA stand for in computer technology?

11. What in Australia is a hutchie?

12. What type of serviceman uses a ditty bag for their personal belongings?

13. What, in the Australian parliament, is a Dorothy Dixer?

14. What, in the British military, does D.C.M. stand for?

15. What would you do with a felucca - sail it or wear it?

ANSWERS 1. Dado **2.** A casino (Place your bets!) **3.** A single woman **4.** Sit on it - it's a low padded seat **5.** DDT **6.** Doona **7.** Jackstraws **8.** A type of sheepdog **9.** Doppelganger **10.** Direct Memory Access **11.** A groundsheet draped over a pole making a temporary shelter **12.** A sailor **13.** A question asked by a member of the government allowing a prepared reply **14.** Distinguished Conduct Medal **15.** Sail it - it's a narrow vessel of the Mediterranean

GENERAL KNOWLEDGE

1. What is the name given to the Scottish dish of boiled chicken, poached eggs and spinach?

2. In which year was Queen Elizabeth I born?

3. What actor was born Reginald Truscott-Jones?

4. In which year was Isaac Newton born?

5. In which year was Ted Hughes appointed poet laureate?

6. Who won the 1964 Nobel peace prize?

7. The novel *From Here to Eternity* derives its name from a line in a poem by whom?

8. On which river does Washington D.C. stand?

9. In which year was Kenyan political leader Tom Mboya assassinated?

10. What is a genipap - a type of hat or a tree?

11. On what date was Easter Sunday in 1901?

12. What is the standard monetary unit of Georgia?

13. In which city is Napier University?

14. In which year was the Hiroshima A-bomb dropped?

15. Who was the father of Achilles in Greek mythology?

ANSWERS 1. Howtowdie **2.** 1533 **3.** Ray Milland **4.** 1642 **5.** 1984 **6.** Martin Luther King Jnr. **7.** Kipling **8.** Potomac **9.** 1969 **10.** A tree **11.** April 7 **12.** Lari **13.** Edinburgh **14.** 1945 **15.** Peleus.

ENTERTAINMENT

1. Which was voted Best Film at the 1978 Cannes Film Festival?

2. Which D.J. played Peter Morgan in 1961 sitcom *Happily Ever After*?

3. Which U.S. film actress was the highest paid in 1935?

4. In which year was T.V. journalist John Pilger born?

5. Who plays Estella as a young girl in 1946 film *Great Expectations*?

6. Who composed the oratorio *A Child of Our Time*?

7. Who played 'The Sheriff of Nottingham' in the children's sitcom *Maid Marian and Her Merry Men*?

8. What is the name of the lead animal in 1980 monster movie *Alligator*?

9. Who wrote comedy show *Rutland Weekend Television*?

10. Which English composer's works include the ballet *Café des Sports*?

11. Who starred in 1960 film *Peeping Tom*?

12. In which office environment was 1983 sitcom *The Happy Apple* set?

13. Who played Kate Starling in 1960's sitcom *Marriage Lines*?

14. Who stars as Capt. Miller in 1997 film *Event Horizon*?

15. Who composed the musical work *A Faust Symphony*?

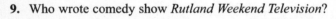

SPORT

1. Whose figures of 17 for 159 against South Africa in Johannesburg in 1913/14 were only surpassed in 1956?

2. Which male squash player won the British Amateur title from 1967-9?

3. Which Paraguay-born swimmer was 1992 Olympic men's 200m breaststroke champion?

4. What was tennis player Richard Alonzo Gonzales better known as?

5. Which club won the World Bowl in 1998 in American Football?

6. Which British team won the 1983 European Cup Winners' Cup?

7. Who was 1997 world men's singles table tennis champion?

8. Who won the men's London Marathon from 1994-96?

9. Who won the 1997 U.S. Open golf championship?

10. With which sport would you associate a 'Lonsdale Belt'?

11. At what sport was Wong Peng Soon an All-England champion from 1950-2?

12. What is the name of Montreal's baseball team?

13. Who won the 1930 World Cup in football?

14. Who won the 1964 Olympic men's 1500m title?

15. At what were Russians Alexeyev and Zhabotinsky Olympic champions?

Peter Snell 15. Weight-lifting.
Ernie Els 10. Boxing 11. Badminton 12. Montreal Expos 13. Uruguay 14.
Pancho 5. Rhein Fire 6. Aberdeen 7. Jan-Ove Waldner 8. Dionicio Ceron 9.
ANSWERS 1. Sidney Barnes 2. Jonah Barrington 3. Mike Barrowman 4.

POP MUSIC

1. Which duo had a Top 20 hit single in 1992 with *Miserere*?

2. Which male vocalist's first Top 20 hit single was 1960's *Image of a Girl*?

3. Which female singer had a 1977 No.1 hit single with *Free*?

4. Which Manchester band split in February 1993 but reformed for a series of gigs in 1999?

5. Whose albums include 1998's *Supposed Former Infatuation Junkie*?

6. Which group recorded 1999 album *Beaucoup Fish*?

7. Which band comprises Welch, Bush, Chipperfield and Frischmann?

8. Sophie Ellis-Bextor is lead singer with which group?

9. Danny and Richard McNamara are members of which group?

10. Gaz Coombes is lead singer with which group?

11. Which duo had a 1967 Top 10 single called *With a Little Help From My Friends*?

12. Who released the album *13* in 1999?

13. With which five-piece group did Jason Orange sing?

14. In which year did Al Stewart have a hit single with *Year of the Cat*?

15. What was the title of R.E.M.'s 1998 hit album?

ANSWERS 1. Zucchero and Luciano Pavarotti **2.** Mark Wynter **3.** Deniece Williams **4.** Happy Mondays **5.** Alanis Morissette **6.** Underworld **7.** Elastica **8.** Theaudience **9.** Embrace **10.** Supergrass **11.** Young Idea **12.** Blur **13.** Take That **14.** 1977 **15.** Up.

SCIENCE

1. How many grams of fat per 100 grams are there in baked beans?

2. What did Carl Anderson and Patrick Blackett discover independently of each other in 1932?

3. Which French physicist was the founder of thermodynamics?

4. What atomic number has the element curium?

5. In which year did German physicist Hans Geiger die?

6. Which element's symbol is Am?

7. What is china clay also known as?

8. What is the perimeter of a circle also called?

9. What nationality was physicist Niels Bohr?

10. What is the name given to the back part of the skull?

11. What was formerly known as 'fixed air'?

12. What vitamin is also called riboflavin?

13. In which century did Robert Bunsen, inventor of the Bunsen burner, live?

14. What colour is the mineral chlorite?

15. Which English scientist born in 1891 worked on the Manhattan Project to develop the atomic bomb?

ANSWERS 1. 0.5 2. The positron 3. Nicholas Carnot 4. 96 5. 1945 6. Americium 7. Kaolin 8. The circumference 9. Danish 10. Occiput 11. Carbon dioxide 12. B2 13. 19th 14. Green 15. Sir James Chadwick.

GENERAL KNOWLEDGE

1. What bird is also called a cushat?

2. What profession is associated with Frenchman André Le Nôtre?

3. In which year did writer and actor John Wells die?

4. What is the approximate population of Baghdad in millions - 2, 3 or 4?

5. In which century did the German botanist Leonard Fuchs live?

6. Which dramatist wrote the play *Absurd Person Singular*?

7. Of which country was George William Forbes prime minister from 1930-35?

8. Who was the husband of Mary I of England and Ireland?

9. Who authored 1673 play *The Country Wife?*

10. By what initials is Chronic Fatigue Syndrome usually known?

11. In the New Testament, who was the high priest during the trial of Jesus?

12. In which country is the wine region of Medoc?

13. Which zodiac sign covers parts of December and January?

14. On what date is the feast day of St. George?

15. Which politician was born Goldie Mabovich?

ANSWERS 1. Wood pigeon 2. Landscape gardener 3. 1998 4. 4 million 5. 16th 6. Alan Ayckbourn 7. New Zealand 8. Philip II of Spain 9. William Wycherley 10. ME 11. Caiaphas 12. France 13. Capricorn 14. April 23rd 15. Golda Meir.

ENTERTAINMENT

1. What was voted Best Film at the 1976 Cannes Film Festival?

2. Who played Officer Muldoon in sitcom *Car 54, Where Are You?*?

3. What is Victor Henry's job in 1969 film *All Neat in Black Stockings*?

4. Who played waitress Nicola in BBC drama *Pie in the Sky*?

5. Who starred as *The Great Gatsby* in a 1949 film?

6. What is the name of the central family in comedy *Married...With Children*?

7. Who played Chachi in comedy series *Happy Days*?

8. Which cast member of *Friends* appeared in the film *The Opposite of Sex*?

9. Who choreographed the 1937 ballet *Horoscope*?

10. Who directed the film *The Thin Red Line*?

11. Which actor played Merlin in the 1981 film *Excalibur*?

12. Who played artist Dora Carrington in the 1995 film *Carrington*?

13. Who authored the 1985 sitcom *Happy Families*?

14. Who directed the 1996 film *Everyone Says I Love You*?

15. What nationality was pianist Edwin Fischer who died in 1960?

ANSWERS 1. Taxi Driver **2.** Fred Gwynne **3.** Window cleaner **4.** Samantha Janus **5.** Alan Ladd **6.** Bundy **7.** Scott Baio **8.** Lisa Kudrow **9.** Frederick Ashton **10.** Terrence Malick **11.** Nicol Williamson **12.** Emma Thompson **13.** Ben Elton **14.** Woody Allen **15.** Swiss.

SPORT

1. Who won the 1986 World Professional Snooker Championship?

2. What nationality was world Formula 1 motor racing champion Jody Scheckter?

3. Who were All-Ireland hurling champions in 1982 & '83?

4. Who has won the British Open golf championship most times?

5. At which course is the St. Leger run?

6. What sport commences with a 'bully-off'?

7. Which British team were National Cup winners in basketball in 1998?

8. In which U.S. state was Olympic swimming champion Brian Goodell born?

9. Who was women's British Open squash champion 1993-98?

10. Who were 1998 Super League champions in rugby league?

11. What is cricketer Graham Gooch's middle name?

12. Who rode 1857 Epsom Derby-winning horse Blink Bonny?

13. Who rode 1973 Cheltenham Gold Cup winner The Dikler?

14. Which former onion-picker defeated 'Sugar Ray' Robinson to win the world middleweight boxing title in 1957?

15. For which country did Grant Batty play international rugby union from 1972-77?

ANSWERS 1. Joe Johnson 2. South African 3. Kilkenny 4. Harry Vardon 5. Doncaster 6. Hockey 7. Thames Valley 8. California 9. Michelle Martin 10. Wigan Warriors 11. Alan 12. Jack Charlton 13. Ron Barry 14. Carmen Basilio 15. New Zealand.

POP MUSIC

1. Roger Troutman was shot dead in May 1999. With which group did he chart in 1986?

2. With which song did Sue Wilkinson have a Top 30 hit in 1980?

3. Which group recorded the 1998 album *Deserter's Songs*?

4. Of which group is James Dean Bradfield a member?

5. Which group backed Dave Stewart on 1990 hit *Jack Talking*?

6. Which duo had a 1994 Christmas hit with *Them Girls Them Girls*?

7. Who is lead singer in group Placebo?

8. On which record label did Rod Stewart record 1975's *This Old Heart of Mine*?

9. Which group did singer Dave Randall quit in December 1998?

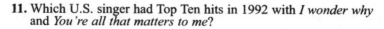

10. Which boyband had a 1998 hit album with *Where we belong*?

11. Which U.S. singer had Top Ten hits in 1992 with *I wonder why* and *You're all that matters to me*?

12. Which group's 1998 album was called *Version 2.0*?

13. Graham Coxon and Damon Albarn are members of which group?

14. Who is the lead singer with group *Republica*?

15. With which group did Pete Wylie have a hit single in 1991 with *Sinful*?

ANSWERS 1. Zapp **2.** You gotta be a hustler if you wanna get on **3.** Mercury Rev **4.** Manic Street Preachers **5.** The Spiritual Cowboys **6.** Zig and Zag **7.** Brian Molko **8.** Riva **9.** Lo-Fidelity Allstars **10.** Boyzone **11.** Curtis Stigers **12.** Garbage **13.** Blur **14.** Saffron **15.** The Farm.

THE ULTIMATE PUB QUIZ BOOK

PEOPLE

1. Who is the manager of Manchester United F.C.?

2. Who married Prince Edward in 1999?

3. Who was made Secretary of State for Defence in May 1997?

4. Who succeeded John Major as leader of the Conservative Party?

5. Which former T.V. star was jailed in May 1999 for nine months for supplying cocaine and cannabis?

6. Which title did Jennifer Forwood assume in 1999 following a lengthy court battle?

7. What job did Séverine Caneele have prior to winning joint Best Actress Award at the 1999 Cannes Film Festival?

8. Bob Ayling is chief executive of which airline?

9. By what name was U.S. outlaw William H. Bonney better known?

10. What was English pirate Edward Teach better known as?

11. Who did John Wilkes Booth assassinate in 1865?

12. Which politician did Arthur Herman Bremer shoot in May 1972?

13. How was serial killer Ted Bundy executed in 1989?

14. What was U.S. outlaw Robert Leroy Parker better known as?

15. Which woman founded the Christian Science Movement?

THE ULTIMATE PUB QUIZ BOOK

GENERAL KNOWLEDGE

1. The shape of what capital letter does a planoconvex lens most resemble?

2. In which year did Henry V die?

3. In ancient Rome, what would you have done in a room called a caldarium?

4. In which month of the year is St. Cuthbert's feast day?

5. What were the forenames of H.G. Wells?

6. Who authored the play *Dear Brutus*?

7. Who was British prime minister 1835-41?

8. Which writer's home from 1858-70 was Gads Hill Place?

9. Which country's flag is a yellow cross on a blue background?

10. In cricket, what do the initials h.w. stand for?

11. The schilling is the monetary unit of which European country?

12. In which year was Gamblers Anonymous founded in the U.S.?

13. What is the collective noun for a group of crows?

14. Who was the eldest son of Queen Victoria?

15. Who wrote the poem *Tam O'Shanter*?

ENTERTAINMENT

1. What was voted Best Film at the 1974 Cannes Film Festival?

2. What was the 1964 film *Carry on Jack* called in the U.S.?

3. Which actress played Tom Cruise's girlfriend in 1983 film *All the Right Moves*?

4. Who played Alison Mackenzie in 1960's T.V. drama *Peyton Place*?

5. Who played Major Frank Burns in the sitcom *M*A*S*H*?

6. Who directed the 1940 film *The Great McGinty*?

7. What is Caroline Duffy's job in the sitcom *Caroline in the City*?

8. In which city was U.S. comedian Martin Mull born?

9. Who composed the opera *From the House of the Dead*?

10. In which year was comedian Mike Harding born?

11. Who starred as a boxing reporter in 1956 film *The Harder They Fall*?

12. What nationality is composer Carlisle Floyd?

13. Who played the painter *Rembrandt* in a 1936 film?

14. Which French actor starred in the 1990 film *Green Card*?

15. Who directed the 1973 film *The Exorcist*?

SPORT

1. In which European capital city was Canadian swimmer Alex Baumann born?

2. Which athlete won the men's 1500m title at the 1974 Commonwealth Games?

3. Bob Beamon was the first long jumper to exceed 29 feet. Who was the first to exceed 28 feet?

4. Which cricket team won the 1998 AXA Life League?

5. Who were British basketball men's league champions from 1990-92?

6. What did Sandy Lyle score in the First Round of the 1999 U.S. Masters?

7. Which women's team won the European Club Champions Cup in hockey from 1983-7?

8. Who won the men's 400m title at the 1993, '95 & '97 IAAF World Championships?

9. Which cricket team won the 1992 Benson & Hedges Cup?

10. Which man won the New York Marathon from 1976-79?

11. Who was world women's singles table tennis champion in 1995 & '97?

12. Which horse won the Oaks in 1996?

13. How old was Gary Kasparov when he became World Chess champion?

14. What is the name of Detroit's American Football team?

15. Which cricketer stood against Jim Callaghan in the 1964 election?

ANSWERS 1. Prague 2. Filbert Bayi 3. Beamon, in the same jump 4. Lancashire 5. Kingston 6. 71 7. HGC Wassenaar 8. Michael Johnson 9. Hampshire 10. Bill Rodgers 11. Deng Yaping 12. Lady Carla 13. 22 14. Detroit Lions 15. Ted Dexter.

POP MUSIC

1. Of which chart-topping group is Tjinder Singh a member?

2. Who recorded the 1998 album *Mutations*?

3. What was the title of Stiltskin's No.1 single in 1994?

4. Which trio of producers charted in 1987 with *Roadblock*?

5. Which film star provided group Stump with a surprise hit in 1988?

6. What was Supertramp's first Top Ten U.K. single?

7. Which group had a 1971 No.1 single with *Hey girl don't bother me*?

8. How many U.K. No.1 singles did The Temptations have?

9. Which duo recorded 1983 album *Battle Hymns for Children Singing*?

10. What was J.J. Barrie's only No.1 single called?

11. Which comedy group caused hilarity with their 1983 hit *Buffalo Bill's Last Scratch*?

12. Which item of clothing provided The John Barry Seven with a 1960 Top 30 single?

13. Which northern soul favourite had hits in 1965 with *1-2-3* and *Cry Like a Baby*?

14. Which band's Top Ten singles include *One Love* and *Elephant Stone*?

15. Martin Rossiter is the lead singer with which group?

ART AND LITERATURE

1. The waif Heathcliff is picked up by Mr. Earnshaw in which city in the novel *Wuthering Heights*?

2. Who wrote the novel *Beau Geste*?

3. Which Bulgarian-born artist's projects include wrapping up sections of the Australian coastline?

4. In which century did the French artist Charles-Francois Daubigny live?

5. Which cult author wrote the novel *Post Office*?

6. In which controversial novel does the Korova Milkbar appear?

7. Which U.S. comic thriller writer's Florida-based works include *Double Whammy* and *Stormy Weather*?

8. Who is credited with the authorship of *The Iliad*?

9. What was painter Augustus John's middle name?

10. In which city was the painter Kandinsky born?

11. In which city was Sir Eduardo Paolozzi born?

12. Which Spanish Cubist painter's father was an art teacher?

13. Which Surrealist artist died in Brussels in 1967?

14. Who wrote the thriller book *The Partner*?

15. What is the name of Arundhati Roy's Booker Prize-winning best seller?

ANSWERS 1. Liverpool 2. P.C. Wren 3. Christo 4. 19th 5. Charles Bukowski 6. A Clockwork Orange 7. Carl Hiaasen 8. Homer 9. Edwin 10. Moscow 11. Edinburgh 12. Picasso 13. Magritte 14. John Grisham 15. The God of Small Things.

GENERAL KNOWLEDGE

1. On which island of New York City is the park called The Battery?

2. Tapetus is a satellite of which planet?

3. Of what whole number is 24.494897 the square root?

4. Which U.S. state is nicknamed the Garden State?

5. In which Shakespeare play would you find the character Caliban?

6. What was the 'month of buds' in the French revolutionary calendar?

7. Who composed the film soundtrack for *Once Upon a Time in the West*?

8. Who composed the operetta *The Count of Luxembourg*?

9. In which country is Melton Mowbray?

10. How did bank robber Ned Kelly die?

11. In what country is the mountain Aconcagua?

12. When was the first London to Brighton veteran car rally?

13. Which Athenian dramatist authored the play *The Ill-Tempered Man*?

14. What sort of creature is a babirusa?

15. Which item of clothing did Mary Phelps Jacob patent?

ANSWERS 1. Manhattan Island **2.** Saturn **3.** 600 **4.** New Jersey **5.** The Tempest **6.** Germinal **7.** Ennio Morricone **8.** Franz Lehar **9.** Leicestershire **10.** He was hanged **11.** Argentina **12.** 1927 **13.** Menander **14.** A wild pig **15.** The bra.

ENTERTAINMENT

1. Who composed 1830 comic opera *Fra Diavolo?*

2. Which Australian comedian scripted and starred in 1990 film *Almost an Angel?*

3. What is the real name of comic Harry Hill?

4. Who did Laurence Naismith play in T.V. show *The Persuaders!?*

5. What was voted Best Film at the 1971 Cannes Film Festival?

6. Who played Simon Harrap in 1980's sitcom *Me & My Girl?*

7. Who directed 1974 film *The Cars That Ate Paris?*

8. What was Gail's maiden name in *Coronation Street?*

9. What nationality is composer Keith Humble?

10. Who played Jo Grant in T.V. show *Doctor Who?*

11. Which comedian was born Bob Davies in Birmingham in 1945?

12. Who directed 1940 film *The Philadelphia Story?*

13. Who directed 1990 film *The Grifters?*

14. Who plays *Expresso Bongo* in a 1959 film?

15. Which actor played Tom Chance in sitcom *Chance in a Million?*

ANSWERS 1. Daniel Auber 2. Paul Hogan 3. Matthew Hall 4. Judge Fulton 5. The Go-Between 6. Richard O'Sullivan 7. Peter Weir 8. Potter 9. Australian 10. Katy Manning 11. Jasper Carrott 12. George Cukor 13. Stephen Frears 14. Cliff Richard 15. Simon Callow.

SPORT

1. In which town was Tony Jacklin born?

2. With which sport do you associate Jack Kramer?

3. For which modern Olympics was the flame first carried from Greece?

4. Whose first winner as an amateur jockey in 1986 was Gulfland?

5. In which year was the first British motor racing Grand Prix held?

6. For which Cup did 'Magic' compete with 'Cambria' in 1870?

7. Who beat Romania 51-0 in their first rugby union game of 1993/4?

8. Who was women's world Open judo champion from 1980-86?

9. Who won rugby league's Challenge Cup in 1998?

10. Which man won the New York Marathon from 1980-82?

11. Who were runners-up from 1986-88 in the British men's basketball league?

12. How many times did Bill Beaumont captain England rugby union side?

13. Which German football league club did Franz Beckenbauer play for from 1980-2?

14. Who was the first German winner of the Wimbledon men's singles tennis championship?

15. In which city was 1970's distance runner David Bedford born?

POP MUSIC

1. What was R & J Stone's 1976 hit single?

2. Rebecca Storm's 1985 single *The Show* was the theme tune of which T.V. series?

3. Of which group is Bobby Gillespie a member?

4. Which group's hit singles include 1980's *Bear Cage* and *Who wants the world?*

5. Which instrumental group charted in 1963 with *Wipe Out?*

6. Which duo had a hit in 1963 with the song *Deep Purple?*

7. Which group had Top Ten hits with *The Dean and I* and *Wall Street Shuffle?*

8. What was the title of Justin Hayward and John Lodge's 1975 hit L.P.?

9. What was the alliterative 1975 No.1 single of the Bay City Rollers?

10. Which group had a 1990 No. 1 single with *Dub be good to me?*

11. Bedrocks charted in 1968 with which song by the Beatles?

12. Who is the lead singer of the band Garbage?

13. Who recorded the 1998 album *Mezzanine?*

14. *16 Bars* was the last Top Ten single, in 1976, for which vocal group?

15. After their 1967 No.1 *Massachusetts*, the Bee Gees charted with similarly titled songs. What were they called?

ANSWERS 1. We do it **2.** Connie **3.** Primal Scream **4.** The Stranglers **5.** The Surfaris **6.** Nino Tempo and April Stevens **7.** 10 c.c. **8.** Blue Jays **9.** Bye Bye Baby **10.** Beats International **11.** Ob-la-di, Ob-la-da **12.** Shirley Manson **13.** Massive Attack **14.** The Stylistics **15.** 'World', and 'Words'.

GEOGRAPHY

1. Which mountain range is known as the 'backbone of England'?

2. In which U.S. state is the town of Albuquerque?

3. In what is Bounty Island, New Zealand, covered?

4. What is the capital of the Central American republic of Panama?

5. On which river is Newport, Isle of Wight?

6. Montevideo is the capital of which South American country?

7. What is the name of the garden suburb S.W. of Birmingham founded by George Cadbury in 1897?

8. What is the longest river in Scotland?

9. What is the name of the strait separating the Isle of Wight from Hampshire?

10. On which river is the Pennsylvania port of Pittsburgh?

11. In which county of the Southwest is Portishead?

12. What is the chief island of the Society Islands in French Polynesia?

13. What is the seaport capital of the Falkland Islands?

14. In which ocean is the Sargasso Sea?

15. Which is longer - the River Rhône or the River Rhine?

ANSWERS 1. The Pennine Range **2.** New Mexico **3.** Guano (it is uninhabited) **4.** Panama City **5.** Medina **6.** Uruguay **7.** Bourneville **8.** River Tay **9.** The Solent **10.** Ohio River **11.** Somerset **12.** Tahiti **13.** Stanley **14.** Atlantic Ocean **15.** River Rhine.

GENERAL KNOWLEDGE

1. What type of food is badderlocks?

2. What is the name given to the nest or hollow where a hare lives?

3. In which year did Louis Bleriot first cross the English Channel by aeroplane?

4. What is Ido?

5. How many U.S. presidents have had George as their first name?

6. Who was the chief character in Johnny Speight's *Till Death Us Do Part?*

7. In which year was Julius Caesar assassinated?

8. Which king authored 1604's *A Counterblast to Tobacco?*

9. Where is the Sea of Rains?

10. Which U.S. journalist authored 1919 book *The American Language?*

11. Which island was once called Van Diemen's Land?

12. Which element's symbol is Md?

13. Which cartoonist created the strip *Peanuts?*

14. Which religious figure is carried on the gestatorial chair?

15. What would you do with a callop - eat it or ride in it?

ENTERTAINMENT

1. Who composed 1746 oratorio *Judas Maccabaeus?*

2. Who won Best Actress award at the 1979 Cannes Film Festival?

3. Who directed 1965 film *Alphaville?*

4. How were the actors Bill and Jon Pertwee related?

5. What was Milo O'Shea's character name in comedy show *Me Mammy?*

6. What are comedians Paul and Barry Elliot better known as?

7. Who directed 1999 film *eXistenZ?*

8. Who directed 1942 film *Casablanca?*

9. Who played Phyllis Pearce in *Coronation Street?*

10. What nationality was composer Engelbert Humperdinck?

11. What job did Ian Lavender do in sitcom *Have I Got You...Where You Want Me?*

12. Who directed 1998 film *Rounders?*

13. Which comedian stars in the 1963 sketch *Same Procedure As Last Year* which is shown annually in Scandinavia at New Year?

14. Which comic actor plays Mr. Grocer in 1997 film *Grosse Pointe Blank?*

15. Who stars as a fashion photographer in the film *Eyes of Laura Mars?*

ANSWERS 1. Handel **2.** Sally Field **3.** Jean-Luc Godard **4.** They were cousins **5.** Bunjy Kennefick **6.** The Chuckle Brothers **7.** David Cronenberg **8.** Michael Curtiz **9.** Jill Summers **10.** German **11.** Dentist **12.** John Dahl **13.** Freddie Frinton **14.** Dan Aykroyd **15.** Faye Dunaway.

SPORT

1. Which male won the badminton singles at the 1972 Olympics when it was a demonstration sport?

2. How many caps did David Duckham win for England at rugby union?

3. Who was men's British Open squash champion 1958-61?

4. With which club side did French footballer Alain Giresse end his career?

5. By what score did Dennis Priestley beat Eric Bristow in the 1991 World Professional Darts Championship?

6. Which club won the world bowl in American Football in 1997?

7. Who was the 1998 U.S. Open golf champion?

8. Which club lost the 1981 European Cup Winners' Cup Final?

9. Which woman was 1979 World Student 100m champion?

10. How many runs did cricketer Neil Harvey score in his 79 Tests for Australia from 1948-63?

11. Who won the men's 800m event at the 1995 & '97 IAAF World Championships?

12. Who was the first Indian bowler to take 200 Test wickets?

13. What was cricketer Alec Bedser's twin brother called?

14. Who was 1986 European Footballer of the Year?

15. Which New Zealander won the 1984 World Outdoor Singles title at bowls?

ANSWERS 1. Rudy Hartono 2. 36 3. Azam Khan 4. Marseille 5. 6-0 6. Barcelona Dragons 7. Lee Janzen 8. Carl Zeiss Jena 9. Marlies Göhr 10. 6149 11. Wilson Kipketer 12. Bishen Bedi 13. Eric 14. Igor Belanov 15. Peter Belliss.

POP MUSIC

1. Which group recorded the album *Good Morning Spider?*

2. On which record label did The *Sugarcubes* record 1992 hit *Hit?*

3. What was the title of Five Star's 1986 No.1 album?

4. On which record label was Fleetwood Mac's 1968 album *Fleetwood Mac* released?

5. Who recorded the 1984 album *How Men Are?*

6. Which group recorded 1986 album *London 0 Hull 4?*

7. Which singer recorded 1980 L.P. *The Up Escalator?*

8. Frantz, Weymouth, Harrison, Byrne - which group?

9. Which group recorded the 1980 album *Sandinista?*

10. What was Freddie Bell and the Bellboys' only U.K. single hit?

11. What was trumpet player Eddie Calvert's second No.1 single?

12. Who had a 1986 Top Ten single with *Word Up?*

13. In which year was *Happy Talk* a No.1 single for Captain Sensible?

14. Whose Top Ten singles include 1988's *Circle in the Sand* and *I Get Weak?*

15. Which group recorded the 1998 album *Celebrity Skin?*

ANSWERS 1. Sparklehorse 2. One Little Indian 3. Silk and Steel 4. Blue Horizon 5. Heaven 17 6. The Housemartins 7. Graham Parker 8. Talking Heads 9. The Clash 10. Giddy-up-a-ding-dong 11. Cherry Pink and Apple Blossom White 12. Cameo 13. 1982 14. Belinda Carlisle 15. Hole.

HISTORY

1. In which year did the Klondike gold rush begin?

2. In which year was Sydney Harbour Bridge officially opened?

3. What annual event started in Islington in 1886 before moving to Olympia and Earl's Court?

4. In which year was Mary, Queen of Scots executed?

5. In which century was the Supreme Court of the U.S.A. established?

6. In which year did Friends of the Earth form?

7. In which year did work begin on the Suez Canal?

8. In which year did George II of England die?

9. In which county is Tolpuddle, home of the Tolpuddle Martyrs?

10. In which year did Prince Albert die?

11. In which year did the Korean War begin?

12. In which city was the United Nations charter signed in June, 1945?

13. Paragraph 31 of the Magna Carta concerns the taking of what, without consent?

14. What was the name of the merchant who first signed the American Declaration of Independence?

15. Who became Empress of Russia in 1762?

GENERAL KNOWLEDGE

1. In which year was Jean-Paul Marat assassinated?

2. Who did William Shakespeare marry in 1582?

3. Who was born first - Laurel or Hardy?

4. In which year did inventor John Logie Baird die?

5. In radio terminology what does the abbreviation CW stand for?

6. In which U.S. state is Fort Lauderdale?

7. What is ghee?

8. LS is the abbreviation for which postcode area?

9. On November 27, 1970, Pope Paul VI was nearly attacked by a knifeman in which airport?

10. What is the standard monetary unit of Laos?

11. Where in Hampshire is the National Motor Museum?

12. Who invented the Kenwood Chef electric food mixer?

13. Who wrote the novel *Absalom, Absalom!?*

14. What is the name of the scientific study of sound and sound waves?

15. Which poet authored *The Cotter's Saturday Night?*

ANSWERS 1. 1793 2. Anne Hathaway 3. Laurel 4. 1946 5. Continuous waves 6. Florida 7. Clarified butter used in Indian cookery 8. Leeds 9. Manila 10. Kip 11. Beaulieu 12. Ken Wood 13. William Faulkner 14. Acoustics 15. Robert Burns.

ENTERTAINMENT

1. Which comic actor played Dr. Rex Regis in 1994 sitcom *Health and Efficiency?*

2. Who was named Best Actor at the 1978 Cannes Film Festival?

3. Who directed the 1989 film *Always?*

4. Which actress plays Kat in 1995 film *Casper?*

5. Who played Ivy Tilsley in *Coronation Street?*

6. Who plays a cynical weatherman in the film *Groundhog Day?*

7. What was Wolfie's girlfriend called in the show *Citizen Smith?*

8. Who played Jim Wilkins in one-off 1975 T.V. comedy show *Milk-O?*

9. Who composed the opera *The Ice Break*, produced at Covent Garden in 1977?

10. Who won Best Actress award at the 1975 Cannes Film Festival?

11. Who directed 1955 film *House of Bamboo?*

12. On whose book is 1987 film *Castaway* based?

13. Who played Jamie McCrimmon in *Doctor Who?*

14. Who composed the series of percussive works entitled *Imaginary Landscape?*

15. What was the profession of *Clarence* in the Ronnie Barker sitcom?

(146)

THE ULTIMATE PUB QUIZ BOOK

SPORT

1. Which United States threesome won the 1993 Dunhill Cup in golf?

2. Which teams competed in the 1993 baseball World Series?

3. In which year was athlete Carl Lewis born?

4. Which horse won the 1984 Irish Derby?

5. At what weight was Chris Finnegan Olympic boxing champion in 1968?

6. Who was 1960 Olympic men's 100m champion?

7. Which man won the 1984 and '85 New York Marathon?

8. What did the Rumbelows League Cup in football become in 1993?

9. Which team won the 1993 Benson & Hedges Cup in cricket?

10. Which British women's basketball team were runners-up in the league in 1997 & '98?

11. What was New Zealand rugby union player Sid Going's middle name?

12. Who rode 1998 Epsom Derby-winning horse High-Rise?

13. Who was 1996 Wimbldeon men's singles tennis champion?

14. Who won the Five Nations championship in rugby union in 1998?

15. Who knocked out Yum Dong-Kyun in 1977 to win the WBC super-bantamweight boxing title?

ANSWERS 1. Payne Stewart, John Daly & Fred Couples 2. Toronto Blue Jays and Philadelphia Phillies 3. 1961 4. El Gran Senor 5. Middleweight 6. Armin Hary 7. Orlando Pizolato 8. Coca-Cola Cup 9. Derbyshire 10. Thames Valley Ladies 11. Milton 12. Olivier Peslier 13. Richard Krajicek 14. France 15. Wilfredo Gomez.

POP MUSIC

1. Who recorded the 1998 album *There's Something Going On?*

2. From which country did band Sutlans of Ping F.C. hail?

3. Which group recorded 1980 album *Strange Boutique?*

4. Who produced the album *End of the Century* by the Ramones?

5. Which group recorded 1980 album *Sound Affects?*

6. What was the name of Madonna's 1998 album?

7. Who duetted on 1979 hit single *No More Tears (Enough is Enough)?*

8. Which artist recorded 1981 hit single *Bette Davis Eyes?*

9. How many U.K. No.1 singles did The Carpenters have?

10. Who scored a 1978 Top ten single with *Do it do it again?*

11. David Cassidy's 1973 No. 1 *Daydreamer* was a double A-side with which song?

12. Who recorded the 1983 album *North of a Miracle?*

13. Which entertainer had a hit with *Little White Berry* in 1960?

14. Which entertainer had a hit with *Little White Bull* in 1959'?

15. Who recorded the song collection *10 Bloody Marys and 10 How's Your Fathers?*

ANSWERS 1. Babybird **2.** Ireland **3.** The Monochrome Set **4.** Phil Spector **5.** The Jam **6.** Ray of Light **7.** Donna Summer and Barbra Streisand **8.** Kim Carnes **9.** None **10.** Raffaella Carra **11.** The Puppy Song **12.** Nick Heyward **13.** Roy Castle **14.** Tommy Steele **15.** Elvis Costello.

WORDS

1. What in Russia is a kibitka?

2. Lactic refers to which liquid?

3. What ancient Roman unit of weight corresponded to a pound?

4. Which board game derives its name from the Latin 'I play'?

5. What sort of creature is a wobbegong - a shark or a bird of prey?

6. What is the Greek word for finger-nail?

7. What is a kier?

8. What would you do with laksa in Malaysia - eat it or drink it?

9. What sort of creature is a limpkin?

10. What is the sixth letter in the Greek alphabet?

11. What is the wildebeest also known as?

12. What nickname was given to Sir Robert Peel when Chief Secretary for Ireland between 1812-1818?

13. What, in Islam, is the word for the will of Allah?

14. What would you do with langoustine - paint with it or eat it?

15. Which type of pasta is named after the Italian phrase 'small tongues'?

GENERAL KNOWLEDGE

1. In which town is Keele University?

2. Who assassinated prime minister Spencer Perceval in 1812?

3. On which part of the body would you wear a ghillie?

4. Where in Dorset is there a museum housing 300 tanks?

5. In which year was the Battle of Marengo?

6. How old was Buddy Holly when he died?

7. Which U.S. president was present at the Yalta Conference?

8. Calpe was the ancient name for which limestone promontory?

9. How old was Frank Sinatra when he died?

10. In which year was Indian film producer Ismail Merchant born?

11. Costa Smeralda is a resort area of which Mediterranean island?

12. Of which country is 'Waitangi Day' the national day?

13. Who wrote the letter *De Profundis* to Lord Alfred Douglas?

14. Which imaginary country features in *The Prisoner of Zenda?*

15. Which U.S. state is nicknamed the 'Diamond State'?

ANSWERS 1. Newcastle under Lyme 2. John Bellingham 3. On the foot - it is a shoe 4. Bovington Camp 5. 1800 6. 22 7. Franklin D. Roosevelt 8. Rock of Gibraltar 9. 82 10. 1936 11. Sardinia 12. New Zealand 13. Oscar Wilde 14. Ruritania 15. Delaware.

ENTERTAINMENT

1. Who played *The Amazing Dr. Clitterhouse* in a 1938 film?

2. Who played schoolteacher Eileen in T.V. drama *Pennies From Heaven?*

3. Who was Best Actress award winner at the 1973 Cannes Film Festival?

4. Which pair of actors starred in 1993 film *Grumpy Old Men?*

5. Which director did Ian McKellen portray in the film *Gods and Monsters?*

6. In which year was comedian Julian Clary born?

7. Which comic actor played *The Climber* in a 1983 sitcom?

8. Who played Percy Sugden in *Coronation Street?*

9. Who directed 1989 film *Casualties of War?*

10. Who did Ann George play in *Crossroads?*

11. Who played Colin in the sitcom *Colin's Sandwich?*

12. In which year was Spike Milligan born?

13. Who composed what 1900 opera *Our Lady's Juggler?*

14. What was awarded Best Film accolade at the 1969 Cannes Film Festival?

15. In which year was actor Nicholas Parsons born?

SPORT

1. In which U.S. state is the Preakness Stakes horse race run?

2. Which Australian state side did cricketer Richie Benaud captain from 1955-64?

3. Stellan Bengtsson won the 1971 world singles table tennis title. Which country did he represent?

4. In which city was former world light-welterweight champion boxer Wilfred Benitez born?

5. Which Italian boxer won the 1960 Olympic welterweight title?

6. How many caps did England rugby union player William Wavell-Wakefield win for his country?

7. Which English football team lost in the 1966 European Cup Winners' Cup Final?

8. Irene de Kok was women's light-heavyweight judo champion in 1986 & '87. Which country did she represent?

9. Which Mexican man won the 1994 & '95 New York Marathon?

10. What did Nick Faldo score in the First Round of the 1999 U.S. Masters golf tournament?

11. Which horse won the Oaks in 1997?

12. Who was 1998 Wimbledon women's singles tennis champion?

13. Who won rugby union's European Cup in the 1997/98 season?

14. Which British women's basketball team were league champions from 1996-98?

15. Who led Pakistan to victory in the 1992 cricket World Cup?

ANSWERS 1. Maryland **2.** New South Wales **3.** Sweden **4.** New York **5.** Nino Benvenuti **6.** 31 **7.** Liverpool **8.** Netherlands **9.** German Silva **10.** 80 **11.** Reams of Verse **12.** Jana Novotna **13.** Bath **14.** Sheffield Hatters **15.** Imran Khan.

POP MUSIC

1. What was Stevie Wonder's only 1973 Top Ten single?

2. Who recorded the 1998 album *Voice of an Angel?*

3. Nina Persson is lead singer with which group?

4. Which child star had a 1974 hit with *Ma, he's making eyes at me?*

5. Who had a 1975 hit single with *Sending out an S.O.S.?*

6. The video for whose single, *Temper Temper*, was banned in 1998 by the B.B.C.?

7. Which Radio One disc jockey was awarded the O.B.E. in June 1998?

8. Whose debut solo album was *Unfinished Monkey Business?*

9. Which group backed Dave Edmunds on 1981 single *The race is on?*

10. From which European country do Technotronic originate?

11. What was the only U.K. hit, in 1964, of Helmut Zacharias?

12. Which Australian vocalist had a Top Ten hit in 1978 with *Love is in the air?*

13. Who recorded the 1998 album *What another man spills?*

14. Which U.S. singer drowned in the Mississippi River in June 1997?

15. What was Womack and Womack's 1988 Top Ten single?

SCIENCE

1. Whose work in synthesizing DDT won him the 1948 Nobel prize for medicine?

2. In the Mohs scale of hardness what is No. 7?

3. Who authored 1988's *A Brief History of Time?*

4. What is the name given to a rock fragment between 0.2-2.3 inches in diameter?

5. Which element has the atomic number 50?

6. In which year did astronomer Edmund Halley die?

7. What is the melting point of plutonium in °C?

8. Who discovered carbolic acid in 1834?

9. A hyper arid area is one which experiences no rainfall in a 12 month period. Approximately what percentage of the world's land area is hyper arid?

10. What in chemistry does HPLC stand for?

11. Which element's symbol is Ho?

12. In which century did Dutch mathematician Christiaan Huygens live?

13. What is the name given to the point on the Earth's surface directly above the focus of an earthquake?

14. Which English physician discovered vaccination?

15. Which dinosaur's name derived from the phrase 'earthquake lizard'?

GENERAL KNOWLEDGE

1. What colour are the trunk and branches of the ghost gum tree?

2. What does the abbreviation IFF mean in military parlance?

3. What shape is a converging meniscus lens?

4. In which year did France last recapture Calais from England?

5. In which year was the horse Shergar stolen?

6. Which actress became Greek minister of Culture in 1985?

7. Which French chef was known as 'The King of Cooks'?

8. What is the international car registration for Cyprus?

9. In which county is the town of Gillingham?

10. In what year was the storming of the Bastille?

11. Hg is the symbol of which element?

12. Which military leader was known as the 'Corsican ogre'?

13. In what year was the St. Valentine's Day massacre?

14. Who was born first - John Lennon or Yoko Ono?

15. What type of clothing was an acton in medieval Europe?

ANSWERS 1. White 2. Identification, Friend or Foe? 3. Crescent-shaped 4. 1558 5. 1983 6. Melina Mercouri 7. Escoffier 8. CY 9. Kent 10. 1789 11. Mercury 12. Napoleon 13. 1929 14. Yoko Ono 15. A jacket or jerkin.

THE ULTIMATE PUB QUIZ BOOK

ENTERTAINMENT

1. *The Ambushers* was third in a series of films starring Dean Martin as which spy?

2. Who played Simon Templar in t.v. show *The Return of the Saint?*

3. Which actress plays the widow of a U.S. president in 1994 film *Guarding Tess?*

4. On whose novel is 1989 film *Cat Chaser* based?

5. What was awarded Best Film accolade at the 1970 Cannes Film Festival?

6. Who played Zoe Herriot in *Doctor Who?*

7. Who composed the 3-Act opera *Treemonisha?*

8. Who played Adam Chance in *Crossroads?*

9. Which duo starred on t.v. as *The Odd Couple?*

10. Which comic actress starred in 1977 sitcom *Come Back Mrs. Noah?*

11. Who played Lou Beale in *EastEnders?*

12. Who was musical accompanist on t.v. comedy *Hello Cheeky?*

13. Which member of the Monty Python team co-wrote and starred in 1991 film *American Friends?*

14. In which U.S. city is the Juilliard School of Music?

15. Which country singer co-stars in 1971 film *A Gunfight?*

SPORT

1. Who in 1992 won both the Tour de France and the Giro d'Italia?

2. Who did Chelsea defeat in the 1971 European Cup Winners' Cup Final?

3. Who won the men's 800m at the 1987 & '91 IAAF World Championships?

4. What was the nickname of England rugby union player C.H. Pillman?

5. Which team won the 1994 Benson & Hedges Cup in cricket?

6. In which year did French rugby union player Pierre Berbizier make his international debut?

7. For which motor racing team did Gerhard Berger drive from 1990-92?

8. For which team did baseball player Yogi Berra play in 14 World Series?

9. In which year was footballer George Best born?

10. Which female tennis player won the 1946 Wimbledon & U.S. singles tennis titles?

11. In which year was the Davis Cup first competed for?

12. In which American state was golfer Ben Hogan born?

13. With what sport would you associate Pat Pocock?

14. What distinction did boxer Henry Armstrong acheive in 1938?

15. What is the nationality of snooker player Kirk Stevens?

POP MUSIC

1. Which male duo had a novelty hit in 1975 with their spoof of the song *If?*

2. On which record label do B*Witched record?

3. Rob Pilatus died in 1998. With which group did he achieve notoriety?

4. What was Barbra Streisand's first U.K. Top 20 single?

5. Only one of the Top Ten singles by The Wombles refrained from using the words 'Womble' or 'Wombling'. What was it?

6. Which U.S. dance group featured on Teenage Fan Club's 1994 single *Fallin?*

7. Which female vocalist recorded 1969 album *Postcard?*

8. Who recorded the 1998 album *Moon Safari?*

9. Of which group is Ben Ottewell a member?

10. What was country star Faron Young's only Top Ten U.K. single?

11. Which female singer featured on 1987 single *The Rhythm Divine* by Yello?

12. Who is the female vocalist with the group Catatonia?

13. Who recorded the 1998 album *This is Hardcore?*

14. Which group recorded 1975 Top 20 single *Why Did You Do It?*

15. Which female singer recorded 1998 album *Is This Desire??*

ANSWERS 1. Yin and Yan **2.** Epic **3.** Milli Vanilli **4.** Second Hand Rose **5.** Banana Rock **6.** De La Soul **7.** Mary Hopkin **8.** Air **9.** Gomez **10.** It's Four in the Morning' **11.** Shirley Bassey **12.** Cerys Matthews **13.** Pulp **14.** Stretch **15.** P.J. Harvey.

PEOPLE

1. Which Chancellor of the Exchequer nationalised the Bank of England in 1946?

2. Who wrote the music for the film *Genevieve?*

3. What was the middle name of U.S. vice-president Spiro Agnew?

4. Which saint was known as the Apostle of Northumbria?

5. Which astronaut walked in space for over 5 hours during the Gemini 12 mission?

6. Which Chilean politician won the presidency in 1970?

7. Which German neuropathologist lends his name to the disease of presenile dementia?

8. Who is chief executive of Channel Four television?

9. Which religious leader was appointed to the Order of Merit in May 1999?

10. Rudolph Guiliani is mayor of which U.S. city?

11. Whose final film as director was *Eyes Wide Shut?*

12. Who is the actress wife of Tom Cruise?

13. Who was made Secretary of State for Wales in May 1997?

14. Which Norwegian explorer's ships included *Fram* and *Maud?*

15. In which year was photographer David Bailey born?

ANSWERS 1. Hugh Dalton **2.** Larry Adler **3.** Theodore **4.** St. Aidan **5.** 'Buzz' Aldrin **6.** Salvador Allende **7.** Alzheimer **8.** Michael Jackson **9.** Cardinal Basil Hume **10.** New York **11.** Stanley Kubrick **12.** Nicole Kidman **13.** Ron Davies **14.** Roald Amundsen **15.** 1938.

GENERAL KNOWLEDGE

1. Which U.S. financier and diplomat won the 1925 Nobel peace prize?

2. Who was the Roman goddess of fortune?

3. In which year was the Penny Post introduced?

4. From which country did the U.S. buy Florida?

5. On which island would you find the animal called an indris?

6. What does RADAR stand for?

7. Of what number is 30 the square root?

8. What monarch is found on a Penny Black stamp?

9. In what year was Harrods founded?

10. In what year was the Jarrow hunger march?

11. Camoodi is a Caribbean name for which snake?

12. What is the name of the woollen fabric which covers a billiard table?

13. What was the name of the half man/half fish god worshipped by the Philistines in the Bible?

14. Who played the third television *Doctor Who?*

15. Who is James Bond's service chief?

ANSWERS 1. Charles Dawes 2. Fortuna 3. 1840 4. Spain 5. Madagascar 6. Radio detection and ranging 7. 900 8. Queen Victoria 9. 1849 10. 1936 11. Anaconda 12. Baize 13. Dagon 14. Jon Pertwee 15. M.

ENTERTAINMENT

1. Who played television's *Comrade Dad?*

2. Who played 'Dex' Dexter in *Dynasty?*

3. For which pop group was 1965 film *Catch Us If You Can* a vehicle?

4. Who played Steven Taylor in *Doctor Who?*

5. In which year was actor Leonard Nimoy born?

6. Who played Leroy in t.v. show *Fame?*

7. Which actor played *The Misfit* in a 1970's ITV sitcom?

8. In which year was comedian Brian Conley born?

9. What was the character name of Lee Majors in drama series *The Fall Guy?*

10. *The Jumping Frog of Calaveras County* is a Monty Python sketch - true or false?

11. Who played Mr. Roarke in t.v. show *Fantasy Island?*

12. In which year did comedian Dickie Henderson die?

13. Who played Mary Smith in *EastEnders?*

14. In 1970's sitcom *Miss Jones and Son* who played Miss Jones?

15. Who directed 1973 film *American Graffiti?*

THE ULTIMATE PUB QUIZ BOOK

SPORT

1. Which team won the 1974 European Cup Winners' Cup?

2. How many caps did Peter Jackson win for England at rugby union from 1956-63?

3. Which U.S. basketball team won the NBA title from 1952-54?

4. What nationality was cyclist Felice Gimondi?

5. By what score did John Lowe defeat Leighton Rees in the 1979 World Professional Darts championship?

6. Who was runner-up in the 1969 & '70 World Formula 1 motor racing championship?

7. Who won the 1996 British Open Golf Championship?

8. Which team won the World Bowl in American Football in 1996?

9. At which course was the 1997 British Open golf championship held?

10. Who did rugby league star Brian Bevan play for after his 16 years at Warrington?

11. At what field event did Udo Beyer win gold at the 1976 Olympics?

12. Which jockey won the 1967 Cheltenham Gold Cup on Woodland Venture?

13. What was unusual about the shoes Abebe Bikila wore to win the 1960 Olympic marathon?

14. In which U.S. state was Olympic swimming champion Matt Biondi born?

15. Who was captain of the U.S. basketball 'Dream Team' at the 1992 Olympics?

ANSWERS 1. Magdeburg **2.** 20 **3.** Minneapolis Lakers **4.** Italian **5.** 5-0 **6.** Jacky Ickx **7.** Tom Lehman **8.** Scottish Claymores **9.** Royal Troon **10.** Blackpool Borough **11.** Shot put **12.** Terry Biddlecombe **13.** Their absence - he ran barefoot **14.** California **15.** Larry Bird.

POP MUSIC

1. Which record provided Thin Lizzy with their highest singles chart placing?

2. Which group recorded the album *Emotional Rescue?*

3. Dennis Greaves was singer/guitarist with which early 1980's blues band?

4. Who was lead singer in the group Dead or Alive?

5. Who was bass player in The Clash?

6. How many No.1 singles did Yazoo have?

7. Which record provided punk band X-Ray Spex with their highest singles chart placing?

8. Which member of the Rolling Stones had a solo hit single with *(si si) Je suis un rock star?*

9. Which group recorded the *Shortsharpshock* E.P. in 1993?

10. What was the first record bought by Siouxsie Sioux, according to an interview with magazine *The Face* in 1980?

11. Which actor had a hit single in 1971 with *The Way You Look Tonight?*

12. Which song by The Jam was inspired by a poem entitled *Entertainment?*

13. How many solo No.1 singles has Stevie Wonder had?

14. Which 1973 Christmas hit featured vocal backing by, among others, the Stockland Green Bilateral School First Year Choir?

15. Who recorded 1981 album *Don't Follow Me, I'm Lost Too?*

ART AND LITERATURE

1. Which French painter's works include *The Cheat with the Ace of Diamonds?*

2. Of what did artist Yves Klein die in 1962, at the age of 34?

3. In which city was artist Frida Kahlo born?

4. Which author's thrillers include *Hornet's Nest* and *Unnatural Exposure?*

5. Who wrote the novel *Toward the End of Time?*

6. Who wrote the thriller *Manchester Slingback?*

7. Which English artist's animal pictures include *The Cat's-Paw?*

8. Why was Henri de Toulouse-Lautrec stunted in his growth?

9. Which writer of nonsense verse began as a zoological draughtsman?

10. Who wrote *The Prisoner of Zenda?*

11. Which book opens 'My desert-island, all-time, top five most memorable split-ups...'?

12. Which comedian wrote 1997 novel *The Detainees?*

13. What did artist Helmut Herzfelde change his name to during World War I?

14. What is the term for a sculpture or painting showing the Virgin Mary supporting the dead Christ on her lap?

15. In which European city is the Pitti Palace art gallery?

GENERAL KNOWLEDGE

1. In which year did Winston Churchill die?

2. On which island was singer Freddie Mercury born?

3. What is the name of the decorated dart thrust into a bull's neck or shoulder in bullfighting?

4. What is the Jewish holiday Yom Kippur also known as?

5. What type of creature is a gilthead - a snake or a fish?

6. What is the Latin name for Switzerland?

7. What is the name of the Grand Canal in Venice?

8. How long, approximately, is Route 66?

9. In mythology, how many heads did the giant Geryon have?

10. What was the name of King Arthur's magic sword?

11. Who are the feuding families in the play *Romeo and Juliet?*

12. What was the name of the league of ten cities including Damascus established in 63 B.C. by Pompey?

13. What in U.S. history was a forty-niner?

14. What is the standard monetary unit of Lesotho?

15. In which year was Mrs. Marcos stabbed and injured in Pasay City, Philippines?

ANSWERS 1. 1965 2. Zanzibar 3. Banderilla 4. Day of Atonement 5. Fish 6. Helvetia 7. Grand Canal 8. 2,200 miles 9. Three 10. Excalibur 11. Montagues and Capulets 12. Decapolis 13. A prospector in the 1849 California gold rush 14. Loti 15. 1972.

ENTERTAINMENT

1. Who played Marilyn Gates in *Crossroads?*

2. Who directed 1951 film *An American in Paris?*

3. What was comedian Ernie Wise's real name?

4. Who played Purdey in *The New Avengers?*

5. On whose play is 1958 film *Cat On A Hot Tin Roof* based?

6. Who played Dreyfus in 1958 film *I Accuse?*

7. Which writing duo scripted television's *Yes, Minister?*

8. In which year was writer and interviewer Daniel Farson born?

9. Who composed the nocturnes *Liebesträume?*

10. In which year was actress Farrah Fawcett born?

11. Who played *The Mistress* in a BBC2 sitcom of the 1980's?

12. In which town was comedian Lenny Henry born?

13. Which actress played the lead role in 1964 film *The Americanization of Emily?*

14. Who is the male star of 1932 film *I Am A Fugitive From a Chain Gang?*

15. Who played Pte. Mick Hopper in Dennis Potter's drama series *Lipstick on Your Collar?*

SPORT

1. Who in American Football was 'the Gipper'?

2. Who won the 1998 men's hockey world cup?

3. In which year did Marc Girardelli make his Olympic debut?

4. Which French team lost the 1976 European Champions Cup Final to Bayern Munich?

5. What did manager Joe McCarthy call baseball star Gabby Hartnett?

6. Which English team lost the 1976 European Cup Winners' Cup Final to Anderlecht?

7. Which country are football team Deportivo La Coruna from?

8. At what sport does Mary Joe Fernandez compete?

9. Who refereed the 1993 Holland v England World Cup qualifier?

10. Who won the 16th game in the 1993 PCA World Chess championship?

11. In what sport is the Lugano Cup competed for?

12. In which year did Helsinki stage the Summer Olympic Games?

13. What nationality was tennis champion Jean Borotra?

14. Who in boxing was known as 'the Black Cloud'?

15. Who were 1988 Superbowl champions in American Football?

ANSWERS 1. George Gipp **2.** Netherlands **3.** 1988 **4.** St. Etienne **5.** The Perfect Catcher **6.** West Ham United **7.** Spain **8.** Tennis **9.** Karl-Josef Assenmacher **10.** Nigel Short **11.** Walking **12.** 1952 **13.** French **14.** Larry Holmes **15.** Washington Redskins.

POP MUSIC

1. Which duo had a 1990 hit with *Birdhouse in Your Soul*?

2. Which duo penned Chris Farlowe's hit *Out Of Time*?

3. Which rock singer remarked that 'the largest flying land mammal is the absent mind'?

4. Whose albums include 1979's *Squeezing Out Sparks*?

5. Which group recorded the 1980 album *Freedom Of Choice*?

6. Who was bass player in The Beatles?

7. Which actor had a No.2 single in 1987 with *Under the Boardwalk*?

8. Which guitar instrumental provided Mason Williams with a 1968 hit single?

9. Whose only U.K. hit single was 1984's *Break My Stride*?

10. How many No.1 singles has Kim Wilde had?

11. Which duo charted in 1986 with *The Skye Boat Song*?

12. Which group recorded 1980 album *Ska'N'B*?

13. Which vocalist had a 1984 single hit with *High Energy*?

14. Which group's early singles included *Jumping Someone Else's Train*?

15. Which member of The Who recorded solo album *Empty Glass*?

GEOGRAPHY

1. In which country is the rice-growing town of Budge-Budge?

2. Lanzarote and Tenerife belong to which island group?

3. In which English county is the picturesque village of Clovelly?

4. In which European country is the village of Blenheim, scene of a 1704 battle?

5. Monta Rosa, the highest mountain in the Pennine Alps, is on the border between which two countries?

6. In which country is the seaport of Aden?

7. In which county of the Republic of Ireland is Arklow?

8. On which of North America's Great Lakes does the city of Buffalo stand?

9. Carson City is the capital of which U.S. state?

10. Which strait connects the Sea of Marmara with the Aegean Sea?

11. Bridgeport is the largest city in which U.S. state?

12. Buganda is a province of which African country?

13. Castries is the capital of which West Indies island?

14. Vienna and Belgrade lie on the banks of which river?

15. On which Scottish island are the Cuillin Hills?

GENERAL KNOWLEDGE

1. What is the fifth book of the New Testament?

2. In which city is the University of Essex?

3. Who authored 1977 novel *Unknown Man No. 89*?

4. On which island of Asia is the village of Bantam?

5. Who wrote the ballad *The Absent-minded Beggar*?

6. In mythology, who was the mother of Arcas?

7. Who was British prime minister 1905-8?

8. The Corbillon Cup is competed for by women at which sport?

9. Approximately how many million people in the world spoke Tamil in 1993?

10. At which castle was Mary Queen of Scots executed in 1587?

11. In which year did *Coronation Street* begin on ITV?

12. What was county town of the former county of Merioneth?

13. To which island is the bird called a mesite confined?

14. Who composed the song-cycle *Dichterliebe*?

15. What is a Sam Browne?

ANSWERS 1. Acts of the Apostles **2.** Colchester **3.** Elmore Leonard **4.** Java **5.** Rudyard Kipling **6.** Callisto **7.** Henry Campbell-Bannerman **8.** Table tennis **9.** 68 **10.** Fotheringay Castle **11.** 1960 **12.** Dolgellau **13.** Madagascar **14.** Schumann **15.** A military belt.

ENTERTAINMENT

1. Who played *Cattle Queen of Montana* in a 1954 film?

2. Which comedian appeared in a 1989 series of *The Krypton Factor* as a number of different characters?

3. Who directed 1997 film *The Ice Storm*?

4. Who presents the quiz show *Fifteen to One*?

5. Who created the character *Mog*, played on T.V. by Enn Reitel?

6. Which reggae artist played Spring in children's show *Here Come the Double Deckers*?

7. Who presented the *Film '71* series before Barry Norman?

8. Who composed the symphony *The Song of the Earth*, which was first performed in 1911?

9. What is the middle name of Bob Monkhouse?

10. In which year did Tommy Cooper die?

11. Who was lead puppet in the series *Fireball XL5*?

12. What was presenter Ayshea's surname in pop show *Lift Off*?

13. In which county was the drama *Flambards* set?

14. Who plays an Italian restaurant owner in 1990 film *I Love You to Death*?

15. Who directed 1953 film *I Confess*?

ANSWERS 1. Barbara Stanwyck 2. Steve Coogan 3. Ang Lee 4. William G. Stewart 5. Peter Tinniswood 6. Brinsley Forde 7. Jacky Gillott 8. Mahler 9. Alan 10. 1984 11. Colonel Steve Zodiac 12. Brough 13. Essex 14. Kevin Kline 15. Alfred Hitchcock.

SPORT

1. Which country were 1980 Olympic men's basketball champions?

2. In which year was the World Professional Darts championship first held?

3. Of which country was David Houghton a Test cricket captain?

4. Who scored Leeds United's consolation goal in the 1965 F.A. Cup Final?

5. Which team won the 1995 Benson & Hedges Cup in cricket?

6. Who won the men's 1500m title at the IAAF World Championships in 1991, '93 & '95?

7. Which Kenyan won the 1997 & '98 men's New York Marathon?

8. Which U.S. basketball team won the NBA title eight years in a row from 1958-66?

9. Who beat Rudy Hartono to win the 1975 All-England badminton championships?

10. In which year did Ray Illingworth take over as England Test cricket captain from Colin Cowdrey?

11. Which year saw the first replay in a European Cup Winners' Cup Final in football?

12. Who captained Spurs to their Cup and League double of 1961?

13. In which country was French rugby union star Serge Blanco born?

14. Dutch triple jumper Jan Blankers was coach, and later husband, to which athlete?

15. Which footballer made 109 appearances for the USSR from his debut in 1972?

ANSWERS 1. Yugoslavia 2. 1978 3. Zimbabwe 4. Billy Bremner 5. Lancashire 6. Noureddine Morceli 7. John Kagwe 8. Boston Celtics 9. Svend Pri 10. 1969 11. 1962 12. Danny Blanchflower 13. Venezuela 14. Fanny Koen 15. Oleg Blokhin.

POP MUSIC

1. Who recorded the 1986 album *Deep in the Heart of Nowhere*?

2. Which U.S. vocalist's albums include *Breakaway* and *Water Mark*?

3. Which U.S. vocalist recorded the albums *I Want You* and *Let's Get It On*?

4. Which group recorded the 1965 album *Ferry Cross the Mersey*?

5. Which member of the Gibb family recorded 1984 solo album *Now Voyager*?

6. Who recorded the 1980 album *Never Forever*?

7. Which group recorded 1979 single *Where's Captain Kirk?*?

8. Which group were Kevin Rowland and Al Archer in prior to Dexy's Midnight Runners?

9. What was Wham's first No.1 single?

10. Who had a 1987 Top Forty single with *Ba-Na-Na-Bam-Boo*?

11. Which guitarist reached the Top Ten singles chart in 1959 with *Guitar Boogie Shuffle*?

12. Which group had a top Thirty single in 1984 with *The Lion's Mouth*?

13. Which solo male singer hit the charts in 1964 with *Boys Cry*?

14. Which comic actor had a 1953 Top Ten hit with *Wonderful Copenhagen*?

15. Who recorded 1959 No.1 single *Here Comes Summer*?

ANSWERS 1. Bob Geldof **2.** Art Garfunkel **3.** Marvin Gaye **4.** Gerry and the Pacemakers **5.** Barry **6.** Kate Bush **7.** Spizz Energi **8.** The Killjoys **9.** Wake Me Up Before You Go Go **10.** Westworld **11.** Bert Weedon **12.** Kajagoogoo **13.** Eden Kane **14.** Danny Kaye **15.** Jerry Keller.

HISTORY

1. In which year did Blondin first walk across the Niagara Falls on a tightrope?

2. In which year did Peter Abelard become tutor to Héloïse?

3. Who succeeded Antoninus Pius as Roman emperor in 161 A.D.?

4. Who was regent of the Netherlands from 1559-67?

5. In which year did Karl Marx die?

6. In which year did the Korean War end?

7. King John, who died in 1216, was the youngest son of which king?

8. In which year did Richard the Lionheart set forth on the Third Crusade?

9. Which U.S. president was born in Stonewall, Texas, in 1908?

10. Who was British prime minister from 1852-55?

11. Who was Conservative secretary of state for social services from 1970-74?

12. Which U.S. abolitionist published the newspaper 'The Liberator' in 1831?

13. Who was the mother of Mary, Queen of Scots?

14. Who was U.S. secretary of state from 1949-53?

15. In which year was Bacon's rebellion, a protest of farmers against the governor of Virginia?

GENERAL KNOWLEDGE

1. What colour are the stripes on a barber's pole?

2. How many golfers take part in a four-ball?

3. In law, what is the name given to the essential point of an action?

4. In which city is Cartwright Hall Art Gallery?

5. On what does a leopard snake mostly feed?

6. Which of the wives of Henry VIII was executed in 1542?

7. Which two types of dog appear in Landseer's painting *Dignity and Impudence*?

8. Which German battleship sank HMS Hood?

9. What is the professional organisation of British magicians called?

10. The Discobolus is a 5c B.C. sculpture by Myron of what type of athlete?

11. Who authored the novel *Mrs. de Winter*?

12. In which present day country does the ancient region of Mesopotamia lie?

13. In which city was artist Pierre Auguste Renoir born?

14. Who was 38th president of the U.S.?

15. What is the international car registration for Iraq?

ANSWERS 1. Red and white **2.** Four **3.** The gist **4.** Bradford **5.** Rodents **6.** Catherine Howard **7.** A bloodhound and a Scotch terrier **8.** Bismarck **9.** The Magic Circle **10.** Discus thrower **11.** Susan Elizabeth Hill **12.** Iraq **13.** Limoges **14.** Gerald Ford **15.** IRQ.

ENTERTAINMENT

1. Who played *The American President* in a 1995 film?

2. Which Scottish comedian started his career as Bing Hitler?

3. Who plays Lee Simon in 1998 Woody Allen film *Celebrity*?

4. Who played Thelma Ferris in *Whatever Happened to the Likely Lads?*?

5. What was the surname of the dance instructors in the sitcom *Hi-de-Hi*?

6. Who was producer on 1966 adventure series *Flipper*?

7. In which year was comedian Hugh Laurie born?

8. In which year did comedian Ernie Wise die?

9. Who composed the 1866 operetta *Light Cavalry*?

10. In which year did comedian Leslie Crowther die?

11. What were the names of *The Flowerpot Men*?

12. In which year was the London String Quartet formed?

13. In which year was t.v. cook Keith Floyd born?

14. What was Mindy's surname in the sitcom *Mork and Mindy*?

15. Who played 'the Colonel' in children's drama *Follyfoot*?

SPORT

1. Who was world rallying champion in 1984?

2. By what score did Valencia beat Arsenal on penalties in the 1980 European Cup Winners' Cup Final?

3. Which U.S. basketball team won the NBA title from 1996-98?

4. Who retained her U.S. Open tennis singles title in 1955?

5. Which horse won the Oaks in 1998?

6. Who was Wimbledon ladies singles tennis champion in 1997?

7. In which year did Geoff Hurst sign as a professional for West Ham United?

8. Which cyclist won the Tour de France three times in a row from 1953-5?

9. In which U.S. state was Olympic figure skating champion Brian Boitano born?

10. Which golfer won the British Amateur title three times in a row, 1968-70?

11. On which island was Australian Test cricketer David Boon born?

12. Which horse won the 1993 Melbourne Cup?

13. Which game was patented in the year 1874 under the name of Sphairistike?

14. Who won the 1993 Skoda Snooker Grand Prix?

15. Who won the 1993 Madrid Open in golf?

POP MUSIC

1. Which member of the Gibb family recorded the 1978 album *Shadow Dancing*?

2. Who was lead singer with the group Sham 69?

3. Derwood and Mark Laff were members of which punk group?

4. Which group recorded 1980 album *Hypnotised*?

5. Which U.S. vocalist had a 1962 hit with *Send Me the Pillow That You Dream On*?

6. What was singer Tiny Tim's only U.K. hit single?

7. On which label did The Timelords record their No.1 *Doctorin' the Tardis*?

8. Who charted in 1987 with *The Future's So Bright I Gotta Wear Shades*?

9. Who had a hit in 1982 with *The Lion Sleeps Tonight*?

10. Which comic actor had a 1983 Christmas hit with *Christmas Countdown*?

11. Under what name did Jonathan King record 1972 hit *Loop di Love*?

12. What was the last No.1 single, in 1966, for The Kinks?

13. Which comedian had a 1968 Top Forty hit with *On Mother Kelly's Doorstep*?

14. Which fictional character did Landscape sing of in a 1981 hit?

15. Which group's 1980 hit singles included *Dance Yourself Dizzy* and *Substitute*?

WORDS

1. Oster-monath was the Anglo Saxon name of which month?

2. What would you do in Russia with a kissel - use it for building or eat it?

3. On which part of the body would you wear a larrigan?

4. What is liquidambar - a tree or an artificial language?

5. What sort of creature is a luderick?

6. What in English is a WH question?

7. What was an oriflamme?

8. Which part of the body is also known as the genu?

9. What would you do with a lava-lava - cook it or wear it?

10. What does the Latin phrase loco citato mean?

11. What would you keep in a lota - fruit or water?

12. What is the name of the astronomical toy showing the relative movements of the planets?

13. What sort of food is a kneidel in Jewish cookery?

14. What is a lazy Susan?

15. What in the circus is a liberty horse?

ANSWERS 1. April 2. Eat it - it is a dessert 3. The foot, it is a boot 4. A tree 5. A fish 6. One requiring other than a yes-no answer, i.e. why, where, when etc. 7. A scarlet flag adopted as the national banner of France in the Middle Ages 8. The knee 9. Wear it - it's a skirt 10. In the place quoted 11. Water 12. An orrery 13. Dumpling 14. A revolving tray for holding condiments 15. A riderless horse that moves to verbal commands.

GENERAL KNOWLEDGE

1. What type of creature is a grassquit - a crab or a bird?

2. What does the abbreviation RUC stand for in the world of Irish politics?

3. In which year did Hurricane Allen result in 272 deaths?

4. What is the standard monetary unit of Spain?

5. Which shipping forecast area is due east of Sole?

6. In which year was the Salvation Army founded?

7. What is the colour of the traffic light used as a warning between red and green?

8. On which gulf is the Nigerian port of Lagos?

9. Who was the minstrel in Robin Hood's band of merry men?

10. Who was Melody Maker's British Female Jazz Vocalist of the Year 1964-70?

11. Which London hotel won Egon Ronay Hotel of the Year title in 1970?

12. Who won the 1960 Queen's Gold Medal for Poetry?

13. What is bohea?

14. Who won 1980's *Mastermind* title?

15. Corinium was the Latin name of which English market town?

ANSWERS 1. A bird 2. Royal Ulster Constabulary 3. 1980 4. Peseta 5. Plymouth 6. 1865 7. Amber 8. Gulf of Guinea 9. Allan-a-Dale 10. Cleo Laine 11. The Inn on the Park 12. John Betjeman 13. A black Chinese tea 14. Fred Housego 15. Cirencester.

ENTERTAINMENT

1. Who directed the 1997 film *Amistad*?

2. Who composed the 1877 drawing-room ballad *The Lost Chord*?

3. In which country was comedian Mort Sahl born?

4. Which knockabout comedian played the Janitor in 1949 sitcom *Cuckoo College*?

5. What did t.v. presenter Keith Fordyce study at Cambridge?

6. Who played Frazer in *Dad's Army*?

7. Who played Soames in 1967 drama *The Forsyte Saga*?

8. At what early age did comedian Bill Hicks die in 1994?

9. Which actress played Amy Wilde in t.v. drama *The Wilde Alliance*?

10. Who composed the opera *Love for Three Oranges*?

11. Who wrote and directed the 1993 film *Century*?

12. Who produced the 1960 puppet series *Four Feather Falls*?

13. Which Scottish comedian played *Mr. Majeika* in a children's t.v. series?

14. Which entertainer's real name is Daniel Patrick Carroll?

15. Who played Sgt. Blaketon in t.v show *Heartbeat*?

ANSWERS 1. Steven Spielberg 2. Arthur Sullivan 3. Canada 4. Norman Wisdom 5. Law 6. John Laurie 7. Eric Porter 8. 32 9. Julia Foster 10. Prokofiev 11. Stephen Poliakoff 12. Gerry Anderson 13. Stanley Baxter 14. Danny La Rue 15. Derek Fowlds.

SPORT

1. With which sport is coach Don Shula associated?

2. Where were the 1928 Summer Olympics held?

3. In what sport is the MacRobertson Shield competed for?

4. Which sport do the San Diego Padres compete in?

5. Who captained the Australia cricket side in their 1987 World Cup win?

6. How many sets did Bjorn Borg lose in his 1976 Wimbledon singles title win?

7. How old was golfer Julius Boros when he won the 1968 USPGA?

8. Which French tennis player was known as the 'Bouncing Basque'?

9. Which England rugby union player died on May 5, 1915, killed by a sniper's bullet?

10. Who won the 1987 men's 5,000m title at the IAAF World Championships?

11. Which Briton won the 1991 women's New York Marathon?

12. Billy Hardin competed at the 1964 Olympics in the 400m hurdles. At which Olympics did his father win the same event?

13. Who were English league champions in rugby union in the 1997/98 season?

14. Who retained her U.S. Open tennis singles title in 1961?

15. What was the nickname of Canadian ice hockey star Michael Bossy?

POP MUSIC

1. What was Lord Rockingham's XI's 1958 No. 1 single?

2. Who had a Top Twenty single in 1986 with *Amityville (The House on the Hill)*?

3. What was Paul McCartney's first solo U.K. Top Ten single?

4. Which actor and actress had a 1990 Top Five single with *Kinky Boots*?

5. In which year did Madonna have a No.1 single with *Vogue*?

6. Who recorded 1992 single *Motorcycle Emptiness*?

7. What was Pigmeat Markham's only U.K. hit single, in 1968?

8. What was the B-Side of Lee Marvin's No.1 single *Wand'rin' Star*?

9. Whose first chart single was 1984's *Get Out Of Your Lazy Bed*?

10. What was Matthews' Southern Comfort's only No.1 single?

11. Which vocal duo had a 1987 No.1 single with *Respectable*?

12. Which punk band had hit singles with *Offshore Banking Business* and *The Sound of the Suburbs*?

13. With whom did Freddie Mercury duet on 1987 single *Barcelona*?

14. Which biblical pair scored a 1972 Top 30 hit for Middle of the Road?

15. How many No.1 hit singles did The Monkees have?

ANSWERS 1. Hoots Mon 2. Lovebug Starski 3. Another Day 4. Patrick MacNee and Honor Blackman 5. 1990 6. Manic Street Preachers 7. Here Comes the Judge 8. 'I Talk To the Trees' by Clint Eastwood 9. Matt Bianco 10. Woodstock 11. Mel and Kim 12. The Members 13. Montserrat Caballé 14. Samson and Delilah 15. One.

SCIENCE

1. What in physical geography is a nunatak?

2. Which German astronomer's Third Law stated that 'the square of a planet's periodic time is proportional to the cube of its mean distance from the sun'?

3. What is the symbol for the element thulium?

4. What is the colouring agent E102 also called?

5. What sort of creature was the prehistoric creature a smilodon?

6. What is the name given to a straight line that joins two points on the circumference of a circle?

7. How many grams of fat per 100 grams are there in a Mars bar?

8. Approximately what percentage of a chocolate biscuit is sugar?

9. In which year was Cordelia, a satellite of Uranus, discovered?

10. Which element is to the immediate left of Antimony in the Periodic table?

11. In which century did English physicist James Joule live?

12. Is the element Polonium radioactive?

13. What is the name of the larger of the two bones in the lower section of the arm?

14. What is the atomic number of silver?

15. What is the name given to the highest point of a triangle?

ANSWERS 1. An isolated mountain peak projecting through the surface of surrounding glacial ice 2. Johann Kepler 3. Tm 4. Tartrazine 5. A sabre-toothed cat 6. Chord 7. 19 8. 33% 9. 1986 10. Tin 11. 19th 12. Yes 13. Ulna 14. 47 15. Apex.

GENERAL KNOWLEDGE

1. Who won Member to Watch award at the 1987 Parliamentarian of the Year luncheon?

2. Lyons is the capital of which French department?

3. In which German-occupied country were the EAM the leftist resistance in World War II?

4. In Israel, what monetary unit is one-hundredth of a shekel?

5. What in Hindu mythology is amrita?

6. Which Scottish psychiatrist wrote the book *The Divided Self*?

7. Who was Melody Maker's Top Male Jazz Singer 1955-68?

8. What is the official language of Libya?

9. Who authored the novel *A Laodicean*?

10. Otalgia is the technical name for what illness?

11. What is the chief port of Tanzania?

12. Which musical instrument is also called a sweet potato?

13. Which London hotel won Egon Ronay Hotel of the Year award in 1978?

14. What is the name of the secret intelligence agency of Israel?

15. To whom did the Crime Writers' Association award the Diamond Dagger in 1991?

ANSWERS 1. Gordon Brown 2. Rhône 3. Greece 4. Agora 5. Food of the gods which bestows immortality 6. R.D. Laing 7. Frank Sinatra 8. Arabic 9. Thomas Hardy 10. Earache 11. Dar es Salaam 12. Ocarina 13. The Ritz 14. Mossad 15. Ruth Rendell.

ENTERTAINMENT

1. Who played Supt. Tom Lockhart in the T.V. drama *No Hiding Place*?

2. What was the character name of Lewis Collins in the comedy series *The Cuckoo Waltz*?

3. In which year did comic actor Bill Fraser die?

4. In which year was cellist Yo-Yo Ma born?

5. Who played Chad Hanna in a 1940 film?

6. What type of animal was television puppet Fred Barker?

7. In which year did Richard Hearne, a.k.a. Mr. Pastry, die?

8. Which actress played air hostess Shona Spurtle in the 1995 sitcom *The High Life*?

9. In which year did ITV comedy show *Game for a Laugh* begin?

10. Which actress played Charlotte Cavendish in the T.V. drama *Lovejoy*?

11. What are comedy duo George Logan and Patrick Fyffe better known as?

12. Who hosted BBC T.V. show *Gardening Club* from 1955-67?

13. In which year was musician Paul McCartney born?

14. Which actor was born James Baumgarner in 1928?

15. Who directed the 1959 film *Anatomy of a Murder*?

ANSWERS 1. Raymond Francis 2. Gavin Rumsay 3. 1987 4. 1955 5. Henry Fonda 6. Dog 7. 1979 8. Siobhan Redmond 9. 1981 10. Caroline Langrishe 11. Hinge and Bracket 12. Percy Thrower 13. 1942 14. James Garner 15. Otto Preminger.

SPORT

1. In which Welsh city was rugby league star Billy Boston born?

2. Who was 1960 Olympic men's long jump champion?

3. For which county cricket team did Ian Botham play from 1987-91?

4. In which year did Geoffrey Boycott make his Yorkshire debut?

5. Of the eleven women's New York Marathons between 1978 & '88, how many did Grete Waitz win?

6. Who was basketball's leading scorer in the NBA from 1953-55?

7. In which year did Sir Len Hutton make his Test debut?

8. What is rugby union player William Henry Hare known as?

9. Who was women's world middleweight judo champion from 1982-86?

10. Which team won the 1996 Benson & Hedges Cup in cricket?

11. Which female U.S. Olympic volleyball player died in 1986 of Marfan's Syndrome?

12. In which year did cyclist Reg Harris die?

13. Which former Olympic women's 200m silver winner was disqualified in a 1976 semi-final for two false starts?

14. Who defeated Max Baer to win the world heavyweight title in 1935?

15. Who was captain of South Australia's cricket team from 1935-48?

ANSWERS 1. Cardiff 2. Ralph Boston 3. Worcestershire 4. 1962 5. Nine 6. Neil Johnston 7. 1937 8. Dusty 9. Brigitte Deydier 10. Lancashire 11. Flo Hyman 12. 1992 13. Raelene Boyle 14. James Braddock 15. Donald Bradman.

POP MUSIC

1. From which country did duo Mouth and MacNeal hail?

2. Who had Top Ten singles with *We Are Glass* and *She's Got Claws*?

3. Mike Barson was keyboard player with which band from 1978-83?

4. Which Welsh rock band's albums include 1976's *The Welsh Connection*?

5. What is singer Derek Dick better known as?

6. Which singer/songwriter recorded the 1973 L.P. *Solid Air*?

7. Which city do Massive Attack come from?

8. In which year was John Mayall born?

9. In which city was Curtis Mayfield born?

10. In which city was Meat Loaf born?

11. In what year did producer Joe Meek commit suicide?

12. Which 'Goth' band released the albums *Carved in Sand* and *Grains of Sand*?

13. Which Canadian singer was born Roberta Joan Anderson?

14. In which city was Alanis Morrisette born?

15. What is rock musician Ian Kilminster better known as?

PEOPLE

1. Which circus clown, born in 1910, was a star attraction of the Blackpool Tower Circus for 39 years?

2. What was frontierswoman Martha Jane Burke better known as?

3. Which English speedboat racer died in 1967 when his hydroplane Bluebird crashed on Lake Coniston?

4. In which year did gangster Al Capone die?

5. In which Italian city was French fashion designer Pierre Cardin born?

6. Who is Artistic Director of the National Theatre?

7. What is the name of the chief schools inspector embroiled in controversy in 1999?

8. Which folk musician was recovering in hospital in April 1999 when told of his obituary in the Daily Telegraph?

9. Who is leader of political group Plaid Cymru?

10. Who is Chairman of the B.B.C.?

11. Who is president of Sinn Fein?

12. Which former newspaper editor runs Talk Radio?

13. Which young leading actor had to swim for his life whilst filming *The Beach* in 1999?

14. Who did Ted Hughes succeed as poet laureate?

15. Which actress is girlfriend of actor Hugh Grant?

ANSWERS 1. Charlie Cairoli 2. Calamity Jane 3. Donald Campbell 4. 1947 5. Venice 6. Trevor Nunn 7. Chris Woodhead 8. Dave Swarbrick 9. Dafydd Wigley 10. Christopher Bland 11. Gerry Adams 12. Kelvin MacKenzie 13. Leonardo DiCaprio 14. John Betjeman 15. Elizabeth Hurley.

GENERAL KNOWLEDGE

1. In which European country is the region of Graubünden?

2. Who won Member to Watch award at the 1991 Parliamentarian of the Year luncheon?

3. Who won Pipe Smoker of the Year award in 1988?

4. What is the island of Fernando Po now called?

5. What sort of creature is a cisco - a bird or a fish?

6. In which year was a controversial glass pyramid erected in the forecourt of the Louvre art gallery?

7. Who is the hero of the novel *Kidnapped* by R.L. Stevenson?

8. Which saint was the first English martyr?

9. The Chianti mountain range is in which mountain group?

10. Ameslan is a communications system. Of what is the word a corruption?

11. What nationality was orchestral conductor Eugen Jochum?

12. Who was Muse of History in Greek mythology?

13. Which model at Madame Tussauds was voted Hero of Entertainment in 1984?

14. To whom did the Crime Writers' Association award the Diamond Dagger in 1989?

15. What is the approximate area of Easter Island in square miles - 32, 64 or 128?

ENTERTAINMENT

1. Which comedian starred in the 1983 sitcom *Cuffy*?

2. On whose novel was the 1996 film *The Chamber* based?

3. Who played Captain Steve Burton in the 1960s science fiction series *Land of the Giants*?

4. Which actor played prime minister Harold Wilson in the one-off 1969 ITV comedy *Mrs. Wilson's Diary*?

5. Which comedian played Jim Nelson in the Channel Four drama series *GBH*?

6. In which year was comic performer Cyril Fletcher born?

7. Which actor played *Dad* in the 1997 BBC T.V. sitcom?

8. Who scripted the 1968 film *Inadmissible Evidence* from his own play?

9. Who played Douglas Fairbanks in the 1992 film *Chaplin*?

10. Who played T.V.'s *Gemini Man* in 1976?

11. What nationality was the composer Bruno Maderna?

12. Who played *Mulberry* in the T.V. sitcom?

13. Who voiced Fred Flintstone in the cartoon series *The Flintstones*?

14. Who played Nurse Hilda Price in the long-running ITV drama *General Hospital*?

15. Who directed the 1945 film *And Then There Were None*?

THE ULTIMATE PUB QUIZ BOOK

SPORT

1. How many caps did rugby union player Mike Gibson win for Ireland from 1964-79?

2. In which year was badminton player Gillian Gilks born?

3. Which former holder of the men's 400m & 800m world record was killed whilst fighting in World War II in March 1944?

4. Which team won the World Bowl in American Football in 1995?

5. Which year saw Feyenoord's only European Champions Cup win?

6. Which basketball player was leading scorer in the NBA in 1956 & '59?

7. By what score did Eric Bristow beat Dave Whitcombe in the 1986 World Professional Darts Championship?

8. At which course was the 1998 British Open golf championship held?

9. How many caps did W.J.A. 'Dave' Davies win for England at rugby union?

10. By what score did Europe win the 1995 Ryder Cup?

11. Who scored a hat-trick for Blackpool in their 1953 F.A. Cup Final win?

12. What was the score in the England v Sweden 1999 European Championship qualifier in football?

13. Which horse won the 1996 2,000 Guineas?

14. Who was men's British Open squash champion 1976-81?

15. Which team won the 1997 Benson & Hedges Cup in cricket?

ANSWERS **1.** 69 **2.** 1950 **3.** Rudolf Harbig **4.** Frankfurt Galaxy **5.** 1970 **6.** Bob Pettit **7.** 6-0 **8.** Royal Birkdale **9.** 22 **10.** 14 and a half - 13 and a half **11.** Stan Mortensen **12.** 0-0 **13.** Mark of Esteem **14.** Geoff Hunt **15.** Surrey.

POP MUSIC

1. Which female vocalist had a hit in August 1997 with *4 Page Letter*?

2. Which group released the 1999 album *The Days of our Nights*?

3. Which duo had a 1998 hit with *Long Time Coming*?

4. Which folk singer recorded the 1999 album *Ravenchild*?

5. Which member of group Dave Dee, Dozy, Beaky, Mick and Tich was John Dymond?

6. Which U.S. group released the album *Echo* in 1999?

7. Who had a 1996 No. 1 with *Breakfast at Tiffany's*?

8. Who co-wrote 1970s track *Abdulmajid* with David Bowie?

9. Which French duo had a 1994 hit single with *Sweet Lullaby*?

10. On which studio album does Bob Dylan's *One More Cup of Coffee* appear?

11. Which 1970s group released the album *Something for the Weekend* in 1999?

12. Which group recorded the album *Crooked Rain, Crooked Rain*?

13. On which studio album by Neil Young and Crazy Horse does the song *Piece of Crap* appear?

14. In which year was Human League singer Phil Oakey born?

15. Which Australia-based rock group had a minor hit in 1996 with *Hail Caesar*?

ANSWERS 1. Aaliyah **2.** Luna **3.** Bump & Flex **4.** Maddy Prior **5.** Beaky **6.** Tom Petty and the Heartbreakers **7.** Deep Blue Something **8.** Brian Eno **9.** Deep Forest **10.** Desire **11.** Stackridge **12.** Pavement **13.** Sleeps with Angels **14.** 1955 **15.** AC/DC.

ART AND LITERATURE

1. Who wrote the thriller novel *Birds of Prey*?

2. Who wrote the thriller books *Black Market* and *Midnight Club*?

3. Whose novels include *Other People's Children*?

4. Which American artist's works include 1960's *People in the Sun*?

5. Whose works of art include 1956's *Just What Is It That Makes Today's Homes So Different, So Appealing*?

6. What are the forenames of art duo Proesch and Passmore?

7. Whose books include *The World According to Garp*?

8. In which novella by Henry James do the characters Mrs. Grose and Miss Jessel appear?

9. Which French author wrote *Bel-Ami*?

10. Which Cubist artist made the abstract film *Le Ballet Mechanique* in 1924?

11. With which visual art movement is American Roy Lichtenstein associated?

12. Which Scottish portrait painter's works include *Rev. Robert Walker skating*?

13. Which horror writer penned *The Green Mile*?

14. Which poet's volumes include *Birthday Letters*?

15. Which novel inspired Jean Rhys's *Wide Sargasso Sea*?

ANSWERS 1. Wilbur Smith 2. James Patterson 3. Joanna Trollope 4. Edward Hopper 5. Richard Hamilton 6. Gilbert and George 7. John Irving 8. The Turn of the Screw 9. Guy de Maupassant 10. Fernand Léger 11. Pop Art 12. Sir Henry Raeburn 13. Stephen King 14. Ted Hughes 15. Jane Eyre.

GENERAL KNOWLEDGE

1. Who wrote the 1699 poem *The Dispensary*?

2. In which year did Kenya join the United Nations?

3. In which year did painter Francis Bacon die?

4. Who was president of the Philippines from 1965-86?

5. Who wrote the play *A Doll's House*?

6. In which county is the port of Watchet?

7. As what is the plant *Amaranthus caudatus* better known?

8. In which year was Grand Duchess Anastasia of Russia believed to have been executed?

9. What is the more familiar name of the fish called the bummalo?

10. Which pop singer of the 1970's was formerly known as Shane Fenton?

11. What is a Joey Hooker - a snake or a plant?

12. What is the capital of Moldova?

13. Who was Melody Maker Top Female Jazz Singer 1957-70?

14. Who wrote the novel *Castle Rackrent*?

15. In which Welsh village was the TV series *The Prisoner* filmed?

ENTERTAINMENT

1. Who played Ma Larkin in the T.V. drama series *The Darling Buds of May*?

2. Who directed the 1950 film *In A Lonely Place*?

3. Which actor played Dixie Dean in the T.V. drama *Boys from the Blackstuff*?

4. Who played Lord Rustless in the 1972 sitcom *His Lordship Entertains*?

5. Who played Commander George Gideon in the police drama series *Gideon's Way*?

6. What was Eddie Munster's middle name in the T.V. comedy *The Munsters*?

7. Who directed the 1968 film *The Charge of the Light Brigade*?

8. What was Starsky's forename in *Starsky and Hutch*?

9. In which city was comic Les Dawson born?

10. What was John Wayne's character name in the 1956 film *The Searchers*?

11. Which actor played Hauptmann Reinicke in World War II T.V. drama *Enemy at the Door*?

12. What was Ryan O'Neal's character name in the 1970 film *Love Story*?

13. In which city did composer Gustav Mahler die?

14. Who directed the 1997 film *In & Out*?

15. Who directed the 1990 film *An Angel At My Table*?

SPORT

1. Which U.S. tennis player won the 1960 French women's singles title?

2. Who was 1998 U.S. Open women's singles tennis champion?

3. Which cricketing all-rounder was known as the 'W.G. Grace of Australia'?

4. For which four Italian teams did footballer Liam Brady play?

5. Who scored from the penalty spot for Tottenham in their 1962 F.A. Cup Final win?

6. Of his 31 matches as England Test captain, how many did Mike Brearley lose?

7. Who won the 1993 & '95 men's 5,000m title at the IAAF World Championships?

8. Baseball player Harry Breechen was nicknamed after which animal?

9. In which year did motor racing champion James Hunt die?

10. Who was women's world bantamweight judo champion from 1993-97?

11. Who scored the only goal in the 1990 football World Cup Final?

12. Who scored for West Germany in both the 1974 & '82 World Cup Finals?

13. Who in boxing was 'the Boston Gob'?

14. In which American state was jockey Steve Cauthen born?

15. What nationality was motor racing driver Bruce McLaren?

POP MUSIC

1. Which group had a 1998 hit with *Kung Fu Fighting*, featuring Carl Douglas?

2. Which Canadian singer/songwriter released the 1999 album *Whereabouts*?

3. Which singer released the albums *Imperial Bedroom* and *Trust*?

4. Which Swedish group had a Top Ten single in 1998 with *Life is a Flower*?

5. In which country was singer Engelbert Humperdinck born?

6. With which single did Abba have a No. 1 in the U.K. and the U.S.?

7. Which Scottish group recorded the 1998 Scotland World Cup song *Don't Come Home Too Soon*?

8. Which single by the Spice Girls entered at No. 1 in the singles chart in December 1998?

9. Which female singer had a hit single in 1969 with *Walk on Gilded Splinters*?

10. Which group recorded the albums *Wild Honey* and *Smiley Smile*?

11. Who recorded the album *Oedipus Schmoedipus*?

12. Who recorded the album *Odelay!*?

13. From which country does singer Youssou N'Dour come?

14. Which act had a 1998 hit with single *Paradise City*?

15. From which European country do duo A.D.A.M. featuring Amy come?

GEOGRAPHY

1. Lake Titicaca is on the border of which two South American countries?

2. Which island of the Inner Hebrides houses Fingal's Cave?

3. In which U.S. state is the Sequoia National Park?

4. The seaport of Port Gentil is in which African country?

5. Paphos is an ancient city on which Mediterranean island?

6. In which ocean is the island republic of Nauru?

7. In which English county is the holiday resort of Minehead?

8. Horney Peak is the highest point of which U.S. mountain range?

9. In which African country is the state of Tigré?

10. Split is a seaport on which European sea?

11. What is the name of the peninsula at the head of the Red Sea?

12. In which county of northern England is the market town of Shap?

13. The Ile de Ré is off the coast of which French seaport?

14. On which British island is the seaport of Ramsey?

15. In which European country is the region of Transylvania?

ANSWERS 1. Peru and Bolivia 2. Staffa 3. California 4. Gabon 5. Cyprus 6. Pacific Ocean 7. Somerset 8. Black Hills 9. Ethiopia 10. Adriatic Sea 11. Sinai Peninsula 12. Cumbria 13. La Rochelle 14. Isle of Man 15. Romania.

GENERAL KNOWLEDGE

1. What type of creature is a green leek?

2. Which cartoonist created the character Colonel Blimp?

3. Which political group killed USAF captain John Birch in 1945?

4. What is the name given to a tooth having one point?

5. To whom did the Crime Writers' Association award the Diamond Dagger in 1988?

6. What mollusc is also called a sea-ear?

7. Who played *Superman* in a 1978 film?

8. Who won Pipe Smoker of the Year award in 1987?

9. Approximately how large in area is Andorra in square miles - 80, 180 or 280?

10. What is the French equivalent of the English surname Wood?

11. What is the standard monetary unit of Samoa?

12. Which shipping forecast area is due north of German Bight?

13. What is the Religious Society of Friends also called?

14. Which essayist wrote *Essays of Elia*?

15. In which country was athlete Eric Liddell born?

ENTERTAINMENT

1. Which actor starred as Ernest Springer in the 1982 sitcom *Dead Ernest*?

2. Who directed the 1991 film *The Indian Runner*?

3. Who directed the 1979 film *Mad Max*?

4. In which year was composer Henry Mancini born?

5. Who played Fitz in the 1980 sitcom *Holding the Fort*?

6. Who played Everton Bennett in the 1970's drama *Empire Day*?

7. Who played Augusto Odone in the 1992 film *Lorenzo's Oil*?

8. Which comedienne played nurse Elaine Dobbs in the 1993 T.V. drama *Tender Loving Care*?

9. Who plays Albert Finney's secretary in the 1968 film *Charlie Bubbles*?

10. Who played Joe Sugden in *Emmerdale Farm*?

11. Who played T.V.'s *Murphy Brown*?

12. Who composed the 4-Act opera *Manon Lescaut*?

13. Who co-wrote and starred in the sitcom *Dear Mother...Love Albert*?

14. Who directed the 1937 film *Lost Horizon*?

15. Who directed the 1987 film *Angel Heart*?

THE ULTIMATE PUB QUIZ BOOK

SPORT

1. Who was Champion National Hunt jockey in 1966/7 & '67/8?

2. Which basketball player was leading scorer in the NBA from 1974-76?

3. What was baseball star James A. Hunter known as?

4. Which team won the 1998 Benson & Hedges Cup in cricket?

5. With which British speedway team did Barry Briggs end his career?

6. For what country did rugby union player Colin Meads play?

7. In which year was the 'Suffragettes' Derby when Emily Davison died?

8. Which football club was originally called Singers F.C.?

9. Who was the first black boxer to win the world heavyweight title?

10. Which country finished third in the 1954 World Cup in football?

11. Which Briton was 1993 world men's individual modern pentathlon champion?

12. With which team did ice hockey star Tim Horton end his career?

13. What is the middle name of cricketer Merv Hughes?

14. In which city was rugby player Ellery Hanley born?

15. How many caps did John Pullin win for England at rugby union?

ANSWERS 1. Josh Gifford **2.** Bob McAdoo **3.** Catfish **4.** Lancashire **5.** Hull **6.** New Zealand **7.** 1913 **8.** Coventry City **9.** Jack Johnson **10.** Austria **11.** Richard Phelps **12.** Buffalo Sabres **13.** Gregory **14.** Leeds. **15.** 42.

POP MUSIC

1. Which U.K. group charted in 1997 with *Swallowed* and *Bone Driven*?

2. Which was Spacedust's 1998 No. 1 single?

3. Which Jamaican act had a minor 1996 hit with *Every kinda people*?

4. Which group recorded the album *If You're Feeling Sinister*?

5. Which U.S. rock act had a 1997 hit with *Falling in Love (Is Hard on the Knees)*?

6. Which group had a 1997 Top 20 single with *Step into my World*?

7. Which group released the 1998 album *Flying Low*?

8. Which late singer recorded the 1994 album *Grace*?

9. Which group recorded the 1996 album *Murder Ballads*?

10. Which group released the album *Looking for a Day in the Night*?

11. Which country songwriter recorded the album *Old No. 1*?

12. Which group's albums include *Abacab*?

13. Which group recorded the album *Look Mom No Head!*?

14. Which group's only singles chart hit was 1970's *Vehicle*?

15. From which European country do instrumental duo Age of Love hail?

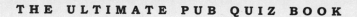

HISTORY

1. In which year was Pompeii buried by the eruption of Mount Vesuvius?

2. In which year did the SALT 1 talks begin?

3. Mary of Teck was wife of which British king?

4. Who captured Babylon in 539 B.C. and incorporated it into the Persian Empire?

5. In which year did British Columbia join the Dominion of Canada?

6. Which African politician authored the 1962 book *Zambia Shall Be Free*?

7. Thomas of Woodstock was the youngest son of which king?

8. Who commanded the troops at Fort Sumter that fired the first shots by the North in the U.S. Civil War?

9. In which year was the Battle of Lepanto?

10. Which Palestinian guerrilla group seized 11 Israelis at the 1972 Munich Olympics?

11. In which year did gangster John Dillinger die?

12. In which year was Abraham Lincoln assassinated?

13. Who was king of Spain from 1759-88?

14. Which king of Greece died in 1964?

15. In which year was the cruise ship the Achille Lauro hijacked by the P.L.O.?

ANSWERS 1. 79 A.D. 2. 1969 3. George V 4. Cyrus the Great 5. 1871 6. Kenneth Kaunda 7. Edward III 8. Abner Doubleday 9. 1571 10. Black September 11. 1934 12. 1865 13. Charles III 14. Paul I 15. 1985.

GENERAL KNOWLEDGE

1. What does the Latin phrase *bona fide* mean?

2. In which year was Charles I of England executed?

3. Who wrote the play *All God's Chillun Got Wings*?

4. In which country is the ancient city of Ecbatana?

5. Who won the title of World's Strongest Man in 1993?

6. To whom did the Crime Writers' Association award the Diamond Dagger in 1987?

7. Which model at Madame Tussauds was voted Hero of Entertainment in 1986?

8. In which year did saxophone player Sidney Bechet die?

9. In which year did Hurricane Hugo claim 504 lives?

10. Who authored *The World is Full of Married Men*?

11. In which country are the Lammermuir Hills?

12. Who created the strip cartoon *Blondie*?

13. In what field of entertainment might you win the Maskelyne award?

14. Who wrote novel *Rosemary's Baby*?

15. Who designed the Volkswagen motor car?

ANSWERS 1. Good faith 2. 1649 3. Eugene O'Neill 4. Iran 5. Gary Taylor 6. P.D. James 7. Benny Hill 8. 1959 9. 1989 10. Jackie Collins 11. Scotland 12. Chic Young 13. Magic 14. Ira Levin 15. Ferdinand Porsche.

(205)

THE ULTIMATE PUB QUIZ BOOK

ENTERTAINMENT

1. For which singer was the 1994 film *Angie* originally written?

2. Who played *Irma La Douce* in a 1963 film'?

3. What was the 1987 follow up to the sitcom *Up the Elephant and Round the Castle*?

4. Who played Ding Bell in the film *It's a Mad, Mad, Mad, Mad, World*?

5. Who won Best Actor Oscar for his performance as *Charly* in 1968?

6. Who played Teddy Barnes in the 1985 film *Jagged Edge*?

7. Who played the Earl of Essex in the 1971 BBC T.V. drama *Elizabeth R*?

8. What was James Stewart's character name in the film *It's A Wonderful Life*?

9. What was conductor Annunzio Paolo better known as?

10. Who played villainess Rosa Klebb in the film *From Russia With Love*?

11. What is the French national anthem?

12. Who directed the 1988 film *Frantic*?

13. In which year was comedian Jack Dee born?

14. Who played Carr Gomm in the 1980 film *The Elephant Man*?

15. Who played Tim O'Hara in the 1960's sitcom *My Favourite Martian*?

ANSWERS 1. Madonna 2. Billy Wilder 3. Home James! 4. Mickey Rooney 5. Cliff Robertson 6. Glenn Close 7. Robin Ellis 8. George Bailey 9. Mantovani 10. Lotte Lenya 11. La Marseillaise 12. Roman Polanski 13. 1962 14. John Gielgud 15. Bill Bixby.

SPORT

1. When did Haile Gebrselassie win the first of his 10,000m titles at the IAAF World Championships?

2. In the 12 years from 1987-98, how many times did Michael Jordan finish top scorer in the NBA?

3. At which club was Roger Uttley when he won 23 rugby union caps for England from 1973-80?

4. In which city was judo star Karen Briggs born?

5. In which athletics field event might you see a 'Brill bend'?

6. What was the nickname of Boston Bruins ice hockey star Frankie Brimsek?

7. Which Pakistan cricketer in 1952 became the world's youngest Test wicket-keeper?

8. Who were Welsh League champions in rugby union in 1997/98?

9. In which year was Canadian ice hockey star Gordie Howe born?

10. Who won the 3,000m steeplechase at the IAAF World Championships three times from 1991-95?

11. Which Canadian rower was nicknamed 'the Boy in Blue'?

12. Which cyclist won the Vuelta A España in 1998?

13. Which Canadian ice hockey star was nicknamed 'the Golden Jet'?

14. Which brothers were world double sculls rowing champions in 1978 & '79?

15. Which world Formula 1 motor racing champion died in 1992 of a heart attack?

POP MUSIC

1. Which duo had a 1995 Top Ten hit with *Yes*?

2. Which model had a minor hit in 1994 with *Love and Tears*?

3. Which duo had a 1998 Xmas hit with *Especially for you*?

4. With which single did The Animals have a No. 1 both in the U.K. and U.S.?

5. Which eccentric pop artist wrote the comic opera *Stinkfoot*?

6. Whose 1999 album is called *Viva El Amor*?

7. With which song did Robbie Williams have a September 1998 No. 1 single?

8. What name do duo Benoit Dunkel and Nicolas Godin record under?

9. Which solo artist recorded the album *Here Come the Warm Jets*?

10. Sharleen Spiteri is lead singer with which group?

11. Which female vocal group had a 1998 Top Twenty single with *Telefunkin*?

12. Which singer/songwriter released the 1999 album *Thanksgiving*?

13. With which John Lennon song did Jimmy Nail have a 1995 Top 40 hit?

14. What was Billy Idol's first solo chart single in 1982?

15. What was the name of Jewel Aken's only Top 30 single, in 1965?

WORDS

1. What type of animal is a kob?

2. What does LCD stand for in electrical equipment?

3. What is the part of the body called the lumbus also known as?

4. When in Russia would you eat zakuski - before or after the main dish?

5. What sort of creature is a whippoorwill?

6. What would you do with orts - wear them or eat them?

7. What sort of animal is a kulan?

8. What number does the letter L represent in Roman numerals?

9. What in cricket is a long-hop?

10. What, in Australia and New Zealand, is a zambuck?

11. What would you do with waragi - fry it or drink it?

12. 'An old parrot does not mind the stick' is the Latin equivalent of which proverb?

13. What is the name given to a piece of music opening a concert?

14. What in the theatre is an 'oyster part'?

15. What sort of creature is a Leghorn?

ANSWERS 1. An antelope 2. Liquid Crystal Display 3. Loin 4. Before, they are hors d'oeuvres 5. A bird 6. Eat them - they're scraps 7. Wild ass 8. 50 9. An easily hit short-pitched ball 10. A St. John ambulance attendant 11. Drink it - it is an alcoholic drink 12. Old Dogs will not Learn New Tricks 13. Overture 14. An actor who appears or speaks only once 15. A domestic fowl.

GENERAL KNOWLEDGE

1. Of which country was Bülent Ecevit prime minister from 1978-79?

2. Gregory's powder is a laxative. From what plant is it made?

3. In which year did actor Burt Lancaster die?

4. In what county of the Republic of Ireland is Lifford?

5. What unit in meteorology is used to measure cloud cover?

6. To whom did the Crime Writers' Association award the Diamond Dagger in 1986?

7. Who composed *The Sorcerer's Apprentice*?

8. Who became Home Secretary in 1997?

9. Who won Pipe Smoker of the Year award in 1985?

10. Who wrote play *Man and Superman*?

11. Who composed television opera *Tobias and the Angel*?

12. Which pop group had a 1974 hit with *Costafine Town*?

13. Which Scottish film director coined the word 'documentary'?

14. In which county is Loughborough?

15. In which year was the Battle of Balaclava?

ENTERTAINMENT

1. Who played Nancy Belasco in the 1994 sitcom *Honey For Tea*?

2. Who played Anna in the 1946 film *Anna and the King of Siam*?

3. Who played Alfredo in the 1989 film *Cinema Paradiso*?

4. Who played Joey Harris in the sitcom *My Two Dads*?

5. Which British actress starred in the 1970's U.S. sitcom *Diana*?

6. Who directed the 1981 film *Chariots of Fire*?

7. Who directed the 1966 film *The Chase*?

8. What was Robert Mitchum's character name in the 1962 film *Cape Fear*?

9. Who played Disraeli in the 1975 drama *Edward the Seventh*?

10. Who played King Arthur in the 1967 musical *Camelot*?

11. In which city was composer Steve Martland born?

12. What was Harrison Ford's character name in the film *Blade Runner*?

13. Who plays photo-journalist Nora Wilde in the sitcom *The Naked Truth*?

14. Who directed the 1929 film *Blackmail*?

15. Who played Alan Bradley in *Coronation Street*?

SPORTS

1. Which 1980 Olympic swimming champion was nicknamed 'Bones'?

2. Which Dallas player was MVP in Superbowl XXVIII in 1994?

3. Which football team won the European Champions Cup in 1971?

4. Who was 1998 World Professional Billiards Champion?

5. Who scored Arsenal's winner in the 1936 F.A. Cup Final against Sheffield United?

6. Which horse won the 1997 2,000 Guineas?

7. Who won the 1978 WBC world heavyweight boxing title by beating Ken Norton?

8. Who was world professional darts champion from 1984-86?

9. Which men's doubles tennis partnership won the Australian title from 1946-50?

10. In which city was equestrian star David Broome born?

11. Which tennis player won all three ladies titles at the U.S. championships from 1912-14?

12. Who won the women's 100m & 200m at the 1972 Olympics?

13. In which sport might you see a Double Lutz?

14. How many points does red score in archery?

15. How high off the ground in feet is a basketball hoop?

ANSWERS 1. Ute Geweniger **2.** Emmitt Smith **3.** Ajax **4.** Geet Sethi **5.** Ted Drake **6.** Entrepreneur **7.** Larry Holmes **8.** Eric Bristow **9.** Adrian Quist & John Bromwich **10.** Cardiff **11.** Mary Browne **12.** Renate Stecher **13.** Ice dancing **14.** Eight **15.** Ten feet.

POP MUSIC

1. Which vocalist featured on the 1995 hit *Fee Fi Fo Fum* by Candy Girls?

2. Which female artist had a 1997 Top 20 single with *Waterloo Sunset*?

3. What was the title of the 1998 No.1 single by Manic Street Preachers?

4. Which female vocalist had a hit in May 1998 with *Where are you*?

5. Which group recorded the album *The Light user Syndrome*?

6. From which European country do duo Nalin & Kane hail?

7. Which group's albums include *Voyage to the Bottom of the Road*?

8. Which U.S. rapper had a 1996 Top 20 with *If I Ruled the World*?

9. Which group had a Top 40 hit in 1998 with *Ain't goin' to Goa*?

10. In which year did Scottish singer Karl Denver die?

11. What was Natalie Imbruglia's first Top Ten single?

12. From which European country does the act Natural Born Grooves come?

13. Which group released 1999 album *The Hush*?

14. Who recorded the album *Wolf Songs for Lambs*?

15. Which song by Rick Astley was a No.1 in both the U.K. and U.S.?

ANSWERS 1. Sweet Pussy Pauline 2. Cathy Dennis 3. If you tolerate this your children will be next 4. Imaani 5. The Fall 6. Germany 7. Half Man Half Biscuit 8. Nas 9. Alabama 3 10. 1998 11. Torn 12. Belgium 13. Texas 14. Jonathan Fire*Eater 15. Never Gonna Give You Up.

SCIENCE

1. What is the name of the outermost layer in the earth's mantle?

2. What in physical geography is a drumlin?

3. How many square metres are there in an are?

4. Which Englishman won the 1935 Nobel prize for physics for confirming the existence of the neutron?

5. Why is tungsten so called?

6. In which year was Uranus discovered?

7. Which acid constitutes the preservative E210?

8. Which two scientists won the 1951 Nobel prize for physics?

9. Which Russian physicist led the team that exploded the first soviet atomic bomb?

10. From what phrase did the dinosaur triceratops derive its name?

11. Who discovered the planet Pluto in 1930?

12. Which scientist constructed the first cyclotron?

13. What nationality was biologist Anton von Leeuwenhoek?

14. On the Mohs scale of hardness what is No. 2?

15. What is lignite also known as?

ANSWERS 1. Lithosphere 2. A small hill formed by the action of a glacier 3. 100 4. Sir James Chadwick 5. After the Swedish phrase 'heavy stone' 6. 1781 7. Benzoic acid 8. Ernest Walton and John Cockcroft 9. Igor Kurchatov 10. Three-horned 11. Clyde Tombaugh 12. Ernest Lawrence 13. Dutch 14. Gypsum 15. Brown coal.

GENERAL KNOWLEDGE

1. Which U.S. president was known as JFK?

2. In which year was Princess Anne born?

3. Who was king of France from 1498-1515?

4. Who was the mother of Richard II, who was also known as the Fair Maid of Kent?

5. Which D.J. was host of Melody Maker's Radio Show of the Year award winner, 1974-78?

6. What is Job's-tears - a type of grass or a type of wine?

7. Which comedian won the 1981 Laurence Olivier Best Comedy Performance of the Year award?

8. In which year was cult leader Charles Manson born?

9. What does the New Zealand expression 'up the boohai' mean?

10. To whom did the Guild of Professional Toastmasters award the accolade of Best After-Dinner Speaker of the Year in 1989?

11. Who won the 1977 *Mastermind* title?

12. What was U.S. president Grover Cleveland's first name?

13. In which year did King Edward VIII die?

14. Which town was awarded the Resort of the Year title in 1992 by the English Tourist Board?

15. In which year did Mao Tse-tung die?

ANSWERS 1. John Fitzgerald Kennedy **2.** 1950 **3.** Louis XII **4.** Joan **5.** Alan Freeman **6.** Grass **7.** Rowan Atkinson **8.** 1934 **9.** Completely lost **10.** Margaret Thatcher **11.** Sir David Hunt **12.** Stephen **13.** 1972 **14.** Bournemouth **15.** 1976.

ENTERTAINMENT

1. Who played Arthur Fowler in *EastEnders*?

2. Which madcap pop group were regulars on the comedy series *Do Not Adjust Your Set*?

3. Who played Liz in the 1963 film *Billy Liar*?

4. Who composed the opera *The Mask or Orpheus*?

5. Who played Fidel Castro in the 1969 film *Che!*?

6. Who directed the 1988 film *Big*?

7. Which writing duo created the sitcom *Nearest and Dearest*?

8. Who directed the 1991 film *Backdraft*?

9. What was the character name of Barry Evans in the sitcom *Doctor in the House*?

10. Who played Anne Boleyn in the film *Anne of the Thousand Days*?

11. Who played Sheila Grant in *Brookside*?

12. How were comedians Hope and Keen related?

13. Who played Blake Carrington in the soap *Dynasty*?

14. In which year was comedian Tim Brooke-Taylor born?

15. Who played *Anna Karenina* in a 1948 film?

SPORT

1. Which West Indies bowler took 26 wickets in the 1973 Test series against Australia?

2. Who was 1998 French Open men's singles tennis champion?

3. Who in 1987 became the first woman to win two singles titles at the World Badminton championships?

4. How many players are in a volleyball team?

5. With which sport would you associate John Naber and Peter Rocca?

6. Which Olympic sportswoman married athlete Valery Borzov?

7. Who was 1989 world amateur snooker champion?

8. In which year did Jan Kodes win the men's singles at Wimbledon?

9. With which team did Rogers 'Rajah' Hornsby begin his baseball career?

10. Which year saw the first replay in the European Champions Cup in football?

11. What did football's Littlewoods Cup become in 1991?

12. Which American won the men's 110m hurdles title at the IAAF World Championships in 1983, '87, and '91?

13. By what score did Europe win the 1997 Ryder Cup?

14. What was the nickname of Jacques Brugnon, doubles ace of the 'Four Musketeers' tennis group?

15. Who was president of the International Olympic Committee from 1952-72?

ANSWERS 1. Lance Gibbs **2.** Carlos Moya **3.** Han Aiping **4.** Six **5.** Swimming **6.** Lyudmila Tourischeva **7.** Ken Doherty **8.** 1973 **9.** St. Louis Cardinals **10.** 1974 **11.** Rumbelows League Cup **12.** Greg Foster **13.** 14 and a half - 13 and a half **14.** Toto **15.** Avery Brundage.

POP MUSIC

1. From which African country does singer Alberta hail?

2. Which group had a 1997 No.2 single with *Lovefool*?

3. Which group had a 1997 hit with *Barrel of a Gun*?

4. Which group had a 1998 No.1 with the song *Bootie Call*?

5. Which U.S. duo had a 1983 hit with *Last Night a D.J. Saved My Life*?

6. Which singer's albums include *Tupelo Honey*?

7. Which group's debut L.P. is *Songs for a Barbed Wire Fence*?

8. Which was the only single by the Beach Boys to hit No. 1 in both the U.K. and U.S.?

9. Which duo sang the minor 1994 hit *The Day I Fall in Love*?

10. Which female singer featured on the 1996 hit *One and One* by Robert Miles?

11. Which group's L.P.s include *Huevos* and *Up on the Sun*?

12. Which group recorded the album *Baby's Got a Gun*?

13. In which year did singer Ricky Nelson die?

14. With which song did Madonna have a 1998 No. 1 single?

15. From which European country does the singer Alda come?

PEOPLE

1. Who became the Duke of Edinburgh's first woman equerry in 1999?

2. What is the name of the former deputy prime minister of Malaysia sentenced in 1999 to six years in jail for misuse of power?

3. Which film director presided over the international jury at the 1999 Cannes Film Festival?

4. Which celebrity married Anna Ottewill in 1999?

5. Which Scottish bacteriologist discovered penicillin in 1928?

6. Which comedy duo host the surreal T.V. game show *Families at War*?

7. Which British actress played Mel Gibson's wife in *Braveheart*?

8. In which country was the industrialist and philanthropist Andrew Carnegie born?

9. Which Conservative politician was secretary general of NATO from 1984-88?

10. Which Norfolk-born Egyptologist discovered the tomb of Tut'ankhamun in 1922?

11. Who won a place in the Guinness Book of Records for writing 26 books in 1983?

12. Which supermodel had a cameo role in Spike Lee's film 'Girl 6'?

13. Which talk-show host was the mayor of Cincinatti?

14. Who played *Peyton* in Aaron Spelling's T.V. saga *Savannah*?

15. In which year did industrialist Howard Hughes die?

GENERAL KNOWLEDGE

1. What was Toy of the Year in 1966?

2. What are the Carmelites also known as?

3. Which Italian football club did Diego Maradona join in 1984?

4. *The Monocled Mutineer* is the story of which person?

5. What is the name of the nine-headed monster in Greek mythology?

6. In which year did French engineer A.G. Eiffel die?

7. As what is the Book of Changes more commonly known?

8. What is the second name of film director D.W. Griffith?

9. Who was the 1972 U.S. Open men's singles tennis champion?

10. Which mime artist is associated with the character 'Bip'?

11. Who starred as *Gregory's Girl* in 1982?

12. Who won Pipe Smoker of the Year award in 1984?

13. What bird is also called a titlark?

14. Who wrote the novel *The Top of the Hill*?

15. Who wrote the play *Entertaining Mr. Sloane*?

ANSWERS 1. Action Man **2.** White Friars **3.** Napoli **4.** Percy Toplis **5.** Hydra **6.** 1923 **7.** I Ching **8.** Wark **9.** Ilie Nastase **10.** Marcel Marceau **11.** Dee Hepburn **12.** Henry Cooper **13.** Pipit **14.** Irwin Shaw **15.** Joe Orton.

ENTERTAINMENT

1. In which suburb of Liverpool was Ken Dodd born?

2. What is Thomas Sweeney better known as in *Brookside*?

3. Who directed the 1967 film *The Chelsea Girls*?

4. Who created T.V. sleuth Paul Temple?

5. Which writing duo created the 1970's sitcom *Don't Drink the Water*?

6. Who directed the 1988 film *Another Woman*?

7. Who did Michelle Herbert play in *Grange Hill*?

8. In which 1986 sitcom did Robert Hardy play dual roles of Twiggy Rathbone and Russell Spam?

9. What was the name of the taking golden flute in the T.V. show *H.R.Pufnstuf*?

10. Who directed the 1966 film *Chimes at Midnight*?

11. In which year was T.V. presenter David Letterman born?

12. Who composed the 1-Act opera *Master Peter's Puppet Show*?

13. Who played Vivienne Cooper in the BBC drama *The Newcomers*?

14. In which year was comedian Bob Newhart born?

15. Who played *Annie* in a 1982 film?

SPORT

1. Who won the 1957 Wimbledon women's singles tennis championship?

2. Which team did American Football star Paul Hornung play for after leaving Notre Dame in 1956?

3. Who scored both goals for Newcastle United in the 1951 F.A. Cup Final?

4. Who in fencing was 1997 & '98 world foil champion?

5. How high in feet and inches is the net in volleyball?

6. Which Yorkshire-born bowls player was awarded the CBE in 1980?

7. At which fencing discipline did Georges Buchard win three individual world titles between 1927 and 1933?

8. Whose record of 27 English classic winners did Lester Piggott surpass in 1984?

9. Who, on 20th July, 1984, became the first man to throw over 100m with a javelin?

10. Which cyclist won the 1996 & '97 Vuelta A España?

11. In which year did Mike Teague win his 27th and final rugby union cap for England?

12. Who took 30 wickets in his debut Test series for the West Indies against India in 1958/9?

13. Who won the men's high jump at the 1993 & '97 IAAF World Championships?

14. In which country did England Test cricketer Walter Hammond settle after his retirement?

15. At what was Dmitri Svatkovsky men's individual world champion in 1994 & '95?

ANSWERS 1. Althea Gibson 2. Green Bay Packers 3. Jackie Milburn 4. Serey Golubitsky 5. Seven feet one inch 6. David Bryant 7. Épée 8. Frank Buckle 9. Uwe Hohn 10. Alex Zülle 11. 1993 12. Wes Hall 13. Javier Sotomayor 14. South Africa 15. Modern Pentathlon.

POP MUSIC

1. Which female vocalist had a 1998 Top ten single with *My All*?

2. Which U.S. rap duo charted in 1998 with *Halls of Illusion*?

3. Which female vocalist had a 1998 chart hit with *What's Your Sign*?

4. How many singles by the Beatles got to No.1 in both the U.S. and U.K.?

5. Which country singer recorded the album *Grievous Angel*?

6. Which songwriter recorded the 1971 album *Magnetic South*?

7. From which European country does singer Neja hail?

8. Which group had a 1995 No. 2 hit with the song *Don't give me your life*?

9. Which U.K. singer had a 1995 Top 30 with *Rough with the Smooth*?

10. Who had a No.1 single in 1998 with *You Make Me Wanna*?

11. Which group's albums include *Trompe Le Monde*?

12. Which vocal group had a 1998 Top Five single with *No, no, no*?

13. In which year did singer Michael Hutchence die?

14. Which was David Bowie's only single to reach No.1 in the U.S. and U.K.?

15. With which song did The Verve have a No.1 single in 1997?

The Drugs Won't Work.

15. Let's Dance **14.** 1997 **13.** Destiny's Child **12.** The Pixies **11.** Usher **10.**
Shara Nelson **9.** Alex Party **8.** Italy **7.** Michael Nesmith **6.** Gram Parsons
5. 12 **4.** Des'Ree **3.** Insane Clown Posse **2.** Mariah Carey **1.** **ANSWERS**

ART AND LITERATURE

1. Whose romance books include *The Ranch* and *The Ghost*?

2. Who authored the novel *Armadillo* about loss adjustor Lorimer Black?

3. What in the world of art is a polyptych?

4. Which British gallery houses *When Did You Last See Your Father?* by W.F. Yeames?

5. In which year did sculptor Elisabeth Frink die?

6. Which British artist's collages include 1961's *The First Real Target*?

7. Who wrote the poem *The Wreck of the Hesperus*?

8. In which novel do the characters William Dobbin and Rawdon Crawley appear?

9. In which year did artist Jackson Pollock die?

10. Which London-born artist's forenames were Joseph Mallord William?

11. Who wrote *Moby-Dick*?

12. '1801 - I have just returned from a visit to my landlord' are the opening lines of which book?

13. Which U.S. thriller writer's books include *The Postman Always Rings Twice*?

14. Napoleon and Snowball are creatures in which satirical novel?

15. Which English playwright authored the comic novel *Head to Toe*?

GENERAL KNOWLEDGE

1. After which king of France was Louisville, Kentucky named?

2. What is the standard monetary unit of Romania?

3. In which year was the Free Church of Scotland formed?

4. Why might you not welcome a visit from a boomslang?

5. Which shipping forecast area is N.W. of Faeroes?

6. Clichy is an industrial suburb of which French city?

7. What is the approximate mileage from Land's End to John O'Groats by road?

8. Which pair of British aviators made the first non-stop transatlantic flight in 1919?

9. What was Toy of the Year in 1969?

10. The Marie Celeste left New York before being found abandoned. Which was its port of destination?

11. On what Mediterranean island is Syracuse?

12. Who won Pipe Smoker of the Year award in 1983?

13. In which year did Anne of Cleves marry Henry VIII?

14. What is the approximate area in square miles of the island of Elba - 86, 186 or 286?

15. Who keeps *The Diary of a Nobody*?

ENTERTAINMENT

1. Who did John Barrett play in the sitcom *The Dustbinmen*?

2. Who did Susan Tully play in *Grange Hill*?

3. In which city was comedian Frankie Howerd born?

4. Which future Labour M.P. appeared on the science show *Don't Ask Me*?

5. Who directed the 1974 film *Chinatown*?

6. Who plays P.T. Barnum in the 1934 biopic *The Mighty Barnum*?

7. What in film making is a dolly?

8. Which comic actor played Edgar Briggs in the 1974 sitcom *The Top Secret Life of Edgar Briggs*?

9. Which actor played Dr. Tony Latimer in the sitcom *Don't Wait Up*?

10. What was Admiral Nelson's forename in the T.V. show *Voyage to the Bottom of the Sea*?

11. Who composed the nocturne *Paris:The Song of a Great City*?

12. Which T.V. presenter was born Nicholas Henty Dodd?

13. Who played Flt. Lt. Phil Carrington in the T.V. show *Colditz*?

14. In which year did jazz player Charlie Parker die?

15. The American consul Sharples appears in which opera?

SPORT

1. Who were Scottish League champions in rugby union in the 1997/8 season?

2. Which skier won the 1984 Olympic 5km, 10km and 20km cross-country golds?

3. Who was 1996 World Professional Billiards champion?

4. Which U.S. cyclist won the 1988 Giro d'Italia?

5. Who took 28 wickets for the West Indies on the 1976 England tour?

6. Who was men's pole vault champion in the IAAF World Championships from 1983-97?

7. For which Italian club side did Swedish footballer Kurt Hamrin sign in 1956?

8. Which controversial athlete married Mike Pieterse in 1989?

9. Who won all three men's tennis titles at Wimbledon in 1937?

10. At what Olympic sport did Romanian Olga Bularda win medals?

11. Who did Craig Brown replace as Scotland football manager?

12. With which sport is Cedric Pioline associated?

13. What nationality is golfer Joakim Haeggman?

14. From which club did Manchester United sign goalkeeper Mark Bosnich in 1999?

15. With which sport is Desmond Douglas associated?

ANSWERS 1. Watsonians **2.** Marja-Liisa Hämäläinen **3.** Mike Russell **4.** Andy Hampsten **5.** Michael Holding **6.** Sergey Bubka **7.** Juventus **8.** Zola Budd **9.** Don Budge **10.** Rowing **11.** Andy Roxburgh **12.** Tennis **13.** Swedish **14.** Aston Villa **15.** Table tennis.

POP MUSIC

1. Which female vocalist hit the charts in 1998 with the song *Uh la la la*?

2. Which female singer had a 1996 Top Ten with *In too deep*?

3. In which year was Janet Jackson born?

4. Which vocal group had a 1995 Top Ten single with *I Need You*?

5. What was the title of Run-DMC vs Jason Nevin's 1998 No. 1 single?

6. Which group recorded the 1971 album *There's a Riot Goin' On*?

7. On which label did Moby release the 1999 album *Play*?

8. In which year did New Edition chart with the single *Hit me off*?

9. Which female singer duetted with Big Dee Irwin on the 1963 hit *Swinging on a Star*?

10. Which group recorded the live album *Severe Tire Damage*?

11. Which group recorded the 1994 album *San Francisco*?

12. With which song did Tatyana Ali have a hit in November 1998?

13. Which group's last chart hit single was 1967's *Green Street Green*?

14. With what song did Michael Jackson score a 1997 No.1 single?

15. Which singer recorded the album *The Cult of Ray*?

GEOGRAPHY

1. In which African country is the seaport of Dar-es-Salaam?

2. On which river is Ilkley, West Yorkshire?

3. In which ocean is the former penal settlement of Devil's Island?

4. In which Central American republic is the volcano Irazu?

5. On which river is the German port of Dresden?

6. Irian Jaya forms the western part of which island?

7. In which European country are the forested highlands of Hunsrück?

8. Carantuohil is the highest peak of which mountain group?

9. In which country is the airport town of Dum-Dum?

10. On which West Indies island would you find the ports of Kingston and Montego Bay?

11. Which strait lies between the Persian Gulf and the Gulf of Oman?

12. In which English county is the River Lyn, scene of severe flooding in 1952?

13. On which U.S. river is the Hoover Dam?

14. Which is larger - Luxembourg or Liechtenstein?

15. Lusaka is the capital of which African country?

ANSWERS 1. Tanzania 2. River Wharfe 3. Atlantic Ocean 4. Costa Rica 5. River Elbe 6. New Guinea 7. Germany 8. Macgillicuddy's Reeks 9. India 10. Jamaica 11. Strait of Hormuz 12. Devon 13. Colorado 14. Luxembourg 15. Zambia.

GENERAL KNOWLEDGE

1. What in Devon is a grockle?

2. What was Toy of the Year in 1980?

3. Which Austrian-born film director made the thriller *The Testament of Dr. Mabuse*?

4. Who authored the children's book *The Ghost of Thomas Kempe*?

5. Of which country was Joseph Coates prime minister from 1925-28?

6. What is the name of the female demon in Jewish folklore who attempts to kill new-born children?

7. What was the nickname of Richard de Clare, Earl of Pembroke?

8. In which country was artist George Grosz born?

9. What does the children's book of verse *Struwwelpeter* translate as?

10. EX is the abbreviation for which postcode area?

11. Which operetta by Sigmund Romberg features *The Drinking Song*?

12. Which D.J.'s show won Melody Maker Radio Show of the Year award 1984-93?

13. What name was given to Holy Roman Emperor Frederick II?

14. In which city is George Eliot's novel *Romola* set?

15. What was the pen-name of Sir Arthur Quiller-Couch?

ANSWERS 1. A tourist **2.** Rubik's Cube **3.** Fritz Lang **4.** Penelope Lively **5.** New Zealand **6.** Lilith **7.** Strongbow **8.** Germany **9.** Shock-headed Peter **10.** Exeter **11.** The Student Prince **12.** John Peel **13.** Stupor Mundi **14.** Florence **15.** Q.

ENTERTAINMENT

1. Who directed the 1983 film *Christine*?

2. Which Australian operatic soprano made her debut in Brussels in 1887?

3. Which comedian was born Charles Springall in 1925?

4. Which Benjamin Britten opera was premiered at Aldeburgh in June 1960?

5. In which year did actor Peter Cushing die?

6. In which opera does the aria *Nessun Dorma* appear?

7. What nationality was baritone Titta Ruffo?

8. Ffynnon Garw Hill is central to the plot of which 1995 film?

9. Which writing duo created the sitcom *Drop the Dead Donkey*?

10. Which folk singer was born in Okemah, Oklahoma?

11. Which member of the Monty Python team scripted the 1983 film *The Missionary*?

12. Which actress played 'Annie Oakley' in a 1935 film?

13. Who played Tom Joad in the film *The Grapes of Wrath*?

14. Which actor was born Bernard Schwarz?

15. Who is the lead singer/songwriter with the group Wilco?

ANSWERS 1. John Carpenter **2.** Dame Nellie Melba **3.** Charlie Drake **4.** A Midsummer Night's Dream **5.** 1994 **6.** Turandot **7.** Italian **8.** The Englishman Who Went Up a Hill but Came Down a Mountain **9.** Andy Hamilton & Guy Jenkin **10.** Woody Guthrie **11.** Michael Palin **12.** Barbara Stanwyck **13.** Henry Fonda **14.** Tony Curtis **15.** Jeff Tweedy.

SPORT

1. In which sport did Haydn Bunton and Haydn Bunton, Jr. win the Sandover Medal?

2. In which city was cyclist Beryl Burton born?

3. Which baseball player died in 1941 of the disease amyotrophic lateral schlerosis, which was later named after him in the U.S.?

4. Which Dallas player was MVP in Superbowl XXX in 1996?

5. At which individual sport was Hans Deutgen world champion from 1947-50?

6. Which football team were runners-up in the 1966 European Champions Cup?

7. Who won the 1992 Nat West Trophy in cricket?

8. Which tennis player won the 1956 U.S. singles title, denying Lew Hoad the Grand Slam in the Final?

9. Who, in fencing, was 1998 world sabre champion?

10. Which team did Sheffield United defeat to win the 1925 F.A. Cup Final?

11. Which horse won the 1993 Breeders Cup Classic?

12. In which year was the first women's cricket Test match?

13. Who was the founder of the modern Olympic Games?

14. Who was Olympic heavyweight boxing champion in 1968?

15. In what year was the Modern Pentathlon introduced into the Olympics?

ANSWERS 1. Australian Rules Football 2. Leeds 3. Lou Gehrig 4. Larry Brown 5. Archery 6. Partizan Belgrade 7. Northants 8. Ken Rosewall 9. Luigi Tarantino 10. Cardiff City 11. Arcangues 12. 1934 13. Baron de Coubertin 14. George Foreman 15. 1912.

POP MUSIC

1. Which female singer had a 1996 Top ten single with *Escaping*?

2. Which single by Phil Collins reached No.1 both in the U.K. and U.S.?

3. Which duo's debut chart hit was 1996's *I am I feel*?

4. Which singing duo had a 1995 hit with *Had to be*?

5. On which label did Dinosaur Jr. chart in 1994 with the song *Feel the Pain*?

6. What was the title of Oasis's only No.1 single in 1997?

7. Who is the singer with the group *Nine Inch Nails*?

8. Which group's debut L.P. in 1975 was *Late Night Movies, All Night Brainstorms*?

9. Which indie group recorded the album *When Animals Attack*?

10. What was the first No.1 single for the group All Saints?

11. Which U.K. vocal group's first U.K. Top Ten single was 1996's *Don't Make Me Wait*?

12. Which male singer had a 1998 Top Ten with the song *Crazy Little Party Girl*?

13. Which male singer featured on the 1998 hit *True to your Heart* by 98 Degrees?

14. Who recorded the album *Gorgeous George*?

15. Which group recorded the 1997 Top 20 hit *Spiderwebs*?

ANSWERS 1. Dina Carroll **2.** A Groovy Kind of Love **3.** Alisha's Attic **4.** Cliff Richard & Olivia Newton-John **5.** Bianco Y Negro **6.** D'You Know what I Mean? **7.** Trent Reznor **8.** The Doctors of Madness **9.** Cable **10.** Never Ever **11.** 911 **12.** Aaron Carter **13.** Stevie Wonder **14.** Edwyn Collins **15.** No Doubt.

HISTORY

1. Which king of Mercia killed King Oswald of Northumbria in 642?

2. Which Jewish sect seized the fortress of Masada in 66 A.D.?

3. Who was elected president of France in June 1969?

4. Which English children's author married Trotsky's secretary Evgenia Shelepin?

5. Which American was president of the Screen Actors' Guild from 1947-52?

6. At which castle was the investiture of the Prince of Wales in 1969?

7. Which king founded Trinity College, Cambridge?

8. In which year did Canberra officially become capital of Australia?

9. Who was the first Archbishop of Canterbury?

10. Who formed the Cato Street Conspiracy of 1820?

11. In which year was nurse Edith Cavell executed by the Germans in World War I?

12. In which year was the First Factory Act passed?

13. In which year did the Spanish Civil War end?

14. In which year was the Falklands War?

15. At the end of which year did the farthing cease to be legal tender?

GENERAL KNOWLEDGE

1. On which island was actress Lillie Langtry born?

2. On what river is the city of Lima, Peru?

3. What was Toy of the Year in 1986?

4. Who were the legendary founders of Rome?

5. What is the site of the French Foreign Office in Paris?

6. What type of animal is a Border Leicester?

7. Which Italian actress received an honorary Academy Award in 1991?

8. Which fictional detective was aided by the Baker Street Irregulars?

9. For what is *cocky's joy* Australian slang?

10. Adam's Bridge links the island of Mannar to which country?

11. Who was Best Actress winner at the 1987 Laurence Olivier Awards?

12. What does the Latin phrase *cogito, ergo sum* translate as?

13. Who was the second son of Noah in the Old Testament?

14. Who was British prime minister 1763-65?

15. In which year did Qatar join the U.N.?

ENTERTAINMENT

1. Which comedian played Sherlock Holmes in the one-off 1973 T.V. comedy *Elementary, My Dear Watson*?

2. In which year was comedian Roy Hudd born?

3. Who played Cleopatra in the 1972 film *Antony and Cleopatra*?

4. Who played Christopher Columbus in a 1949 film?

5. Who played the 'Wife' in the US T.V. series *Macmillan and Wife*?

6. 'This Machine Kills Fascists' was a slogan on whose guitar?

7. What was Michael Landon's character name in *Highway to Heaven*?

8. In which year did comedian Dick Emery die?

9. Who directed the 1965 film *Mickey One* which starred Warren Beatty?

10. Who composed the 1819 opera *The Twin Brothers*?

11. Who directed the 1935 film *Bride of Frankenstein*?

12. Which Australian comedian took over from Ron Moody as Fagin in the London stage production of *Oliver*'

13. Dawn Ralph sang lead vocals on what pop hit?

14. Who authored the 1975 sitcom *I Didn't Know You Cared*?

15. Which D.J. was known as 'The Hairy Cornflake'?

ANSWERS 1 John Cleese **2.** 1936 **3.** Hildegard Neil **4.** Fredric March **5.** Susan Saint James **6.** Woody Guthrie **7.** Jonahan Smith **8.** 1983 **9.** Arthur Penn **10.** Schubert **11.** James Whale **12.** Barry Humphries **13.** Grandma We Love You **14.** Peter Tinniswood **15.** Dave Lee Travis.

SPORT

1. Which footballer took over the captaincy of Real Madrid in 1964 following the departure of Di Stefano?

2. Which jockey won the 1997 & '98 2,000 Guineas?

3. Who was men's shot champion at the 1987, '91 & '93 IAAF World Championships?

4. Who was 1998 French Open tennis women's singles champion?

5. What was the nickname of Canadian ice hockey player Bernard Geoffrion?

6. Which U.S. Olympic swimming champion was known as 'Mr. Machine'?

7. How many Scottish international caps did Sir Matt Busby win?

8. Which Spanish footballer scored four against Denmark in their 1986 World Cup Finals game?

9. What was the nickname of Canadian ice hockey player Glenn Hall?

10. Which batsman was the first to reach 4,000 runs and 5,000 runs in Test cricket?

11. Who in 1960 became the first man to win gold medals at six successive Olympic Games?

12. For which international side did footballer Germano de Figuereido play?

13. Who was 1996 world matchplay golf champion?

14. Who won the 1993 Paris Indoor tennis title?

15. Who won the 1993 Australian Grand Prix in Formula 1?

ANSWERS 1. Francisco Gento 2. Mick Kinane 3. Werner Günthör 4. Arantxa Sánchez Vicario 5. Boom-Boom 6. Mike Burton 7. One 8. Emilio Butragueno 9. Mr. Goalie 10. Jack Hobbs 11. Aladar Gerevich 12. Portugal 13. Ernie Els 14. Goran Ivanisevic 15. Ayrton Senna.

POP MUSIC

1. With which group did Celine Dion record the 1998 hit *Immortality*?

2. Which female vocalist had a Top Ten hit in 1997 with the song *You Might Need Somebody*?

3. Which duo had a 1985 No.1 single with *Dancing in the Street*?

4. Which group recorded the 1999 album *The Unauthorised Biography of Reinhold Messner*?

5. Which Australian group had a 1991 hit with *I Touch Myself*?

6. Which was the only single by Ray Charles to reach No.1 in both the U.S. and U.K. charts?

7. Which singer had a 1998 No.1 single with *Deeper Underground*?

8. Who had a 1997 No.1 single with *You're Not Alone*?

9. Which U.S. group had a minor hit in 1993 with *Johnny Mathis' Feet*?

10. Which Oasis copyists charted in 1996 with *I'd Like to Teach the World to Sing*?

11. Which singer recorded the album *Brutal Youth*?

12. Whose debut album is 1999's *Avant Hard*?

13. Which group had a 1997 Top Ten with *I'm a Man not a Boy*?

14. Which song gave James a Top Ten single in 1997?

15. What was the real name of rapper Notorious B.I.G.?

ANSWERS 1. The Bee Gees 2. Shola Ama **3.** David Bowie and Mick Jagger **4.** Ben Folds Five **5.** Divinyls **6.** I Can't Stop Loving You **7.** Jamiroquai **8.** Olive **9.** American Music Club **10.** No Way Sis **11.** Elvis Costello **12.** Add N to X **13.** North and South **14.** She's a Star **15.** Christopher Wallace.

WORDS

1. What word meaning 'belonging to a village' has come to mean a heathen?

2. 'The black ox has never trod upon his foot' refers to a man who is not what?

3. What in Australia is a wagga - a bed covering or a poisonous berry?

4. For what do North American Indians use a watap - smoking or sewing?

5. What would you do with kummel - soak clothes in it or drink it?

6. What article of clothing is named after the German for 'leather trousers'?

7. From what phrase does the 'loran' navigation system derive its name?

8. What in Spain is a zapateado?

9. Yite is the Scottish word for which bird?

10. Which German phrase meaning 'wonder child' is given to a child prodigy?

11. What does VDU stand for in computer terminology?

12. What sort of creature is a wentletrap - a dog or a mollusc?

13. Is wowser Australian slang for a drunkard or a teetotaller?

14. What is belly-timber?

15. What is a Blindman's Lantern?

GENERAL KNOWLEDGE

1. What was Toy of the Year in 1967?

2. Which actress was the *Girl with the Million Dollar Legs*?

3. What is the name of the alcoholic drink consisting of half burgundy, half champagne?

4. Who succeeded Ahab as king of Israel?

5. Who led the Paramount Jazz Band?

6. From which illness did author Katherine Mansfield die?

7. Which Radio D.J. won the Pipe Smoker of the Year award in 1982?

8. What is the brightest star in the constellation Scorpius?

9. Who played Father Dougal in the T.V. show *Father Ted*?

10. Which actress was 'The Vamp'?

11. What is the most famous work of sculpture by Gutzon Borglum?

12. Who wrote the 1922 story collection *Tales of the Jazz Age*?

13. Who authored the 1938 novel *The Yearling*?

14. Of what is an Elsan a portable variety?

15. What type of creature is a guan - a lizard or a bird?

ANSWERS 1. Spirograph **2.** Betty Grable **3.** Cold duck **4.** Jehu **5.** Acker Bilk **6.** Tuberculosis **7.** Dave Lee Travis **8.** Antares **9.** Ardal O'Hanlon **10.** Theda Bara **11.** The carved busts of the U.S. presidents on Mount Rushmore **12.** F. Scott Fitzgerald **13.** Marjorie Kinnan Rawlings **14.** Lavatory **15.** Bird.

ENTERTAINMENT

1. What is Woody Allen's character initial in the animated film *Antz*?

2. Which U.S. sitcom starred Elliott Gould as an ear-nose-and-throat specialist?

3. Who played Mary Shelley in the 1935 film *Bride of Frankenstein*?

4. Who starred as *The Cincinnati Kid* in 1965?

5. *Orville's Song* was written by which winner of the T.V. show *Opportunity Knocks*?

6. Who did Mark Slade play in the western series *The High Chaparral*?

7. Oliver Bendt was lead singer with which chart-topping group?

8. Who directed the 1984 film *Micki & Maude*?

9. Which D.J. and comedian was born Maurice Cole?

10. What was Hilary Lester's chart-topping alter ego?

11. Who starred as *Cinderfella* in a 1960 film?

12. Who wrote the pop song *Grandad*?

13. In which year did entertainer Adge Cutler die?

14. Who authored the sitcom *Fairly Secret Army*?

15. Who played Steed in the T.V. show *The Avengers*?

SPORT

1. Who was 1952 & '56 Olympic Modern Pentathlon champion?

2. Who was 1998 Australian Open men's singles tennis champion?

3. Which golfer won the 1950 U.S. Open, a year after a serious car accident?

4. In what year did Sonny Liston die?

5. Who won the 1993 World Rally Drivers championship?

6. Which cricket team finished bottom in the 1992 & '93 county championship?

7. Which England rugby union centre won 28 consecutive caps between 1953 and 1959?

8. Who trained the 1936 Epsom Derby winner Mahmoud?

9. At what field event did Tamara Bykova set three world records in 1983-4?

10. What was the nickname of American Football star Elroy Hirsch?

11. Who won the men's discus title at the IAAF World Championships from 1991 to 1997?

12. Who was 1994 World Professional Billiards champion?

13. Who was 1996 World Outdoor Bowls men's champion?

14. Which cyclist won the Vuelta A España in 1995?

15. Which American was 1956 & '60 Olympic men's 110m hurdles champion?

ANSWERS 1. Lars Hall 2. Petr Korda 3. Ben Hogan 4. 1970 5. Juha Kankkunen 6. Durham 7. Jeff Butterfield 8. Frank Butters 9. High jump 10. Crazy Legs 11. Lars Riedel 12. Peter Gilchrist 13. Tony Allcock 14. Laurent Jalabert 15. Lee Calhoun.

POP MUSIC

1. Which female vocalist had a 1994 hit with *Cornflake Girl*?

2. Which male singer had a minor chart hit in 1992 with *Machine + Soul*?

3. In which city was Celine Dion born?

4. What was Oasis's first No.1 single?

5. Which singer had a minor hit in 1993 with *London's Brilliant*?

6. Which group's 1996 Top Ten singles included *Walkaway* and *Sandstorm*?

7. Which member of Stump recorded the solo L.P. *Stolen Jewels*?

8. Who had a No.1 single in 1997 with *Don't Speak*?

9. Which Italian artist had a 1996 hit with *X-Files*?

10. What was Ocean Colour Scene's first Top Ten single?

11. Which single by Culture Club reached No.1 in the U.K. and U.S.?

12. Which U.K. group had a 1996 Top Ten hit with *Good Enough*?

13. Which group recorded the album *Retreat from Memphis*?

14. Which female singer had a 1998 hit with song *Maybe I'm Amazed*?

15. Which act had a minor hit in July 1998 with *Nagasaki Badger*?

SCIENCE

1. How many vertices has a cube?

2. What nationality was the scientist Copernicus?

3. How many kilogrammes are in 1 quintal?

4. What sort of creature was the prehistoric mammal a procoptodon?

5. What nationality was scientist Johann Lambert?

6. Which four main blood groups did Karl Landsteiner identify in 1901?

7. How many gallons are in a peck?

8. In which year was Charon, satellite of Pluto, discovered?

9. What is the term for air that has a temperature of 0°C or less?

10. Which U.S. physicist constructed the first working laser?

11. How many centilitres are there in one decilitre?

12. In which Italian city was Marconi born?

13. Which 19c Austrian monk discovered the basic principles of heredity?

14. Which element is directly above antimony in the Periodic table?

15. In which continent is the Brickfielder a very hot N.E. wind?

ANSWERS 1. Eight 2. Polish 3. 100 4. Kangaroo 5. German 6. A,O,B, and AB 7. 2 8. 1978 9. Air frost 10. Theodore Maiman 11. 10 12. Bologna 13. Gregor Mendel 14. Arsenic 15. Australia.

GENERAL KNOWLEDGE

1. Around which island do a group of Brittany sailors fish in a famous series of novels by Pierre Loti?

2. Who was Best Actress winner at the 1992 Laurence Olivier awards?

3. What was the pseudonym of the crime writer Edith Pargeter?

4. How many packs of cards are used in the game boston?

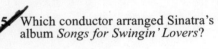

5. Which conductor arranged Sinatra's album *Songs for Swingin' Lovers*?

6. In which year did Oklahoma join the Union?

7. What was Toy of the Year 1987-89?

8. Which green alcoholic drink has a high wormwood content?

9. What is the hedge sparrow also called?

10. Which English poet and critic authored *Seven Types of Ambiguity* in 1930?

11. Who was the legendary wife of King Arthur?

12. What is the standard monetary unit of Nicaragua?

13. What type of bird is a lanner - a swan or a falcon?

14. On which bay is the Cyprus port of Limassol?

15. What is the Land of the Long White Cloud?

ENTERTAINMENT

1. Who plays Philo Beddoe in the 1980 film *Anyway Which Way You Can*?

2. What was Lynda Bellingham's character name in the 1996 series *Faith in the Future*?

3. Which U.S. president was the subject of a 1987 opera by John Adams?

4. Which comic starred in the BBC sitcom *Here's Harry*?

5. Which opera was premiered at Cairo Opera House on Christmas Eve 1871?

6. What was the trade of the two leads in the U.S. sitcom *I'm Dickens, He's Fenster*?

7. Benjamin Britten, Peter Pears and Eric Crozier founded a music festival in which Suffolk town in 1948?

8. Who scripted the 1995 film *Circle of Friends*?

9. Who composed the opera *Fierrabras*?

10. Which children's T.V. show was called *Le Maison de Tu Tu* in its native France?

11. In which year did comedian Arthur Haynes die?

12. Who directed the 1996 action film *Maximum Risk*?

13. In which year did the Stuttgart Chamber Orchestra give their first performance?

14. By what initials was John Barron's character known in *The Fall and Rise of Reggie Perrin*?

15. What was unusual about the opera *Amahl and the Night Visitors*?

ANSWERS 1. Clint Eastwood **2.** Faith Grayshot **3.** Richard Nixon **4.** Harry Worth **5.** Aida **6.** Carpenters **7.** Aldeburgh **8.** Andrew Davis **9.** Schubert **10.** Hector's House **11.** 1966 **12.** Ringo Lam **13.** 1945 **14.** C.J. **15.** It was the first opera written for television.

SPORT

1. Which French rugby union player scored 30 points against Zimbabwe in the 1987 World Cup?

2. Why did motor racer Malcolm Campbell call his cars *Bluebird*?

3. Which Ireland rugby union player scored 21 points against Scotland in 1982?

4. In which year was Australia rugby union star David Campese born?

5. Which cricketer in 1906 scored 2,385 runs and took 208 wickets in a first class season?

6. Who won the men's hammer event at the 1983 & '87 IAAF World Championships?

7. Who was 1996 World Outdoor Bowls women's champion?

8. Who were All-Ireland League rugby union champions in the 1997/98 season?

9. Who was 1997 & '98 men's individual world modern pentathlon champion?

10. Who was 1998 Australian Open women's singles tennis champion?

11. At what Olympic sport did Mexican Ernesto Campo win gold in 1984?

12. At what Olympic sport did Mexican Joaquin Capilla win gold in 1956?

13. For what country did Antonio Carbajal play in the football World Cup finals five times from 1950-66?

14. Who won the 1993 Volvo Masters golf championship?

15. For which country did Hasely Crawford win the 1976 Olympic 100m?

ANSWERS 1. Didier Cambérabéro **2.** After a play by Maeterlinck **3.** Ollie Campbell **4.** 1962 **5.** George Hirst **6.** Sergey Litvinov **7.** Carmelita Anderson **8.** Shannon **9.** Sébastien Deleigne **10.** Martina Hingis **11.** Walking **12.** Diving **13.** Mexico **14.** Colin Montgomerie **15.** Trinidad & Tobago.

THE ULTIMATE PUB QUIZ BOOK

POP MUSIC

1. On which label did Catatonia chart with the 1998 hit *Mulder and Scully*?

2. Which group released the 1999 album *The Soft Bulletin*?

3. From which European country did instrumental group Don Pablo's Animals come?

4. Which single by Dexy's Midnight Runners reached No.1 in the U.K. and U.S.?

5. What was the title of White Town's 1997 No.1 single?

6. What was Peter Andre's first No.1 hit single?

7. Which song gave Duran Duran a No.1 hit in the U.K. and U.S.?

8. Which U.S. vocal group had a 1998 Top Ten hit with *How Deep is your Love*?

9. With which song did Prodigy have a November 1996 No.1 hit?

10. Which pop musician was born Keigo Oyamada?

11. Which duo had a 1995 Top 30 hit with *Secret Love*?

12. Who had a 1998 Top Ten hit with the song *Hard Knock Life (Ghetto Anthem)*?

13. Which group released the 1984 album *Learning to Crawl*?

14. Which guitarist had a minor 1994 hit with *Hibernaculum*?

15. Who had a Top Ten single in 1998 with *Gone Till November*?

ANSWERS 1. Blanco Y Negro **2.** Flaming Lips **3.** Italy **4.** Come on Eileen **5.** Your Woman **6.** Flava **7.** The Reflex **8.** Dru Hill **9.** Breathe **10.** Cornelius **11.** Daniel O'Donnell and Mary Duff **12.** Jay-Z **13.** The Pretenders **14.** Mike Oldfield **15.** Wyclef Jean.

PEOPLE

1. Who is disc jockey Zoë Ball's father?

2. Who is Madam Speaker of the House of Commons?

3. Which soap actress and singer once worked as an assistant in store 'Knickerbox'?

4. Who captained England's cricket team for the 1999 World Cup?

5. Which model and actress is daughter of singer Steve Tyler and model Bebe Buell?

6. Which *Blue Peter* presenter was sacked in 1998 after allegations of drug use?

7. Who was the female star of the film 'Clueless'?

8. What nationality is actress Famke Janssen?

9. Which Irish patriot and author of 'the Black Diaries' was hanged for high treason in 1916?

10. Who murdered John Lennon in 1980?

11. Charles the Fat was king of which country from 884 A.D.?

12. Which English publisher compiled a famous *Peerage of England, Scotland and Ireland*?

13. Which French general wrote the 1940 book *The Army of the Future*?

14. Which judge held the inquiry into the resignation of politician John Profumo?

15. Kindred is the middle name of which American science fiction author?

ANSWERS 1. Johnny Ball **2.** Betty Boothroyd **3.** Martine McCutcheon **4.** Alec Stewart **5.** Liv Tyler **6.** Richard Bacon **7.** Alicia Silverstone **8.** Dutch **9.** Sir Roger Casement **10.** Mark Chapman **11.** France **12.** John Debrett **13.** Charles de Gaulle **14.** Lord Denning **15.** Philip K. Dick.

GENERAL KNOWLEDGE

1. Who authored the poem *The Rime of the Ancient Mariner*?

2. Which of the Canary Islands is known for its *Mountains of Fire*?

3. In which year was the first Aldermaston march?

4. Alan Saldanha was 1993 British champion at which board game?

5. Which musician won the Pipe Smoker of the Year award in 1981?

6. Who was world professional snooker champion in 1982?

7. What was the 1981 TV Show of the Year in the Melody Maker Polls?

8. In which county is Bosworth Field, site of a 1485 battle?

9. In which year was the U.S. battleship Maine blown up in Havana Harbor?

10. Who was Best Actor award winner at the 1986 Laurence Olivier awards?

11. Which magician won the 1993 Carlton Award for Comedy?

12. What was the first name of French tyre manufacturer Michelin?

13. Who composed the opera *Eugene Onegin*?

14. Who authored *Tess of the D'Urbervilles*?

15. In which play does Algernon Moncrieff court Cecily Cardew?

ANSWERS 1. Samuel Taylor Coleridge **2.** Lanzarote **3.** 1958 **4.** Scrabble **5.** James Galway **6.** Alex Higgins **7.** Tiswas **8.** Leicestershire **9.** 1898 **10.** Albert Finney **11.** Ali Bongo **12.** André **13.** Tchaikovsky **14.** Thomas Hardy **15.** The Importance of Being Earnest.

ENTERTAINMENT

1. Who directed the 1979 film *Apocalypse Now*?

2. Which Philadelphia-born contralto died in 1993?

3. Who was the photographer on the 1941 film *Citizen Kane*?

4. In which Verdi opera does the Anvil Chorus appear?

5. In which year did Arthur Sullivan die?

6. Which singer played John McVicar in a 1980 biopic?

7. Who directed the 1974 film *The Texas Chainsaw Massacre*?

8. Which actor played Alex P. Keaton in the sitcom *Family Ties*?

9. In which century did the composer Thomas Arne live?

10. Who starred as Godfrey Spry in the 1993 sitcom *If You See God, Tell Him*?

11. Who wrote the 1736 opera *Atalanta*?

12. What nationality is baritone Jonathan Summers?

13. Who wrote the 1925 1-Act opera *At the Boar's Head*?

14. Which comedian starred in the 1992 film *Memoirs of an Invisible Man*?

15. In which city was opera singer Dame Joan Sutherland born?

SPORT

1. At which sport did American Tommy Hitchcock excel in the 1920s and '30s?

2. At what sport was Vicki Cardwell British Open champion in 1983?

3. Which Irish footballer captained the Rest of Europe against Great Britain in Glasgow in 1947?

4. Who was 1988 & '97 World Indoor Bowls men's champion?

5. In which year was former England rugby union captain Will Carling born?

6. How were Indian opening batsmen Gundappa Viswanath and Sunil Gavaskar related?

7. Which Green Bay player was MVP in Superbowl XXXI?

8. Who in 1961 became the youngest ever world champion 250cc motor cyclist?

9. Who was world individual fly fishing champion in 1992 & '96?

10. Which French cyclist was nicknamed 'the Badger'?

11. Which football team were runners-up in the 1960 European Champions Cup?

12. In which country were the first modern Winter Olympics held?

13. What sport do you associate with Drew Henry?

14. In how many Tests did David Gower captain England?

15. Which country won the 1993 Heineken World Cup in golf?

ANSWERS 1. Polo **2.** Squash **3.** Johnny Carey **4.** Hugh Duff **5.** 1965 **6.** Brothers-in-law **7.** Desmond Howard **8.** Mike Hailwood **9.** Pierluigi Coccito **10.** Bernard Hinault **11.** Eintracht Frankfurt **12.** France **13.** Snooker **14.** 32 **15.** U.S.A.

POP MUSIC

1. What was Dave Angel's minor hit single in 1997?

2. Which single reached No.1 in the U.S. and U.K. for Foreigner?

3. Who recorded the album *Hard Nose the Highway*?

4. Which actor had a 1962 Top 20 single with *Love Me Tender*?

5. Which singer had a 1969 Top Ten single with *Good Morning Starshine*?

6. Which U.S. group had a 1991 Top Forty hit with *The King is Half Undressed*?

7. Which male singer had a 1997 Top 40 single with *Golden Brown*?

8. Which group had a minor hit in 1995 with the single *I Hate Rock 'N' Roll*?

9. Which act had a 1998 Top Ten with the song *Kung Fu*?

10. Which rapper had a 1997 Top 40 single with *You Can't Stop the Reign*?

11. What was Italian vocalist Drupi's first U.K. hit single?

12. Which group had a 1997 hit with *Toxygene*?

13. Which group had a 1996 hit with *Walking on the Milky Way*?

14. What was the title of Mark Morrison's 1996 No.1 single?

15. Which group had 1997 Top Ten singles with *Satan* and *The Saint*?

ANSWERS 1. Tokyo Stealth Fighter **2.** I Want to Know What Love is **3.** Van Morrison **4.** Richard Chamberlain **5.** Oliver **6.** Jellyfish **7.** Omar **8.** Jesus and Mary Chain **9.** 187 Lockdown **10.** Shaquille O'Neal **11.** Vado Via **12.** The Orb **13.** Orchestral Manoeuvres in the Dark **14.** Return of the Mack **15.** Orbital.

ART AND LITERATURE

1. *Down the Rabbit-Hole* is the opening chapter in which book?

2. The author of Booker Prize-winning novel *The Sea, the Sea* died in 1999. Who was she?

3. Whose novels include *Nostromo*?

4. Who wrote the novel *Absolute Beginners*?

5. In which century did Rembrandt live?

6. Who painted 1864's *Symphony in White No.2: Little White Girl*?

7. Which portrait painter was born the son of a clergyman in Plympton St. Maurice, Devon, in 1723?

8. In which century did Vincent van Gogh live?

9. In which book does Mr. Worldly Wiseman appear?

10. In which Shakespeare play does the petty constable Verges appear?

11. In which novel by Charles Dickens does Mr. Wopsle appear?

12. Who was Phileas Fogg's valet in the novel *Around the World in Eighty Days*?

13. What nationality was Pop Artist Jim Dine?

14. Which artist's studio was known as 'The Factory'?

15. In which museum and art gallery is the statue *Venus de Milo* housed?

ANSWERS 1. Alice's Adventures in Wonderland **2.** Dame Iris Murdoch **3.** Joseph Conrad **4.** Colin MacInnes **5.** 17th **6.** James Whistler **7.** Sir Joshua Reynolds **8.** 19th **9.** Pilgrim's Progress **10.** Much Ado About Nothing **11.** Great Expectations **12.** Passepartout **13.** American **14.** Andy Warhol's **15.** The Louvre.

THE ULTIMATE PUB QUIZ BOOK

GENERAL KNOWLEDGE

1. Where would you write an apostil?

2. Which French novelist wrote the *Gigi*?

3. In Arthurian legend who was the faithful wife of Geraint?

4. Which British actor starred as an Interpol agent in the 1972 film *Kill! Kill! Kill!*?

5. At approximately what altitude in feet is the city of La Paz - 10,000, 20,000 or 30,000?

6. What was once drunk in the British navy to prevent scurvy?

7. Who was Best Actor winner at the 1991 Laurence Olivier awards?

8. What was Melody Maker TV Show of the Year in their 1993 polls?

9. Which shipping forecast area is due south of Viking?

10. On which island does the aye-aye live?

11. What fish is *Anguilla anguilla*?

12. Who composed the opera *Pimpinone*?

13. What is the surname of *Lucky Jim* in the novel by Amis?

14. Of which country was Guzman Blanco president from 1873 to 1877?

15. Which ocean liner was brought to Long Beach, California in 1967?

ANSWERS 1. In a margin (it is a marginal note) 2. Colette 3. Enid 4. 1605 5. James Mason 6. Lime juice 7. Nigel Hawthorne 8. Red Dwarf 9. Forties 10. Madagascar 11. Eel 12. Georg Telemann 13. Dixon 14. Venezuela 15. Queen Mary.

ENTERTAINMENT

1. In which year did the Sydney Opera House open?

2. Which actor played Patrick Glover in the sitcom *Father, Dear Father*?

3. Who plays Jack Swigert in the 1995 film *Apollo 13*?

4. In which South American city was conductor Daniel Barenboim born?

5. Who produced and directed the 1931 film *City Lights*?

6. Which English conductor was born in St. Helens in 1879?

7. Who wrote the words to *The Beggar's Opera*?

8. What was the name of Dougal's pet rabbit in the sitcom *Father Ted*?

9. Which English composer wrote the 1965 opera *The Mines of Sulphur*?

10. Who conducted the U.S. premiere of the opera *Peter Grimes*?

11. What are the forenames of comedy team Punt & Dennis?

12. Which comedian starred in the 1958 film *Merry Andrew*?

13. In which opera does the stevedore Crown appear?

14. Which opera is set aboard HMS Indomitable?

15. Which opera of Bizet's was Tchaikovsky's favourite?

ANSWERS 1. 1973 **2.** Patrick Cargill **3.** Kevin Bacon **4.** Buenos Aires **5.** Charlie Chaplin **6.** Sir Thomas Beecham **7.** John Gay **8.** Sampras **9.** Richard Rodney Bennett **10.** Leonard Bernstein **11.** Steve & Hugh **12.** Danny Kaye **13.** Porgy and Bess **14.** Billy Budd **15.** Carmen.

SPORT

1. Which swimmer won the 1984 Olympic men's 100m & 200m backstroke?

2. Who scored San Marino's goal in their 1993 football World Cup qualifier against England?

3. How many African teams were at the 1994 football World Cup Finals?

4. Who won the 1st Test in the 1993 cricket series between Australia and New Zealand?

5. In which year was Billie-Jean King born?

6. Which motor racing driver's sister, Pat, did rally star Erik Carlsson marry in 1964?

7. In which year did heavyweight boxing champion Primo Carnera die?

8. At what weight was Georges Carpentier world champion from 1920 to 1922?

9. Who was 1964 Olympic men's 200m champion?

10. Which team did Sheffield United beat 3-0 to win the 1915 F.A. Cup Final?

11. Who won the 1993 Nat West Trophy in cricket?

12. Which rider won the 1998 Badminton horse trials?

13. Which Middlesex cricketer is known as 'Bloodaxe'?

14. Which horse won the 1996 1,000 Guineas?

15. How many times did Wigan rugby league player Kenneth Gee play for England?

ANSWERS 1. Rick Carey 2. Davide Gualtieri 3. Three 4. It was a draw 5. 1943 6. Stirling Moss 7. 1967 8. Light-heavyweight 9. Henry Carr 10. Chelsea 11. Warwickshire 12. Chris Bartle 13. Mark Ramprakash 14. Bosra Sham 15. 33.

POP MUSIC

1. Which female vocalist featured on Paul Anka's 1974 hit *(You're) Having My Baby?*

2. Which group had a 1998 No.1 single with *Freak Me?*

3. Which group had a 1997 hit with *North Country Boy?*

4. Which U.K. group had chart success in 1996 with *Not So Manic Now?*

5. Which group had a minor hit in 1998 with *Iloverocknroll?*

6. Which single by the Four Tops reached No.1 in the U.K. and U.S.?

7. Which group had a 1976 hit single with *Sunshine Day?*

8. Who had a 1996 No.1 single with *Jesus to a Child?*

9. In which year was Donny Osmond born?

10. Which duo had a 1992 No.1 hit with *Would I Lie To You?*

11. With which song did Simply Red have a No.1 single in 1995?

12. Which group scored a chart hit in 1995 with a cover of song *White Lines (Don't Do It?*

13. In which year was singer Gilbert O'Sullivan born?

14. What was Rickie Lee Jones's only hit single?

15. Which group recorded the 1993 album *There is No-one What Will Take Care of You?*

ANSWERS 1. Odia Coates **2.** Another Level **3.** The Charlatans **4.** Dubstar **5.** The Jesus and Mary Chain **6.** Reach Out I'll Be There **7.** Osibisa **8.** George Michael **9.** 1957 **10.** Charles and Eddie **11.** Fairground **12.** Duran Duran **13.** 1946 **14.** Chuck E's in Love **15.** The Palace Brothers.

GEOGRAPHY

1. In which state is the Australian seaport of Bunbury?

2. Which dance is the state capital of West Virginia?

3. The Crimea Peninsula is part of which European country?

4. East London is a seaport and holiday resort in which African country?

5. Which insect is the largest river of Papua New Guinea?

6. On which island is the volcano of Hekla?

7. In which Canadian province is the Jasper National Park?

8. Which peninsula of China lies opposite Hong Kong Island?

9. In which eastern European country is the university city of Lublin?

10. In which American country is the Mesa del Norte plateau?

11. The Painted Desert lies in which U.S. state?

12. On which Mediterranean island is the seaport of Palermo?

13. In which English county is the market town of Rugby?

14. On which river is the Russian city of Tomsk?

15. What town is the capital of the Seychelles?

ANSWERS 1. Western Australia 2. Charleston 3. Ukraine 4. South Africa
5. Fly River 6. Iceland 7. Alberta 8. Kowloon Peninsula 9. Poland 10.
Mexico 11. Arizona 12. Sicily 13. Warwickshire 14. River Tom 15.
Victoria.

GENERAL KNOWLEDGE

1. Which U.S. state is known as the 'Badger State'?

2. Who wrote the novel *Not To Disturb*?

3. What is a mangosteen - a piece of armour or a tree?

4. From which club did Manchester United sign Andy Cole?

5. Which drink consists of pineapple juice, rum and coconut?

6. Who did Roger Moore play in TV drama *The Persuaders*?

7. What do Australians refer to as the Apple Isle?

8. What was the Roman counterpart of the Greek goddess Eos?

9. Who wrote the 1968 play *Plaza Suite*?

10. What was the birthplace of writer Dr. Johnson?

11. What is the peepul tree also known as?

12. What is the name of the black-and-yellow beetle which is a serious pest of potatoes?

13. What is the name of Princess Anne's daughter?

14. Who composed the opera *The Cunning Little Vixen*?

15. What sort of creature is a habu?

ANSWERS 1. Wisconsin 2. Muriel Spark 3. Tree 4. Newcastle United 5. Piña Colada 6. Brett Sinclair 7. Tasmania 8. Aurora 9. Neil Simon 10. Lichfield 11. The bo tree 12. Colorado beetle 13. Zara 14. Leos Janacek 15. Snake.

ENTERTAINMENT

1. Which actor was Oscar-nominated for the 1997 film *The Apostle*?

2. What was the surname of the Major in the sitcom *Fawlty Towers*?

3. Who played *Mary of Scotland* in the 1936 film?

4. What was the subtitle of the 1994 film *City Slickers II*?

5. Ernest Bloch's only opera was a version of which Shakespeare play?

6. Who played Skeletor in the 1987 film *Masters of the Universe*?

7. Which 1896 Puccini opera is set in the Latin Quarter of Paris?

8. Who directed the 1998 film *The Faculty*?

9. In which year did comedian Marty Feldman die?

10. Which English bass created the role of Swallow in the opera *Peter Grimes*?

11. Who directed the 1959 film *Porgy and Bess*?

12. What dance does Salome perform in the opera *Salome* by Strauss?

13. "I don't think we're in Kansas anymore" - which 1939 film?

14. Who is Prince Ramiro's valet in the Rossini opera *La Cenerentola*?

15. In which city was composer Frederick Delius born?

ANSWERS 1. Robert Duvall 2. Gowen 3. Katharine Hepburn 4. The Legend of Curly's Gold 5. Macbeth 6. Frank Langella 7. La Bohème 8. Robert Rodriguez 9. 1982 10. Owen Brannigan 11. Otto Preminger 12. The Dance of the Seven Veils 13. The Wizard of Oz 14. Dandini 15. Bradford.

SPORT

1. What was the nickname of American football star George Halas?

2. Who was the 1997 World Matchplay golf champion?

3. Which country won the 1997 Davis Cup?

4. Who was runner-up to Daley Thompson in the 1984 Olympic decathlon?

5. Who was 1995 & '96 125cc motor cycling world champion?

6. Who won an Olympic Nordic skiing gold medal in 1960 at the age of 35 years and 52 days?

7. Who won the 1993 County Cricket Championship?

8. Who was the 1960 Olympic men's 5,000m champion?

9. Which Australian rugby union player was capped 36 times from 1968-82?

10. Which jockey won the 1980 Epsom Derby on Henbit?

11. In which city was tennis player Rosemary Casals born?

12. Which male tennis player won the 1982 Junior singles title at Wimbledon?

13. Which golfer won the 1970 U.S. Masters tournament?

14. Which race horse trainer's first Classic winner was Bolonski in 1975?

15. What nationality is motor cycling champion Alberto 'Johnny' Cecotto?

ANSWERS 1. Papa Bear 2. Vijay Singh 3. Sweden 4. Jürgen Hingsen 5. Haruchika Aoki 6. Veikko Hakulinen 7. Middlesex 8. Murray Halberg 9. John Hipwell 10. Willie Carson 11. San Francisco 12. Pat Cash 13. Billy Casper 14. Henry Cecil 15. Venezuelan.

POP MUSIC

1. Which male singer had a Top 40 hit in 1995 with the song *Wonderful*?

2. Which male vocal group had Top 20 hits in 1997 with *Let Me In* and *All Out Of Love*?

3. In which year did Tom Jones have a hit single with *The Young New Mexican Puppeteer*?

4. What was the debut L.P. from Bristol-based group Straw?

5. Who had a 1995 No. 1 single with *Boombastic*?

6. Whose only chart hit was 1959's *A Pub with No Beer*?

7. Which group recorded the album *OK Computer*?

8. Which group had a 1997 chart hit with *Hey Child*?

9. Which single by Marvin Gaye was a No. 1 hit in the U.K. and U.S.?

10. Which group had a No. 4 single in 1998 with *Lost in Space*?

11. Which group had a No. 6 single in 1998 with *Lost in Space*?

12. Which group had a minor 1997 hit with *Chemical # 1*?

13. Which group recorded the album *The Royal Scam*?

14. Which of Jive Bunny's three No. 1 singles went straight into the chart at that position?

15. In which year did Joy Division first chart with the single *Love Will Tear Us Apart*?

ANSWERS 1. Adam Ant 2. OTT 3. 1972 4. Shoplifting 5. Shaggy 6. Slim Dusty 7. Radiohead 8. East 17 9. I Heard it Through the Grapevine 10. Apollo Four Forty 11. The Lighthouse Family 12. Jesus Jones 13. Steely Dan 14. Let's Party 15. 1980.

HISTORY

1. In which year did J. Edgar Hoover become Director of the F.B.I.?

2. In which year was the Festival of Britain?

3. Which king was the intended victim of Fieschi's Plot in 1835?

4. The International Monetary Fund was established by the Bretton Woods Agreement of which year?

5. Which international criminal police organization was established in 1923 in Vienna?

6. In which year was the island of Iwo Jima returned to Japan by the U.S.?

7. In which year was the mountain K-2 first climbed?

8. What was the year of the Louisiana Purchase?

9. In which century was the Taj Mahal built?

10. Who opened the 'Bloody Assize' in Taunton in 1685?

11. Which famous rail bridge disaster happened on December 28th, 1879?

12. The Anti-Saloon League of America was succeeded in 1948 by which organization?

13. In which year did the Pilgrim Fathers establish Thanksgiving Day?

14. In which year in the 18c was Lisbon devastated by an earthquake?

15. Gudrun Esslin was a founder member of which German terrorist group?

ANSWERS 1. 1924 2. 1951 3. Louis Philippe of France 4. 1944 5. Interpol 6. 1968 7. 1954 8. 1803 9. 17th 10. Judge Jeffreys 11. Tay Bridge disaster 12. Temperance League of America 13. 1621 14. 1755 15. Baader-Meinhof Gang.

THE ULTIMATE PUB QUIZ BOOK

GENERAL KNOWLEDGE

1. In which year was Longchamps horse racecourse created?

2. Which artist and writer founded the Kelmscott Press?

3. Baldy Mountain is the highest point of which Canadian province?

4. Who wrote the novel *Empire of the Sun*?

5. What would you do with a brisling - eat it or wear it?

6. Which of the Seven Wonders of the World was destroyed by an earthquake in 225 B.C.?

7. In music, what is four-four time also known as?

8. In which century did Nell Gwyn live?

9. Who wrote *The Silmarillion*?

10. Which English county's administrative centre is Dorchester?

11. On what part of the body would you wear a jandal?

12. Which former Jamaican prime minister died in 1997?

13. Which two actors starred in the 1974 film *Freebie and the Bean*?

14. What is the name of the female reproductive part of a flower?

15. Who was president of the Central African Republic from 1972-76?

ANSWERS 1. 1857 2. William Morris 3. Manitoba 4. J.G. Ballard 5. Eat it - it's a fish 6. Colossus of Rhodes 7. Common time 8. 17th 9. J.R.R. Tolkien 10. Dorset 11. On the foot 12. Michael Manley 13. James Caan and Alan Arkin 14. Pistil 15. Jean Bokassa.

ENTERTAINMENT

1. What was the spin-off from the TV series *Please, Sir!* called?

2. Who directed the 1988 film *Appointment with Death* which starred Peter Ustinov as the detective Poirot?

3. Who composed the 1899 opera *The Devil and Kate*?

4. Who was the writer of the ITC sitcom *Is it Legal?*?

5. In which city was Placido Domingo born?

6. Who directed the 1952 film *Clash by Night*?

7. Who composed the opera *Don Giovanni*?

8. Who composed the opera *Lucia di Lammermoor*?

9. What was the character name of Michael Bates in the sitcom *It Ain't Half Hot Mum*?

10. In which city was U.S. soprano Emma Eames born in 1965?

11. Who directed the 1986 film *Matador*?

12. On whose drama was the 1933 opera *The Emperor Jones* based?

13. On whose novella was the 1998 film *Apt Pupil* based?

14. Who directed the 1932 film *The Old Dark House*?

15. Which actor played twins in the 1988 film *Dead Ringers*?

SPORT

1. At what age did Alex Higgins win the 1972 World Professional Snooker championships?

2. Who was the USPGA golf champion from 1924-7?

3. Who was men's javelin champion at the 1993 & '95 IAAF World Championships?

4. Who was 1994 & '95 men's World Indoor Bowls champion?

5. Which cyclist won the 1994 Vuelta A España?

6. Who was world 250cc motor cycling champion in 1988 & '89?

7. Who won rugby union's Pilkington Cup from 1984-7?

8. Who in 1961 became the first American to win the world Formula 1 motor racing title?

9. For which international rugby union side did Michel Celaya play?

10. Who did Marcel Cerdan knock out in 1948 to take the world middleweight boxing title?

11. What was Indian bowler Bhagwant Chandrasekhar's highest batting score in Tests?

12. In which city was footballer Herbert Chapman born in 1875?

13. Who succeeded Ian Chappell as Australian Test cricket captain?

14. What are jockey Willie Carson's middle names?

15. At what sport does Austrian Tomas Stangassinger compete?

THE ULTIMATE PUB QUIZ BOOK

POP MUSIC

1. What was Aqua's third No. 1 single?

2. Which female vocalist had a 1994 Top 20 single with *Reach*?

3. What was the title of Blur's 1995 No. 1 single?

4. Which group released the 1999 single *Get the Keys and Go*?

5. Which single by Gloria Gaynor was a No. 1 hit in the U.K. and U.S.?

6. Which group had hit singles in 1980 with *United* and *Breaking the Law*?

7. Which group revisited the charts after a six year absence with 1997's *Nothing Lasts Forever*?

8. Which group recorded the album *I Should Coco*?

9. From which country does singer Tina Arena come?

10. Which ex-member of Take That had solo success in 1996 with *Child*?

11. What was Patti Page's only singles chart hit, in 1953?

12. Which female singer featured on the 1997 hit *All My Time* by Paid and Live?

13. Which group charted in 1983 with *Scatterlings of Africa*?

14. Which indie group had a Top 20 hit in 1995 with *Great Things*?

15. Which U.S. vocal group had a 1995 hit with *Freek 'N You*?

ANSWERS 1. Turn Back Time 2. Judy Cheeks 3. Country House 4. Llama Farmers 5. I Will Survive 6. Judas Priest 7. Echo and the Bunnymen 8. Supergrass 9. Australia 10. Mark Owen 11. (How Much is) That Doggie in the Window 12. Lauryn Hill 13. Juluka 14. Echobelly 15. Jodeci.

WORDS

1. In Australia, what is a woodchop - a type of bird or a wood-chopping competition?

2. The German phrase meaning 'world pain' is used to denote melancholy. What is the phrase?

3. On a ship, what did the phrase 'to paint the lion' mean?

4. What is the plant deadly nightshade also called?

5. What is belomancy?

6. What is a corroboree?

7. What is the Swiss equivalent of John Bull, the typical Englishman?

8. What is the name given to the tail of a fox?

9. What does the Latin term 'Bona fide' mean?

10. Which alcoholic drink is known as 'blue ruin'?

11. What is 'black strap' to a sailor?

12. What does the phrase 'beside the cushion' mean?

13. 'Cucumber Time' is the dull season in which trade?

14. What type of animal is a grivet - a monkey or an antelope?

15. What would you do with a sackbut - play it or drive it?

ANSWERS 1. A wood-chopping competition 2. Weltschmerz 3. To strip a person naked and then smear the body with tar 4. Belladonna, or dwale 5. Divination by arrows 6. An Australian wardance 7. Colin Tampon 8. Brush 9. In good faith 10. Gin 11. Bad liquor 12. Not to the point 13. Tailoring 14. A monkey 15. Play it - it is a musical instrument.

GENERAL KNOWLEDGE

1. Which member of the pumpkin family might you find in a bathroom?

2. Which order of insects includes the beetles?

3. What is the name of the French national theatre opened in Paris in 1680?

4. In which year did the British submarine Thetis sink in Liverpool Bay?

5. What is the standard monetary unit of Mexico?

6. On which island was cricketer Brian Lara born?

7. On which river is the town of Limerick?

8. What is the most famous novel of Erich Maria Remarque?

9. Which BBC soap opera was set in the village of Los Barcos?

10. Who directed the 1993 film *The Piano*?

11. Which philosopher wrote *The Rights of Man*?

12. Which horse won the 1995 Grand National?

13. Who is the detective in the novel *The Moonstone*?

14. Which bird is also known as an apteryx?

15. Of which country was Sir John Hall prime minister from 1879-82?

ANSWERS 1. Loofah 2. Coleoptera 3. Comédie Française 4. 1939 5. Peso 6. Trinidad 7. Shannon 8. All Quiet on the Western Front 9. Eldorado 10. Jane Campion 11. Thomas Paine 12. Royal Athlete 13. Sergeant Cuff 14. Kiwi 15. New Zealand.

ENTERTAINMENT

1. Which actors played Jack and Hugo in the sitcom *Ffizz*?

2. Who starred as *The Arab* in the 1924 film?

3. Who directed the 1994 film *Clear and Present Danger*?

4. Who directed the 1974 Bond film *The Man with the Golden Gun*?

5. Who wrote the sitcom *Filthy, Rich and Catflap*?

6. Which family live next door to *The Simpsons* in the cartoon series?

7. Who created and starred in the 1980s sitcom *It Takes a Worried Man*?

8. Who played Caesar in the 1963 film *Cleopatra*?

9. Who played *Marlowe* in the 1969 film based on the novel *The Little Sister*?

10. Who directed the 1998 film *Armageddon*?

11. Which actress starred in the two series of comedy playlets *About Face*?

12. Which comedy sketch series featured the villagers of Stoneybridge?

13. What were the surnames of Adam and Joe in *The Adam and Joe Show*?

14. Which character did Ken Weatherwax play in television's *The Addams Family*?

15. Who played Sarah France in the T.V. sitcom *After Henry*?

SPORT

1. Who won the world middleweight boxing title in 1980 by defeating Alan Minter?

2. Who was World Formula 1 motor racing championship runner-up from 1963-5?

3. Which American won the decathlon title at the 1991, '93 & '95 IAAF World Championships?

4. Which member of the Chappell family played only three Tests for Australia, in 1981?

5. Who did Bob Charles beat in a play-off to win the 1963 British Open golf tournament?

6. In which city was world heavyweight boxing champion Ezzard Charles born?

7. By what score did Ronnie O'Sullivan win the 1993 U.K. snooker final?

8. Which greyhound's life story was told in the 1935 film *Wild Boy*?

9. Which trainer was associated with the horse Red Rum?

10. Which Brazilian scored in every game of the 1970 World Cup Finals?

11. Who won the 1993 RAC Rally?

12. Which country won both men and women's team archery golds at the 1988 Olympics?

13. Which country won the 1976 European championships in football?

14. Who was men's world cross country champion from 1986-9?

15. Who were the first cricket county champions in 1864?

ANSWERS **1.** Marvelous Marvin Hagler **2.** Graham Hill **3.** Dan O'Brien **4.** Trevor **5.** Phil Rodgers **6.** Chicago **7.** 10-6 **8.** Mick the Miller **9.** Ginger McCain **10.** Jairzinho **11.** Juha Kankkunen **12.** South Korea **13.** Czechoslovakia **14.** John Ngugi **15.** Surrey.

POP MUSIC

1. Who charted in 1998 with the single *Because I Got It Like That*?

2. Which duo released the album *Fear of Fours* in 1999?

3. What was the only solo single by John Lennon to reach No. 1 in the U.K. and U.S. charts?

4. In which year was singer Billy Joel born?

5. From which country does D.J. and producer Armin hail?

6. Who had a No. 1 single in 1995 with *Boom Boom Boom*?

7. Which duo had a 1996 hit with *Live Like Horses*?

8. Which singer recorded the album *Frank's Wild Years*?

9. Under which name did Isaac Hayes have a 1998 Christmas hit single?

10. What was the title of Jennifer Paige's 1998 hit single?

11. Which group recorded the 1997 hit *Novocaine for the Soul*?

12. Which singer had a minor hit single in 1994 with *Girl U Want*?

13. In which year did Louise Nurding leave the group Eternal?

14. Which pop group helped out Nottingham Forest F.C. on the single *We've Got the Whole World in Our Hands*?

15. Which group recorded the 1995 album *Bite It*?

ANSWERS 1. The Jungle Brothers 2. Lamb 3. (Just Like) Starting Over 4. 1949 5. Holland 6. Outhere Brothers 7. Elton John & Luciano Pavarotti 8. Tom Waits 9. Chef 10. Crush 11. The Eels 12. Robert Palmer 13. 1995 14. Paper Lace 15. Whiteout.

SCIENCE

1. Which Scottish mathematician devised logarithms?

2. Is the element selenium radioactive?

3. What is the name given to the areas of ocean between 40° and 50° latitude in the southern hemisphere?

4. In the abbreviation cDNA what does c stand for?

5. What is the name given to an experiment carried out on a living body?

6. In pressure how many pascals equal 1 millibar?

7. Which element's symbol is Y?

8. What is the name given to a change of wind direction in an anticlockwise manner?

9. What is the equation of the Perfect Gas Law?

10. Which Scottish scientist's nickname at school was 'Dafty'?

11. Which English scientist constructed the first practical electromagnet?

12. Which element is directly below tin in the Periodic table?

13. What is flaschenblitz a form of?

14. What was inventor Thomas Edison's middle name?

15. In which year did Foucault construct the gyroscope?

ANSWERS 1. John Napier 2. No 3. Roaring Forties 4. Complementary 5. In vivo 6. 100 7. Yttrium 8. Backing 9. pV=nRT 10. James Clerk Maxwell 11. William Sturgeon 12. Lead 13. Lightning 14. Alva 15. 1852.

GENERAL KNOWLEDGE

1. Aqua fortis is an obsolete name for which liquid?

2. In chess, what does the abbreviation e.p. mean?

3. What was the annual boarding fee in 1997 at the Oratory School, Woodcote, Berkshire?

4. Who wrote the story collection *You Know Me, Al*?

5. To which genus does the cobra belong?

6. From which football club did Chelsea sign Gianluca Vialli?

7. In which country is the parliament called the boule?

8. In which U.S. state is the Comstock Lode, an extensive gold and silver vein?

9. On what date is Hallowe'en?

10. In which year was Russian author Mikhail Lermontov killed in a duel?

11. Who wrote the novel *Psycho*?

12. Which blind soothsayer in Greek mythology disclosed the crimes of Oedipus?

13. Which position did Manny Shinwell hold from 1950-51 in the Labour Government?

14. Which European coastal plant's Latin name is *Crambe maritima*?

15. Who was artistic director of the Ballet Rambert from 1981-6?

ANSWERS 1. Nitric acid **2.** En passant **3.** £13,635 **4.** Ring Lardner **5.** Naja **6.** Juventus **7.** Greece **8.** Nevada **9.** October 31st **10.** 1841 **11.** Robert Bloch **12.** Tiresias **13.** Minister of Defence **14.** Sea kale **15.** Robert North.

ENTERTAINMENT

1. Which comedian was the host of the 1997 comedy series *500 Bus Stops*?

2. Who created *The Simpsons*?

3. Who played Brian Webber in the 1980s sitcom *Sink or Swim*?

4. Who directed the 1959 film *Ben-Hur*?

5. Which comedy duo's stage shows included *At the Drop of a Hat*?

6. Which Oscar-winning actress played *The Flying Nun* in the 1970 U.S. sitcom?

7. Who directed the 1966 film *Grand Prix*?

8. Which actress played Ada in the sitcom *For the Love of Ada*?

9. Who played *Marnie* in the 1964 Alfred Hitchcock film?

10. What was the character name of Maria Charles in the sitcom *Agony*?

11. Who played Victorian patriarch Albert in the 1970 sitcom *Albert and Victoria*?

12. In which city was comedian Alexei Sayle born?

13. Which two actresses starred in the ITV sketch show *Alfresco*?

14. Which actor played Henry in the ITV sitcom *All at No. 20*?

15. What was Derek Nimmo's character name in the sitcom *All Gas and Gaiters*?

THE ULTIMATE PUB QUIZ BOOK

SPORT

1. Who was top scorer for Australia in their 1999 cricket World Cup Group B game against New Zealand?

2. Which footballer was the 1990 BBC Sports Personality of the Year?

3. How many wickets did Joel Garner take in the 1984 Test series against Australia?

4. What nationality is Anders Gärdebud, winner of the 1976 Olympic 3,000m steeplechase title?

5. In which year was cricketer Rachel Heyhoe-Flint born?

6. In which year was cricketer Mike Gatting born?

7. Which Denver player was MVP in the XXXII Superbowl in 1998?

8. Which Estonia-born wrestler was known as 'the Russian Lion'?

9. Who was world individual fly fishing champion in 1994 & '97?

10. Which footballer scored a consolation goal for the Czech Republic in the 1996 European Championship Final?

11. In which year was footballer John Charles born?

12. How many international caps did Bobby Charlton win for England?

13. Which Somerset cricketer is known as Skirlog?

14. Who won the 1994 Nat West Trophy in cricket?

15. Which rider won the 1997 Badminton Horse Trials?

ANSWERS 1. Darren Lehmann 2. Paul Gascoigne 3. 31 4. Swedish 5. 1939 6. 1957 7. Terrell Davis 8. George Hackenschmidt 9. Pascal Cognard 10. Berger 11. 1931 12. 106 13. Adrian Pierson 14. Worcestershire 15. David O'Connor.

POP MUSIC

1. What was Arsenal F.C.'s 1998 Top Ten hit single?

2. Which duo charted in 1987 with *Another Step (Closer To You)*?

3. Which female vocalist had a No. 1 in 1998 with *Believe*?

4. Which was the first single by Madonna to reach No. 1 in the U.K. and U.S.?

5. Who had a No. 1 in 1995 with *Cotton Eye Joe*?

6. Which group's debut hit single in 1989 was called *Getting Away With It*?

7. Which vocal group had a 1992 Top Ten hit with *I'm Doing Fine Now*?

8. Which vocal duo had a 1957 hit with *Gonna Get Along Without Ya Now*?

9. Which group had a minor hit in 1998 with the song *Madagasga*?

10. What was the group Pearl Jam's only U.K. Top Ten single, in 1994?

11. Which singer fetaured on the 1992 single *I Like It* by Overweight Pooch?

12. Which rapper had a 1998 Top 20 single with *Beep Me*?

13. Which group charted in 1998 with *Keep on Dancin' (Let's Go)*?

14. Which group recorded the album *Freaky Trigger*?

15. Which group had a 1998 hit single with *Come Back to What You Know*?

PEOPLE

1. What was Walt Disney's middle name?

2. Which British statesman was the 1st Earl of Beaconsfield?

3. Which Plymouth-born naval commander died at Porto Rico in 1595?

4. What is polar explorer Sir Ranulph Fiennes' full name?

5. Actresses Madonna and Kim Basinger walked out on the making of which 1993 film?

6. Who was the father of Jemima Khan?

7. Which footballer is married to actress Leslie Ash?

8. In what does actress Mira Sorvino have a degree from Harvard?

9. With which illusionist was Claudia Schiffer romantically linked in the mid 1990s?

10. On which date in the calendar was model Helena Christensen born?

11. What was the stage name of sharpshooter Phoebe Anne Oakley Moses?

12. What was the middle name of actor Laurence Olivier?

13. What was the middle name of Greek-born ship owner Aristotle Onassis?

14. Which Australian media proprietor created World Series Cricket?

15. What was the name of the Swedish prime minister assassinated in 1986?

THE ULTIMATE PUB QUIZ BOOK

GENERAL KNOWLEDGE

1. Which secretary-general of the United Nations won the 1961 Nobel peace prize?

2. What was the name in Roman mythology for the gods who guarded the store cupboard?

3. Which English businessman was associated with the 1982 Skytrain project?

4. In which year did Belgian songwriter Jacques Brel die?

5. Who wrote the poem *Gunga Din*?

6. What is the name for an eighth part of a circle?

7. Who was elected M.P. for Berwick-upon-Tweed in 1997?

8. What is the approximate maximum depth in feet of Loch Ness?

9. Which zodiac sign is also called the Water Carrier?

10. In which year was the Lockerbie disaster?

11. What type of creature is the congo eel?

12. What was the nationality of architect Arne Jacobsen?

13. In which year did postcard artist Donald McGill die?

14. Which female singer recorded the 1971 album *Tapestry*?

15. Which actor directed the 1992 film *Hoffa*?

ANSWERS 1. Dag Hammarskjöld 2. Penates 3. Freddie Laker 4. 1978 5. Rudyard Kipling 6. Octant 7. Alan Beith 8. 755 9. Aquarius 10. 1988 11. Salamander 12. Danish 13. 1962 14. Carole King 15. Danny DeVito.

ENTERTAINMENT

1. Which actress appeared as Samantha Ryder-Ross in the 1971 sitcom *It's Awfully Bad For Your Eyes, Darling...*?

2. What was the title of the third *Evil Dead* film?

3. Who directed the 1993 film *Cliffhanger*?

4. Which film director played Michael Stivic in the sitcom *All In the Family*?

5. Which Irish comedian born in 1936 was a Butlin's Redcoat at Skegness?

6. The search for which painting featured frequently in the sitcom *'Allo 'Allo!*?

7. *Beane's of Boston* was a U.S. version of which British sitcom?

8. Who played *Madame Curie* in the 1943 film?

9. Who played Niles Crane in T.V.'s *Frasier*?

10. Who played the patriarch in the family sitcom *The Fosters*?

11. Who directed the 1942 film *The Magnificent Ambersons*?

12. Who played Mickey Finn in the 1937 film *Way Out West*?

13. Which singer had a cameo as a piano player in the 1956 film *Around the World in Eighty Days*?

14. Which comedy duo wrote the 1997 sketch show *It's Ulrika!*?

15. Who directed the 1944 film *Arsenic and Old Lace*?

ANSWERS 1. Joanna Lumley **2.** Army of Darkness **3.** Renny Harlin **4.** Rob Reiner **5.** Dave Allen **6.** The Fallen Madonna with the Big Boobies **7.** Are You Being Served? **8.** Greer Garson **9.** David Hyde Pierce **10.** Norman Beaton **11.** Orson Welles **12.** James Finlayson **13.** Frank Sinatra **14.** Vic Reeves and Bob Mortimer **15.** Frank Capra.

THE ULTIMATE PUB QUIZ BOOK

SPORT

1. Who lost the 1975 World Snooker championship to Ray Reardon, 31-30?

2. Who in 1987 became the first Australian to win the world 500cc motor cycling title?

3. Which horse won the 1997 1,000 Guineas?

4. What was Brazilian footballer Manoel Francisco do Santos better known as?

5. Which Olympic athlete became an ITV newscaster in September 1955?

6. Which Mexican boxer was WBC super-featherweight champion from 1984-87?

7. In which country was footballer Eusebio born?

8. In which American state was tennis player Chris Evert born?

9. Which two events did Jackie Joyner-Kersee win at the 1988 Olympics?

10. Which All Black scored three tries against Scotland on his debut in 1993?

11. What Olympic event is Dwight Stones associated with?

12. Which Dane won the 1971 World Individual speedway title?

13. Who finished third in the 1974 football World Cup?

14. In which year did Jack Charlton win his first England cap?

15. When did John McEnroe win his first Wimbledon men's singles tennis title?

ANSWERS 1. Eddie Charlton 2. Wayne Gardner 3. Sleepytime 4. Garrincha 5. Chris Chataway 6. Julio Cesar Chavez 7. Mozambique 8. Florida 9. Long jump and heptathlon 10. Jeff Wilson 11. High jump 12. Ole Olsen 13. Poland 14. 1965 15. 1981.

POP MUSIC

1. Which rap group had hits in 1998 with *Jayou* and *Concrete Schoolyard*?

2. Which group released the 1999 live album *Mad for Sadness*?

3. On which record label was Keith Emerson's *Honky Tonk Train Blues* a hit?

4. Which group had a 1997 hit with *A Life Less Ordinary*?

5. Which was the only single by Meat Loaf to reach No. 1 in the U.K. and the U.S.?

6. Which male vocalist had a 1989 Top Ten single with *Americanos*?

7. Which male singer had Top Ten singles in 1998 with *Save Tonight* and *Falling in Love Again*?

8. Who had a 1991 chart hit with *It's Grim Up North*?

9. Which duo had a 1994 Top 40 hit with *True Love Ways*?

10. Which group won a Mercury Music Prize for the L.P. *Elegant Slumming*?

11. What was the title of Ellis, Beggs and Howard's only singles chart entry?

12. Which female singer recorded the 1989 album *Strange Angels*?

13. In which year was singer Howard Jones born?

14. From which European country does singer Leila K come?

15. Which group recorded the 1995 album *The Honeymoon Suite*?

ART AND LITERATURE

1. In which century did U.S. sculptor Hiram Powers live?

2. In which European city is the Prado museum of art?

3. Who wrote the novel *The Woodlanders*?

4. What kind of animal is the Empress of Blandings in stories by P.G. Wodehouse?

5. Which French artist's studies of ballet dancers include *The Rehearsal* of 1873-4?

6. Which Romania-born sculptor created 1907's *The Kiss*?

7. Who created the character Moll Flanders?

8. "Now, what I want is, Facts". The opening line of which novel by Charles Dickens?

9. Which book takes place in Laputa and Brobdingnag, among other places?

10. Who wrote the novel *The Mosquito Coast*?

11. Which female British artist born in 1931 is associated with the Op Art movement?

12. Which sculptor's only equestrian statue, *General Lynch*, was destroyed by a revolution in Chile?

13. Who painted *The Raft of the Medusa*?

14. Whose thriller books include *Best Laid Plans*?

15. Who is the author of the *Harry Potter* series of books?

GENERAL KNOWLEDGE

1. What doesn't the port of Hammerfest in Norway have between November 21st and January 21st?

2. Who, in German legend, is the Knight of the Swan?

3. What is the name given to the housing of a ship's compass?

4. In which year did conductor Sir Adrian Boult die?

5. Who was the Muse of love poetry in Greek mythology?

6. Who wrote the novel *The Good Earth*?

7. Who wrote and directed the 1986 film *House of Games*?

8. In which year did singer Jim Reeves die in a plane crash?

9. In which year did Laurens Hammond invent the Hammond organ?

10. Who did Leonard Nimoy play in the T.V. show *Star Trek*?

11. Who composed the *Laudon Symphony*?

12. In which year was golfer Lee Trevino born?

13. Which horse racecourse is near Chichester, Sussex?

14. What type of creature is a manakin?

15. Who wrote the book of light verse *A Bad Child's Book of Beasts*?

ANSWERS 1. Sunlight 2. Lohengrin 3. Binnacle 4. 1983 5. Erato 6. Pearl Buck 7. David Mamet 8. 1964 9. 1934 10. Spock 11. Haydn 12. 1939 13. Goodwood 14. Bird 15. Hilaire Belloc.

ENTERTAINMENT

1. Who directed the 1987 film *Wall Street*?

2. Who played Neville Leggit in the sitcom *Son of the Bride*?

3. Who starred as the composer *Mahler* in the 1974 biopic?

4. What was the profession of Henry Nunn in the sitcom *Sorry, I'm a Stranger Here Myself*?

5. Who composed the score for the 1981 film *Arthur*?

6. Who wrote the 1996 sitcom *Sometime, Never*?

7. Who starred as Alison Holmes in the 1978 sitcom *A Soft Touch*?

8. Who was television's *Foxy Lady* in the 1980s comedy show?

9. What were the forenames of entertainers The Smothers Brothers?

10. Who directed the 1953 film *The Man Between*?

11. Who played D.J. Dave 'Nicey' Nice on T.V.?

12. Who directed the 1998 film *An Autumn Tale*?

13. In which year was comedian Freddie 'Parrot Face' Davies born?

14. Which actors played highwaymen *Plunkett and MacLeane* in the 1999 film?

15. Who played Bulldog in the comedy series *Frasier*?

SPORT

1. What is the nationality of golfer Roberto De Vicenzo?

2. In which year was racing driver Jackie Stewart born?

3. Over what distance in metres is the Prix de L'Arc de Triomphe run?

4. Who won the Tour de France from 1969-72?

5. Which cycling Luxembourger was nicknamed 'the Angel of the Mountains'?

6. Who rode the 1973 Epsom Derby winner Morston?

7. In which year was Sir Richard Hadlee born?

8. Which three Germans have each scored twice in football's European Championship Final?

9. Which club were runners-up in Football's Premier League in 1996 & '97?

10. Who was the 1998 World matchplay golf champion?

11. Who won the 1994 County Cricket Championship?

12. In which institution did jockey Sam Chifney die in 1807?

13. At what sport did Eddy Choong, 'the Pocket Prodigy from Penang' excel?

14. For which international football team did Hector Chumpitaz play?

15. What was the nickname of Australian rugby league star Clive Churchill?

ANSWERS 1. Argentinian 2. 1939 3. 2,400m 4. Eddie Merckx 5. Charly Gaul 6. Edward Hide 7. 1951 8. Müller (1972), Hrubesch (1980) and Bierhoff (1996) 9. Newcastle United 10. Mark O'Meara 11. Warwickshire 12. Fleet Prison in London 13. Badminton 14. Peru 15. The Little Master.

POP MUSIC

1. Which group had a 1998 Christmas hit with *I Am in Love With the World*?

2. Whose only singles chart hit was 1965's *Bye Bye Blues*?

3. Which group recorded the 1969 album *Younger Than Yesterday*?

4. Which group's minor hits in 1998 included *Buzzin'* and *Black White*?

5. In which year did The Clash release their debut L.P.?

6. Which female vocalist's only chart entry was 1966's *Witches' Brew*?

7. Which duo had a U.K. and U.S. No. 1 single with *I Knew You Were Waiting (For Me)*?

8. Which boxer featured on the 1996 hit *Walk Like a Champion* by Kaleef?

9. Under what name did Colin Blunstone record the 1969 hit *She's Not There*?

10. Which D.J. released the 1996 album *Archive One*?

11. Which group had a 1997 No. 2 single with *Tubthumping*?

12. Which U.S. group recorded the 1971 album *Nantucket Sleighride*?

13. Who is lead singer with the Manchester band M People?

14. Which duo had a 1958 No. 1 single with the song *When*?

15. From which European country does instrumentalist and producer Atgoc come?

ANSWERS 1. Chicken Shed Theatre **2.** Bert Kaempfert **3.** The Byrds **4.** Asian Dub Foundation **5.** 1977 **6.** Janie Jones **7.** George Michael & Aretha Franklin **8.** Prince Naseem **9.** Neil MacArthur **10.** Dave Clarke **11.** Chumbawamba **12.** Mountain **13.** Heather Small **14.** Kalin Twins **15.** Italy.

GEOGRAPHY

1. In which town in Kent would you find the promenade The Pantiles?

2. The Shatt-al-Arab river is formed by the union of which two rivers?

3. Riga is the capital of which European country?

4. Naxos is the largest of which group of Greek islands?

5. On which German river is the porcelain town of Meissen?

6. Which six countries border the Black Sea?

7. On which river does Berlin stand?

8. Mount Marcy is the highest peak of which North American mountain range?

9. In which bay is the former prison island of Alcatraz?

10. What did the country of Upper Volta become in 1984?

11. The commercial centre of which city in Illinois is called 'The Loop'?

12. What crop accounts for 75% of Cuba's exports?

13. To which South American country do the Galapagos Islands belong?

14. Which is longer - the River Forth or the River Tees?

15. The Atlantic coastal resort of Hollywood is in which U.S. state?

ANSWERS 1. (Royal) Tunbridge Wells 2. Tigris & Euphrates 3. Latvia 4. Cyclades 5. River Elbe 6. Bulgaria, Georgia, Romania, Russia, Turkey & Ukraine 7. River Spree 8. Adirondack Mountains 9. San Francisco 10. Burkina Faso 11. Chicago 12. Sugar 13. Ecuador 14. Forth 15. Florida.

GENERAL KNOWLEDGE

1. What are the three main components of bourbon whisky?

2. What was the pseudonym of author John Griffith Chaney?

3. Who was rugby league's 1990 Man of Steel winner?

4. In which year was Nelson Mandela born?

5. What was the river of forgetfulness in Greek legend?

6. What sort of creature is known in Australia as a sea wasp?

7. The fungus *Claviceps purpurea* causes what disease of cereals?

8. Which horse won the 1968 Epsom Derby?

9. Which actress was the second wife of playwright John Osborne?

10. Which actor played Adam Cartwright in the T.V. show *Bonanza*?

11. What was the principal language of the world in 1993, with 827 million native speakers?

12. In which year did the French submarine *Eurydice* sink in the Mediterranean?

13. What is the standard monetary unit of Myanmar?

14. In which year was the disease Lassa fever first described?

15. What sort of creature is a limpkin - a mollusc or a bird?

ANSWERS 1. Maize, malt and rye 2. Jack London 3. Shaun Edwards 4. 1918 5. Lethe 6. Jellyfish 7. Ergot 8. Sir Ivor 9. Mary Ure 10. Pernell Roberts 11. Mandarin 12. 1970 13. Kyat 14. 1969 15. Bird.

ENTERTAINMENT

1. Who directed the 1997 film *As Good As It Gets*?

2. Who played *Sabrina the Teenage Witch* on T.V.?

3. Who directed the 1986 film *Manhunter*?

4. What are the names of Marge's sisters in *The Simpsons*?

5. Who did James Cagney play in the 1957 film *Man of a Thousand Faces*?

6. Who played Vince Tulley in the 1990s sitcom *Side by Side*?

7. Who directed the 1987 film *The Last Emperor*?

8. Who wrote the 1991 sitcom *The Sharp End*?

9. Who played Yetta Feldman in the sitcom *So Haunt Me*?

10. Which comedians were Channel 4's *S and M* in 1991?

11. Who directed the 1971 film *A Clockwork Orange*?

12. Which comic's catchphrases include "What are the chances of that happening, eh?"?

13. Who directed the 1931 film *M*?

14. What nationality is composer Sven-Erik Bäck?

15. Which Yorkshire composer wrote 1921's *Twilight Pieces*?

ANSWERS 1. James L. Brooks **2.** Melissa Joan Hart **3.** Michael Mann **4.** Patty & Selma **5.** Lon Chaney **6.** Gareth Hunt **7.** Bernardo Bertolucci **8.** Roy Clarke **9.** Miriam Karlin **10.** Tony Slattery and Mike McShane **11.** Stanley Kubrick **12.** Harry Hill **13.** Fritz Lang **14.** Swedish **15.** William Baines.

SPORT

1. What nationality is Olympic gymnast Yukio Endo?

2. At what diving discipline did Ingrid Engel retain her Olympic title in 1964?

3. Which South African rugby union winger won 33 caps from 1960-69?

4. At which sport did Phil and Tony Esposito excel?

5. How many goals did Eusebio score in his 64 internationals for Portugal?

6. From which state does U.S. Olympic swimmer Janet Evans hail?

7. Who ran 61.5 yards in 10 seconds before scoring for Manchester United against Arsenal in April 1999?

8. In Superbowls XI, XIV, XVII and XXI the attendance topped 100,000. What was the venue on all four occasions?

9. Where were the 1983 IAAF World Championships held?

10. Which country did Martin Fiz represent in winning the marathon at the 1995 IAAF World Championships?

11. Which two Italian teams contested the 1995 UEFA Cup Final?

12. Who was men's singles World badminton champion in 1987 & '89?

13. Who scored the only goal in the 1996 F.A. Cup Final?

14. Who won the 1968 Olympic men's 400m title?

15. Which Olympic skier did tennis player Chris Evert marry in 1988?

ANSWERS 1. Japanese 2. Springboard diving 3. Jan Engelbrecht 4. Ice hockey 5. 41 6. California 7. Ryan Giggs 8. Pasadena 9. Helsinki 10. Spain 11. Parma and Juventus 12. Yang Yang 13. Eric Cantona 14. Lee Evans 15. Andy Mill.

POP MUSIC

1. Which single by The Monkees reached No. 1 in the U.K. and U.S.?

2. Which U.S. vocal group had a 1997 hit with *Don't Let Go (Love)*?

3. Which record in 1998 gave Linda McCartney her only singles chart success?

4. Which Scottish poet recorded the album *Dandruff*?

5. In which West Midlands town were Ned's Atomic Dustbin formed?

6. In which town was Bill Nelson of Be Bop Deluxe born?

7. Which duo had a 1992 hit with the single *Runaway Train*?

8. Who was the featured singer on the 1997 hit *I Wanna Be the Only One* by Eternal?

9. How many solo No. 1 singles has Paul McCartney had?

10. Who scored a 1995 Top Ten single with *Here Comes the Hotstepper*?

11. Which group had a minor hit in 1993 with the song *Lenny Valentino*?

12. What was Deee-Lite's 1990 hit album called?

13. From which country does vocalist Mory Kante come?

14. In which year did the Eurythmics have a No. 1 hit with *There Must Be An Angel (Playing With My Heart)*?

15. Which group had a 1989 hit album with *3 Feet High and Rising*?

HISTORY

1. Which Scottish castle did Prince Albert purchase in 1852?

2. In which year did Peter the Great of Russia die?

3. In which year was the Tiananmen Square uprising in Beijing?

4. In which French port did Beau Brummel die in 1840?

5. Which French general became professor of strategy at the École Supérieure de Guerre in 1894?

6. In which year did Richard Byrd become the first person to fly over the South Pole?

7. In which century was badminton invented at Badminton House?

8. In which country was al-Fatah, the militant Palestinian organization, founded in 1962?

9. In which year was journalist and M.P. John Wilkes expelled from the House of Commons?

10. In which year was the European Court of Justice established?

11. Which future president of the U.S. served as governor general of the Philippines in 1901?

12. Which politician published the best-selling book *Greater Britain* in 1868?

13. Who was responsible for the Education Act of 1944?

14. Who was appointed commander of the New Model Army in 1645?

15. In which year was the American Declaration of Independence?

ANSWERS 1. Balmoral 2. 1725 3. 1989 4. Caen 5. Ferdinand Foch 6. 1929 7. 19th 8. Kuwait 9. 1764 10. 1957 11. William Howard Taft 12. Sir Charles Wentworth Dilke 13. R.A. Butler 14. Thomas Fairfax 15. 1776.

THE ULTIMATE PUB QUIZ BOOK

GENERAL KNOWLEDGE

1. What would you do with an Aldis lamp?

2. In which century did philosopher Saint Thomas Aquinas live?

3. In old Irish law, what was an eric?

4. In which year was actor Marlon Brando born?

5. What is the largest country of South America?

6. What was entertainer Sir Harry Lauder's real first name?

7. Who directed the 1994 film *Shallow Grave*?

8. At which school would a Harrovian have been educated?

9. What does the Latin word 'conubium' mean?

10. Who was the ninth president of the U.S.?

11. What was the annual boarding fee in 1997 at Winchester College?

12. Who composed the song *St. Louis Blues*?

13. On which Loch is the Scottish village of Ullapool?

14. Who composed the opera *Le Grand Macabre*?

15. On which river is the city of Lincoln?

ANSWERS 1. Transmit Morse code **2.** 13th **3.** A fine paid by a murderer to the family of his victim **4.** 1924 **5.** Brazil **6.** Hugh **7.** Danny Boyle **8.** Harrow **9.** Marriage **10.** William Henry Harrison **11.** £15,345 **12.** W.C. Handy **13.** Loch Broom **14.** Gyorgy Ligeti **15.** River Witham.

ENTERTAINMENT

1. Which comedian's real name is Robert Harper?

2. Which U.S. actor starred in the 1985 comedy film *Macaroni*?

3. Which Jane Austen novel loosely inspired the 1995 film *Clueless*?

4. Who played Tara King in *The Avengers*?

5. Who directed the 1998 film *Pleasantville*?

6. In which city was choreographer George Balanchine born?

7. Who directed the 1998 film comedy *Waking Ned*?

8. Who played Trotsky in the 1972 film *The Assassination of Trotsky*?

9. Who played Michael Faraday in the 1998 film *Arlington Road*?

10. Which comedian's characters include Portuguese singer Tony Ferrino?

11. Who directed the 1998 film *A Simple Plan*?

12. Who played Garth Algar in the 1992 film *Wayne's World*?

13. Who played Harry in the film *When Harry Met Sally*?

14. What are the forenames of the comedy duo French and Saunders?

15. Who did Bob Hoskins play in the film *Who Framed Roger Rabbit??*

ANSWERS 1. Bobby Ball **2.** Jack Lemmon **3.** Emma **4.** Linda Thorson **5.** Gary Ross **6.** St. Petersburg **7.** Kirk Jones **8.** Richard Burton **9.** Jeff Bridges **10.** Steve Coogan **11.** Sam Raimi **12.** Dana Carvey **13.** Billy Crystal **14.** Dawn and Jennifer **15.** Eddie Valiant.

SPORT

1. Whose first of six St. Leger winners as a trainer was 1962's Hethersett?

2. Which was the first country to stage football's European Championship finals twice?

3. Which cyclist won the 1994 Giro d'Italia?

4. Which country did 1998 Olympic 5,000m speed skating champion Tomas Gustafson represent?

5. Which team won the men's 4 x 100m relay at the 1995 & '97 IAAF World Championships?

6. Which horse won the 1998 1,000 Guineas?

7. Who won rugby union's Pilkington Cup in 1998?

8. Who was Olympic 1000m sprint cycling champion in 1984 & '88?

9. How many internationals did footballer Giacinto Facchetti play for Italy between 1962-77?

10. What is Nick Faldo's middle name?

11. What was world Formula 1 motor racing champion Juan Fangio's middle name?

12. Who took 6-52 and 6-46 for Pakistan in 1954 against England at the Oval?

13. What was the nickname of baseball star Bob Feller?

14. At what event was Adhemar Ferreira da Silva an Olympic champion in 1952 & '56?

15. Which individual fencing gold did Anja Fichtel take at the 1988 Olympics?

POP MUSIC

1. What was Katrina and the Waves's 1997 Top Ten single?

2. Which single by Roy Orbison reached No. 1 in the U.K. and the U.S.?

3. Which singer's first singles success was 1996's *Crazy Chance*?

4. Which male singer had a minor hit in 1992 with the single *Lover Lover Lover*?

5. Who is the female member of the group New Order?

6. Which group had a 1997 Top Ten single with *Hard To Say I'm Sorry*?

7. Which group did Dave Grohl form after Nirvana split?

8. Which duo had a Top 30 hit in 1995 with 'Haunted'?

9. Who was the original drummer in the group Oasis?

10. Which U.S. artist recorded the album *Tit...an opera*?

11. In which year did Janet Key first chart with *Silly Games*?

12. Which female singer recorded the album *I Do Not Want What I Haven't Got*?

13. Which female singer had a Top 20 hit in 1998 with the song *Adia*?

14. Which traditional song did Don McLean record on the album *American Pie*?

15. Which group recorded the album *Pioneer Soundtracks*?

ANSWERS 1. Love Shine a Light 2. Oh Pretty Woman 3. Kavana 4. Ian McCulloch 5. Gillian Gilbert 6. Az Yet 7. Foo Fighters 8. Shane MacGowan and Sinead O'Connor 9. Tony McCarroll 10. Dogbowl 11. 1979 12. Sinead O'Connor 13. Sarah McLachlan 14. Babylon 15. Jack.

WORDS

1. What is the name of the syrup made from pomegranate juice used in various drinks?

2. What is the name for a small group of whales or seals?

3. What sort of food is sapsago?

4. What sort of animal is a saki?

5. What sort of bird is a culver?

6. What does the theatrical expression 'to get the big bird' mean?

7. Monetarily speaking, how much was a bender?

8. Why wouldn't 'blue beans' do you any good?

9. What is a 'cat-o'-nine-tails'?

10. Which country is known as the 'cockpit of Europe'?

11. What is botanomancy?

12. On which part of the body would you wear a bendigo?

13. What is the name given to a large stone resting on two others like a table?

14. From what is the Japanese drink sake made?

15. What is a Salvo in Australian slang?

ANSWERS 1. Grenadine 2. Pod 3. Cheese 4. Monkey 5. Pigeon 6. To be hissed on stage 7. Sixpence 8. They're bullets 9. A nine-lash whip 10. Belgium 11. Divination by leaves 12. The head, it is a hat 13. A cromlech 14. Rice 15. A member of the Salvation Army.

GENERAL KNOWLEDGE

1. Which bird is *Gallinago gallinago*?

2. In which year was the Paris landmark the Arc de Triomphe completed?

3. On which shore of Lake Geneva is the town of Lausanne?

4. What nationality was naval surgeon James Lind?

5. In which year did Arthur Scargill become president of the NUM?

6. Who wrote the play *Riders to the Sea*?

7. Which building on Muswell Hill was known as 'Ally Pally'?

8. Who was the second wife of Henry VIII?

9. Which artist designed the cover for the Beatles' LP *Sergeant Pepper's Lonely Hearts Club Band*?

10. In which city is the novel *The Aspern Papers* set?

11. Which city on the Rio Grande lies opposite Ciudad Juarez?

12. Who was England Test cricket captain 1966-67?

13. On which survey ship did Charles Darwin sail from 1831-36?

14. What nationality was the novelist Knut Hamsun?

15. Which forest features in Shakespeare's play *As You Like It*?

ANSWERS 1. Snipe 2. 1836 3. North 4. Scottish 5. 1981 6. J.M. Synge 7. Alexandra Palace 8. Anne Boleyn 9. Peter Blake 10. Venice 11. El Paso 12. Brian Close 13. H.M.S. Beagle 14. Norwegian 15. Forest of Arden.

ENTERTAINMENT

1. Who played Douglas MacArthur in the 1977 film biopic *MacArthur*?

2. Who played Mona in the 1998 film *Hi-Lo Country*?

3. Which actor played Jack Geller in the comedy show *Friends*?

4. Who played Sally in *When Harry Met Sally*?

5. What was Nicolas Cage's character name in the film *Wild At Heart*?

6. Which Australian comedian's characters include Sir Les Patterson?

7. Who wrote the score for the film *Atlantic City*?

8. Who played Daryl Van Horne in the film *The Witches of Eastwick*?

9. Who directed the 1998 film *American History X*?

10. What was the nickname of Marion Cobretti, played by Sylvester Stallone, in a 1986 film?

11. What was Dorothy's surname in the film *The Wizard of Oz*?

12. Who played Gerald Crich in the 1969 film *Women in Love*?

13. In which year was Canadian sports commentator Kent Walton born?

14. Who played Macduff in the 1948 film *Macbeth* by Orson Welles?

15. Who directed the 1975 film *At Long Last Love*?

SPORT

1. What nationality is Olympic skiing champion Michela Figini?

2. By how many seconds did Greg LeMond beat Laurent Fignon to win the 1989 Tour de France?

3. In which English county was world heavyweight boxing champion Bob Fitzsimmons born?

4. At what field event was John Flanagan Olympic champion from 1900-1908?

5. Which country did 1964 Olympic skiing champion Christl Haas represent?

6. Which Australian pair won the 1962 Wimbledon men's doubles tennis championship?

7. Who was manager of Watford F.C. during the 1998/9 season?

8. At what weight did boxer Kaosai Galaxy win a 1984 world title?

9. In which city was Superbowl XXXII played in 1998?

10. What nationality was figure skater Sonja Henie?

11. Which country won the World Team Freshwater Angling title in 1987 & '88?

12. Who was 1976 & '80 Olympic men's marathon winner?

13. Which world Formula 1 motor racing champion was the son of a Scottish sheep farmer?

14. For which ice hockey team did Bobby Clarke play from 1969-84?

15. In which city is the headquarters of the English Basketball Association?

ANSWERS 1. Swiss **2.** Eight **3.** Cornwall **4.** Hammer **5.** Austria **6.** Fred Stolle & Bob Hewitt **7.** Graham Taylor **8.** Bantamweight **9.** San Diego **10.** Norwegian **11.** England **12.** Waldemar Cierpinski **13.** Jim Clark **14.** Philadelphia Flyers **15.** Leeds.

POP MUSIC

1. From which South American country did instrumental group Azymuth come?

2. Which male vocalist had a 1997 Top Ten hit with the song *Gotham City*?

3. Which duo from the group U2 had a 1996 hit with *Theme from Mission: Impossible*?

4. Which album was the first release on Virgin Records?

5. Which group's first singles chart hit was *Punka* in 1996?

6. Which band formed in 1978 consisted of the duo Paul Humphries and Andy McCluskey?

7. Which single by the Pet Shop Boys reached No. 1 in both the U.K. and the U.S.?

8. In which town was singer John Otway born?

9. Which U.S. singer had a 1998 No. 3 single with *Stranded*?

10. Which group recorded the 1988 album *Nothing's Shocking*?

11. Which female vocal group had a 1998 hit with *Life Ain't Easy*?

12. Which Irish group had a minor chart hit in 1997 with *Mexican Wave*?

13. Who was the featured vocalist on the 1997 No. 1 *I'll Be Missing You* by Puff Daddy?

14. What was singer Sean Maguire's first singles chart entry in 1994?

15. On which record label did Madonna record the 1998 single *Ray of Light*?

ANSWERS 1. Brazil 2. R. Kelly 3. Adam Clayton and Larry Mullen 4. Tubular Bells 5. Kenickie 6. Orchestral Manoeuvres in the Dark 7. West End Girls 8. Aylesbury 9. Lutricia McNeal 10. Jane's Addiction 11. Cleopatra 12. Kerbdog 13. Faith Evans 14. Someone to Love 15. Maverick.

THE ULTIMATE PUB QUIZ BOOK

SCIENCE

1. How many faces has a regular tetrahedron?

2. What is the radius of the Earth's inner core in kilometres?

3. What unit of length is equal to 0.9144 of a metre?

4. At which Cambridge college did Isaac Newton study?

5. Which scientist delivered the 1953 Reith Lectures?

6. Who became professor of chemistry at the Sorbonne in 1867?

7. How many seconds are there in a solar day?

8. Which element composes approximately 36% of the Earth?

9. In which year was English molecular biologist Francis Crick born?

10. Which element is directly below silver in the Periodic table?

11. What is the name given to a DNA molecule that is able to replicate in a cell?

12. What is the word 'smog' a corruption of?

13. What nationality was the doctor and alchemist Paracelsus?

14. How many minutes are there in a degree of an angle?

15. Which Italian mathematician born in 1858 promoted the universal language interlingua?

GENERAL KNOWLEDGE

1. Who was elected M.P. for Beckenham in 1997?

2. On which river is the resort town of Llangollen?

3. Which German philosopher won the 1908 Nobel prize for Literature?

4. What in Scotland are breeks?

5. Who wrote the 1922 play cycle *Back to Methuselah*?

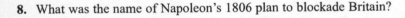

6. In which country was the French fashion illustrator Erté born?

7. Which is the third largest city in Sweden?

8. What was the name of Napoleon's 1806 plan to blockade Britain?

9. What type of creature is an oribi?

10. What type of creature is a jacksmelt?

11. What was the name of the former secret police of East Germany?

12. In which year did Nigeria join the U.N.?

13. Which character did Kathy Staff play in T.V.'s *Last of the Summer Wine*?

14. In which year did Hawaii join the Union?

15. Who directed the 1966 TV film *Cathy Come Home*?

ANSWERS 1. Piers Merchant 2. Dee 3. Rudolph Eucken 4. Trousers 5. George Bernard Shaw 6. Russia 7. Malmö 8. The Continental System 9. Antelope 10. Fish 11. Stasi 12. 1960 13. Nora Batty 14. 1959 15. Ken Loach.

ENTERTAINMENT

1. Which music-hall performer born in 1832 wrote the song *Pretty Polly Perkins of Paddington Green*?

2. The play *Waiting for Lefty* is about a strike by which body of workers?

3. In which year did the Royal Lyceum Theatre, Edinburgh, open?

4. Which German dramatist wrote the play *Woyzeck*?

5. In which 1841 play does the character Lady Gay Spanker appear?

6. What was comedian Arthur Askey's middle name?

7. Which husband and wife team starred in the BBC sitcom *B-and-B*?

8. Which actor was television's *The Baldy Man*?

9. What was Lucille Ball's character name in *I Love Lucy*?

10. In which year was comedian Stanley Baxter born?

11. In which year was entertainer Michael Barrymore born?

12. Who directed the 1967 film *The Dirty Dozen*?

13. Who narrated the Woody Allen film *Radio Days*?

14. Who directed the 1975 film *Nashville*?

15. Who played D'Artagnan in the 1939 film *The Three Musketeers*?

ANSWERS 1. Harry Clifton **2.** Taxi-drivers **3.** 1883 **4.** Georg Büchner **5.** London Assurance **6.** Bowden **7.** Bernard Braden & Barbara Kelly **8.** Gregor Fisher **9.** Lucy Ricardo **10.** 1926 **11.** 1952 **12.** Robert Aldrich **13.** Woody Allen **14.** Robert Altman **15.** Don Ameche.

SPORT

1. Who scored 163 points on the 1957 All Blacks rugby union tour of Australia?

2. In which year was the first European Championship in football?

3. Who was the 1992 Olympic women's high jump champion?

4. Who won the 1995 Nat West Trophy in cricket?

5. Who were runners up in football's Division One from 1970-72?

6. Which Essex cricketer is known as Jimmy Widges?

7. Which rider won the 1995 Badminton Horse Trials?

8. Which Scotland international footballer killed himself in June 1957 by throwing himself in front of a train?

9. Which team won the men's 4 x 400m relay title at the 1993, '95 & '97 IAAF World Championships?

10. Which country did 1984 Olympic gymnastics gold medal winner Koji Gushiken represent?

11. Who was the 1994 USPGA golf champion?

12. In which year was Australian distance runner Ron Clarke born?

13. At what team sport did Leslie Claudius win three Olympic golds?

14. For which baseball team did Roberto Clemente play his entire career from 1955-72?

15. Who in 1949 became England's youngest ever Test cricketer?

POP MUSIC

1. Which singer featured on Melanie B's No. 1 single *I Want You Back*?

2. Which single by the Police reached No. 1 in both the U.K. and the U.S.?

3. Which duo had a 1987 Top Ten hit with *Rise to the Occasion*?

4. Which group recorded the 1998 album *Munki*?

5. Which female vocalist had a 1997 Top 30 hit with *100%*?

6. Which group's debut L.P. was 1996's *At the Club*?

7. Which group recorded the 1975 album *Handsome*?

8. Which 1978 hit was subtitled *The Telephone Answering Machine Song*?

9. In which town was singer Robert Palmer born?

10. What was Kicks Like A Mule's 1992 Top Ten hit single?

11. Which group had a No .1 hit in 1998 with *Rollercoaster*?

12. What was the debut L.P. of the group Graham Parker and the Rumour?

13. Which pop singer was born Barry Pincus in 1946?

14. From which European country do the group Clubhouse come?

15. What was Elvis Presley's first single to reach No. 1 in both the U.S. and U.K. charts?

ANSWERS 1. Missy 'Misdemeanour' Elliot **2.** Every Breath You Take **3.** Climie Fisher **4.** The Jesus and Mary Chain **5.** Mary Kiani **6.** Kenickie **7.** Kilburn & the High Roads **8.** Hello this is Joanie (by Paul Evans) **9.** Batley **10.** The Bouncer **11.** B*Witched **12.** Howlin' Wind **13.** Barry Manilow **14.** Italy **15.** All Shook Up.

PEOPLE

1. Which American bank robber penned the poem 'The Story of Suicide Sal'?

2. Which American wit died alone in her apartment with her dog Troy by her side?

3. Which Conservative politician had an affair with his secretary Sara Keays?

4. Which French film pioneer produced the cliff-hanger series *The Perils of Pauline*?

5. Which U.S. soldier was known as 'Old Blood and Guts'?

6. Which French soldier's defence of Verdun in World War I made him a national hero?

7. In which country was British double agent Kim Philby born?

8. Which Canadian-born film actress was known as 'the World's Sweetheart'?

9. Which detective foiled a plot in 1861 to assassinate Abraham Lincoln?

10. Which American Indian princess married John Rolfe in 1613?

11. What was French entertainer Joseph Pujol known as?

12. Which member of the royal family presented the Best Video Award at the 1998 MTV Europe Awards?

13. Which pop singer changed his name to Abdul Rahman in 1998?

14. Which Canadian socialite wrote the book *Beyond Reason* in 1979?

15. Which son of Theodore Roosevelt wrote *War in the Garden of Eden* in 1919?

ANSWERS 1. Bonnie Parker 2. Dorothy Parker 3. Cecil Parkinson 4. Charles Pathé 5. George Patton 6. Henri Pétain 7. India 8. Mary Pickford 9. Allan Pinkerton 10. Pocahontas 11. Le Petomaine 12. Sarah Ferguson 13. Mark Morrison 14. Margaret Trudeau 15. Kermit Roosevelt.

GENERAL KNOWLEDGE

1. In American Indian legend what is the name of the paradise to which a person passes after death?

2. What in computing does LAN stand for?

3. What type of creature is a sauger?

4. Which country was the world's largest arms importer in 1989?

5. In which city is the University of Teeside?

6. What was the middle name of tennis player Rod Laver?

7. Approximately how long did Charles Lindbergh take to fly from New York to Paris in 1927?

8. Which U.S. state is nicknamed the 'Aloha State'?

9. In which South American country is the city Arequipa?

10. Who wrote the 1970 novel *Blue Movie*?

11. Which creature is also called a honey bear or potto?

12. What was the first name of U.S. president Calvin Coolidge?

13. What was the forename of Mr. Yale, American locksmith?

14. Who wrote *The Screwtape Letters*?

15. In which comic would you marvel at the exploits of Desperate Dan?

ANSWERS 1. Happy hunting ground **2.** Local area network **3.** Fish **4.** Saudi Arabia **5.** Middlesbrough **6.** George **7.** 33 and a half hours **8.** Hawaii **9.** Peru **10.** Terry Southern **11.** Kinkajou **12.** John **13.** Linus **14.** C.S. Lewis **15.** The Dandy.

ENTERTAINMENT

1. Which Oscar-winning actress was born in Walton-on-Thames in 1935?

2. Which comedian discovered Swedish actress Ann-Margret when she was a nightclub singer and dancer?

3. What was silent film star 'Fatty' Arbuckle's real first name?

4. Who replaced Gene Kelly in the 1948 film *Easter Parade* after he was injured?

5. Which film director won the Bancroft Medal at RADA in 1942?

6. *A.J. Wentworth, B.A.* was the last T.V. series of which comedy star?

7. In which T.V. show did the character Captain 'Howling Mad' Murdoch appear?

8. Which comedian's characters included secret agent Basildon Bond?

9. Which comedians were *Mr. Don and Mr. George* in 1993?

10. Which music-hall perfomer born in 1851 was billed as the 'Vital Spark'?

11. What was Sir Laurence Olivier's middle name?

12. Which comic actress made her New York debut in 1947 as Lady Bracknell in *The Importance of Being Earnest*?

13. Which music-hall performer born in 1866 is associated with the songs *Boiled Beef and Carrots* and *Hot Tripe and Onions*?

14. Which Dublin theatre reopened in 1977 with *John, Paul, George, Ringo... and Bert*?

15. What is the middle name of playwright Peter Shaffer?

SPORT

1. In which year did footballer Brian Clough win his two caps for England?

2. On which Scottish loch was motor racing driver John Cobb killed in 1952?

3. What was unusual about Henri Cochet's 1927 Wimbledon men's singles title win?

4. From which university did Sebastian Coe get a degree in economics?

5. Which Chinese diver became the first woman to score over 600 points in a springboard competition in 1988?

6. When was the only European Championship final in football to result in a replay?

7. Which New York Yankees baseball star was known as 'Old Reliable'?

8. In which year did Watford finish runners-up to Liverpool in Division One?

9. Who won the 1967 Belgian motor racing Grand Prix?

10. Who finished first in the women's 200m final at the 1995 IAAF World Championships but was later disqualified?

11. Who won the 1995 County Cricket Championship?

12. At what age did figure skater Cecilia Colledge appear in the 1932 Winter Olympics?

13. Which British speedway rider won the 1976 World Individual championship?

14. What age was gymnast Nadia Comaneci when she competed at the 1976 Montreal Olympics?

15. With which baseball team did Earle Combs play his entire career, from 1924-35?

POP MUSIC

1. In which year was Adam Faith born?

2. Which group recorded the album *Arthur, or the Decline and Fall of the British Empire*?

3. Which group had a 1994 Top 40 single with *Millennium*?

4. Which duo had a 1998 Top 20 single with *Burning*?

5. Under which name did Jonathan King record the 1971 hit *Sugar Sugar*?

6. Which group had a 1998 Top 20 single with *The Dope Show*?

7. Which band backed Neil Young on the 1995 album *Mirror Ball*?

8. Which duo comprise The Pet Shop Boys?

9. Which group charted in 1998 with the single *Bad Old Man*?

10. In which year did John Lennon release the live album *Some Time in New York City*?

11. Which group recorded the album *Larks' Tongues in Aspic*?

12. What was the 1962 singles chart entry for the Clyde Valley Stompers?

13. *Laughing All the Way to the Cleaners* was the debut single of which band?

14. Which punk singer guested on Leftfield's single *Open Up*?

15. Which group had a 1998 hit single with *God is a D.J.*?

ART AND LITERATURE

1. Who was the author of the thriller novel *10lb Penalty*?

2. Who painted the portrait *Mme Gautreau* which was exhibited in 1884?

3. Who wrote *Madame Bovary*?

4. "To begin at the beginning: It is spring, moonless night in the small town, starless and bible-black..." Which poem?

5. Who wrote the novel *Oranges Are Not the Only Fruit*?

6. Who painted 1642's *The Night Watch*?

7. What was the name of the 1956 art exhibition at the Whitechapel Art Gallery which was influential in the development of Pop Art?

8. Who was the author of the novel *My Legendary Girlfriend*?

9. Which English woodcarver, born in 1648, became Master Carver in Wood to the Crown under Charles II?

10. Which detective writer's books include *LaBrava* and *Cat Chaser*?

11. What was Helen Zahavi's controversial 1991 novel called?

12. Which American novelist wrote 1963's *Cat's Cradle*?

13. What is the name of the brown pigment made from the ink of cuttlefish?

14. In which decade was the art movement The Brotherhood of Ruralists conceived?

15. Which French painter worked with the Paris Customs Office from 1871-93?

ANSWERS 1. Dick Francis 2. John Singer Sargent 3. Gustave Flaubert 4. Under Milk Wood 5. Jeanette Winterson 6. Rembrandt 7. This is Tomorrow 8. Mike Gayle 9. Grinling Gibbons 10. Elmore Leonard 11. Dirty Weekend 12. Kurt Vonnegut Jr. 13. Sepia 14. 1970s 15. Henri Rousseau.

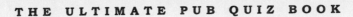

GENERAL KNOWLEDGE

1. Which politician was Chancellor of the Exchequer 1916-19?

2. How many goals did footballer Gary Lineker score for England?

3. To which genus does the aspen tree belong?

4. What in Australia is a brigalow?

5. Of which African protectorate was Hargeisa capital from 1941-60?

6. Which poet wrote *The Bride of Abydos*?

7. Who is the twin sister of Sebastian in the play *Twelfth Night*?

8. What was Dame Nellie Melba's original name?

9. Who played Stan Ogden in *Coronation Street*?

10. In which novel by Walter Scott does gypsy Meg Merrilies appear?

11. Who was elected Labour M.P. for Bolsover in 1997?

12. Who was the god of war in Greek mythology?

13. What is the name of the ship in the book *Treasure Island*?

14. In which town in Galilee did Jesus change water into wine?

15. Who was England Test cricket captain 1988-93?

ANSWERS 1. Andrew Bonar Law **2.** 48 **3.** Populus **4.** Tree **5.** British Somaliland **6.** Lord Byron **7.** Viola **8.** Helen Porter Mitchell **9.** Bernard Youens **10.** Guy Mannering **11.** Dennis Skinner **12.** Ares **13.** Hispaniola **14.** Cana **15.** Graham Gooch.

ENTERTAINMENT

1. Which music-hall performer born in 1870 was known for his musical monologues such as *The Green Eye of the Little Yellow God?*

2. Which modern playwright acted under the name David Baron?

3. Which annual dramatic event is held at Niagara-on-the-Lake, Ontario?

4. Which comedy actress played *The Bed-Sit Girl* in the 1960s BBC sitcom?

5. Which comedian was *The Man From Auntie?*

6. Who played the butler *Benson* in the U.S. sitcom?

7. Who starred as Beryl in the 1970s sitcom *Beryl's Lot?*

8. Who played Jane Hathaway in the 1960s sitcom *The Beverly Hillbillies?*

9. Which quartet wrote and performed the satirical show *Beyond the Fringe?*

10. Who made his last stage appearance as Elwood P. Dowd in the play *Harvey* in 1949?

11. In which year was La Comédie-Française founded by Louis XIV?

12. Who was Artistic Director of Nottingham Playhouse from 1973-8?

13. Which theatre director's first wife was actress Janet Suzman?

14. Which Irish dramatist wrote the play *Red Roses For Me?*

15. In which city was the Octagon Theatre opened in 1967?

SPORT

1. What was the name of Denis Compton's elder brother who kept wicket for Middlesex?

2. What was the nickname of ice hockey player Lionel Conacher?

3. Which French rugby union club side did Jean Condom move to in 1986?

4. In which city was U.S. triple jumper Mike Conley born?

5. Which boxer was world light-heavyweight champion from 1939-41?

6. What was the profession of American yachtsman Dennis Conner's father?

7. Who scored a consolation goal for Holland in their 1978 World Cup Final defeat?

8. Which Australian wicket-keeper played in 51 Tests from 1957-66?

9. Who was the last player to score for the losing team in a football World Cup Final?

10. Who was the 1972 Olympic men's 200m breaststroke swimming champion?

11. Which cyclist won the 1995 Giro d'Italia?

12. Who was world 250cc motor cycling champion from 1994-97?

13. Which Swedish tennis player designed the Stockholm stadium for the 1912 Olympics?

14. Which team won rugby union's Swalec Cup from 1991-3?

15. Which country were the 1996 world ice hockey champions?

ANSWERS 1. Leslie 2. Big Train 3. Biarritz 4. Chicago 5. Billy Conn 6. Tuna fisherman 7. Nanninga 8. Wally Grout 9. Rudi Völler, in 1986 10. John Hencken 11. Tony Rominger 12. Massimiliano Biaggi 13. Torben Grut 14. Llanelli 15. Czech Republic.

POP MUSIC

1. Which was Lionel Richie's only single to hit No. 1 in the U.K. and U.S.?

2. Which vocalist featured on Babyface's 1997 hit *How Come, How Long*?

3. Which D.J. recorded the 1991 album *Words Escape Me*?

4. Which Dutch duo are also known as Itty Bitty Boozy Woozy?

5. Which group had a 1996 Top 40 hit with *Tishbite*?

6. Which act had a Top Five hit in 1992 with *Iron Lion Zion*?

7. Which group had a 1997 Top Ten single with *Choose Life*?

8. Who was the drummer of the group Led Zeppelin?

9. Who had a 1996 Top Ten single with *Blurred*?

10. Which guitarist had a minor chart hit in 1996 with the single *Cannibals*?

11. Whose first solo album was entitled *She's So Unusual*?

12. Which group scored a Top 30 single hit in 1997 with *Debaser*?

13. Which act charted in 1996 with *The Boy with the X-Ray Eyes*?

14. What are the forenames of k.d. lang?

15. Under which name did Jonathan King record the 1976 hit *It Only Takes a Minute*?

GEOGRAPHY

1. Which is the largest of the Channel Islands?

2. To which European country does the island of Lampedusa belong?

3. What is the island in the Bristol Channel about 20km northwest of Hartland Point?

4. Which strait lies between the Italian mainland and Sicily?

5. Mount Palomar is in which U.S. state?

6. The Pevensey Levels is a marshy area of which English county?

7. In which Australian state is the former uranium site of Rum Jungle?

8. Kigali is the capital of which African republic?

9. In which U.S. state is Lake Winnebago?

10. In which county of the Republic of Ireland is the Twelve Pins mountain range?

11. Cardiff stands on the mouth of which river?

12. Which is the smallest of Japan's four main islands?

13. Melbourne, Australia, is at the mouth of which river?

14. In which eastern European country is the city of Lodz?

15. On which river does Norwich stand?

GENERAL KNOWLEDGE

1. In which country was D.H. Lawrence's novel *The Plumed Serpent* set?

2. What nationality was botanist Carolus Linnaeus?

3. What is the fruit of the tree *Prunus persica*?

4. Who created the cartoon character Old Bill?

5. Who wrote the novel *The Monkey King*?

6. Who composed the opera *Rigoletto*?

7. Which sea lies between Korea and the Philippines?

8. What sort of creature is an ariel?

9. Who was elected M.P. for Bassetlaw in 1997?

10. In which African country is the city of Iwo?

11. In which year did Little Rock become state capital of Arkansas?

12. The card game cooncan resembles which familiar game?

13. In which year was Babington's plot against Elizabeth I?

14. In which ocean are the Maldives?

15. To which genus does the goat belong?

ANSWERS 1. Mexico **2.** Swedish **3.** Peach **4.** Bruce Bairnsfather **5.** Timothy Mo **6.** Verdi **7.** China Sea **8.** Gazelle **9.** Joe Ashton **10.** Nigeria **11.** 1821 **12.** Rummy **13.** 1586 **14.** Indian Ocean **15.** Capra.

ENTERTAINMENT

1. Which actress was the third wife of Sir Laurence Olivier?

2. Which actor who died in 1989 founded the Compass touring company in 1983?

3. Who wrote the 1936 comedy play *French Without Tears*?

4. Which comic actor played the title role in Robert Bolt's play *Gentle Jack* in 1963?

5. Which music-hall comedian appeared as Falstaff in *Henry IV* part I in 1935 at His Majesty's Theatre?

6. What was Edina's surname in the T.V. comedy *Absolutely Fabulous*?

7. Who was the arch enemy of television's Adam Adamant?

8. Who did Peter Adamson play in *Coronation Street*?

9. Who played the Sheriff of Nottingham in the late 1950s T.V. series *The Adventures of Robin Hood*?

10. Who created the puppet Twizzle?

11. Which actor married Lauren Bacall in 1961?

12. Who played *Baby Doll* in the 1956 film?

13. On whose novel was the 1972 film *The Getaway* based?

14. Who played *Mame* in the 1974 film?

15. Who played *Cleopatra* in the 1917 film?

ANSWERS 1. Joan Plowright **2.** Sir Anthony Quayle **3.** Terence Rattigan **4.** Kenneth Williams **5.** George Robey **6.** Monsoon **7.** The Face **8.** Len Fairclough **9.** Alan Wheatley **10.** Roberta Leigh **11.** Jason Robards Jr. **12.** Carroll Baker **13.** Jim Thompson **14.** Lucille Ball **15.** Theda Bara.

SPORT

1. For which Italian football club did Ruud Gullit sign in July 1993?

2. Which cricketer scored over 3000 first-class runs three times, in 1923, '28 & '33?

3. Which was the first country to host football's World Cup finals twice?

4. What nationality is former world speed skating champion Erik Gundersen?

5. In which year did Stephen Hendry win his first World Professional snooker title?

6. Who won the 1956 Olympic men's hammer competition?

7. Who was Wimbledon ladies singles champion 1952-54?

8. Which American male tennis star retired in 1992 after winning 109 singles titles?

9. At which field event did Italian Adolfo Consolini win Olympic gold in 1948?

10. For which Lancashire League cricket side did Sir Learie Constantine play for ten years?

11. Which horse won the 1993 Grand National at Aintree?

12. Which team won the 1988 F.A. Cup Final?

13. At which sport were Tom Morris Snr. and Tom Morris Jnr. successful?

14. When was the last all-British women's singles final at Wimbledon?

15. In which U.S. state was Ed Moses born?

ANSWERS 1. Sampdoria 2. Patsy Hendren 3. Mexico 4. Danish 5. 1990 6. Hal Connolly 7. Maureen Connolly 8. Jimmy Connors 9. Discus 10. Nelson 11. None did - it was abandoned 12. Wimbledon 13. Golf 14. 1961 15. Ohio.

POP MUSIC

1. Which male vocal group had a 1997 Top 30 hit with *Can We Talk...*?

2. Which group had hits in 1993 with *Why Are People Grudgeful* and *Behind the Counter*?

3. Which U.S. group recorded the album *Kick Out the Jams*?

4. Which U.S. group had a 1997 hit single with *A.D.I.D.A.S.*?

5. Which male vocal group first charted in 1995 with the single *We've Got It Goin' On*?

6. Which was the first single by The Rolling Stones to reach No. 1 in the U.S. and U.K.?

7. Which group's debut chart hit in 1983 was *Destination Zululand*?

8. Which actor/singer's first chart hit was 1998's *The Heart's Lone Desire*?

9. Which male singer had a 1995 Top 30 single with *Like Lovers Do*?

10. From which city were the group The La's?

11. Which male singer had a 1995 hit single with *Rock and Roll is Dead*?

12. Which female vocalist featured on the 1998 single *One* by Busta Rhymes?

13. Which Japanese group charted in 1997 with the single *Mon Amour Tokyo*?

14. What is funk bass player Robert Bell's nickname?

15. Which U.S rapper featured on Goldie's 1997 hit *Digital*?

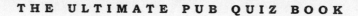

HISTORY

1. Who was king of Castile from 1035-65?

2. Leaders of which plot to kill Queen Elizabeth were executed in 1586?

3. In which year was Sir Thomas Wentworth, 1st Earl of Stafford, beheaded following a charge of high treason?

4. Who succeeded to the U.S. presidency on the death of Zachary Taylor?

5. In which year of World War II did Donald Bailey invent the Bailey Bridge?

6. In which year was Robespierre executed?

7. Which composer famously visited Staffa in 1829?

8. Anastasio Bustamante was president of which country from 1837-41?

9. Who was prime minister of the Bulgarian People's Republic from 1946-49?

10. In which year did the Folies-Bergère Theatre open in Paris?

11. In which year of year of World War II was the battleship Admiral Graf Spee scuttled?

12. Which future president of the U.S. served as governor of Massachusetts from 1919-20?

13. In which year did William III land at Torbay?

14. Where in 1854 was there a rebellion of Australian miners?

15. In which year did Gerald Ford become president of the U.S.?

ANSWERS 1. Ferdinand I 2. Babington's Plot 3. 1641 4. Millard Fillmore 5. 1941 6. 1794 7. Mendelssohn 8. Mexico 9. Georgi Dimitrov 10. 1869 11. 1939 12. John Calvin Coolidge 13. 1688 14. Eureka Stockade, Ballarat 15. 1974.

GENERAL KNOWLEDGE

1. In which year was the British Legion founded?

2. What is the port of Smyrna now known as?

3. Between which two countries was the region of Livonia divided in 1918?

4. Which Agatha Christie detective features in *Evil Under the Sun*?

5. What is the Euxine Sea better known as?

6. In which year was Martin Luther King Jnr. assassinated?

7. In which play by Henrik Ibsen is Mrs. Alving a character?

8. Which seaport is at the head of the Shannon estuary?

9. Which book of the Bible features the story of Noah's ark?

10. To what animal does the adjective corvine refer?

11. What line on a map connects places having an equal period of sunshine?

12. What is the major religion of Mali?

13. On which part of the body would you have worn a buskin in Ancient Greece?

14. How many ounces are there in a pound?

15. In what year did racing car designer Enzo Ferrari die?

ANSWERS 1. 1921 2. Izmir 3. Latvia and Estonia 4. Hercule Poirot 5. Black Sea 6. 1968 7. Ghosts 8. Limerick 9. Genesis 10. Crow 11. Isohel 12. Muslim 13. Foot 14. 16 15. 1988.

ENTERTAINMENT

1. What is the screen name of actress Camille Javal?

2. Which actress is the elder sister of Warren Beatty?

3. Who delivered Alan Bennett's 1988 television monologue *A Cream Cracker Under the Settee*?

4. Who directed the 1989 film *Driving Miss Daisy*?

5. Who played *Joan of Arc* in the 1948 film?

6. Which dramatist wrote *The Odd Couple*?

7. In which city was the French workers' co-operative group Théâtre du Soleil formed?

8. Which Nigerian playwright and Nobel prize winner studied English at Leeds University?

9. Which character did John Bentley play in *Crossroads*?

10. Which ventriloquist's dolls include Lord Charles and Ali Cat?

11. In which soap opera did The Waterman's Arms feature?

12. Who did Terence Alexander play in T.V.'s *Bergerac*?

13. Who played Siegfried Farnon in the T.V. show *All Creatures Great and Small*?

14. Which U.S. comedy series was based on *Till Death Us Do Part*?

15. The French town of Nouvion was the setting of which sitcom?

ANSWERS 1. Brigitte Bardot **2.** Shirley MacLaine **3.** Thora Hird **4.** Bruce Beresford **5.** Ingrid Bergman **6.** Neil Simon **7.** Paris **8.** Wole Soyinka **9.** Hugh Mortimer **10.** Ray Alan **11.** Albion Market **12.** Charlie Hungerford **13.** Robert Hardy **14.** All in the Family **15.** 'Allo, 'Allo.

SPORT

1. For which French club side did rugby union player Jean Gachassin become player/trainer in 1969?

2. Who in 1980 won all five men's Olympic speed skating titles?

3. In which city was Superbowl XXXI played in 1997?

4. Which country won the World Team Freshwater Angling title in 1996 & '97?

5. Geoff Hurst famously scored three goals in the 1966 World Cup Final. How many players had scored twice in the final prior to that?

6. Who won the 1996 Nat West Trophy in cricket?

7. Who won the women's 200m title at the 1993 & '95 IAAF World Championships?

8. Which rider won the 1994 Badminton Horse Trials?

9. Which Essex cricketer is known as Dic Dic?

10. Who became world flyweight boxing champion in 1960?

11. Who were runners-up in football's Division 1 from 1891-93?

12. Who was the 1995 USPGA golf champion?

13. For which side did ice hockey player Bill Cook play his entire NHL career?

14. In which round did Henry Cooper floor Muhammad Ali in their 1963 fight?

15. Which Huddersfield rugby league player scored ten tries against Keighley in 1951?

POP MUSIC

1. What was Fat Les's 1998 Christmas hit?

2. Which group had a minor hit in 1992 with the single *Armchair Anarchist*?

3. From which country does singer Ricky Martin hail?

4. Which U.S. vocalist scored a 1997 hit with *Where Have All the Cowboys Gone*?

5. Who had a 1998 Top 10 single with *The Rockafeller Skank*?

6. From which country does singer Merril Bainbridge hail?

7. What was Kula Shaker's first Top 10 single?

8. Which was the first single by Rod Stewart to reach No. 1 in the U.K. and U.S.?

9. From which country does singer k.d. lang come?

10. Which group recorded the album *Made From Technetium*?

11. Which U.K. singer had a 1998 hit single with *Little Bit of Lovin'*?

12. Which duo charted in 1996 with the single *Better Watch Out*?

13. Which duo had a 1998 Top 30 single with *Most High*?

14. Which D.J. recorded the 1994 album *One Step Ahead of the Spider*?

15. Which group charted in 1996 with the single *Release the Pressure*?

ANSWERS 1. Naughty Christmas (Goblin in the Office) **2.** Kingmaker **3.** Mexico **4.** Paula Cole **5.** Fatboy Slim **6.** Australia **7.** Tattva **8.** Maggie May **9.** Canada **10.** Man or Astro-Man? **11.** Kele Le Roc **12.** Ant and Dec **13.** Page and Plant **14.** MC 900 FT Jesus **15.** Leftfield.

WORDS

1. What is the name of the weight in bowls which makes them deviate from the straight line?

2. A billy is a name for a pocket handkerchief. What then is a 'blue billy'?

3. To be 'stabbed with a Bridport dagger' is to be killed by what method?

4. What is the literal meaning of the word candidate?

5. When are one's 'cap-and-feather' days?

6. What sort of fish is a Severn capon?

7. What metal is named after the German word for 'gnome'?

8. What sort of animal is a saiga?

9. What is the name of a person who manufactures salt?

10. What would you do with a sampan - fly it or sail it?

11. What sort of animal is a sassaby - a kangaroo or an antelope?

12. From what is the Chinese drink samsara made?

13. What is the motto of the U.S.A.?

14. What is guano?

15. What was a 'guinea pig' on a ship?

ANSWER 1. Bias 2. A blue pocket handkerchief with white spots 3. Hanging 4. Clothed in white 5. Childhood 6. A sole 7. Cobalt 8. An antelope 9. A salter 10. Sail it 11. An antelope 12. Rice 13. E Pluribus Unum 14. Bird droppings 15. A midshipman.

GENERAL KNOWLEDGE

1. In which year did jazz player Louis Armstrong die?

2. Who wrote *The Last of the Mohicans*?

3. In which English county is Farnborough?

4. What is an 'eye dog'?

5. Which U.S. film actress was born Harlean Carpentier?

6. What is the gestation period in months of a llama?

7. Which publishing firm did Carmen Calill found in 1973?

8. Who composed the opera *Artaxerxes* which was first performed in 1762?

9. Which organization was formerly known as the Spastics Association?

10. What breed of dog is also called a Persian greyhound?

11. Who directed the 1978 film *Pretty Baby*?

12. Who was president of the U.S. from 1881-85?

13. Which French dish translates as 'cock with wine'?

14. On which river is the town of Evesham?

15. Why is a heart cherry so called?

ANSWERS 1. 1971 **2.** James Fenimore Cooper **3.** Hampshire **4.** One trained to control sheep by staring at them **5.** Jean Harlow **6.** Eleven **7.** Virago **8.** Thomas Arne **9.** Scope **10.** Saluki **11.** Louis Malle **12.** Chester A. Arthur **13.** Coq au vin **14.** Avon **15.** Because of its shape.

ENTERTAINMENT

1. Which Italian dramatist wrote the play *Trumpets and Raspberries*?

2. Which English actress born in 1874 founded a school for the stage training of children?

3. Which Welsh actor appeared as *Hamlet* in New York in 1964?

4. Which 1969 Samuel Beckett play lasts for approximately half a minute?

5. Who played Gabriel Oak in the 1967 film *Far From the Madding Crowd*?

6. Which U.S. film director was born William Berkeley Enos?

7. Which actress has been married to actor Rod Steiger and author Philip Roth?

8. Who appeared on T.V. as Roald Dahl in 1981's *The Patricia Neal Story*?

9. Who in 1924 was described by Louise Brooks as "a slim boy with charming manners"?

10. Who directed the 1977 film *Exorcist II: The Heretic*?

11. Which Oscar-winning actor married Ethel Merman in 1964?

12. Which French actor killed himself in 1978, two days after his wife died?

13. In which city was actor Kenneth Branagh born?

14. In which year did actor Jean-Louis Barrault die?

15. Which poet's first play was 1935's *The Dance of Death*?

SPORT

1. Which husband and wife team won the 1986 Commonwealth Games small bore rifle pairs title?

2. Which Italian cyclist won the Giro d'Italia in 1953?

3. Who was the first man to win the world heavyweight boxing title under the Marquess of Queensbury Rules?

4. With what sport would you associate Joe Namath?

5. In which year was Pete Sampras born?

6. Which of the two equestrian Schockemöhle brothers is the elder?

7. What are Seattle's American football team called?

8. Which boxer was nicknamed 'the Fighting Marine'?

9. In which year was Alf Ramsey made England's football manager?

10. What was U.S. Olympic swimming champion Rowdy Gaines's real name?

11. Which British woman swimmer won the 1956 Olympic 100m backstroke title?

12. Who was the 1960 Olympic women's figure skating champion?

13. Who scored Holland's consolation goal in the 1974 World Cup Final?

14. Who were runners-up in football's Division 1 from 1947-49?

15. Who won the women's 400m titles at the 1991 & '95 IAAF World Championships?

POP MUSIC

1. Which vocalist had a minor 1996 hit with *The Mill Hill Self Hate Club*?

2. Who sang the theme song to the James Bond film *License to Kill*?

3. Who duetted with Fish on the 1995 single *Just Good Friends*?

4. What was Collapsed Lung's 1998 hit single?

5. Gene Simmons and Paul Stanley formed which band in 1972?

6. Which female singer recorded the album *Deadline on My Memories*?

7. Which vocalist featured on Pato Banton's 1995 hit *Bubbling Hot*?

8. Which group had a minor chart hit in 1994 with *Big Gay Heart*?

9. Which blues guitarist's guitar is named Lucille?

10. Which female vocalist had single success in 1992 with *Walking on Broken Glass*?

11. Which heavy metal band did Rob Halford join in 1971?

12. Which group's debut Top Ten single was 1997's *Nancy Boy*?

13. Which group recorded the 1987 album *Crooked Mile*?

14. What was Gary Barlow's second solo No. 1 single?

15. Which was the only single by The Supremes to reach No. 1 in the U.K. and the U.S.?

SCIENCE

1. What does B.t.u. stand for in terms of heat?

2. What in meteorology is graupel?

3. How many gallons of beer are in an anker?

4. What type of cement did Joseph Aspdin patent in 1824?

5. What in computing does DPI stand for?

6. In which country does the hot wind khamsin blow in early summer?

7. How many hundredweights make up a ton?

8. What in computing does GIF stand for?

9. How many edges has a regular octahedron?

10. During which period of geological time did trilobites become extinct?

11. Of what is hypnophobia a fear?

12. Which German won the 1905 Nobel prize for medicine for his research on tuberculosis?

13. How many °F is 17°C?

14. Which French scientist founded the branch of physics that he named electrodynamics?

15. Who shared the 1903 Nobel prize for physics with the Curies?

ANSWERS 1. British thermal unit 2. Soft partially melted hail 3. 10 4. Portland cement 5. Dots per inch 6. Egypt 7. Twenty 8. Graphic image format 9. 12 10. Permian 11. Sleep 12. Robert Koch 13. 63° 14. André Ampère 15. Antoine Becquerel.

GENERAL KNOWLEDGE

1. Which Canadian humorist wrote *Sunshine Sketches of a Little Town*?

2. Which creature did Fafnir become in Norse mythology?

3. On which river is the Austrian city of Linz?

4. LPG is an alternative to petrol. For what do the initials stand?

5. What was the name given to the 1623 massacre by the Dutch of English merchants in the Spice Islands?

6. Which Scottish river reaches the North Sea at Berwick?

7. Who wrote the play *Top Girls*?

8. Who directed the 1980 film *Kagemusha*?

9. What is the international car registration for Bahrain?

10. What type of creature is a gayal?

11. Who wrote the 1516 work *Utopia*?

12. What is the capital of Chad?

13. What is the musical instrument an English horn better known as?

14. Who wrote the novel *The Dark Arena*?

15. The island Corregidor lies at the entrance to which bay?

ANSWERS 1. Stephen Leacock 2. Dragon 3. Danube 4. Liquid petroleum gas 5. Amboina massacre 6. Tweed 7. Caryl Churchill 8. Akira Kurosawa 9. BRN 10. Ox 11. Sir Thomas More 12. Ndjamena 13. Cor anglais 14. Mario Puzo 15. Manila Bay.

ENTERTAINMENT

1. Which playwright's radio works include *Embers* and *All That Fall*?

2. Who designed and directed the 1960 London production of Ionesco's play *Rhinoceros*?

3. Who was the author of the 1975 play *Alphabetical Order*?

4. What was the clown Karl Adrien Wettach better known as?

5. In which year did comic actress Joyce Grenfell die?

6. Which Liverpool theatre opened in 1964?

7. Who presented the British improvisation show *Whose Line Is It Anyway*?

8. Which medical drama was set at St. Angela's Hospital, Battersea?

9. Which comic actor's catch-phrase was "I'm free"?

10. *Bootsie and Snudge* was a spin-off from which sitcom?

11. What was the name of the chimpanzee in the T.V. show *Daktari*?

12. Which 1960s drama series was called *Secret Agent* in the U.S.?

13. Who voiced Penfold in the cartoon series *Dangermouse*?

14. Who is the wife and assistant of magician Paul Daniels?

15. In which year was sports presenter Dickie Davies born?

ANSWERS 1. Samuel Beckett **2.** Orson Welles **3.** Michael Frayn **4.** Grock **5.** 1979 **6.** Everyman **7.** Clive Anderson **8.** Angels **9.** John Inman **10.** The Army Game **11.** Judy **12.** Danger Man **13.** Terry Scott **14.** Debbie McGee **15.** 1933.

SPORT

1. How many Test wickets did Fred Trueman take for England?

2. Who was the first sub 3 mins 50 secs miler?

3. Who won the 1980 World Professional Snooker championship?

4. How many players are in a rugby league side?

5. Who won her 25th golfing title at the 1993 Australian Ladies Masters?

6. Who in 1974 rode Cannonade to victory in the 100th Kentucky Derby?

7. In which year was England rugby union player Fran Cotton born?

8. Who won the 1948 British Open golf tournament?

9. Which golfer won the 1992 U.S. Masters golf tournament?

10. Who became world featherweight boxing champion in 1946?

11. Who won the 1996 County Cricket Championship?

12. Which jockey rode 1994 Epsom Derby winner Erhaab?

13. For which international rugby union side did John Gainsford play from 1960-67?

14. What was the nickname of swimmer Michael Gross?

15. What time did David Hemery run in winning the 1968 Olympic 400m hurdles?

ANSWERS 1. 307 2. John Walker 3. Cliff Thorburn 4. 13 5. Laura Davies 6. Angel Cordero 7. 1947 8. Henry Cotton 9. Fred Couples 10. Willie Pep 11. Leicestershire 12. Willie Carson 13. South Africa 14. The albatross 15. 48.12 secs.

THE ULTIMATE PUB QUIZ BOOK

POP MUSIC

1. Which singer guested on the 1995 single *Just the One* by the Levellers?

2. In which year did singer Janis Joplin die?

3. Which Scottish singer had a 1995 hit with *A Girl Like You*?

4. Which woman singer released the mini-L.P. *Girl at Her Volcano*?

5. Which singer's albums include 1993's *Too Long in Exile*?

6. Who left Jethro Tull in 1969 to form Blodwyn Pig?

7. Which vocal group's chart debut was 1997's *Slam Dunk (Da Funk)*?

8. Which singer had a 1995 hit with *R to the A*?

9. Which group recorded the album *In Utero*?

10. Which singer had a 1996 Top Ten hit with *Dance into the Light*?

11. Which group charted in 1995 with the single *Downtown Venus*?

12. Which easy-listening combo got to No. 2 in December 1995 with a cover of *Wonderwall* by Oasis?

13. Who was lead singer with the group Jesus Jones?

14. Which duo from *Coronation Street* had a minor hit in 1995 with *Something Stupid*?

15. How are Steve Jansen and David Sylvian of the group Japan related?

PEOPLE

1. Who is the president of the World Professional Billiards and Snooker Association?

2. Who in May 1999 became the first Briton to climb 11 of the world's 14 highest mountains?

3. Who is the Metropolitan Police Commissioner?

4. Which singer won the 1999 Eurovision Song Contest?

5. What is terrorist Ilich Ramirez Sanchez better known as?

6. Which Australian ballerina created the role of *Pineapple Poll* in the 1951 ballet?

7. Which actor did German director Werner Herzog plot to kill on the set of the film *Fitzcarraldo*?

8. What is the nickname of James Gardner, friend of footballer Paul Gascoigne?

9. Former Walt Disney studio chief Jeffrey Katzenberg now works for which studio?

10. Which actress played the younger Diana Dors in the 1999 T.V. film *The Blonde Bombshell*?

11. Which actress played the older Diana Dors in the 1999 T.V. film *The Blonde Bombshell*?

12. Who was the French presenter of T.V.'s *Le Show*?

13. Who became the new Poet Laureate in 1999?

14. Who was appointed first minister of Scotland in 1999?

15. Which large Scottish island was formerly owned by Keith Schellenberg?

GENERAL KNOWLEDGE

1. From what is haslet made?

2. In which year was Germany admitted to the League of Nations?

3. What would you do with a 'lira da braccio' ?

4. In which year did the Ferris wheel make its debut?

5. Whose story was told in the TV drama *The Naked Civil Servant*?

6. Who was elected Labour M.P. for Hackney North and Stoke Newington in 1997?

7. What is the New Zealand manuka also called?

8. Who wrote *The Hound of the Baskervilles*?

9. Which singer had a No. 1 single with the song *Begin the Beguine* in 1981?

10. On which river is the Scottish city of Perth?

11. Which town in New York is the seat of Cornell University?

12. Which cartoonist created the schoolgirls of St. Trinian's?

13. What date is Oak-Apple Day in Britain?

14. In which year was James I of Scotland murdered?

15. Approximately how long in miles is Lebanon from north to south - 75, 125 or 175?

ANSWERS 1 Cooked minced pig's offal **2.** 1926 **3.** Play it **4.** 1892 **5.** Quentin Crisp **6.** Diane Abbott **7.** Tea tree **8.** Arthur Conan Doyle **9.** Julio Iglesias **10.** Tay **11.** Ithaca **12.** Ronald Searle **13.** May 29 **14.** 1437 **15.** 125.

ENTERTAINMENT

1. Which comedy impresionist's real name is Robert Nankerville?

2. Who played Miss Jones in the comedy show *Rising Damp*?

3. Annabelle Hurst and Stewart Sullivan were characters in which late 1960s T.V. drama?

4. In which year was T.V. presenter Anne Diamond born?

5. What was Dick Van Dyke's character name in *The Dick Van Dyke Show*?

6. Who played *The District Nurse* in the BBC television series?

7. Which brothers played *The Fabulous Baker Boys* on film?

8. Who starred as a psychiatrist in the 1977 film *Equus*?

9. Which film director's 1972 autobiography was *The Name Above the Title*?

10. Who played Bathsheba Everdene in the 1967 film *Far From the Madding Crowd*?

11. Who played secret agent Flint in the 1965 film *Our Man Flint*?

12. Which western hero did Kevin Costner play in a 1994 Lawrence Kasdan film?

13. Who is actor Tom Cruise's second wife?

14. Which actor was born Charles Buchinsky?

15. What was Mel Brooks's 1977 Alfred Hitchcock parody called?

ANSWERS 1. Bobby Davro 2. Frances de la Tour 3. Department S 4. 1954 5. Rob Petrie 6. Nerys Hughes 7. Jeff & Beau Bridges 8. Richard Burton 9. Frank Capra 10. Julie Christie 11. James Coburn 12. Wyatt Earp 13. Nicole Kidman 14. Charles Bronson 15. High Anxiety.

SPORT

1. In which city was snooker's 1993 European Open held?

2. With which sport is the Austrian Christian Mayer associated?

3. In what year did Danny Blanchflower join Tottenham Hotspur?

4. What length in metres did Mike Powell jump at the 1991 IAAF World Championships?

5. When did Red Rum land his last Grand National victory?

6. In which year did Ray Reardon last win the World Professional snooker title?

7. Who in boxing was 'the Bronx Bull'?

8. For which international side did footballer Socrates play?

9. Which event did Guy Drut win at the 1976 Olympics?

10. Who lost the 1991 U.S. Open men's singles tennis final?

11. What was the nickname of Canadian ice hockey star Yvan Cournoyer?

12. In which city was figure skater Robin Cousins born?

13. Which Italian won the 1984 Olympic men's 10,000m title?

14. Which cricketer captained Kent from 1957-71?

15. Why was U.S. Olympic swimming champion Buster Crabbe not allowed to compete at water polo in the 1936 Olympics?

ANSWERS 1. Antwerp **2.** Skiing **3.** 1954 **4.** 8.95m **5.** 1977 **7.** Jake La Motta **8.** Brazil **9.** 110m hurdles **10.** Jim Courier **11.** The roadrunner **12.** Bristol **13.** Alberto Cova **14.** Colin Cowdrey **15.** Because he had appeared in advertisments.

POP MUSIC

1. Which group's albums include 1993's *Why Do They Call Me Mr. Happy?*?

2. Which group recorded the 1970 album *Home*?

3. Which pop group's debut L.P. was *Yo! Bum Rush the Show*?

4. What was the first singles chart entry for The Pogues?

5. Who is better known as Jamiroquai?

6. Who recorded the albums *Bad* and *Thriller*?

7. Who in 1989 recorded the album *Heart-Shaped World*?

8. Which rap artist recorded the album *Nature of a Sista*?

9. Which female vocalist featured on the song *History Repeating* by The Propellerheads?

10. Which group recorded the album *Pablo Honey*?

11. Which group had a Top 30 entry in 1997 with the song *Battle of Who Could Care Less*?

12. Who replaced Paul Di'anno as vocalist of Iron Maiden?

13. Whose second album was *In-a-gadda-da-vida*?

14. Which group's hit singles included *Saturn 5* and *This Is How It Feels*?

15. What is singer William Broad better known as?

ANSWERS 1. Nomeansno 2. Procol Harum 3. Public Enemy 4. A Pair of Brown Eyes 5. Jason Kay 6. Michael Jackson 7. Chris Isaak 8. Queen Latifah 9. Shirley Bassey 10. Radiohead 11. Ben Folds Five 12. Bruce Dickinson 13. Iron Butterfly 14. Inspiral Carpets 15. Billy Idol.

ART AND LITERATURE

1. The painting *Do Not Go Gentle Into That Good Night* by Ceri Richards was inspired by a poem by whom?

2. Which Scottish painter's works included *Village Politicians*?

3. Who created Winnie-the-Pooh?

4. Who wrote the novel *Hemlock and After*?

5. Who wrote the play *A Streetcar Named Desire*?

6. Vladimir and Estragon are tramps in which play?

7. In which Thomas Hardy novel does Eustacia Vye appear?

8. From which country did artist Kurt Schwitters flee to England from the Nazis in 1940?

9. Which British painter is associated with the village Cookham?

10. Which Paris-born artist lived in Tahiti from 1891?

11. Which Russian author's stories included *The Death of Ivan Ilyich*?

12. Which female author wrote the 1982 novel *The President's Child*?

13. Whose thriller books include *Executive Orders*?

14. Who wrote the crime novel *Road Rage*?

15. What was the title of Irvine Welsh's 1998 novel about a corrupt policeman?

ANSWERS 1. Dylan Thomas **2.** Sir David Wilkie **3.** A.A. Milne **4.** Angus Wilson **5.** Tennessee Williams **6.** Waiting for Godot **7.** The Return of the Native **8.** Norway **9.** Sir Stanley Spencer **10.** Paul Gauguin **11.** Tolstoy **12.** Fay Weldon **13.** Tom Clancy **14.** Ruth Rendell **15.** Filth.

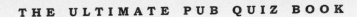

GENERAL KNOWLEDGE

1. What do the initials a.s.a.p. mean?

2. A hebdomad is a group of how many?

3. P.O. Box 369, Jebb Avenue, London is the address of which institution?

4. According to the Koran, what instrument will Israfil play on the Day of Judgment?

5. In which year did Bolivia join the U.N.?

6. Who wrote the poem *The Yarn of the Nancy Bell*?

7. In which year was the Battle of the Little Big Horn?

8. What is the major religion in Malaysia?

9. In which year was the Battle of Gettysburg?

10. What was the original name of political activist Malcolm X?

11. What sort of creature is a brolga?

12. How many universities make up the Ivy League group of the U.S.?

13. In which year did Arizona join the Union?

14. In which year did King Farouk I of Egypt abdicate?

15. What is the name given to a leading dancer of a corps de ballet?

ANSWERS 1. as soon as possible 2. Seven 3. Brixton prison 4. Trumpet 5. 1945 6. W.S. Gilbert 7. 1876 8. Muslim 9. 1836 10. Malcolm Little 11. A bird - it's a type of crane 12. Eight 13. 1912 14. 1952 15. Coryphée.

THE ULTIMATE PUB QUIZ BOOK

ENTERTAINMENT

1. Which actor played *Arthur of the Britons* in the 1970s T.V. series?

2. Which comedian played *Mr. Bean*?

3. Which actor/singer played Wayne in the drama *Auf Wiedersehen, Pet*?

4. In which children's show did Professor Yaffle appear?

5. Who played Inspector Wexford in *The Ruth Rendell Mysteries* on television?

6. Which comedienne's catchphrase was "She knows you know"?

7. Which philosophy graduate and ex-trapeze artist appeared in the 1960 film *The Magnificent Seven*?

8. Who played the killer in the 1954 film *Rear Window*?

9. Who played *Edward Scissorhands*?

10. Who played Sonny in the 1972 film *The Godfather*?

11. Who played police chief Rheinlander Waldo in the 1981 film *Ragtime*?

12. Who played *Alfie* in the 1966 film?

13. Who was described by Frank Muir as "the thinking man's crumpet"?

14. Which children's show featured the catch phrase "Hold the Bus!"?

15. Cheese and Egg and Heavy Breathing were characters in which sitcom?

ANSWERS 1. Oliver Tobias **2.** Rowan Atkinson **3.** Gary Holton **4.** Bagpuss **5.** George Baker **6.** Hylda Baker **7.** Yul Brynner **8.** Raymond Burr **9.** Johnny Depp **10.** James Caan **11.** James Cagney **12.** Michael Caine **13.** Joan Bakewell **14.** The Banana Splits **15.** The Dustbinmen.

SPORT

1. Which world welterweight boxing champion was born on St. Thomas in the U.S. Virgin Islands in 1938?

2. Who won cycling's Giro d'Italia in 1996?

3. Who won the 1995 & '97 IAAF World Championships women's 800m title?

4. Who won the 1994 women's hockey World Cup?

5. Which country were the 1997 ice hockey world champions?

6. Who was world 500cc motor cycling champion from 1990-92?

7. At what weight did Thomas Hearns win his first world boxing title in 1980?

8. Which U.S. runner won the women's 1500m & 3000m titles at the 1983 IAAF World Championships?

9. Who became world junior lightweight boxing champion in 1931?

10. Which jockey won the 1960 & '63 1,000 Guineas?

11. Who won rugby union's Swalec Cup in 1998?

12. Who was Welsh amateur snooker champion in 1975?

13. Which Australian bowler took 44 wickets in the 1935/36 Test series against South Africa?

14. Who became world lightweight boxing champion in 1942?

15. Which horse won the 1996 Grand National?

ANSWERS 1. Emile Griffith **2.** Pavel Tonkov **3.** Ana Quirot **4.** Australia **5.** Canada **6.** Wayne Rainey **7.** Welterweight **8.** Mary Decker **9.** Kid Chocolate **10.** Roger Poincelet **11.** Llanelli **12.** Terry Griffiths **13.** Clarrie Grimmett **14.** Beau Jack **15.** Rough Quest.

POP MUSIC

1. Which U.S. group had a minor hit in 1995 with *Free, Gay and Happy*?

2. Which group recorded the album *Odyshape*?

3. Which group had a 1997 Top Five single with *Flash*?

4. Which singer recorded the 1983 album *Legendary Hearts*?

5. Which group recorded the 1990 album *Goo*?

6. Which rap singer appeared in the film *Tank Girl* as a kangaroo?

7. Which city were the band The Human League from?

8. What was blues singer Chester Arthur Burnett better known as?

9. Which U.S. group had a 1995 hit single with *'74-'75*?

10. Which group's debut chart single was *This is a Call* in 1995?

11. What was the 1998 Top Five hit for The Beastie Boys?

12. Who had a U.K. and U.S. No. 1 single in 1995 with *Gangsta's Paradise*?

13. Which group promoted themselves as 'The Fourth Best Band in Hull'?

14. *Shine On* was the debut single, in 1987, of which band?

15. Which group's debut album was *The Right to be Italian*?

GEOGRAPHY

1. Which ancient city of Italy, at the mouth of the River Tiber, was once the port of Rome?

2. On which river does Nottingham stand?

3. Which strait separates the Isle of Anglesey from mainland Wales?

4. In which U.S. state is the iron and steel town of Bessemer?

5. Which Asian republic's chief rivers are the Helm and Kabul?

6. In which Australian state is Alice Springs?

7. Which dog is the largest state in Mexico?

8. Ennis is the county town of which county of the Republic of Ireland?

9. What is the French name for the English Channel?

10. In which country is the cheese-producing region of Emmental?

11. What is the highest mountain of Japan?

12. As what is Lake Tiberias better known?

13. Amman is the capital of which Asian kingdom?

14. In which European country is the River Lek?

15. Which island of New York contains the borough of Brooklyn?

GENERAL KNOWLEDGE

1. In which U.S. state is Cape Canaveral?

2. What would a machine called a Fourdrinier make?

3. Which town in Somerset is the reputed burial place of King Arthur?

4. In which English county is Maiden Castle?

5. In which year was the Barebones Parliament?

6. In which year did Roman empress Messalina die?

7. Which animal is *Mephitis mephitis*?

8. In which year was the Brecon Beacons designated a National Park?

9. Who wrote the 1963 novel *The Presidential Papers*?

10. Whose sculptures include the floor piece *Equivalents*?

11. Who makes the doll *Coppélia* in the ballet of the same name?

12. In which year was the artist R.B. Kitaj born?

13. In which city is the HQ of the International Red Cross?

14. In which year did conductor Sir John Barbirolli die?

15. Who wrote *The A.B.C. Murders*?

THE ULTIMATE PUB QUIZ BOOK

ENTERTAINMENT

1. Which comic actor's pen-name was Gerald Wiley?

2. In which western series did Chinese cook Hop Sing appear?

3. Who played Rocky Cassidy in the T.V. drama *Boon*?

4. Who played Rodrigo Borgia in the 1981 drama series *The Borgias*?

5. Which French actress starred in the 1964 film *Father Goose*?

6. Who played Mia Farrow's husband in the film *Rosemary's Baby*?

7. Which singer won a Best Actress Oscar for the film *Moonstruck*?

8. Who played a skinhead in the 1983 T.V. film *Made in Britain*?

9. In which town was actor John Cleese born?

10. Who was seriously injured in a car accident while making the 1957 film *Raintree Country*?

11. Who played *Hamlet* in the 1990 Franco Zeffirelli film?

12. Who played detective Charlie Barlow in *Z Cars*?

13. Which former panellist on *What's My Line* committed suicide in 1980?

14. Who played T.V.'s *The Baron*?

15. Which actress from *Coronation Street* played the title role in the film *Carry On Cleo*?

ANSWERS 1. Ronnie Barker **2.** Bonanza **3.** Neil Morrissey **4.** Adolfo Celi **5.** Leslie Caron **6.** John Cassavetes **7.** Cher **8.** Tim Roth **9.** Weston-super-Mare **10.** Montgomery Clift **11.** Mel Gibson **12.** Stratford Johns **13.** Lady Isabel Barnett **14.** Steve Forrest **15.** Amanda Barrie.

THE ULTIMATE PUB QUIZ BOOK

SPORT

1. What is Barcelona midfielder Fernando Macedo da Silva known as?

2. In which Lancashire town was Australian rugby league player Bozo Fulton born?

3. Which Australian cricketer, who died in 1929, batted in every position in the order in his Test career?

4. Who trained 1956 Epsom Derby-winning horse Lavandin?

5. In which city was Superbowl XXIX played in 1995?

6. Who was world individual freshwater angling champion in 1980 & '83?

7. In which year did Newcastle United win their first Division 1 football title?

8. Which jockey's first win in the Prix de l'Arc de Triomphe was on Bot Mot III in 1966?

9. Which country did Hassiba Boulmerka, 1995 IAAF World Championship women's 1500m winner, represent?

10. Who won the 1997 Nat West Trophy in cricket?

11. Which Sussex cricketer is known as Baba Oily?

12. Which cricketer captained Sussex from 1973-7?

13. Which rider won the 1998 world individual three-day event championship?

14. Who scored the winning goal in West Ham United's 1980 F.A. Cup Final victory?

15. Who became world junior welterweight boxing champion in 1959?

POP MUSIC

1. Which group had a 1997 Top 40 Christmas hit with *I Want an Alien for Christmas*?

2. Which irony-laden group had hits in 1996 with *Rotterdam* and *Don't Marry Her*?

3. Which singer had a 1992 hit with *Feed my Frankenstein*?

4. Which female singer featured on D.J. Milano's 1998 hit *Santa Maria*?

5. Which veteran singing group had a 1997 Top Five single with *Alone*?

6. Which singer had a minor hit in 1996 with *I Come From Another Planet Baby*?

7. Which singer had a 1995 Top Five hit with *Total Eclipse of the Heart*?

8. Niki Sullivan, Jerry J.J. Allison and Joe B. Maudlin comprised which band?

9. In which city was Jimi Hendrix born?

10. *(We Don't Need This) Fascist Groove Thang* was which group's debut single?

11. In which city was Isaac Hayes born?

12. In which year did Hawkwind release their debut L.P.?

13. Which member of the Beatles released the 1981 solo L.P. *Somewhere in England*?

14. Which singer/songwriter penned *When An Old Cricketer Leaves the Crease*?

15. Who wrote the song *If I Were a Carpenter*?

ANSWERS 1. Fountains of Wayne **2.** The Beautiful South **3.** Alice Cooper **4.** Samantha Fox **5.** The Bee Gees **6.** Julian Cope **7.** Nicki French **8.** The Crickets **9.** Seattle **10.** Heaven 17 **11.** Memphis **12.** 1970 **13.** George Harrison **14.** Roy Harper **15.** Tim Hardin.

HISTORY

1. In which year did the European Union replace the European Community?

2. In which year did Diana, Princess of Wales, die?

3. In which county is Chartwell, former home of Sir Winston Churchill?

4. Which princess was the only daughter of King George IV and Caroline of Brunswick?

5. In which year did Parliamentarians capture and sack Corfe Castle, Dorset?

6. What was Spanish soldier Rodrigo Diaz de Vivar better known as?

7. From which city did Sir Francis Chichester begin and end his solo circumnavigation of the world?

8. Which Chinese statesman wrote the book *Summing Up At Seventy* in 1957?

9. In which month of 1944 were the Germans expelled from Dieppe?

10. Who became Conservative M.P. for Oldham in 1900?

11. Which famous climber was the first to ascend the volcano Chimborazo in Ecuador in 1880?

12. In which city was David Lloyd George born in 1863?

13. In which year was the world's worst nuclear power accident, at Chernobyl?

14. Of which country was Porfirio Diaz president from 1884-1911?

15. In which year did the Ivory Coast officially become the Côte d'Ivoire?

ANSWERS 1. 1993 2. 1997 3. Kent 4. Charlotte 5. 1645 6. El Cid Campeador 7. Plymouth 8. Chiang Kai-Shek 9. September 10. Winston Churchill 11. Edward Whymper 12. Manchester 13. 1986 14. Mexico 15. 1986.

GENERAL KNOWLEDGE

1. What is an adder's-mouth?

2. In which country was comedian Spike Milligan born?

3. What is the ninth letter in the Greek alphabet?

4. On which island is the deemster one of the two justices?

5. What is the psychological term for an irresistible urge to steal?

6. What was the forename of Russian composer Stravinsky?

7. Cape Delgado is a headland in which African country?

8. How many balls are used in a golf foursome?

9. In which year was the magazine *Private Eye* founded?

10. Which French composer's works include *Quartet for the End of Time*?

11. Who was the 1986 world professional snooker champion?

12. Who wrote the 1958 novel *The Bell*?

13. Which U.S. state is nicknamed 'The Heart of Dixie'?

14. Which bride of Jason in Greek mythology was murdered on her wedding day by Medea?

15. In which Shakespeare play does Puck appear?

ENTERTAINMENT

1. Who created the puppet fox Basil Brush?

2. Who played the title role in the British sitcom *Dear John*?

3. Who played Egghead in the T.V. series *Batman*?

4. Who did Geoffrey Bayldon play in the children's show *Worzel Gummidge*?

5. Who did Pamela Anderson play in *Baywatch*?

6. Who played barber Desmond in the sitcom *Desmond's*?

7. In which city was Sean Connery born?

8. Which western hero did Gary Cooper play in *The Plainsman*?

9. Which two actors starred in the 1960s T.V. show *I Spy*?

10. Who appeared uncredited as a drunken coroner in the film *Touch of Evil*?

11. *Mommie Dearest* is a biography of which film actress?

12. In which city was director David Cronenberg born?

13. Who did Bing Crosby play in the 1944 film *Going My Way*?

14. Which late newsreader's father invented the googly in cricket?

15. Who played the title role in T.V.'s *Father Dowling Investigates*?

ANSWERS 1. Ivan Owen 2. Ralph Bates 3. Vincent Price 4. The Crowman
5. C.J. Parker 6. Norman Beaton 7. Edinburgh 8. Wild Bill Hickok 9. Bill
Cosby & Robert Culp 10. Joseph Cotten 11. Joan Crawford 12. Toronto 13.
Father O'Malley 14. Reginald Bosanquet 15. Tom Bosley.

SPORT

1. What did football's Milk Cup become in 1987?

2. Who was the USPGA golf champion in 1996?

3. Which horse won the 1996 Epsom Derby?

4. For which London Premier League club does Joe Cole play?

5. Which cricketer, known as 'the Black Bradman' became the first black to captain West Indies?

6. For which English speedway team did Ove Fundin spend most of his career competing?

7. Who scored twice for West Germany in the 1954 World Cup Final?

8. In which year did Everton win their first Division 1 football title?

9. Which ice hockey star is known as 'the Great One'?

10. Who became world welterweight boxing champion in 1898?

11. Who won the inaugural women's 5,000m title at the 1995 IAAF World Championships?

12. Who won the 1997 County Cricket championship?

13. Which country won the Federation Cup in tennis in 1998?

14. Which runner won the 1982 Commonwealth Games men's 1,500m title?

15. Which woman swimmer won the 1956 Olympic 400m freestyle title?

ANSWERS 1. Littlewoods Cup 2. Mark Brooks 3. Shaamit 4. West Ham United 5. George Headley 6. Norwich 7. Helmut Rahn 8. 1891 9. Wayne Gretzky 10. Mysterious Billy Smith 11. Sonia O'Sullivan 12. Glamorgan 13. Spain 14. Steve Cram 15. Lorraine Crapp.

POP MUSIC

1. Which male singer had a 1996 hit with *Devil's Haircut*?

2. Which Irish group's first chart single was *Runaway* in 1996?

3. Which group charted in 1996 with *Scooby Snacks*?

4. Which Jamaican singer had a 1998 Top Ten single with *Who Am I*?

5. On which record label do group Belle and Sebastian record?

6. Which group had a 1997 Top 20 hit with *Fired Up!*?

7. Who had a 1996 chart entry with *My Unknown Love*?

8. Which group had a Top 40 hit in 1997 with the song *Mum's Gone to Iceland*?

9. Which group had a 1997 Top 20 hit with the song *We Have Explosive*?

10. What was Bentley Rhythm Aces's 1997 Top 20 single?

11. Whose debut L.P. in 1987 was entitled *Squirrel and G-Man Twenty Four Hour Party People Plastic Face Carnt Smile (White Out)*?

12. Who was lead singer with the group Van Der Graaf Generator?

13. *Back in the D.H.S.S.* was the debut L.P. of which group?

14. William Bailey is the real name of which rock singer?

15. Dave Ball and Richard Norris comprise which electronic duo?

ANSWERS 1. Beck **2.** The Corrs **3.** Fun Lovin' Criminals **4.** Beenie Man **5.** Jeepster **6.** Funky Green Dogs **7.** Count Indigo **8.** Bennet **9.** Future Sound of London **10.** Bentley's Gonna Sort You Out **11.** Happy Mondays **12.** Peter Hammill **13.** Half Man Half Biscuit **14.** Axl Rose **15.** The Grid.

WORDS

1. What would you do with a salmi - eat it or ride it?

2. What in Ireland was the 'Hanging Gale'?

3. Which word meaning a toady do we derive from the Greek phrase 'fig-blabbers'?

4. What would you do with a sarrusophone - play it or say it?

5. What is to 'slick off'?

6. To which part of the body does the adjective sural apply?

7. What would you do with an ocarina?

8. What, architecturally, is an 'oeil-de-boeuf'?

9. What was a sutler?

10. Which finger is the 'ear-finger'?

11. How long, in feet, is Gunter's Chain?

12. What bird is also known as a plantain-eater?

13. Where were the nymphs known as hamadryads supposed to live?

14. What does pps stand for at the end of a letter?

15. What is the name of the Japanese dish consisting of small rice cakes topped with fish?

ANSWERS 1. Eat it - it's a ragout of game **2.** The custom of taking 6 months' grace in the payment of rent **3.** Sycophant **4.** Play it **5.** To finish a job in hand without stopping **6.** The calf of the leg **7.** Play it - it's a musical instrument **8.** A circular window **9.** A merchant who accompanied an army in order to sell provisions **10.** The little finger **11.** Sixty-six **12.** A touraco **13.** Forest-trees **14.** Post postscriptum **15.** Sushi.

THE ULTIMATE PUB QUIZ BOOK

GENERAL KNOWLEDGE

1. Who wrote the 1967 novel *The Fixer*?

2. In which James Bond film did Art Malik play an Afghan freedom fighter?

3. What is the value of the black ball in snooker?

4. From which team did Aston Villa buy footballer Dion Dublin?

5. What is harmonica player Larry Adler's middle name?

6. What fruit is used to make the brandy framboise?

7. In which year did Patricia, wife of former president Nixon, die?

8. In which year was the first human heart transplant?

9. In which year was president Ford shot at by Sara Jane Moore?

10. The abbreviation gld stands for which unit of currency?

11. What is the standard monetary unit of Liechtenstein?

12. In which city is the Jewry Wall Museum?

13. What was Kinshasa formerly known as, until 1966?

14. Who was the faithful companion of Aeneas in the book *The Aeneid*?

15. Who was the Roman counterpart of the Greek goddess Demeter?

ANSWERS 1. Bernard Malamud 2. The Living Daylights 3. Seven points 4. Coventry City 5. Cecil 6. Raspberry 7. 1993 8. 1867 9. 1975 10. Guilder 11. Swiss franc 12. Leicester 13. Léopoldville 14. Achates 15. Ceres.

ENTERTAINMENT

1. Arnold Stang voiced which feline cartoon character?

2. Which northern comedian was born James Whittaker?

3. Television play *A Magnum For Schneider* was the pilot for which spy series?

4. In which year did entertainer Roy Castle die?

5. "It's good, but it's not right" - whose catchphrase?

6. Who did Richard Chamberlain play in *The Thorn Birds*?

7. Who played Godber in the sitcom *Porridge*?

8. Who wrote the T.V. drama *The Beiderbecke Affair*?

9. Which naturalist was television's *The Botanic Man*?

10. Who was the female lead in the 1983 comedy film *Trading Places*?

11. Who played William Randolph Hearst in the 1985 T.V. film *The Hearst and Davies Affair*?

12. Who played Elizabeth I in the 1939 film *The Private Lives of Elizabeth and Essex*?

13. Which politician did Peter Finch play in the 1976 film *Raid on Entebbe*?

14. Who played the lead in the 1970 film *Scrooge*?

15. Which pop star did Laurence Fishburne play in the 1993 film *What's Love Got To Do With It*?

SPORT

1. What is cricketer Gordon Greenidge's first name?

2. In which county was U.K. water skier Mike Hazelwood born?

3. By what score did Brazil win on penalties in the 1994 World Cup Final?

4. Who won cycling's Giro d'Italia in 1997?

5. How many points did Preston North End accumulate in winning the inaugural Division 1 title in 1888/89?

6. Who won the 1994 men's hockey World Cup?

7. Which Leeds United player scored in the 1970 F.A. Cup Final and replay?

8. Who was world 500 c.c. motor cycling champion from 1994-98?

9. Which horse won the 1997 Grand National?

10. Who won the county championship in rugby union in 1957?

11. Which country won the 1978 Davis Cup?

12. Which world champion speedway rider died in 1963 at the age of 29?

13. Which country were the 1998 ice hockey world champions?

14. Who became world middleweight boxing champion in 1911?

15. Who won the 1991 IAAF World Championships women's 10,000m title?

ANSWERS 1. Cuthbert 2. Lincolnshire 3. 3-2 4. Ivan Gotti 5. 40 6. Pakistan 7. Mick Jones 8. Michael Doohan 9. Lord Gyllene 10. Devon 11. Sweden 12. Peter Craven 13. Sweden 14. Cyclone Thompson 15. Liz McColgan.

POP MUSIC

1. What was Billie's second No. 1 hit single?

2. Which act had a 1998 summer Top Five hit with the song *Carnaval de Paris*?

3. From which European country do the chart act Course come?

4. Which group had a 1996 hit with *The Secret Vampire Soundtrack E.P.*?

5. Which Icelandic singer had a 1996 Top Ten hit with *Hyperballad*?

6. Which U.S. singer's only U.K. hit was *It's Better To Have (and Don't Need)*?

7. Which group had a minor 1997 hit with *Native New Yorker*?

8. Who got to No. 1 in 1996 with *Ooh Aah...Just a Little Bit*?

9. Which soul singer's album *Call Me* ended with the track *Jesus is Waiting*?

10. In which year did The Grateful Dead member Pigpen die?

11. Which group had a 1973 hit single with *Radar Love*?

12. Which group released the 1977 live album *Playing the Fool*?

13. Which group formed at Charterhouse public school in 1975?

14. Who was frontman with the group The Boomtown Rats?

15. Who released the 1971 album *What's Going On*?

SCIENCE

1. What type of rock is slate - igneous, metamorphic or sedimentary?

2. Who wrote 1871's *The Descent of Man and Selection in Relation to Sex*?

3. What is the stalk of a leaf also known as?

4. In which year did Humphry Davy die?

5. What is the most common colour of the mineral garnet?

6. Which is larger in area - the Black Sea or the Red Sea?

7. Which French mathematician's last words were reputedly "so my soul, a time for parting"?

8. In which city was German physicist Max Planck born?

9. Which fruit's scientific name is *Citrus limon?*

10. What nationality was physicist Christian Doppler?

11. Which element's symbol is O?

12. What is the chemical in plants that gives them their green colour?

13. Which 19c Swedish scientist pioneered the science of spectroscopy?

14. What nationality was chemist Theodor Svedberg?

15. Which scientist's autobiography was *I Am a Mathematician - the Later Life of a Prodigy*?

ANSWERS 1. Metamorphic **2.** Charles Darwin **3.** The petiole **4.** 1829 **5.** Red **6.** Black Sea **7.** René Descartes **8.** Kiel **9.** Lemon **10.** Austrian **11.** Oxygen **12.** Chlorophyll **13.** Anders Angstrom **14.** Swedish **15.** Norbert Wiener.

GENERAL KNOWLEDGE

1. In which year did television presenter Magnus Pyke die?

2. What did Thomas Carlyle refer to as 'The Dismal Science'?

3. Who wrote the novel *Rich Man, Poor Man*?

4. How old was politician Barry Goldwater when he died in 1998?

5. Who was Foreign Secretary 1919-24?

6. In which sport might you use the Conibear style?

7. Who wrote the 1867 poem *Dover Beach*?

8. In which U.S. state is Cape Cod?

9. Of which country was Süleyman Demirel prime minister from 1965-71?

10. What is the nationality of author Janet Frame?

11. In which year did baritone Tito Gobbi die?

12. In what sport do men compete for the Iroquois Cup?

13. Which actress was known as 'The Divine Sarah'?

14. In which year did Albanian statesman Enver Hoxha die?

15. Which actress starred as Suzette in the 1986 film *Absolute Beginners*?

ANSWERS 1. 1992 2. Economics 3. Irwin Shaw 4. 89 5. Lord Curzon 6. Rowing 7. Matthew Arnold 8. Massachusetts 9. Turkey 10. New Zealander 11. 1984 12. Lacrosse 13. Sarah Bernhardt 14. 1985 15. Patsy Kensit.

ENTERTAINMENT

1. In which city was actress Jeanette MacDonald born?

2. Who directed the film *Desperately Seeking Susan*?

3. Which Oscar-winning actor was born in Kirriemuir, Scotland, in 1910?

4. Who played Archie Lee Meighan in the 1956 film *Baby Doll*?

5. Who played Prince John in the 1938 film *The Adventures of Robin Hood*?

6. Who created the animated T.V. series *Crystal Tipps and Alistair*?

7. Which actor bought the film rights to Anne Tyler's book *The Accidental Tourist*?

8. Who played Cliff Barnes in the T.V. show *Dallas*?

9. In which city was actor Nick Nolte born?

10. Which film director played Alan Brady in *The Dick Van Dyke Show*?

11. Which actress was in love with a monkey in the film *Max, Mon Amour*?

12. Who directed the 1961 film *El Cid*?

13. Who played WPC Liz Harris in *Dixon of Dock Green*?

14. In which country was actor Basil Rathbone born?

15. Who played Anne-Marie Wade in *Crossroads*?

SPORT

1. With which team did American football star Forrest Gregg finish his playing career in 1971?

2. Who in the 1947/48 series against Australia became the first Indian cricketer to hit centuries in each innings of a Test?

3. Who scored twice for France in their 1998 World Cup Final victory?

4. Which football team won four out of five Football League titles from 1895-1900?

5. Who scored Liverpool's consolation goal in the 1971 F.A. Cup Final?

6. Which rugby league club did Andy Gregory join in 1979?

7. Who became world light heavyweight boxing champion in 1916?

8. What was the nationality of 1933 Wimbledon men's singles tennis champion Jack Crawford?

9. In which city was U.S. golfer Ben Crenshaw born?

10. Which Australian rugby league centre was nicknamed 'The Crow'?

11. Who took over the captaincy of the New Zealand Test cricket team in 1990?

12. Who captained Holland in the 1974 football World Cup Final?

13. What was the nickname of American baseball star Sam Crawford?

14. What nationality was Olympic athlete Joaquim Cruz?

15. In billiards, what is Whitechapel?

ANSWERS 1. Dallas Cowboys **2.** Vijay Hazare **3.** Zidane **4.** Aston Villa **5.** Steve Heighway **6.** Widnes **7.** Battling Levinsky **8.** Australian **9.** Austin, Texas **10.** Michael Cronin **11.** Martin Crowe **12.** Johan Cruyff **13.** Wahoo Sam **14.** Brazilian **15.** The act of potting one's opponent's white ball.

POP MUSIC

1. Which Irish group had hits in 1994 with *Zombie* and *Linger*?

2. Which group had a 1996 Top Ten single with *Fat Neck*?

3. On which Bob Dylan studio album does the song *Idiot Wind* appear?

4. Which songwriter's works include *Amsterdam*, *Jojo* and *Orly*?

5. Which singer had a 1997 hit with *Midnight in Chelsea*?

6. Hudson, Manuel, Helm, Danko and Robertson comprised which band?

7. Who recorded the 1985 album *Hounds of Love*?

8. Which vocalist featured on the 1996 hit *No Diggity* by Blackstreet?

9. Donald Fagen and Walter Becker were the songwriting team in which group?

10. Andersson, Faltskog, Lyngstad and Ulvaeus comprised which group?

11. Which male rapper had a 1997 No. 2 single with *I Shot the Sheriff*?

12. Who is lead singer with the group A.B.C.?

13. In which year did Bon Scott of AC/DC die following a drinking binge?

14. Which group had a minor hit in 1993 with *Stresss*?

15. *Dirk Wears White Sox* was the first L.P. from which group?

ANSWERS 1. The Cranberries 2. Black Grape 3. Blood on the Tracks 4. Jacques Brel 5. Jon Bon Jovi 6. The Band 7. Kate Bush 8. Dr. Dre 9. Steely Dan 10. Abba 11. Warren G 12. Martin Fry 13. 1980 14. Blaggers I.T.A. 15. Adam and the Ants.

PEOPLE

1. What is the name of Camilla Parker Bowles's son, who was involved in a 1999 drug scandal?

2. Which politician wrote the 1880 novel *Endymion*?

3. Tejan Kabbah is president of which African country?

4. Which star of the sitcom *Diff'rent Strokes* died in May 1999 of a drug overdose?

5. Which Labour M.P. opened the National Assembly in Cardiff in 1999?

6. Who wrote the 1999 novel *Score!*?

7. Who resigned from the cabinet in December 1998 over a mortgage loan?

8. Which child's death landed nanny Louise Woodward in court in 1998?

9. British yachtsman Glynn Charles was killed during which race in December 1998?

10. Which comedian turned actor starred in the film *Enemy of the State*?

11. Which economist wrote the book *The Crisis of Global Capitalism*?

12. Who played Marion in the 1998 remake of the film *Psycho*?

13. In which country is Jean-Claude 'Baby Doc' Duvalier of Haiti living?

14. Which U.S. radio talk-show host planned Nixon's Watergate break-in?

15. What was the name of the British foster parents who went on the run in January 1999?

GENERAL KNOWLEDGE

1. On which part of the body might you wear a glengarry?

2. What does an isobath connect on a map?

3. In which city is the University of East Anglia?

4. Who composed the opera *Serse*?

5. Who produced the *Carry On* series of films?

6. Who directed the 1963 film *Dr. Strangelove*?

7. In which European country is the port of Västeras?

8. Which West Yorkshire town was the birthplace of Harold Wilson?

9. What was the forename of General Franco?

10. What was the nickname of Holy Roman Emperor Frederick I?

11. To which creature does the adjective ovine refer?

12. What game is referred to as 'aerial pingpong' by Australians?

13. To what genus of trees does the ash belong?

14. Which Dorset resort features in the novel *Persuasion*?

15. Deneb is the brightest star in which constellation?

ANSWERS 1. The head - it's a hat 2. Points of equal underwater depth 3. Norwich 4. Handel 5. Peter Rogers 6. Stanley Kubrick 7. Sweden 8. Huddersfield 9. Francisco 10. Barbarossa 11. Sheep 12. Australian Rules Football 13. Fraxinus 14. Lyme Regis 15. Cygnus.

THE ULTIMATE PUB QUIZ BOOK

ENTERTAINMENT

1. Which actor played Lt. Tom Keefer in the film *The Caine Mutiny*?

2. Which actress married film director Goffredo Alessandrini in 1934?

3. Who played Gabrielle Dragon in the sitcom *George and the Dragon*?

4. Who played the witch wishing to be mortal in the 1957 film *Bell, Book and Candle*?

5. Who played the Contessa di Contini in the T.V. series *The Protectors*?

6. In which U.S. city was actress Dorothy Malone born?

7. Who played the title role of a weapons salesman in the 1971 T.V. series *Hine*?

8. Who played the gangster *Dillinger* in the 1974 film?

9. Who played Commander Adama in the T.V. show *Battlestar Galactica*?

10. To which actress was Alexander Korda married from 1939-45?

11. Who played boxing promoter Eddie Burt in the T.V. drama *Winners and Losers*?

12. Who played Sid Vicious in the 1985 film *Sid and Nancy*?

13. Who was concert chairman on the T.V. show *The Wheeltappers' and Shunters' Social Club*?

14. Who directed the 1954 film *Johnny Guitar*?

15. Which actress was born Vera Jayne Palmer?

THE ULTIMATE PUB QUIZ BOOK

SPORT

1. What are the names of the tennis-playing Williams sisters?

2. By what margin did New Zealand beat Australia in their 1999 Group B World Cup cricket game?

3. Which Huddersfield Town player broke Bradford City player Gordon Watson's leg, resulting in £900,000 damages in a 1999 court decision?

4. For which rugby union club side did Kyran Bracken and George Chuter play in 1999?

5. Who did Leeds rugby union club appoint as successor to coach Graham Murray in 1999?

6. What nationality is cyclist Romans Vainsteins?

7. Who did Watford beat in the 1999 First Division play-off semi-finals?

8. What was tennis player Shirley Fry's first major singles title, in 1951?

9. For which Italian football club did Jimmy Greaves play in 1961?

10. With which team did basketball player Spencer Haywood finish his career?

11. In which city was Superbowl XXVIII played in 1994?

12. In which year did Sandy Lyle win the British Open title?

13. How many international rugby union caps did Willie John McBride get?

14. In which port was runner Liz McColgan born?

15. Which horse was the only Epsom Derby winner of jockey Gordon Richards?

ANSWERS 1. Venus and Serena 2. Five wickets 3. Kevin Gray 4. Saracens 5. Dean Lance 6. Latvian 7. Birmingham 8. French 9. A.C. Milan 10. Los Angeles Lakers 11. Atlanta 12. 1985 13. 80 14. Dundee 15. Pinza.

POP MUSIC

1. Which female vocalist had a 1997 Top Ten single with *Everything*?

2. Which group had a minor hit in 1990 with *The Sex of It*?

3. From which European country does singer Gala come?

4. Which group's Top Ten singles include *Stupid Girl* and *Push It*?

5. Which punk group recorded the song *Gary Gilmore's Eyes*?

6. Which rock singer was born Steven Talarico?

7. Who had a 1992 single with *The Days of Pearly Spencer*?

8. Which female singer recorded the 1996 album *Boys for Pele*?

9. Who was bass player in the group The Animals?

10. On which island was singer Joan Armatrading born?

11. Whose solo albums include 1970's *The Madcap Laughs*?

12. What did Paul McCartney announce on April 10, 1970?

13. Which group's second album was called *Choke*?

14. Who had a hit single in 1967 with *Hi-Ho Silver Lining*?

15. Wilson, Wilson, Pierson, Strickland and Schneider made up which band?

ANSWERS 1. Mary J. Blige **2.** Kid Creole and the Coconuts **3.** Italy **4.** Garbage **5.** The Adverts **6.** Steve Tyler **7.** Marc Almond **8.** Tori Amos **9.** Chas Chandler **10.** St. Kitts **11.** Syd Barrett **12.** The break-up of the Beatles **13.** The Beautiful South **14.** Jeff Beck **15.** The B-52's.

THE ULTIMATE PUB QUIZ BOOK

ART AND LITERATURE

1. Which artist won the 1989 Turner Prize?

2. In which century did the Venetian painter Tintoretto live?

3. What is the art technique of serigraphy better known as?

4. Whose novels include *Jack Maggs* and *Illywhacker*?

5. Which former M.P. wrote the novel *She's Leaving Home*?

6. Who wrote the thriller novel *Drink With the Devil*?

7. Gussie Fink-Nottle and Aunt Agatha are whose comic creations?

8. Which English author's books include *The Loved One* and *Decline and Fall*?

9. 'The Early Married Life of the Morels' is the opening chapter in which novel?

10. What is the dog called in the book *Three Men in a Boat*?

11. In which novel did Hannibal Lecter appear prior to *The Silence of the Lambs*?

12. Which detective writer's stories include *The Big Knockover*?

13. What were the works of painters Michael Andrews, Ron Kitaj, Frank Auerbach, Lucien Freud, Francis Bacon and Leon Kossoff collectively exhibited as in 1987?

14. In which year did the Tate gallery open in Millbank, London?

15. What was E.M. Forster's first novel?

ANSWERS 1. Richard Long **2.** 16th **3.** Silk-screen printing **4.** Peter Carey **5.** Edwina Currie **6.** Jack Higgins **7.** P.G. Wodehouse **8.** Evelyn Waugh **9.** Sons and Lovers, by D.H. Lawrence **10.** Montmorency **11.** Red Dragon **12.** Dashiell Hammett **13.** School of London **14.** 1897 **15.** Where Angels Fear to Tread.

GENERAL KNOWLEDGE

1. In which year did Thatcherite politician Nicholas Ridley die?

2. Who was director of the Covent Garden Opera from 1969-71?

3. What is the plant *Campanula trachelium* better known as?

4. Which city in Mexico is capital of Jalisco state?

5. Which was the first Magnox reactor to open in the U.K. in 1956?

6. Which horse is associated with film actor Roy Rogers?

7. Which unit of area is equal to 2.471 acres?

8. Which husband and wife couple starred in the 1992 film *Far and Away*?

9. What was showman P.T. Barnum's first name?

10. Who composed the 1787 work *Eine Kleine Nachtmusik*?

11. What is the alter ego of the comic book character Batman?

12. Which American consumer rights activist wrote *Unsafe at Any Speed*?

13. What was the name of the most important of the seven hills of Rome?

14. What is the colour of the early-blooming flowers of the plant glory-of-the-snow?

15. Hamal is the brightest star of which zodiacal constellation?

ANSWERS 1. 1993 2. Sir Peter Hall 3. Bats-in-the-belfry 4. Guadalajara 5. Calder Hall 6. Trigger 7. A hectare 8. Tom Cruise & Nicole Kidman 9. Phineas 10. Mozart 11. Bruce Wayne 12. Ralph Nader 13. Capitoline 14. Blue 15. Aries.

THE ULTIMATE PUB QUIZ BOOK

ENTERTAINMENT

1. In which year did the T.V. show *The South Bank Show* begin?

2. Who did Ronald Reagan play in the 1940 film *Knute Rockne, All American*?

3. Who did Peter Hill play in *Crossroads*?

4. Who played Bubber Reeves in the 1966 film *The Chase*?

5. In which year did actor Fredric March die?

6. Who played Archie Rice in the 1960 film *The Entertainer*?

7. Who played Bobby Ewing in *Dallas*?

8. In which city was Sir Michael Redgrave born?

9. Who directed the 1955 film *Lola Montès*?

10. Who did Robert Vaughn play in the series *The Protectors*?

11. Who directed the 1982 film *My Favourite Year*?

12. In which year did the T.V. show *Songs of Praise* start?

13. In which city was actor Al Pacino born?

14. Who wrote the sitcom *Some Mothers Do 'Ave 'Em*?

15. Who is the mother of actress Vanessa Redgrave?

SPORT

1. Which British Open golf champion was born in Goldsboro, North Carolina?

2. Briton Chloe Cowan is a light-heavyweight at which sport?

3. Scottish rugby union player James McLaren plays for which French club?

4. Which U.S. boxer was nicknamed 'The Human Windmill'?

5. Which Durham cricketer is known as 'Dr. Chaplaw'?

6. Who was the world individual freshwater angling champion from 1996-98?

7. Janina Kurkowska was world individual champion at which sport from 1931-4?

8. Out of 129 javelin competitions between 1970-80 how many did Ruth Fuchs win?

9. Which Italian footballer scored a consolation goal in their 1970 World Cup Final defeat?

10. What did the Football League Cup become in 1982?

11. Who became undisputed world cruiserweight boxing champion in 1988?

12. Who won the 1998 Nat West Trophy in cricket?

13. Which cricketer was the second man, after W.G. Grace, to score 100 hundreds?

14. On which horse did Vaughan Jeffries win the 1994 world individual three-day event championship?

15. Who was the 1997 USPGA golf champion?

POP MUSIC

1. Which U.S. singer had a 1997 hit with *A Change Would Do You Good*?

2. Which group had a minor hit in 1996 with *Do Wah Diddy Diddy*?

3. Which food gave Laurent Garnier a minor hit in 1997?

4. Which group's hits include 1998's *Solomon Bites the Worm*?

5. Which group's hits include the 1994 single *Pineapple Head*?

6. Which group had a 1997 No. 1 hit with *Beetlebum*?

7. Which female singer had a 1997 Top Ten hit with the song *Do You Know*?

8. Which male singer had a 1995 hit with *Can I Touch You...There*?

9. Which reformed group had a 1998 hit with *I Just Wanna Be Loved*?

10. Which group had a 1995 hit with *Something for the Pain*?

11. What was Elbow Bones and the Racketeers' 1984 hit single?

12. Which group's highest singles chart entry was the 1996 song *For the Dead*?

13. Which member of the Clash formed Big Audio Dynamite?

14. Which member of the Skids formed Big Country?

15. John Disco, Manda Rin and Sci-Fi Steve comprise which band?

ANSWERS 1. Sheryl Crow **2.** Blue Melons **3.** Crispy Bacon **4.** The Bluetones **5.** Crowded House **6.** Blur **7.** Michelle Gayle **8.** Michael Bolton **9.** Culture Club **10.** Bon Jovi **11.** A Night in New York **12.** Gene **13.** Mick Jones **14.** Stuart Adamson **15.** Bis.

GEOGRAPHY

1. On which river is the French city of Metz?

2. The Salmon River of Idaho is only navigable downstream. What is it also known as?

3. In which European country is the port of Setubal?

4. Part of the boundary between which two U.S. states runs down the middle of the main street of Texarkana?

5. Taipei is the capital of which island in Asia?

6. In which county of the Republic of Ireland is the village of Shillelagh?

7. In which U.S. state is Lake Okeechobee?

8. On which river does Munich stand?

9. In which European country is the publishing centre of Lund?

10. On which river is the village of Beaulieu in Hampshire?

11. What is Bedloe's Island in New York harbour also known as?

12. Which is larger - Tasmania or Bahrain?

13. In which African country is the airport town of Entebbe?

14. In which U.S. state is the seaport of Galveston?

15. Bad Homburg is a spa city in which European country?

ANSWERS 1. Moselle 2. The River of No Return 3. Portugal 4. Texas and Arkansas 5. Taiwan 6. Wicklow 7. Florida 8. Isar 9. Sweden 10. River Beaulieu 11. Liberty Island 12. Tasmania 13. Uganda 14. Texas 15. Germany.

GENERAL KNOWLEDGE

1. How many people partake in a game of mahjong?

2. Who wrote the novel *A Small Town in Germany*?

3. What would you do with a barong?

4. What profession would be followed by a FRCVS?

5. In which European country is the town of Fribourg?

6. Who was American vice president 1969-73?

7. What type of fruit is a Doyenne du Comice?

8. According to the Bible, at what age did Methuselah father Lamech?

9. Which unit of measurement was originally defined as one ten-millionth of the distance from the Equator to the North Pole?

10. In which African country is the market town of Yola?

11. How many galleries are there in the Metropolitan Museum of Art?

12. In which year was the Yom Kippur War?

13. What is the standard monetary unit of Afghanistan?

14. How old was travel writer Dame Freya Stark when she died?

15. In which year did John Hinckley Jnr. shoot Ronald Reagan?

ENTERTAINMENT

1. Which singer/actor was born Dino Paul Crocetti?

2. Who was the announcer on the sitcom *Soap*?

3. In which country was actress Lilli Palmer born?

4. Who played P.C. Henry Snow in the T.V. drama *Softly, Softly*?

5. Who played Mary Bailey in the 1946 film *It's a Wonderful Life*?

6. Who directed the 1990 film *Awakenings*?

7. Who wrote the 1992 sitcom *Sitting Pretty*?

8. Who directed the 1987 film *The Princess Bride*?

9. In which Marx Brothers' film does Groucho say "Love flies out the door when money comes innuendo"?

10. Who directed the 1985 film *Revolution*?

11. Who played Nicola Marlow in the T.V. drama *The Singing Detective*?

12. In which European country was film director Karel Reisz born?

13. In which city was actor George Sanders born?

14. In which year did actor Lee Marvin die?

15. Who directed the 1983 film *Carmen*?

SPORT

1. What was the nickname of American football star Joe Greene?

2. Which England footballer's international career was ended by a car crash in 1962?

3. Who won the 1998 County Cricket championship?

4. Who won the 1998 women's hockey World Cup?

5. Which horse won the 1997 Epsom Derby?

6. Who won cycling's Giro d'Italia in 1998?

7. Who became world heavyweight boxing champion in 1905?

8. Which two Italian teams contested the 1998 UEFA Cup Final?

9. On which island was Viv Richards born?

10. In which year was Hana Mandlikova born?

11. Who won the women's javelin silver at the 1988 Olympics?

12. With what sport would you associate Alberto Tomba?

13. Who did Roberto Duran defeat in his 100th professional fight?

14. Who won the 1993 Johnnie Walker World Championship in golf?

15. Which three teams were in the Republic of Ireland's group in the 1994 World Cup?

ANSWERS 1. Mean Joe 2. Johnny Haynes 3. Leicestershire 4. Australia 5. Benny the Dip 6. Marco Pantani 7. Marvin Hart 8. Internazionale and Lazio 9. Antigua 10. 1962 11. Fatima Whitbread 12. Skiing 13. Tony Menefee 14. Larry Mize 15. Mexico, Norway and Italy.

POP MUSIC

1. Which group's last Top Ten single in the 1990s was *Friday I'm In Love*?

2. Which vocalist featured on the 1994 hit by Bono *In the Name of the Father*?

3. Which U.S. rapper charted in 1997 with *All That I Got Is You*?

4. Which group charted in 1996 with the single *C'mon Kids*?

5. Which indie group had a 1998 Top 40 hit with *Whippin' Piccadilly*?

6. Which group had a Top Ten hit in 1995 with *Shoot Me With Your Love*?

7. Which group had a minor hit in 1964 with *Get Your Feet Out Of My Shoes*?

8. Which indie group had minor hits with *Sweet Johnny* and *Patio Song*?

9. Which male singer had a hit in 1996 with *Hallo Spaceboy*?

10. From which country does rapper Da Hool hail?

11. Which French group had a 1997 hit single with *Around the World*?

12. Which male vocal group had Top Ten hits in 1997 with *Love Guaranteed* and *Wonderful Tonight*?

13. What was the third album by the group Blood, Sweat and Tears?

14. Which band's 1975 live album was called *On Your Feet Or On Your Knees*?

15. What did the band Seymour change their name to for their first single *She's So High*?

HISTORY

1. Who became prime minister of Australia in 1932?

2. In which year did Columbus set sail on his third voyage to the New World?

3. Which historic house is known as the 'Palace of the Peak'?

4. In which year did a German air-raid destroy the 15c Coventry cathedral church?

5. In which century did French philosopher Denis Diderot live?

6. As what was Charles Martel, leader of the Franks, known?

7. In which country was left-wing revolutionary Rosa Luxemburg born?

8. Who was prime minister of Canada from 1957-63?

9. Which U.S. soldier commanded the 42nd (Rainbow) Division in France in World War I?

10. At what age was Bernadette Devlin elected to the House of Commons?

11. In which year was the Battle of Dien Bien Phu?

12. Hearth-money was a 17c tax on which part of a house?

13. In which year was the Diet of Worms at which Martin Luther was asked to recant?

14. Who, in 1921, became Canada's first woman M.P.?

15. Bernardo O'Higgins was president of which country from 1818-23?

GENERAL KNOWLEDGE

1. What type of creature is a Gloucester Old Spot?

2. What is the standard monetary unit of Malawi?

3. In which city is the Lady Lever Art Gallery?

4. Who won the Jerwood prize for painting in September 1997?

5. What is the brightest star in the constellation Lepus?

6. Sir Edmund Barton was the first prime minister of which country?

7. Which was the Underworld 'river of Woe' in Greek mythology?

8. In which year was the Battle of Buena Vista?

9. In which country is the Cariboo, a former gold mining region?

10. On which river is the New York city of Yonkers?

11. What is the dominant religion of Mexico?

12. Which two colours are the sponge sections of a Battenburg cake?

13. From which tree would you get St. John's bread?

14. What branch of physics is abbreviated as MHD?

15. In the phrase a YOP scheme, what did YOP stand for?

ANSWERS 1. Pig 2. Kwachi 3. Liverpool 4. Gary Hume 5. Alpha Leporis 6. Australia 7. Acheron 8. 1847 9. Canada 10. Hudson 11. Roman Catholicism 12. Yellow and pink 13. Carob 14. Magnetohydrodynamics 15. Youth Opportunities Programme.

ENTERTAINMENT

1. Who directed the 1989 film *Mississippi Burning*?

2. In which city was Susan Sarandon born?

3. Who played Joe Orton in the film *Prick Up Your Ears*?

4. Who played Grushenka in the 1957 film *The Brothers Karamazov*?

5. In which Italian city was Pier Paolo Pasolini born?

6. Who played nightclub manager Danny Kane in the T.V. drama *The Paradise Club*?

7. Which U.S. actress was born in Quincy, Massachusetts in 1935?

8. Who played Nicola Freeman in the soap *Crossroads*?

9. Who directed the Marx Brothers in *A Night at the Opera* and *A Day at the Races*?

10. Who played Holly Harwood in *Dallas*?

11. Who directed the 1965 comedy thriller film *Mirage*?

12. In which year did Westward TV come into being?

13. Who directed the 1984 film *City Heat*?

14. Who played Paul Buchet in the T.V. series *The Protectors*?

15. In which year did actor Anthony Perkins die?

THE ULTIMATE PUB QUIZ BOOK

SPORT

1. From which country did World Cup footballer Teofilio Cubillas hail?

2. At which field event did Ludvik Danek win Olympic gold in 1972?

3. On which horse did Bruce Davidson win the 1974 individual world three-day event championship?

4. Who is the only man to have held the world billiards and snooker titles at the same time?

5. Who was the captain of the 1959 British Lions rugby union tour of Australasia?

6. What nationality was world singles badminton champion Flemming Delfs?

7. In which country was motor racing driver Ralph De Palma born?

8. Which former rugby union star became South Africa's ambassador to London in 1979?

9. Which Indian hockey centre-forward won three Olympic golds from 1928-36?

10. Which Brazilian footballer managed the 1970 Peruvian World Cup team?

11. What were the forenames of the D'Inzeo brothers in equestrianism?

12. For which baseball team did Bobby Doerr play his entire career?

13. Was New Zealand Test cricketer Martin Donnelly left-handed or right-handed?

14. On which island was West Indies cricketer Jeffrey Dujon born?

15. Which tennis player won the junior singles titles at all four Grand Slam tournaments in 1983?

POP MUSIC

1. Which vocal group charted in 1997 with the song *4 Seasons of Loneliness*?

2. Which female vocalist's hits include the 1995 Top Five single *Not Over Yet*?

3. Which Israeli's debut chart single was 1998's *Diva*?

4. What was Boyzone's first No. 1 single?

5. Which U.S. singer charted in 1995 with a version of *Big Yellow Taxi*?

6. Which rock guitarist's real name is Saul Hudson?

7. What was the 1997 Top Ten single by the Brand New Heavies?

8. Which band had a 1998 hit with *Not If You Were The Last Junkie On Earth*?

9. Which female singer had a 1998 hit with the single *Have You Ever?*?

10. Which Spandau Ballet member had a 1992 solo hit with *Lost in Your Love*?

11. Which male singer had a minor hit in 1995 with the song *Vibrator*?

12. Tim Simenon is the brains behind which dance group?

13. Which Bon Jovi studio album included *You Give Love a Bad Name*?

14. In which city were the Boo Radleys formed?

15. What is the nickname of soul music bass player Donald Dunn?

ANSWERS 1. Boyz II Men **2.** Grace **3.** Dana International **4.** Words **5.** Amy Grant **6.** Slash **7.** You've Got a Friend **8.** The Dandy Warhols **9.** Brandy **10.** Tony Hadley **11.** Terence Trent D'Arby **12.** Bomb the Bass **13.** Slippery When Wet **14.** Liverpool **15.** Duck.

WORDS

1. What would you do with a sarangi?

2. What does the phrase 'ecce homo' mean?

3. What were Switzers?

4. What would you do with a surrey - ride in it or drink it?

5. What method of transport is a PSV?

6. What is an oenophile?

7. What is the 23rd letter of the Greek alphabet?

8. How many are there in an ogdoad?

9. What is a 'lyke-wake'?

10. What in ancient Rome was a scutum?

11. Why might being hit with a 'salt eel' hurt?

12. To what creature does the adjective lupine refer?

13. What sort of creature is a longspur?

14. What is the U.S. name for a courgette?

15. A parka is a type of coat. What does the word mean in the Aleutian language?

ANSWERS 1. Play it 2. Behold the man 3. Swiss mercenaries 4. Ride in it 5. A public service vehicle 6. A lover of wines 7. Psi 8. Eight 9. A watch over a dead person 10. A large shield 11. It is the end of a rope 12. A wolf 13. A bird 14. Zucchini 15. Skin.

GENERAL KNOWLEDGE

1. In which constellation is the star Denebola?

2. In time keeping what do the initials GMT stand for?

3. In which city is De Montfort University?

4. In which month is the Up-Helly-Aa festival held in the town of Lerwick?

5. Of what is Michelangelo's sculpture *David* of 1501-4 made?

6. Which two liquids combine to make a 'Dog's Nose'?

7. Which is the only Great Lake of North America to be wholly within the USA?

8. What is the standard monetary unit of Japan?

9. Who in Greek mythology granted King Midas's wish that everything he touched be turned into gold?

10. Which German-born architect designed the Seagram Building in New York?

11. What is a yate?

12. Which Scottish philosopher wrote 1861's *Utilitarianism*?

13. Who wrote the play *A View from the Bridge*?

14. What is the 14th letter in the Greek alphabet?

15. In which year did bandleader Glenn Miller disappear over the English Channel?

ENTERTAINMENT

1. In which Yorkshire town was James Mason born?

2. Who directed the 1971 film *Sunday, Bloody Sunday*?

3. Which director's last film was *The Osterman Weekend*?

4. Who directed the 1979 film *American Gigolo*?

5. Who played Elvira in the 1983 film *Scarface*?

6. In which country was Arnold Schwarzenegger born?

7. Who scripted the 1966 film *The Quiller Memorandum*?

8. Who directed the 1993 film *Falling Down*?

9. In which town was actress Miranda Richardson born?

10. What does the initial C stand for in the name of actor George C. Scott?

11. In which country was actor Walter Pidgeon born?

12. Who directed the 1991 film *Thelma and Louise*?

13. In which Yorkshire town was film director Tony Richardson born?

14. In which city was actor Raymond Massey born?

15. In which year did actress Jean Seberg die?

SPORT

1. In which city was figure skater John Curry born?

2. Hurry On was the first Classic winner for which racehorse trainer?

3. In which year was Welsh rugby union star Gerald Davies born?

4. At which sport was New-York born John Davis an Olympic champion?

5. Which U.S. jockey won 8 out of 9 races at Arlington on August 13, 1989?

6. Which cyclist won the 1988 Tour de France?

7. Which U.S. jockey won the 1992 Eclipse Award after winning over $14m?

8. Which New Zealand women's squash player won the British Open from 1984-90?

9. At what sport did Klaus Dibiasi win three Olympic titles from 1968-76?

10. What was the nickname of Olympic hurdles champion Harrison Dillard?

11. For which three international teams did footballer Alfredo Di Stefano play?

12. Which brothers won the Wimbledon men's doubles title from 1897-1905?

13. In which year was Olympic athlete Heike Drechsler born?

14. Which male high jumper won the 1956 Olympic title?

15. In which year was jockey Pat Eddery born?

ANSWERS 1. Birmingham 2. Fred Darling 3. 1945 4. Weightlifting 5. Pat Day 6. Pedro Delgado 7. Kent Desormeaux 8. Susan Devoy 9. Highboard diving 10. Bones 11. Spain, Colombia and Argentina 12. Reggie and Laurie Doherty 13. 1964 14. Charles Dumas 15. 1952.

POP MUSIC

1. Which T.V. comedy actors had a 1963 hit single with *At the Palace (Parts 1 & 2)*?

2. Who charted in 1996 with the single *Un-break My Heart*?

3. Which indie group had a minor hit in 1998 with *Candlefire*?

4. Which vocalist had a Top 20 hit in 1998 with *Sexy Cinderella*?

5. Which new country singer had a hit single in 1994 with *Standing Outside the Fire*?

6. Which Irish singer charted in 1995 with the single *The Snows of New York*?

7. Which former member of The Specials charted in 1997 with the single *Ballad of a Landlord*?

8. Which U.S. singer had a 1997 Top Ten single with *Bitch*?

9. Which group had a debut No. 1 single in 1997 with *Mmmbop*?

10. In which year was singer Bobby Brown born?

11. Who was lead singer with the group A-Ha?

12. What is Boy George's real name?

13. In which town was Billy Bragg born?

14. Who was guitarist in the early 1970s band Kippington Lodge?

15. What was Bronski Beat's debut hit single?

ANSWERS 1. Wilfrid Brambell & Harry H. Corbett 2. Toni Braxton 3. Dawn of the Replicants 4. Lynden David Hall 5. Garth Brooks 6. Chris De Burgh 7. Terry Hall 8. Meredith Brooks 9. Hanson 10. 1969 11. Morten Harket 12. George O'Dowd 13. Barking 14. Brinsley Schwarz 15. Smalltown Boy.

SCIENCE

1. What nationality was physicist Giovanni Venturi?

2. How many vertices has a regular dodecahedron?

3. Why is it wrong to call a tsunami a tidal wave?

4. What do the initials CFC stand for with regard to greenhouse gases?

5. What is the name given to the branch of biology concerned with the classification of organisms?

6. Which is larger in area - the Mediterranean Sea or the Caribbean Sea?

7. What nationality was Jules Bordet, winner of the 1919 Nobel prize for medicine?

8. In which city was the 1992 UNCED conference held, that resulted in Agenda 21?

9. How many °C is 100°F?

10. What element composes approximately 28.5% of the Earth?

11. In which year did inventor Alexander Graham Bell die?

12. Which English chemist wrote 1871's *Select Methods of Chemical Analysis*?

13. Which fruit's scientific name is *Ananas comosus*?

14. What type of rock is shale - igneous, metamorphic, or sedimentary?

15. Which country has the longest coastline?

GENERAL KNOWLEDGE

1. In which year did TV presenter Jess Yates die?

2. In which country is the Ala Dag mountain range?

3. Which politician was the 1st Earl of Stockton?

4. Which murderer was released by Pilate in preference to Jesus?

5. What is the third largest state of the U.S. after Alaska and Texas?

6. What was the middle name of novelist Henry Miller?

7. Which poet wrote the 1637 masque *Comus*?

8. After which war did the Finns surrender the Karelian Isthmus to Russia?

9. In which year was the voluntary organization MIND founded?

10. Gannet Peak is the highest peak of which U.S. mountain range?

11. Which jazz composer's works include *The Black Saint and the Sinner Lady*?

12. Who wrote the novel *Gone With the Wind*?

13. In which year did actor Robert Mitchum die?

14. What is the German name for Bavaria?

15. In which South American country is the port of Cartagena?

ENTERTAINMENT

1. What was Steve McQueen's first name?

2. Who created the T.V. show *The Wheeltappers' and Shunters' Social Club*?

3. Who played Griffin Mill in the 1992 film *The Player*?

4. In which city was actor Omar Sharif born?

5. In which European capital city was Edward G. Robinson born?

6. Which French director made the 1967 film *Le Samourai*?

7. Who played Dr. Gibbon in the T.V. drama *The Singing Detective*?

8. Who directed the 1990 film *Pretty Woman*?

9. Who played undercover cop Mick Raynor in the T.V. drama *99-1*?

10. Which actor's real name is Joe Yule Jr.?

11. Who played Tom Howard in the series *Howard's Way*?

12. Who played Shughie McFee in the soap *Crossroads*?

13. For which actor did Maxwell Anderson write the play *Winterset*?

14. Who played Don Lockwood in *Dallas*?

15. Which actress played Trina in the 1925 film *Greed*?

SPORT

1. Which female swimmer won the 1948 Olympic 400m title?

2. What nationality is Olympic swimming champion Tamas Darnyi?

3. Who was the 1970 Commonwealth Games men's long jump champion?

4. In which year was snooker player Steve Davis born?

5. In which year was skater Christopher Dean born?

6. At which field sport was Luis Delis a Pan-American champion?

7. At what age did U.S. swimmer Donna de Varona compete in the 1960 Olympics?

8. In which city was England cricketer Ted Dexter born?

9. Which football player broke O.J. Simpson's record for rushing yards gained in a season in 1984?

10. Which baseball player was known as 'The Little Professor'?

11. Who coached the Chicago Bears from 1982-93?

12. In which country was cricketer Basil D'Oliveira born?

13. In 1950, Czech-born tennis player Jaroslav Drobny took out citizenship of which country?

14. Which jockey rode West Tip to victory in the 1986 Grand National?

15. In which year was jockey Paul Eddery born?

POP MUSIC

1. Which Australian entertainer had a minor 1996 hit with *Bohemian Rhapsody*?

2. Which U.K. vocalist had a 1998 Top Five single with *My Star*?

3. Lorraine McIntosh was the angelic vocalist with which Scottish chart band?

4. Which female singer had Top 20 hits in 1998 with *You Think You Own Me* and *I Wanna Be Your Lady*?

5. Which comedian had a minor hit in 1996 with *Rockin' Good Christmas*?

6. What was singer Lola's only singles chart success, in 1987?

7. Which group recorded the album *Secret Watchers Built the World*?

8. From which European country did 1998 chart act Los Umberellos come?

9. Which male vocalist had a 1970 solo hit with *My Woman's Man*?

10. Which female vocal duo featured on Suggs's 1996 hit *Cecilia*?

11. What was singer Louise's first solo Top Ten hit single?

12. Who had a hit in 1980 with *Funkin' for Jamaica (N.Y.)*?

13. From which European country does singer Hondy come?

14. Which vocal group had a 1997 Top 20 hit with *5 Miles to Empty*?

15. Which soul singer was born in Barnwell, South Carolina on May 3, 1933?

ANSWERS 1. Rolf Harris **2.** Ian Brown **3.** Deacon Blue **4.** Hinda Hicks **5.** Roy 'Chubby' Brown **6.** Wax the Van **7.** Mazey Fade **8.** Denmark **9.** Dave Dee **10.** Louchie Lou and Michie One **11.** Light of My Life **12.** Tom Browne **13.** Italy **14.** Brownstone **15.** James Brown.

PEOPLE

1. What is the name of Robin Cook's ex-wife, author of *A Slight and Delicate Creature*?

2. How much, in dollars, did Bill Clinton pay to Paula Jones to settle the sexual harassment case against him?

3. Who played *Little Voice* in the 1999 film?

4. Which politician wrote the novel *The Eleventh Commandment*?

5. Which actor starred in, and directed, the film *Bulworth*?

6. Who is the Governor of the Bank of England?

7. Which U.S. chat show host starred in the 1999 film *Beloved*?

8. Melanie Blatt is a singer with which vocal group?

9. Which *Coronation Street* actor died in February 1999 in Shipley?

10. The king of Jordan died in Febraury 1999. What was his name?

11. Who wrote the 1999 novel *Glamorama*?

12. Which comedian is the brains behind the Radio 1 show *Blue Jam*?

13. Which singer won the Best Single and Best Video awards at the 1999 Brits?

14. What were the forenames of the three outlaw Younger Brothers?

15. What was U.S. traitor Iva Toguri d'Aquino better known as?

GENERAL KNOWLEDGE

1. What are the two official languages of the island of Madagascar?

2. To which genus does the mint plant belong?

3. What nationality was mathematician August Ferdinand Möbius?

4. What is the international car registration for Barbados?

5. What is the German name for Vienna?

6. In which year was the Mir space station put into earth orbit?

7. Whittret is a dialect word for which male animal?

8. Which Japanese writer's best known work is the four-volume *The Sea of Fertility*?

9. What is the collective noun for a flock of snipe?

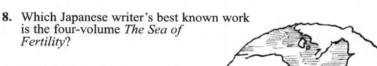

10. Why is the wrybill plover so called?

11. Which European kingdom's islands include Falster and Bornholm?

12. What was the middle name of U.S. poet Robert Frost?

13. In the world of finance, what do the letters GNP stand for?

14. In which year did actor Sir Donald Wolfit die?

15. In which year was the Wolfenden Report, which recommended the legalization of homosexual relations between consenting adults?

ANSWERS 1. French and Malagasy 2. Mentha 3. German 4. BDS 5. Wien 6. 1986 7. Weasel 8. Yukio Mishima 9. Wisp 10. It's bill is deflected to one side 11. Denmark 12. Lee 13. Gross National Product 14. 1968 15. 1957.

ENTERTAINMENT

1. In which year did Anglia Television come into being?

2. Who directed the 1980 film *Nijinsky*?

3. In which city was Sidney Poitier born?

4. Who played Reverend Stephen Young in the T.V. comedy *Our Man at St. Marks*?

5. Who played Lord Toranaga in the 1982 T.V. drama *Shogun*?

6. Which actress starred in the 1992 film *Bitter Moon* and married its director Roman Polanski?

7. Who did Warners call the 'Oomph Girl'?

8. Who wrote the 1968 T.V. play *A Beast with Two Backs*?

9. In which city was actress Bette Midler born?

10. In which country was actress Simone Signoret born?

11. Who played Ophelia in the 1948 film *Hamlet*?

12. Who directed the 1991 film *Whore*?

13. Who played comedian Joe E. Lewis in the 1957 film *The Joker is Wild*?

14. Who played Lou Lewis in the drama series *Shine on Harvey Moon*?

15. Who played the crippled lawyer in the 1948 film *The Lady from Shanghai*?

ANSWERS 1. 1959 **2.** Herbert Ross **3.** Miami **4.** Donald Sinden **5.** Toshiro Mifune **6.** Emmanuelle Seigner **7.** Ann Sheridan **8.** Dennis Potter **9.** Honolulu **10.** Germany **11.** Jean Simmons **12.** Ken Russell **13.** Frank Sinatra **14.** Nigel Planer **15.** Everett Sloane.

SPORT

1. For what fee did Kenny Dalglish join Liverpool from Celtic in 1977?

2. In which year was New Zealand rugby union star Andy Dalton born?

3. From which team did Dixie Dean join Everton in 1925?

4. Who was 1982 & '86 Commonwealth Games men's marathon champion?

5. For which football league team did Jimmy Dickinson play his entire career from 1943-65?

6. What was unusual about the first five horses in the 1983 Cheltenham Gold Cup?

7. Which Olympic swimmer in 1926 became the first woman to swim the English Channel?

8. Who was Middlesex cricket captain from 1953-57?

9. Who won the 1993 European Open in snooker?

10. Who was runner-up in the 1993 Johnnie Walker World Golf championship?

11. Which club signed David Rocastle from Leeds United?

12. When was Charlie Smirke's first Classic success as a jockey?

13. Who was the 1985 English flat race champion jockey?

14. Which country has hosted the Summer Olympics most times?

15. Was Australian cricketer Neil Harvey left-handed or right-handed?

ANSWERS 1. £440,000 **2.** 1951 **3.** Tranmere Rovers **4.** Rob de Castella **5.** Portsmouth **6.** They were all trained by Michael Dickinson **7.** Trudy Ederle **8.** Bill Edrich **9.** Stephen Hendry **10.** Fred Couples **11.** Manchester City **12.** 1934 **13.** Steve Cauthen **14.** U.S.A. **15.** Left-handed.

POP MUSIC

1. What was Dave Dee, Dozy, Beaky, Mick and Tich's only U.K. No. 1?

2. Which vocal group had a Top Ten single in 1998 with *Finally Found*?

3. What is singer Michael Bolton's real name?

4. Which group had Top Ten success in 1997 with *You Showed Me*?

5. Which singer recorded the album *Highway 61 Revisited* in 1967?

6. Which duo had a 1993 Top 40 single with *Gloria*?

7. Which band recorded the 1997 album *Victory Parts*?

8. Which singer recorded the album *Come A Time* in 1978?

9. McGuinn, Clark, Clarke, Crosby & Hillman comprised which band in 1964?

10. Which group had 1998 chart success with *A Nanny in Manhattan*?

11. Which country artist recorded the album of covers entitled *Step Inside This House*?

12. Which Dumbarton-born rock star was lead singer with theband Talking Heads?

13. Which group recorded the album *Possum Trot Plan*?

14. Which female singer had a 1994 Top 40 hit with *Skip to my Lu*?

15. Which singer featured on Malcolm McLaren's 1991 hit *Magic's Back (Theme from The Ghosts of Oxford Street)*?

ART AND LITERATURE

1. Who wrote the novel *The Devil Rides Out*?

2. What is the subtitle of the play *Twelfth Night*?

3. Who wrote the novel *Westward Ho!*?

4. Which artist won the 1995 Turner Prize?

5. Which comedian wrote the 1991 novel *The Liar*?

6. Who wrote the children's book *The Owl Service*?

7. In which 1932 comic novel did Great Aunt Ada Doom appear?

8. Which artist worked from 1795 until his death on drawings concerning the comparative anatomy of *Man, Tiger, and Fowl*?

9. What is the name given to the bottom layer of a painting, such as the canvas?

10. Which painter's subjects included Winston Churchill in 1954 and Somerset Maugham in 1949?

11. Who wrote *Captain Corelli's Mandolin*?

12. What was the title of William Golding's novel about a shipwrecked group of schoolboys?

13. Whose autobiography was *Goodbye to All That*?

14. Who wrote *Jude the Obscure*?

15. "Hale knew they meant to murder him before he had been in Brighton three hours." The opening lines to which novel?

GENERAL KNOWLEDGE

1. In which year was singer Madonna born?

2. What were the forenames of businessman F.W. Woolworth?

3. Which female Canadian singer recorded the album *Mingus*?

4. On which river is the German city of Worms?

5. What in the armed forces does the abbreviation WRNS stand for?

6. In which year was the siege of the Alamo?

7. On which sea is the port of Derbent, which was founded in the 6c?

8. What was the name of the month of fruit in the French Revolutionary calendar?

9. What is a gobo to a singer?

10. In which year was Swedish premier Olaf Palme shot?

11. What is the standard monetary unit of Nauru?

12. In which S. England city is the Pitt Rivers Museum?

13. Who wrote the novel *Across the River and into the Trees*?

14. Who created Doctor Dolittle?

15. Which city was capital of the British East Africa Protectorate from 1888 until 1907?

ANSWERS 1. 1958 2. Frank Winfield 3. Joni Mitchell 4. Rhine 5. Women's Royal Naval Service 6. 1836 7. Caspian Sea 8. Fructidor 9. A shield put around a microphone to exclude unwanted sounds 10. 1986 11. Australian dollar 12. Oxford 13. Ernest Hemingway 14. Hugh Lofting 15. Mombasa.

ENTERTAINMENT

1. Which actress played Vera in the 1963 film *The Servant*?

2. Who played Jesus in the 1969 T.V. play *Son of Man*?

3. Who played Elliott Ness in the 1959 film *The Scarface Mob*?

4. Who played *Baby Face Nelson* in the 1957 film?

5. Which Tarzan was the first husband of actress Vera Miles?

6. In which city was Sylvester Stallone born?

7. Who directed the 1988 film *Track 29*?

8. Who directed the 1984 film *Paris, Texas*?

9. Who played Jan Howard in the T.V. drama *Howard's Way*?

10. What is actor Rod Steiger's middle name?

11. Who played characters based on murderers Leopold and Loeb in the 1959 film *Compulsion*?

12. In which city was director Oliver Stone born?

13. Who played Jim Morrison in the 1991 film *The Doors*?

14. Who played Christopher Cobb in the 1960s western series *Whiplash*?

15. Who played Clifford Leyton in the soap *Crossroads*?

ANSWERS 1. Sarah Miles **2.** Colin Blakely **3.** Robert Stack **4.** Mickey Rooney **5.** Gordon Scott **6.** New York **7.** Nicolas Roeg **8.** Wim Wenders **9.** Jan Harvey **10.** Stephen **11.** Bradford Dillman and Dean Stockwell **12.** New York **13.** Val Kilmer **14.** Peter Graves **15.** Johnny Briggs.

SPORT

1. At which sport did Sadaharu Oh become famous?

2. Who was National Hunt champion jockey from 1949-52?

3. At which circuit was Niki Lauda badly burned in 1976?

4. For which Italian football team did Denis Law play?

5. In which county was England Test cricketer John Edrich born?

6. At what age did Duncan Edwards die following the Munich air disaster in 1958?

7. Who was president of the I.O.C. from 1946-52?

8. Who was captain of the French rugby union side that toured South Africa in 1971?

9. Which U.S. Olympic 110m hurdles champion competed at the 1980 Winter Olympics in the bobsled event?

10. What nationality was world judo champion Brigitte Deydier?

11. Which Poland and Manchester City footballer died in a road accident in 1989?

12. At what age did Gareth Edwards win his first rugby union cap for Wales?

13. At which rugby league club did Joseph Egan become player-coach in 1950?

14. In which year did Joe DiMaggio marry Marilyn Monroe?

15. Who captained France's rugby union team on their 1984 tour of New Zealand?

ANSWERS 1. Baseball 2. Tim Molony 3. Nürburgring 4. Torino 5. Norfolk 6. 21 7. Sigfrid Edström 8. Benoit Dauga 9. Willie Davenport 10. French 11. Kazimierz Deyna 12. 19 13. Leigh 14. 1954 15. Philippe Dintrans.

POP MUSIC

1. Which act had a 1995 Top Five hit with *The Bomb! (These Sounds Fall into My Mind)*?

2. Which band recorded the 1975 album *The Snow Goose*, based on a story by Paul Gallico?

3. Which group recorded the album *Straightaways*?

4. What was Part Four of *The Mole Trilogy* by the Residents?

5. Which band recorded the 1978 album *Candy-O*?

6. Which group had a 1995 No. 1 single with a re-mix of their 1994 hit *Dreamer*?

7. In which year did the New York Dolls release their debut L.P.?

8. Which guitarist recorded the 1989 album *Workbook*?

9. Which Australian singer wrote the novel *And the Ass Saw the Angel*?

10. Which group recorded the album *Electribal Memories*?

11. Tom Rowlands and Ed Simmons make up which electronic duo?

12. Which group's last Top Ten hit, in 1986, was *New Beginning (Mamba Seyra)*?

13. Henry Priestman was the only non-brother in which Liverpool-based 1980s group?

14. Which male singer had a 1997 Top Ten hit with *Phenomenon*?

15. Who recorded the album *Hymns to the Silence*?

GEOGRAPHY

1. On which island of Asia is the resort of Kandy?

2. On which river is the Yugoslavian town of Leskovac?

3. On which sea is the Italian seaport of Leghorn?

4. In which African country is the seaport of Sfax?

5. On which Mediterranean island is the resort town of Sliema?

6. Trim is the county town of which county of the Republic of Ireland?

7. Which river forms most of the boundary between Devon and Cornwall?

8. On which island of Asia is the seaport of Surabaya?

9. Which city is the capital of Costa Rica?

10. Which U.S. state houses the towns of Toledo, Akron, and Dayton?

11. Which is larger - Norway or Finland?

12. In which country is the seaport of Murmansk?

13. In which country of S.W. Asia is the seaport of Abadan?

14. On which river is the Indian city of Agra?

15. What is the capital of Turkey?

ANSWERS 1. Sri Lanka 2. River Morava 3. Ligurian Sea 4. Tunisia 5. Malta 6. Meath 7. Tamar 8. Java 9. San José 10. Ohio 11. Finland 12. Russia 13. Iran 14. Jumna 15. Ankara.

GENERAL KNOWLEDGE

1. In which constellation is the star Bellatrix?

2. What was the country of Lesotho founded as in 1832?

3. Which explorer discovered the St. Lawrence River in Canada?

4. What is the dominant religion of Monaco?

5. Which World War II leader was supposed to have hoarded the 'Treasure of Dongo'?

6. Frederick Whitaker was prime minister of which country from 1882-83?

7. What sort of bird is a whimbrel?

8. Who was first president of independent Algeria?

9. What does the abbreviation ft-lb mean?

10. Mullingar is the county town of which Irish county?

11. What is the dominant religion of Nigeria?

12. In which century did Lady Godiva ride naked through the streets of Coventry?

13. What is the chief export of the island territory of Niue in the South Pacific?

14. Which two designers shared Designer of the Year award in 1997 at the British Fashion Awards?

15. In which city is the University of Central Lancashire?

ENTERTAINMENT

1. Who wrote the 1979 play *Blue Remembered Hills*?

2. In which city was actress Liza Minnelli born?

3. In which year did film director Michael Powell die?

4. Who played Stephanie Rogers in *Dallas*?

5. Who played Amanda Parker in the T.V. drama *Howard's Way*?

6. Who played Nora Charles in the 1934 film *The Thin Man*?

7. In which year was Alan Whicker born?

8. Which comedy actress played Mrs. Crispin in the sitcom *Hugh and I*?

9. Who played 'Geordie' Watson in the drama *When the Boat Comes In*?

10. In which city was actor Tyrone Power born?

11. Who played Catherine Martell in the T.V. drama *Twin Peaks*?

12. Who played Maisie the barmaid in the 1965 T.V. comedy drama *The Flying Swan*?

13. Who played Nurse Mills in the T.V. drama *The Singing Detective*?

14. Who played Veronica in *Shine on Harvey Moon*?

15. Who directed the 1945 film *Yolanda and the Thief*?

ANSWERS 1. Dennis Potter **2.** Los Angeles **3.** 1990 **4.** Lesley-Anne Down **5.** Francesca Gonshaw **6.** Myrna Loy **7.** 1925 **8.** Mollie Sugden **9.** Ian Cullen **10.** Cincinnati **11.** Piper Laurie **12.** Nerys Hughes **13.** Joanne Whalley **14.** Pauline Quirke **15.** Vincente Minnelli.

SPORT

1. Which male athlete won the 1956 & '60 Olympic 400m hurdles title?

2. For which international side did New Zealand-born rugby union player Greg Davis play from 1963?

3. What nationality was Olympic swimming champion Victor Davis, who died in 1989?

4. Which Welsh rugby union player was appointed captain of the Lions tour of New Zealand in 1971?

5. Which world heavyweight boxing champion started his career as 'Kid Blackie'?

6. Which New Zealand batsman was Leicestershire cricket captain from 1936-8?

7. For which baseball team did Larry Doby play the majority of his career?

8. At what Olympic sport did tennis champion Lottie Dod win a medal in 1908?

9. What was the nickname of French rugby union player Amedee Domenech?

10. Who won the 1947 World Snooker Championship?

11. Who did Roberto Duran defeat to take the world lightweight boxing title in 1972?

12. What was the nickname of Australian Rules football star Jack Dyer?

13. What nationality was cyclist Oscar Egg?

14. At what sport was Ilona Elek an Olympic champion?

15. Which Australian rugby union player captained the side on the 1982 tour of New Zealand?

ANSWERS 1. Glenn Davis **2.** Australia **3.** Canadian **4.** John Dawes **5.** Jack Dempsey **6.** Stewart Dempster **7.** Cleveland Indians **8.** Archery **9.** The Duke **10.** Walter Donaldson **11.** Ken Buchanan **12.** Captain Blood **13.** Swiss **14.** Fencing **15.** Mark Ella.

POP MUSIC

1. Baker, Clapton and Bruce - which band?

2. Which Sheffield gas fitter recorded the 1970 live album *Mad Dogs and Englishmen*?

3. With which 1970s pop band did Paul Avron Jeffreys, a victim of the Lockerbie air disaster, achieve fame?

4. Jennifer Warnes's 1987 album *Famous Blue Raincoat* was a collection of covers of which Canadian poet and songwriter's works?

5. Jimmy Somerville and Richard Coles - which duo?

6. Which soul singer was shot dead in Los Angeles in December 1964?

7. What is singer Alice Cooper's real name?

8. Who recorded the 1991 album *Peggy Suicide*?

9. Dolores O'Riordan is lead singer with which band?

10. Which Missouri-born singer's albums include 1993's *Tuesday Night Music Club*?

11. Smith, Tolhurst, Dempset - which punk band?

12. Which band did Eddie Jobson leave when he joined Roxy Music?

13. Who is the 'King of the Surf Guitar'?

14. In which city was Terence Trent D'Arby born?

15. Who was lead singer in the 1980s group Dead or Alive?

ANSWERS 1. Cream **2.** Joe Cocker **3.** Cockney Rebel **4.** Leonard Cohen **5.** The Communards **6.** Sam Cooke **7.** Vincent Furnier **8.** Julian Cope **9.** The Cranberries **10.** Sheryl Crow **11.** The Cure **12.** Curved Air **13.** Dick Dale **14.** New York **15.** Peter Burns.

HISTORY

1. In which year did Napoleon Bonaparte die?

2. What was Welsh dandy Beau Nash's forename?

3. Who was Emperor Nero's mother?

4. Which U.S. naval commander signed the Japanese surrender documents in 1945?

5. Which Irish political leader was known as 'the liberator'?

6. In which year was the Chelsea Flower Show first held?

7. Who became president of Argentina in 1988?

8. In which year was the Suez Canal opened?

9. In which year did Alcoholics Anonymous originate?

10. Who was king of France from 1610-43?

11. In which year did Baden-Powell form the Boy Scouts?

12. In which century did scientist and philosopher Roger Bacon live?

13. Which soldier took Valencia in 1094?

14. In which year was President Clinton's Balanced Budget Act?

15. In which year was William Rufus killed in the New Forest?

GENERAL KNOWLEDGE

1. Which group of radicals were led by John Lilburne, John Wildman and William Walwyn?

2. What was the name of the German Republic that existed from 1919 to Hitler's accession in 1933?

3. What Soviet secret police agency replaced the former OGPU in 1934?

4. What sort of bird is a noddy?

5. In which poem by Edward Lear does the "great Gromboolian plain" appear?

6. Who was elected Conservative M.P. for Worthing West in 1997?

7. In which year did cartoonist Michael Cummings die?

8. What did members of the South Pacific Commission agree to rename their organization in 1997?

9. Which actress was born Ruby Stevens?

10. How many strokes under par for a hole of golf is an albatross?

11. Which Scottish poet famously penned *The Tay Bridge Disaster*?

12. In which year was Sir Roger Casement executed for treason?

13. Which general's ghost haunts *Macbeth* in Shakespeare's play?

14. In which year was Siberian mystic Rasputin murdered?

15. What is former U.S. president Ronald Reagan's middle name?

ENTERTAINMENT

1. What is Gene Wilder's profession in the film *Bonnie and Clyde*?

2. In which cartoon series do the characters Chef and Cartman appear?

3. Who played the lead in the 1993 film *The Positively True Adventures of the Alleged Texas Cheerleader-Murdering Mom*?

4. Who played Caligula in the T.V. drama *I, Claudius*?

5. Who played Morticia in the 1991 film *The Addams Family*?

6. Who played Charles Ryder in the 1981 T.V. series *Brideshead Revisited*?

7. In which T.V. drama series did the characters Richard Barrett and Sharon McCready appear?

8. Which comedy writer wrote the sitcoms *Only When I Laugh* and *The Squirrels*?

9. What was David Doyle's character name in *Charlie's Angels*?

10. In which comedy show did the character Ernie Pantusso appear?

11. On which island was Errol Flynn born?

12. Which cowboy did Henry Fonda play in the 1946 film *My Darling Clementine*?

13. Which comic strip character did Jane Fonda play in a 1968 film?

14. In which city was actor Glenn Ford born?

15. In which city was actor Harrison Ford born?

ANSWERS 1. Undertaker **2.** South Park **3.** Holly Hunter **4.** John Hurt **5.** Angelica Huston **6.** Jeremy Irons **7.** The Champions **8.** Eric Chappell **9.** John Bosley **10.** Cheers **11.** Tasmania **12.** Wyatt Earp **13.** Barbarella **14.** Quebec **15.** Chicago.

SPORT

1. With which American football team did Carl Eller play his last two pro-seasons?

2. What time did Herb Elliott run in his 1960 Olympic 1500m win?

3. Paul Elvstrom won individual medals in the four Olympics from 1948-60. At what sport?

4. For which rugby league team did Keith Elwell play 239 consecutive games as hooker from 1977-82?

5. Who was Australian men's singles tennis champion from 1963-7?

6. Which decathlete did Olympic swimming champion Kornelia Ender marry following the collapse of her marriage to swimmer Roland Matthes?

7. Which sportswoman married Phil Christensen in 1990?

8. In what sport is the TEL machine used?

9. Who was the first black African to win an Olympic gold medal?

10. Who won the 1993 London men's marathon?

11. In which English county was Stanley Matthews born?

12. Where were the 1972 Winter Olympics held?

13. Which boxer was nicknamed 'the Manassa Mauler'?

14. Which team won the World Cup in snooker in 1979 & '80?

15. What was the nickname of boxer Willie Pep?

ANSWERS 1. Seattle Seahawks 2. 3:35.6 3. Yachting 4. Widnes 5. Roy Emerson 6. Steffen Grummt 7. Jayne Torvill 8. Tennis 9. Abebe Bikila 10. Eamonn Martin 11. Staffordshire 12. Sapporo, Japan 13. Jack Dempsey 14. Wales 15. Will o' the Wisp.

POP MUSIC

1. Evans, Simper, Lord, Blackmore and Paice - which band?

2. With which band does Rick Allen drum?

3. Fletcher, Gahan, Gore and Clarke - which 1980s band?

4. Which American punk band included the Casale and Mothersbaugh brothers?

5. Which blues artist's real name is Ellas McDaniel?

6. Which band's albums include *Love Over Gold* and *Communique*?

7. What name does Neil Hannon record under?

8. Which member of group Dr. Feelgood died in 1994?

9. What is singer Malcolm Rebennack better known as?

10. In which city was Thomas Dolby born?

11. Which Scottish singer's songs include *Mellow Yellow* and *Sunshine Superman*?

12. Jim Morrison was lead singer with which 1960s band?

13. *Thank You* was a 1995 covers album by which band?

14. Elston Gunn was an early stage name of which singer?

15. Bernie Leadon, Glenn Frey, Don Henley and Randy Meisner comprised which band?

WORDS

1. What is eisell?

2. In which sport might you use a suplex?

3. What would you do with a parfait - eat it or drive it?

4. What is a 'slug-abed'?

5. What would you do with a lur - cook with it or play it?

6. What in ancient Greece was a scyphus?

7. Of what is a 'nunny bag' made?

8. Why might a lewis be useful in the building trade?

9. Where on your body is the nape?

10. What, in defence, does MIDAS stand for?

11. In which sport might you play a 'long jenny'?

12. What is the male equivalent of a mermaid?

13. What is the name of the enclosed space in a law court where the accused sits?

14. What might you do with a burley - play it or smoke it?

15. By what name is the creature a cachalot also called?

ANSWERS **1.** Wormwood wine **2.** Wrestling - it is a hold **3.** Eat it - it is a dessert **4.** A late riser **5.** Play it - it is a Danish musical instrument **6.** A drinking vessel **7.** Sealskin **8.** It is a device for lifting heavy stones **9.** The back of the neck **10.** Missile Defence Alarm System **11.** Billiards **12.** Merman **13.** Dock **14.** Smoke it **15.** A sperm whale.

GENERAL KNOWLEDGE

1. What was the name of the U.S. architect and engineer born in 1895 who developed the geodesic dome?

2. What would you do with a bergère?

3. What was the informal name given to the British 7th Armoured Division who fought in N. Africa from 1941-42?

4. Which Italian politician was murdered in 1978 by the Red Brigades?

5. Approximately how long in miles is the Khyber Pass?

6. What was the profession of Boston nationalist Paul Revere who made a famous ride in 1775?

7. In which year did politician Cecil Rhodes die?

8. What is a kiekie?

9. Which German aviator commanded the 11th Chasing Squadron in World War I?

10. Which U.S. millionaire founded the Standard Oil Company in 1870?

11. Who succeeded McKinley as U.S. president following his assassination?

12. What was the nickname of German field marshal Erwin Rommel?

13. Who was archbishop of Canterbury 1980-91?

14. In which year was Mount McKinley in Alaska first climbed?

15. How many generals fought in the Wars of the Diodochi for control of the empire of Alexander the Great after his death?

ANSWERS 1. R. Buckminster Fuller 2. Sit in it - it's a type of chair 3. The Desert Rats 4. Aldo Moro 5. 33 miles 6. Silversmith 7. 1902 8. A climbing plant 9. Baron von Richthofen 10. John D. Rockefeller 11. Theodore Roosevelt 12. The Desert Fox 13. Robert Runcie 14. 1913 15. Six.

ENTERTAINMENT

1. Which musical show did Milos Forman film in 1979?

2. Which comedian was portrayed by Dustin Hoffman in a 1974 film?

3. Which actor's only film between 1970 and 1981 was for the Billy Graham Organization?

4. What was Clark Gable's last film?

5. In which city was actor Andy Garcia born?

6. Which comedy team wrote *The Rag Trade* and *On the Buses*?

7. What is the television technique colour separation overlay also called?

8. Who played Julius Caesar in the 1983 T.V. drama *The Cleopatras*?

9. Who narrated the 1972 comedy series *Clochemerle*?

10. Stephanie Beacham, Rula Lenska, Susan George and Joanna Lumley each appeared as which character in what series?

11. Which Oscar-winning Labour M.P. was born in Birkenhead?

12. Which actor voiced Darth Vader in the film *Star Wars*?

13. Who played Gary Gilmore in the 1982 film *The Executioner's Song*?

14. Who played jazz performer Red Nichols in the 1959 film *The Five Pennies*?

15. Which actress played *Annie Hall* in 1977?

ANSWERS 1. Hair **2.** Lenny Bruce **3.** James Fox **4.** The Misfits **5.** Havana, Cuba **6.** Ronald Wolfe and Ronald Chesney **7.** Chroma key **8.** Robert Hardy **9.** Peter Ustinov **10.** Mrs. Peacock, in Cluedo **11.** Glenda Jackson **12.** James Earl Jones **13.** Tommy Lee Jones **14.** Danny Kaye **15.** Diane Keaton.

SPORT

1. Which father and son won Olympic hammer and javelin events respectively?

2. Who was African Footballer of the Year in 1976?

3. At which ground was David Gower's 100th Test match played?

4. Who in boxing was 'the Tylorstown Terror'?

5. At what weight was Pichit Sitbangprachan IBF world champion from 1992-94?

6. Who won rugby league's 1994 Regal Trophy Final?

7. Who won the 1994 Moroccan Open in golf?

8. Which side knocked Liverpool out of the 1994 F.A. Cup?

9. Which pair won the 1964 Monte Carlo Rally?

10. Who was the arch-rival of skater Nancy Kerrigan?

11. In which country were the 1956 Winter Olympics held?

12. Who were the first team to win two World Cups in football?

13. What is the middle name of footballer Jimmy Greaves?

14. When was the World Professional Billiards championship first held?

15. When was the first cricket Test series between India and England?

ANSWERS 1. Imre and Miklos Nemeth **2.** Roger Milla **3.** Headingley **4.** Jimmy Wilde **5.** Flyweight **6.** Castleford **7.** Anders Forbrand **8.** Bristol City **9.** Paddy Hopkirk and Henry Liddon **10.** Tonya Harding **11.** Italy **12.** Italy **13.** Peter **14.** 1870 **15.** 1932.

POP MUSIC

1. Siobhan Fahey and Marcella Detroit comprised which duo?

2. Which group's albums included *The Impossible Dream* and *Tomorrow Belongs to Me*?

3. Singer Henry Samuel is better known as what?

4. In which year was Smokey Robinson born?

5. Glen Matlock, Midge Ure, Rusty Egan and Steve New - which group?

6. Who is the lead singer of R.E.M.?

7. In which year did Otis Redding die?

8. Ricardo Wayne Penniman is better known as whom?

9. Lowell George, Bill Payne, Roy Estrada and Rick Hayward formed which band?

10. In which seaside town were rock band Little Angels formed?

11. Which singer recorded 1970's *Tumbleweed Connection* album?

12. In which year did Buddy Holly die?

13. The Human Beanz became which band in 1967?

14. Who released the 1976 album *Teenage Depression*?

15. In which city did Echo and the Bunnymen form?

SCIENCE

1. In which city was Marie Curie born?

2. What in plant life is a lamina more commonly known as?

3. The Earth is a true sphere. True or false?

4. Who wrote the 1976 book *The Selfish Gene*?

5. Which element's symbol is F?

6. On which Greek island was the reddish-brown clayey earth *terra sigillata* found?

7. What is the SI unit of electrical capacitance?

8. How many chains in a furlong?

9. What in global warming does the abbreviation ODP stand for?

10. What nationality was 18th century scientist Daniel Bernoulli?

11. On the Beaufort scale what is the description of force 3?

12. Of what is cynophobia a fear?

13. During which era was the silurian period of geological time?

14. How many grams of fibre per 100 grams are there in figs?

15. What in acoustics does AM stand for?

ANSWERS 1. Warsaw 2. The blade of a leaf 3. False - it is an ellipsoid 4. Richard Dawkins 5. Fluorine 6. Lemnos 7. Farad 8. 10 9. Ozone depletion potential 10. Swiss 11. Gentle breeze 12. Dogs 13. Palaeozoic 14. 19 15. Amplitude modulation.

GENERAL KNOWLEDGE

1. What was the first name of Nazi leader Joseph Goebbels?

2. Which Italian composer and musical rival of Mozart taught Liszt and Schubert?

3. Which German admiral was commander of the High Sea Fleet at the Battle of Jutland in 1916?

4. Who was chancellor of West Germany 1974-83?

5. A Dick test is used to determine a person's immunity to what disease?

6. Which architect supervised the rebuilding of the House of Commons after World War II?

7. What was the middle name of US Union general William Sherman?

8. The inlet of the Bosporus called the Golden Horn forms the harbour of which city?

9. Which Ukraine-born U.S. engineer built the first successful helicopter?

10. Which English field marshal was governor general of Australia 1953-60?

11. Who was prime minister of Rhodesia 1964-79?

12. Who was prime minister of Portugal 1976-78?

13. Who wrote the 1971 novel *Bear Island*?

14. What sort of creature is a hoopoe?

15. What is the standard monetary unit of Paraguay?

ANSWERS 1. Paul 2. Antonio Salieri **3.** Reinhard Scheer **4.** Helmut Schmidt **5.** Scarlet fever **6.** Giles Gilbert Scott **7.** Tecumseh **8.** Istanbul **9.** Igor Sikorsky **10.** William Joseph Slim **11.** Ian Smith **12.** Mario Soares **13.** Alistair Maclean **14.** Bird **15.** Guarani.

THE ULTIMATE PUB QUIZ BOOK

ENTERTAINMENT

1. Which character did Harvey Keitel play in the 1988 film *The Last Temptation of Christ*?

2. In which year did actress Grace Kelly die?

3. Which Withernsea-born actress died in 1959 of leukemia?

4. Which Shakespearean character did Deborah Kerr play in the 1953 film *Julius Caesar*?

5. Which diminutive actor was born in Hot Springs, Arkansas, in 1913?

6. Who played Jason Colby in *The Colbys*?

7. Who was political editor at the BBC from 1981-92?

8. Who played Fitz in the T.V. series *Cracker*?

9. Which part did Peter Cook play in a 1966 T.V. adaptation of *Alice in Wonderland*?

10. What was Ronnie Corbett's character name in the sitcom *Sorry!*?

11. *Somebody Stole My Girl* was which T.V. bandleader's theme tune?

12. Who played *The Barefoot Contessa* in the 1954 film?

13. Which Shakespearean character did Greer Garson play in the 1953 film *Julius Caesar*?

14. Which Hollywood film star played Danny Zuko on Broadway in *Grease*?

15. Who played *Maverick* in the 1994 film?

ANSWERS 1. Judas **2.** 1982 **3.** Kay Kendall **4.** Portia **5.** Alan Ladd **6.** Charlton Heston **7.** John Cole **8.** Robbie Coltrane **9.** The Mad Hatter **10.** Timothy Lumsden **11.** Billy Cotton **12.** Ava Gardner **13.** Calpurnia **14.** Richard Gere **15.** Mel Gibson.

SPORT

1. Who won the 1990 Badminton horse trials?

2. When did Harry Vardon win the first of his British Open golf titles?

3. Who won the first Olympic men's hockey title?

4. Who was the first Formula 1 motor racing world champion?

5. Which year saw a dead heat in the university boat race?

6. In which year was volleyball introduced into the Olympic Games?

7. What nationality was the runner Kip Keino?

8. Who won the 1994 Regal Welsh Open snooker title?

9. Who scored all of England's points in their Calcutta Cup game in 1984?

10. In which year did Kapil Dev take his first Test wicket?

11. In which year did Graeme Souness take over as Liverpool boss?

12. In which year did golfer Henry Cotton die?

13. In which country was cricketer Colin Cowdrey born?

14. Which golfer won the 1994 Madeira Island Open?

15. Who won the 1994 Houston men's marathon?

ANSWERS 1. Nicola McIrvine **2.** 1896 **3.** England **4.** Nino Farina **5.** 1877 **6.** 1964 **7.** Kenyan **8.** Steve Davis **9.** Jonathan Callard **10.** 1978 **11.** 1991 **12.** 1987 **13.** India **14.** Mats Lanner **15.** Colin Moore.

POP MUSIC

1. Sonya Aurora Madan is lead singer with which group?

2. In which city were electronic band 808 State formed?

3. Who were the three members of group E.L.P.?

4. Who had a No. 1 single with the song *Orinoco Flow*?

5. Vince Clarke and Andy Bell - which electronic duo?

6. Dave Stewart and Annie Lennox - which duo?

7. What are the forenames of the Everly Brothers?

8. Who are Ben Watt and Tracey Thorn?

9. Which band recorded the 1971 album *A Nod's as Good as a Wink...to a Blind Horse*?

10. In which city was Marianne Faithfull born?

11. *Bingo Master's Breakout* was the first single from which Manchester band?

12. Whitney, Grech, Townsend, King and Chapman - which band?

13. From which city does the group The Farm hail?

14. Who was lead singer in the group Frankie Goes to Hollywood?

15. Rodgers, Kirke, Fraser and Kossoff - which group?

PEOPLE

1. What was nun Agnes Gonxha Bojaxhiu better known as?

2. Which comedian formed the band Poor White Trash and the Little Big Horns after performing at Ben Elton's wedding?

3. What was criminal Robert Franklin Stroud also known as?

4. Who played Theodore Roosevelt in the 1962 film *The Longest Day*?

5. Which U.S. criminal was famously killed by Lana Turner's daughter in 1958?

6. Who played Josh Griffiths in the T.V. drama *Casualty*?

7. Which U.S. murderer killed eight student nurses in Chicago in July 1966?

8. Which 1997 film starred the same four principal actors as *A Fish Called Wanda*?

9. Which male wrote the book *Monica's Story*?

10. Who starred as *Trojan Eddie* in the 1996 film?

11. What was the name of the husband and killer of actress/model Dorothy Stratten?

12. Bad Bob, Wendy and Vince are all animated companions of which character?

13. Which U.S. criminal ordered the killing of rival 'Legs' Diamond?

14. What are Clarissa Dickson and Jennifer Paterson better known as?

15. Maureen Rees was the unlikely star of which T.V. documentary series?

GENERAL KNOWLEDGE

1. In which year was Fidel Castro born?

2. Who was lover of Dido in classical mythology?

3. In which century did the Italian playwright Carlo Goldoni live?

4. What is the Italian equivalent of the English surname Brown?

5. In which city is the Kelham Island Industrial Museum?

6. In which city is Aston University?

7. Who in December 1997 won the Turner Prize for modern art?

8. Who won the 1995 Nobel prize for Literature?

9. In which year did Hungarian choreographer Rudolf von Laban die?

10. What is the brightest star in the constellation Taurus?

11. In which year was king Umberto I of Italy assassinated?

12. Which river is the only outlet of Loch Leven?

13. Which Act of 1559 made the Prayer Book the only legal form of worship in England?

14. What does the Latin phrase 'caveat emptor' translate as?

15. What was the nickname of U.S. general Joseph Stilwell?

ANSWERS 1. 1927 **2.** Aeneas **3.** 18th **4.** Bruno **5.** Sheffield **6.** Birmingham **7.** Gillian Wearing **8.** Seamus Heaney **9.** 1958 **10.** Aldebaran **11.** 1900 **12.** River Leven **13.** Act of Uniformity **14.** Let the buyer beware **15.** Vinegar Joe.

ENTERTAINMENT

1. In which year did *Multi-Coloured Swap Shop* end on BBC1?

2. In which country was actor Anthony Quinn born?

3. In which year did *Jim'll Fix It* begin on BBC1?

4. What was Herbert Lom's character name in the medical drama series *The Human Jungle*?

5. Which *Coronation Street* actress played Tracy Glazebrook in the comedy show *Joking Apart*?

6. Who played Betty Smith in the ITV police drama *Hunter's Walk*?

7. In which year did Carlton Television take to the air?

8. Who played hippy Robert Croft in *Coronation Street*?

9. In which country was actress Carmen Miranda born?

10. Who succeeded Johnny Carson as host on NBC's *Tonight Show*?

11. In which city was actor Vincent Price born?

12. What was Chan Kwan better known as in puppet series *Captain Scarlet and The Mysterons*?

13. Who played Messalina in the BBC historical drama *I, Claudius*?

14. Who played Sam Cade in the T.V. police drama *Cade's County*?

15. Who played Morgana in the 1981 film *Excalibur*?

SPORT

1. Which athlete married runner Ann Packer?

2. What is golfer Arnold Palmer's middle name?

3. Which rugby union prop played 55 times for France between 1975-83?

4. In what year was Desert Orchid born?

5. Who beat Tim Henman in the 1998 Wimbledon men's singles tennis semi-final?

6. By what score did Croatia beat Germany in the 1998 World Cup quarter-final?

7. What age was Joe Bugner when he won the WBF world heavyweight title in July, 1998?

8. What was the result of the Third Test between England and South Africa in 1998?

9. From which county cricket club did David Gower retire in 1993?

10. Which horse won the 1992 Grand National?

11. Who won the men's single luge gold at the 1994 Winter Olympics?

12. Which horse won the 1994 Hennessey Gold Cup?

13. By what score did France beat Croatia in their 1998 World Cup semi-final?

14. Which driver won the 1998 British Grand Prix?

15. Which runner took more than a second off the men's 1,500m record in July, 1998?

ANSWERS 1. Robbie Brightwell **2.** Daniel **3.** Robert Paparemborde **4.** 1979 **5.** Pete Sampras **6.** 3-0 **7.** 48 **8.** A draw **9.** Hampshire **10.** Party Politics **11.** Georg Hackl **12.** Jodami **13.** 2-1 **14.** Michael Schumacher **15.** Hicham El Guerrouj.

POP MUSIC

1. Lynval Golding, Neville Staples and Terry Hall - which band?

2. In which year did Peter Gabriel leave Genesis?

3. In which year was Emmylou Harris born?

4. Ian Craig Marsh, Martyn Ware and Glenn Gregory comprised which early 1980s band?

5. Which guitarist recorded the 1976 album *Cry Tough*?

6. Which band recorded the 1967 album *Da Capo*?

7. Which country singer was married to actress Julia Roberts?

8. Which U.S. band is associated with the songs *Freebird* and *Sweet Home Alabama*?

9. Candida Doyle is keyboard player in which group?

10. Who was bass player in the group Queen?

11. Thom Yorke is lead singer in which band?

12. Johnny, Joey, Dee Dee and Tommy - which band?

13. Who was leader of 1970s band The Raspberries?

14. Which group recorded the 1969 album *Let it Bleed*?

15. Which guitarist's first solo album was 1974's *Slaughter on 10th Avenue*?

ART AND LITERATURE

1. Who wrote the 1958 play *Chicken Soup with Barley*?

2. Which novel by H.G. Wells is partly set in the year 802701?

3. Who wrote *The Cloning of Joanna May*?

4. In which year was T.S. Eliot's *The Waste Land* first published?

5. Which American author penned *For Whom the Bell Tolls*?

6. Which Scot wrote the controversial novel *How Late it Was, How Late*?

7. Who wrote the novel *Billy Bathgate*?

8. Whose novels include *Keep the Aspidistra Flying*?

9. Whose sculptures include 1963's *Abstract in White, Ochre and Black*?

10. Whose stories include *Pop. 1280* and *The Killer Inside Me*?

11. Who created the 1963 sculpture *Boomerang*?

12. Which architect published the journal *Frühlicht* from 1920-22?

13. Whose novels include *Going to Meet the Man*?

14. In which year did artist Paul Klee die?

15. In which year did poet Filippo Marinetti die?

GENERAL KNOWLEDGE

1. Who was elected Conservative M.P. for Suffolk South in 1997?

2. Which birth control pioneer wrote the best-selling manual *Married Love* in 1918?

3. What is the crop berseem also called?

4. In which country was bio-chemist Casimir Funk born?

5. In 1933 Joseph Zangara shot and killed the mayor of Chicago. Who was he aiming at?

6. In which town is Brunel University?

7. Who was prime minister of Japan from 1980-82?

8. For which constituency was Mo Mowlam elected M.P. in 1997?

9. Which Conservative politician was minister for trade and industry 1983-85?

10. Which English illustrator is known for his illustrations to Lewis Carroll's *Alice's Adventures in Wonderland*?

11. In which country was film producer Sam Goldwyn born?

12. What is the first name of athlete Carl Lewis?

13. What is ex-prime minister Margaret Thatcher's middle name?

14. What is the middle name of former Canadian prime minister Pierre Trudeau?

15. Which English agriculturist wrote *Horse-Hoeing Husbandry*?

ANSWERS 1. Tim Yeo **2.** Marie Stopes **3.** Egyptian clover **4.** Poland **5.** Franklin D. Roosevelt **6.** Uxbridge **7.** Zenko Suzuki **8.** Redcar **9.** Norman Tebbit **10.** John Tenniel **11.** Poland **12.** Frederick **13.** Hilda **14.** Elliott **15.** Jethro Tull.

ENTERTAINMENT

1. Who did Christopher Coll play in *Coronation Street*?

2. What was Rose's surname in the sitcom *The Golden Girls*?

3. Who did Peter Jeffrey play in the BBC TV drama *By the Sword Divided*?

4. Who played Anthony Mortimer in the soap *Crossroads*?

5. Who directed the 1984 film *The Killing Fields*?

6. Who did Gayle Hunnicutt play in *Dallas*?

7. Who sung the theme song to the series *When the Boat Comes In*?

8. Who played Audrey Horne in the T.V. drama *Twin Peaks*?

9. Who played Huw Evans in the T.V. comedy show *Doctor in the House*?

10. Who directed the film *Jackie Brown*?

11. In which film was Akim Tamiroff's first appearance with Orson Welles?

12. Which Russian film director's works include 1985's *The Sacrifice*?

13. Which comedian was born Jacques Tatischeff?

14. What were the forenames of the leads in the play *Who's Afraid of Virginia Woolf*?

15. Who played a blind Irish violin player in the 1974 film *Blink*?

ANSWERS 1. Victor Pendlebury **2.** Nylund **3.** Oliver Crowell **4.** Jeremy Sinden **5.** Roland Joffe **6.** Vanessa Beaumont **7.** Alex Glasgow **8.** Sherilyn Fenn **9.** Martin Shaw **10.** Quentin Tarantino **11.** Black Magic **12.** Andrei Tarkovsky **13.** Jacques Tati **14.** George & Martha **15.** Madeleine Stowe.

SPORT

1. Who played in goal for Newcastle United in the 1999 F.A. Cup Final?

2. By how many runs did South Africa beat England in their 1999 World Cup Group A cricket game?

3. By how many wickets did Sri Lanka beat Zimbabwe in their 1999 World Cup Group A cricket match?

4. Who won the 1994 Tenerife Open golf title?

5. Who won the 1994 Benson and Hedges Masters snooker title?

6. In which city was golfer Fred Couples born?

7. Who won the men's long jump at the 1964 Olympics?

8. Who is the manager of Liverpool F.C.?

9. Against who, in 1998, was Chris Eubank stopped for the first time in his career?

10. Who lost in a play-off in the 1998 British Open golf tournament?

11. In what position did Justin Rose finish in the 1998 British Open golf tournament?

12. Which horse won the 1998 King George VI and Queen Elizabeth Stakes?

13. Which team bought Ruel Fox from Norwich City?

14. Who was 1992 Olympic welterweight boxing title winner?

15. In which city was Monica Seles stabbed in 1993?

ANSWERS 1. Steve Harper **2.** 122 runs **3.** Four wickets **4.** David Gilford **5.** Alan McManus **6.** Seattle **7.** Lynn Davies **8.** Gerard Houllier **9.** Carl Thompson **10.** Brian Watts **11.** Equal fourth **12.** Swain **13.** Newcastle United **14.** Michael Carruth **15.** Hamburg.

POP MUSIC

1. Malcolm Owen died in 1980. With which band did he sing?

2. Sarah Cracknell is singer with which group?

3. Moore and Prater are the surnames of which soul duo?

4. Which Manchester group recorded the 1982 album *Sextet*?

5. Which group recorded the 1994 album *Ich Bin Ein Auslander*?

6. Which female singer formed All About Eve in 1985?

7. Which reggae star was born Max Elliott in 1960?

8. Which guitarist formed the Amboy Dukes in 1966?

9. In which year was guitarist Chris Rea born?

10. Which group recorded the 1991 album *I am the Greatest*?

11. Which group scored a 1997 Top Ten single with *All Mine*?

12. What was the debut single of group the Anti-Nowhere League?

13. What was the Real Thing's 1976 No. 1 single?

14. In which year did group A.R. Kane form?

15. Which group had a 1971 hit single with *Witch Queen of New Orleans*?

ANSWERS 1. The Ruts **2.** St. Etienne **3.** Sam and Dave **4.** A Certain Ratio **5.** Pop Will Eat Itself **6.** Julianne Regan **7.** Maxi Priest **8.** Ted Nugent **9.** 1951 **10.** A House **11.** Portishead **12.** Streets of London **13.** You To Me Are Everything **14.** 1986 **15.** Redbone.

GEOGRAPHY

1. Aberdeen lies between the mouths of which two rivers?

2. In which American state are the Everglades, an extensive marshy region?

3. On what Mediterranean island is the seaport of Famagusta?

4. Which skiing city is capital of Isère department in France?

5. Which county is known as the 'Garden of England'?

6. Mombasa is the chief seaport of which country?

7. On which river is the Portuguese city of Lisbon?

8. In which Italian hill town is the Palio horse race festival held?

9. What is the highest mountain on the Isle of Man?

10. The Segovia River forms the boundary between which two Central American countries?

11. The city of Nome, centre of a gold rush in 1900, is in which U.S. state?

12. Which river separates Victoria and New South Wales, Australia?

13. The Plains of Abraham are near which Canadian city?

14. In which African country is the seaport of Agadir?

15. In which European country is the town of Altdorf?

GENERAL KNOWLEDGE

1. In which century did English highwayman Dick Turpin live?

2. What was Anne Marie Grosholtz better known as?

3. What on a ship is a futtock?

4. In which year did senator Joe McCarthy die?

5. What type of creature is a karakul?

6. In which year was the Bank of England nationalized?

7. What is the name of Eliza's father in the play *Pygmalion*?

8. What is 25 x 25?

9. What type of fruit is a biffin?

10. Which South African clergyman received the 1984 Nobel peace prize?

11. In which island group is the U.S. naval base of Cavite?

12. Who was the leader of the Peasant's Revolt in 1381?

13. Who was elected Labour M.P. for Oldham West and Royton in 1997?

14. Which English translator of the Bible was burned as a heretic in Belgium in 1536?

15. In which year did French couturier Christian Dior die?

ENTERTAINMENT

1. For which 1984 film did Helen Mirren win a Best Actress prize at Cannes?

2. Who did Noel Howlett play in the comedy series *Please, Sir!*?

3. In which country was actor Lee Strasberg born?

4. Who directed the 1973 film *The Way We Were*?

5. Who played a movie director in the 1970 film *Alex in Wonderland*?

6. Who was the first husband of actress Jessica Tandy?

7. Which actor was born Spangler Arlington Brugh?

8. In which year did actor Tom Mix die?

9. Who played Margaret Schlegel in the 1992 film *Howards End*?

10. What was the subtitle of the 1987 film *Death Wish 4*?

11. Who directed the 1977 film *Fingers*?

12. Which actress is also called Lady Haden-Guest?

13. Who played the female lead in the 1999 film *Notting Hill*?

14. Which actor was born Ivo Livi?

15. Who played T.V.'s *Rumpole of the Bailey*?

ANSWERS 1. Cal **2.** Mr. Cromwell **3.** Austria **4.** Sydney Pollack **5.** Donald Sutherland **6.** Jack Hawkins **7.** Robert Taylor **8.** 1940 **9.** Emma Thompson **10.** The Crackdown **11.** James Toback **12.** Jamie Lee Curtis **13.** Julia Roberts **14.** Yves Montand **15.** Leo McKern.

SPORT

1. Which was Richard Dunwoody's 1000th winner in Britain?

2. Who lost the 1994 Australian Open men's tennis final?

3. Who rode Shergar to victory in the 1981 Epsom Derby?

4. Who won the men's 5,000m and 10,000m at the 1956 Olympics?

5. What was the nickname of tennis player René Lacoste?

6. In which city was footballer Denis Law born?

7. Who won the women's long jump at the 1966 Commonwealth Games?

8. Who won the 1998 Austrian Grand Prix in Formula 1?

9. Who won the 1998 German Grand Prix in Formula 1?

10. By what score did the U.S. beat Great Britain and Ireland in the 1998 Curtis Cup?

11. By what score did Arsenal defeat Manchester United in the 1998 Charity Shield?

12. Which team won Italy's 1998/99 Serie A title?

13. Who retained his WBC welterweight boxing title in May 1999 by beating Oba Carr?

14. Who scored the first goal in the 1999 F.A. Cup Final?

15. Who won the 1998/99 Scottish Premier League football title?

ANSWERS 1. Flakey Dove 2. Todd Martin 3. Walter Swinburn 4. Vladimir Kuts 5. The Crocodile 6. Aberdeen 7. Mary Rand 8. Mika Hakkinen 9. Mika Hakkinen 10. 10-8 11. 3-0 12. A.C. Milan 13. Oscar de la Hoya 14. Teddy Sheringham 15. Rangers.

POP MUSIC

1. Which singer charted in 1984 with the song *Theme From Cheers*?

2. What were the names of the two Allman Brothers?

3. Which blues singer had a minor hit in 1964 with *Shame Shame Shame*?

4. Which Birmingham band recorded the 1981 album *Playing With a Different Sex*?

5. Which duo had a Top 30 single in 1987 with *Soul Man*?

6. Which rap group recorded the 1991 album *The Low End Theory*?

7. Which group had a Top Ten single in 1997 with *Kowalski*?

8. Which group recorded the chart-topping song *Horse with No Name*?

9. Which duo charted in 1993 with the single *Resurrection*?

10. Which former member of The Alarm released the 1994 solo album *Breath*?

11. What was Jim Reeves' first U.K. chart single?

12. Which punk group released the flexi-disc *Love Lies Limp*?

13. Which group backed Vic Reeves on the 1991 hit *Born Free*?

14. What was the Angelic Upstarts' singer Thomas Mensforth known as?

15. Which group had a 1988 Top 40 hit with *Minnie the Moocher*?

ANSWERS 1. Gary Portnoy **2.** Duane and Gregg **3.** Jimmy Reed **4.** Au Pairs **5.** Sam Moore and Lou Reed **6.** A Tribe Called Quest **7.** Primal Scream **8.** America **9.** Brian May & Cozy Powell **10.** Mike Peters **11.** He'll Have To Go **12.** Alternative T.V. **13.** The Roman Numerals **14.** Mensi **15.** Reggae Philharmonic Orchestra.

HISTORY

1. The Evian Accords of the early 1960s resulted in independence for which country?

2. Who did vice-president Aaron Burr kill in a duel in 1804?

3. Who was American secretary of state 1989-92?

4. In which year did Henry II invade Ireland and claim sovereignty?

5. In which year did Jane Seymour, Queen of England die?

6. Who became president of the Czech Republic in 1993?

7. In which city was Israeli statesman Abba Eban born?

8. Which king of Scotland died at the Battle of Flodden Field?

9. In which year was Scottish hero William Wallace defeated by Edward I?

10. Who commanded the Russian force at the Battle of Balaclava?

11. In which year did the War of the Roses begin?

12. In which year did Elizabeth I die?

13. In which year did Richard I of England capture Cyprus?

14. Who was vice-president of the U.S. under Andrew Jackson from 1837-41?

15. The Abbé de Saint-Cyran was a founder of which reform movement in the Roman Catholic Church?

ANSWERS 1. Algeria **2.** Alexander Hamilton **3.** James Addison Baker III **4.** 1171 **5.** 1537 **6.** Vaclav Havel **7.** Cape Town **8.** James IV **9.** 1298 **10.** General Liprandi **11.** 1455 **12.** 1603 **13.** 1191 **14.** Martin van Buren **15.** Jansenism.

GENERAL KNOWLEDGE

1. Which pop star wrote the *Liverpool Oratorio* in 1991?

2. In which county is the resort town of Aldeburgh?

3. Which South African prime minister was assassinated in 1966?

4. Of what is the southern African garment a kaross made?

5. Which Austrian politician was secretary-general of the U.N. from 1972-81?

6. Which U.S. adventurer was briefly president of Nicaragua from 1856-57?

7. A Russian word meaning 'fast' is used to denote a small restaurant. What is it?

8. Who compiled a dictionary entitled *A Table Alphabeticall* in 1604?

9. Who authored the fishing text *The Compleat Angler*?

10. In which year was Kevin Keegan born?

11. Which chief justice of the U.S. supreme court headed the commission that investigated the assassination of President Kennedy?

12. Who wrote the 1954 work *The Doors of Perception*?

13. Who was Ronald Reagan's defense secretary from 1981-87?

14. What type of creature is a keitloa?

15. Which Christian denomination did Thomas and Alexander Campbell found in 1809?

ANSWERS 1. Paul McCartney 2. Suffolk 3. Hendrik Verwoerd 4. Skins 5. Kurt Waldheim 6. William Walker 7. Bistro 8. Robert Cawdrey 9. Izaak Walton 10. 1951 11. Earl Warren 12. Aldous Huxley 13. Caspar Weinberger 14. Rhinoceros 15. The Disciples of Christ.

THE ULTIMATE PUB QUIZ BOOK

ENTERTAINMENT

1. Who did Mädchen Amick play in the T.V. drama *Twin Peaks*?

2. Who directed the 1999 film *Happiness*?

3. In which year did actress Agnes Moorehead die?

4. Who directed the film *Breaking the Waves*?

5. Who played Clay Grainger in the T.V. show *The Virginian*?

6. Who played Det. Supt. Inman in the T.V. drama *Special Branch*?

7. Who played Drusus in the BBC T.V. drama *I, Claudius*?

8. Which actor's feature film debut as director was 1999's *Orphans*?

9. Who played Sandra Gould in *Crossroads*?

10. In which country was actor Paul Muni born?

11. Who did Howard Keel play in the soap *Dallas*?

12. Which actor and war hero's film debut was in 1948's *Beyond Glory*?

13. Who played Dr. Jacoby in the T.V. drama *Twin Peaks*?

14. Who played Cecelia Brady in the 1976 film *The Last Tycoon*?

15. Who directed the 1982 film *48 Hrs*?

ANSWERS 1. Shelly Johnson **2.** Todd Solondz **3.** 1974 **4.** Lars von Trier **5.** John McIntire **6.** Fulton Mackay **7.** Ian Ogilvy **8.** Peter Mullen **9.** Diane Keen **10.** Austria **11.** Clayton Farlow **12.** Audie Murphy **13.** Russ Tamblyn **14.** Theresa Russell **15.** Walter Hill.

SPORT

1. For which country does Jonty Rhodes play cricket?

2. Which team won the 1994 Winter Olympics men's ice hockey gold?

3. Who won the 1994 Andalucian Open in golf?

4. At what age did Judit Polgar become a chess grandmaster?

5. By how many runs did England beat South Africa in the Fifth Test in 1998?

6. Who scored the only goal in Chelsea's 1998 Super Cup victory over Real Madrid?

7. Who won the 1998 Belgian Grand Prix in Formula 1?

8. By what score did Sweden beat England in their European Championship qualifier in September 1998?

9. Where did Wales play their 'home' European Championship qualifier against Italy in September, 1998?

10. Who resigned as German football coach in 1998?

11. What nationality is tennis player Patrick Rafter?

12. Which teams competed in the 1994 Italian Cup Final in football?

13. Who won the men's Giant Slalom Alpine skiing title at the 1994 Olympics?

14. In which year was FIFA founded?

15. What nationality is golfer David Graham?

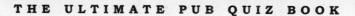

POP MUSIC

1. Which group had a Top 30 single in 1997 with *A Prisoner of the Past*?

2. Which Goth group's debut single was *Ignore the Machine*?

3. What was the only No. 1 single, in 1979, by The Pretenders?

4. Which group recorded the 1986 album *Spreading the Disease*?

5. How many solo No. 1 singles has Alan Price had?

6. Who was lead singer in the group Any Trouble?

7. Which group charted in 1996 with the single *Lump*?

8. What was Elvis Presley's last U.K. No.1 single, in 1977?

9. On which studio L.P. by Tom Waits does the song *In the Neighborhood* appear?

10. Which group had a Top 30 single in 1972 with *Conquistador*?

11. What was the title of Neil Young and Crazy Horse's 1997 live album?

12. Which celebrity learner driver had a minor Christmas hit in 1997?

13. Who was vocalist in the punk group The Dead Boys?

14. What was R.E.M.'s first U.K. chart single entry?

15. In which country did the group Dead Can Dance form?

ANSWERS 1. Prefab Sprout **2.** Alien Sex Fiend **3.** Brass in Pocket **4.** Anthrax **5.** None **6.** Clive Gregson **7.** Presidents of the United States of America **8.** Way Down **9.** Swordfishtrombones **10.** Procol Harum **11.** Year of the Horse **12.** Maureen Rees **13.** Stiv Bators **14.** The One I Love **15.** Australia.

WORDS

1. Who are 'the Slops'?

2. What in printing do the letters u.c. stand for?

3. What are the scopae of a bee?

4. Is gabbro a type of wood or rock?

5. What would you do with a zloty in Poland?

6. What bird is called a menura in Australia?

7. What type of fruit tree is a mazzard?

8. What type of creature is an emmet?

9. Who, or what, is 'small-back'?

10. What sort of creature is a scup?

11. What in medical terms is HRT?

12. What does the Latin phrase 'mea culpa' mean?

13. What is a ziff in Australian parlance?

14. What sort of creatures belong to the family Gadidae?

15. What is an 'enfant terrible'?

ANSWERS 1. The police 2. Upper case 3. The hairs used to collect pollen 4. Rock 5. Spend it 6. Lyre-bird 7. A cherry tree 8. An ant 9. Death 10. A fish 11. Hormone replacement therapy 12. My fault 13. A beard 14. Fish 15. A social or moral nuisance.

GENERAL KNOWLEDGE

1. What colour are the flowers of the Cretan plant dittany?

2. What title is given to Jesus Christ in John 10:11-12 in the New Testament?

3. Who would use a kernmantel rope?

4. Who was the English founder of Methodism?

5. In which year was the battleship HMS Dreadnought launched?

6. Which British Conservative politician was Home Secretary 1979-83?

7. For what is CCTV an abbreviation?

8. Euryale and Stheno were sisters of which character in Greek mythology?

9. What is the name of the room or mat used for the practice of judo?

10. What is the standard onetary unit of Vietnam?

11. Approximately how many million people spoke Norwegian in 1993?

12. In which city is the Glyn Vivian Art Gallery and Museum?

13. Who won the 1997 Nobel prize for Literature?

14. Who was leader of the Labour Party from 1983-92?

15. In which year was rock and roll star Jerry Lee Lewis born?

ANSWERS 1. Pink **2.** Good Shepherd **3.** A mountaineer **4.** John Wesley **5.** 1906 **6.** William Whitelaw **7.** Closed-circuit television **8.** Medusa **9.** Dojo **10.** Dong **11.** Five **12.** Swansea **13.** Dario Fo **14.** Neil Kinnock **15.** 1935.

ENTERTAINMENT

1. What was Doyle's forename in *The Professionals*?

2. Who played *Sexton Blake* in the 1960s children's series?

3. Who played the male lead in the 1999 film *Notting Hill*?

4. Who played Sebastian in the 1960s T.V. police drama *It's Dark Outside*?

5. Who were the two international judges on the show *Jeux Sans Frontières*?

6. Who played Sinclair Yeates in the Channel 4 drama *The Irish R.M.*?

7. Which actress was born Marjorie Robertson in 1904?

8. What was the character name of Roy Thinnes in the T.V. show *The Invaders*?

9. Who played Dr. Kate Westin in the 1975 science fiction series *The Invisible Man*?

10. Who played *The Informer* in the 1960s T.V. series?

11. Who did Roddy McMillan play in the drama *Hazell*?

12. Which actress played Mary Braithwaite in the sitcom *In Loving Memory*?

13. In which city was Paul Newman born?

14. Who played George Webley in the sitcom *Inside George Webley*?

15. Which actress married Franchot Tone in 1935?

SPORT

1. Who lost the final of the 1998 U.S. Open tennis ladies singles?

2. Who won the 1998 Italian Grand Prix in Formula 1?

3. Who lost the final of the 1998 U.S. Open tennis men's singles?

4. Who won women's shot at the 1998 Commonwealth Games?

5. For which Italian football team did Des Walker play in 1992/3?

6. Who won the 1994 Thailand Open in snooker?

7. Who won the 1994 Tour of Murcia in cycling?

8. Who won the 1994 Portuguese Open in squash?

9. What nationality is golfer Nick Price?

10. Who won the 1994 women's British Indoor Bowls title?

11. Who won the 1994 Standard Register Ping golf tournament?

12. Who, in September 1998, broke the men's marathon record?

13. What age was Florence Griffith-Joyner when she died in 1998?

14. Who did Nick Faldo sack as his coach in 1998?

15. Who resigned as Swindon Town manager in September, 1998?

POP MUSIC

1. Which group charted in 1995 with *I'll Be There for You (Theme from Friends)*?

2. On which studio album by David Bowie does the song *Joe the Lion* appear?

3. With which single did Cliff Richard have a Top Ten in 1998?

4. Which group recorded the 1972 album *Machine Head*?

5. What was Renee and Renato's 1983 follow-up to their No. 1 *Save Your Love*?

6. What was the surname of Delaney and Bonnie?

7. Which pair duetted on the 1981 Top Ten single *Endless Love*?

8. In which U.S. city did the group Destroy All Monsters form in 1973?

9. What was Andrew Ridgeley's only solo chart hit, in 1990?

10. What was the title of Dexy's Midnight Runners 1985 album?

11. How many No. 1 singles did Right Said Fred have?

12. What was Prince's first Top Ten single in the U.K.?

13. Which group recorded the 1973 album *Toulouse Street*?

14. Which group backed Kate Robbins on the 1981 hit *More Than in Love*?

15. Which band recorded 1969's *Kip of the Serenes* L.P.?

SCIENCE

1. Chlorine was named after the Greek word for which colour?

2. During the Upper Cretaceous period the land mass of the Earth split into two super-continents. What was the northern one called?

3. What is the symbol of the element rubidium?

4. For what discovery was Harold Urey awarded the 1934 Nobel prize for chemistry?

5. What in mathematics do the initials HCF stand for?

6. In which year did English mathematician Charles Babbage die?

7. What nationality was Ernst Beckmann, after whom a type of thermometer was named?

8. Which is the largest of the seven continents of the world?

9. Which fruit's scientific name is *Musa sapientum*?

10. How many tentacles does an octopus have?

11. What is a reg in a desert?

12. What is the tail fin of a fish also known as?

13. In which year was the Psi Particle discovered?

14. To which genus does the shrimp belong?

15. Which element's symbol is P?

ANSWERS 1. Green **2.** Laurasia **3.** Rb **4.** Heavy hydrogen **5.** Highest common factor **6.** 1871 **7.** German **8.** Asia **9.** Banana **10.** Eight **11.** A sandless area of gravel and rocks **12.** Caudal fin **13.** 1974 **14.** Crangon **15.** Phosphorus.

GENERAL KNOWLEDGE

1. In the *Arabian Nights Entertainments*, what is Ali Baba's job?

2. Who was Australian prime minister from 1972-75?

3. In which year was Ceylon prime minister Solomon Bandaranaike killed?

4. Which U.S. inventor patented the cotton gin in 1793?

5. Who wrote *Bridget Jones's Diary*?

6. Which economist wrote the 1958 book *The Affluent Society*?

7. In which American state is Mount Blackburn?

8. Which English mountaineer made the first ascent of the Matterhorn in 1865?

9. Which English cleric became Lord Chancellor in 1515?

10. What musical instrument is also known as a cembalo?

11. What sort of creature might you catch with a fyke?

12. Which Mormon religious leader founded Salt Lake City?

13. LE is the abbreviation for which postcode area?

14. Which German publisher of foreign travel guides died in 1859?

15. Which Scottish engineer pioneered 'noctovision'?

ANSWERS 1. Woodcutter **2.** Gough Whitlam **3.** 1959 **4.** Eli Whitney **5.** Helen Fielding **6.** J.K. Galbraith **7.** Alaska **8.** Edward Whymper **9.** Thomas Wolsey **10.** Harpsichord **11.** Fish **12.** Brigham Young **13.** Leicester **14.** Karl Baedeker **15.** John Logie Baird.

ENTERTAINMENT

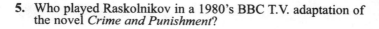

1. Who does James Grout play in T.V.'s *Inspector Morse*?

2. In which year did Fox studios fire Spencer Tracy after a spell in jail?

3. In which year was John Travolta born?

4. Who directed the 1966 film *Who's Afraid of Virginia Woolf?*?

5. Who played Raskolnikov in a 1980's BBC T.V. adaptation of the novel *Crime and Punishment*?

6. Who played a hooker in the 1984 film *Crimes of Passion*?

7. Which French director made the 1981 film *The Last Metro*?

8. Who played *Barton Fink* in the 1991 film?

9. Who played Fay Furillo in the T.V. show *Hill Street Blues*?

10. Which pair of writers penned the 1970s sitcom *Now Look Here...*?

11. What type of television series is an 'oater'?

12. Who played Piso in the BBC drama *I, Claudius*?

13. Who did William Avenell play in *Crossroads*?

14. Who played Gauguin in the 1956 film *Lust for Life*?

15. Who played Mark Graison in the T.V. show *Dallas*?

ANSWERS 1. Chief Supt. Strange **2.** 1935 **3.** 1954 **4.** Mike Nichols **5.** John Hurt **6.** Kathleen Turner **7.** Francois Truffaut **8.** John Turturro **9.** Barbara Bosson **10.** Graham Chapman and Barry Cryer **11.** A western series **12.** Stratford Johns **13.** Mr. Lovejoy **14.** Anthony Quinn **15.** John Beck.

SPORT

1. Which horse won the 1994 Cheltenham Gold Cup?

2. With what sport would you associate Doggett's Coat and Badge?

3. With what sport would you associate 'The Bourda'?

4. For which team did Jos Verstappen drive in the 1994 Grand Prix season?

5. Which team finished bottom in the 1998/99 Serie A in Italy?

6. Which football team won the 1998/99 Spanish league title?

7. Which football team won the 1998/99 German league title?

8. Which referee was pushed to the ground by footballer Paulo Di Canio in 1998?

9. Who did Lennox Lewis defeat in September 1998 to retain the WBC world heavyweight title?

10. Who did Herbie Hide defeat in September 1998 to retain his WBO world heavyweight title?

11. Who finished third in the 1994 Brazilian Grand Prix in Formula 1?

12. In which year did snooker player Joe Davis die?

13. Who won golf's 1994 Lyon Open?

14. Which former athlete was the 1994 London Marathon race organiser?

15. Which which sport would you associate Otilia Badescu?

ANSWERS 1. The Fellow 2. Rowing 3. Cricket 4. Benetton 5. Empoli 6. Barcelona 7. Bayern Munich 8. Paul Alcock 9. Zeljko Mavrovic 10. Willi Fischer 11. Jean Alesi 12. 1978 13. Stephen Ames 14. David Bedford 15. Table tennis.

POP MUSIC

1. In which year did Elvis Presley have a No. 1 U.K. single with *The Wonder of You*?

2. What was the debut L.P. of Dr. Feelgood?

3. Which U.S. singer's first solo chart single, in 1974, was *Just My Soul Responding*?

4. Who was the drummer in the group Dire Straits?

5. Which group had a Top 20 hit with *On a Rope* in 1996?

6. Who produced the album *Q: Are We Not Men? A: We Are Devo!*?

7. In which year did the Rolling Stones last have a U.K. No. 1 single?

8. Which group recorded 1981's *See the Whirl*?

9. Who duetted on the 1987 Top Ten single *Somewhere Out There*?

10. Which group's debut L.P. was called *Fresh Fruit for Rotting Vegetables*?

11. Which singer had a Top Ten single in 1992 with *One Shining Moment*?

12. Which group's second single was *Mattress of Wire*?

13. Which group's debut chart entry was 1996's *Take California*?

14. What was the debut album of Babes in Toyland?

15. Which group had a 1993 Top Ten single with *Almost Unreal*?

PEOPLE

1. Which former M.P. wrote the novel *Venice Midnight*?

2. Who played television's *Jonathan Creek*?

3. In which city did spy Kim Philby die in 1988?

4. Who played *Father Ted* on television?

5. Which Korean is head of the Unification Church?

6. Who was manager of The Beatles in the 1960s?

7. Who did Ramon Mercader assassinate in 1940?

8. Who directed the 1968 cult erotic film *Vixen*?

9. Tonya Flynt Vega is the daughter of which U.S. pornographer?

10. Who is Liberal Democrat M.P. for Yeovil?

11. Which I.R.A. defector, killed in 1999, wrote the book *Killing Rage*?

12. Jeremy Spake was the unlikely star of which T.V. documentary series?

13. Who wrote the play *The Four Alice Bakers*?

14. Who quit in January 1999 as Gordon Brown's press secretary?

15. What is the name of the England rugby union captain embroiled in a 1999 drug scandal?

ANSWERS 1. Gyles Brandreth **2.** Alan Davies **3.** Moscow **4.** Dermot Morgan **5.** Sung Myung Moon **6.** Brian Epstein **7.** Trotsky **8.** Russ Meyer **9.** Larry Flynt **10.** Paddy Ashdown **11.** Eamon Collins **12.** Airport **13.** Fay Weldon **14.** Charlie Whelan **15.** Lawrence Dallaglio.

GENERAL KNOWLEDGE

1. Which movement grew from a Bible study group formed by Charles Taze Russell in 1872?

2. What synthetic plastic was created by Leo Baekeland in 1909?

3. What is the name of Bertie Wooster's club in stories by P.G. Wodehouse?

4. Which German Nazi was expelled from Bolivia in 1983 and convicted of crimes against humanity in France in 1987?

5. Which U.S. circus owner coined the phrase "There's a sucker born every minute"?

6. What does NAAFI stand for?

7. On what date was the Nagasaki bomb dropped?

8. Over what distance is The Oaks flat race run?

9. In which London street is the drama school RADA?

10. The Rag was the old nickname of which club in Pall Mall?

11. In which year did Georgia join the U.N.?

12. Which singer was born Vera Margaret Lewis?

13. What type of creature is a junco - a bird or a snake?

14. Which Russian leaders were known as B & K on their 1956 visit to Britain?

15. Who authored the novel *The Napoleon of Notting Hill*?

ANSWERS 1. Jehovah's Witnesses 2. Bakelite 3. The Drones' Club 4. Klaus Barbie 5. P.T. Barnum 6. Navy, Army and Air Force Institutes 7. August 9, 1945 8. 1 and a half miles 9. Gower Street 10. Army and Navy Club 11. 1992 12. Vera Lynn 13. A bird 14. Bulganin and Khruschev 15. G.K. Chesterton.

ENTERTAINMENT

1. Who played Ruth Ellis in the 1985 film *Dance with a Stranger*?

2. Who directed the 1972 film *The King of Marvin Gardens*?

3. Who did Zeph Gladstone play in *Crossroads*?

4. Who played *The Invisible Man* in the 1933 film?

5. Who directed the 1993 film *In the Name of the Father*?

6. Which actress played the title role in the 1991 film *Whore*?

7. Who played Uncle Joe Grandi in the 1958 film *Touch of Evil*?

8. Who played Sarah in the 1955 film *Guys and Dolls*?

9. Who played Sgt. Lucy Bates in *Hill Street Blues*?

10. Who played *Sir Yellow* in the T.V. sitcom?

11. Who was *Mr. Merlin* in the US T.V. sitcom?

12. Which comedy team starred in the 1957 comedy show *Double Six*?

13. Who did Owen Brenman play in the comedy series *One Foot in the Grave*?

14. Who was quizmaster on *They Think It's All Over*?

15. Who played Sorenson in the show *NYPD Blue*?

SPORT

1. Who won the 1998 Luxembourg Grand Prix in Formula 1?

2. Who defeated the United States in the semi-final of the 1998 Davis Cup?

3. Who succeeded Christian Gross as manager of Tottenham Hotspur?

4. Which former England cricket captain of the 1980s became director of coaching at Middlesex CCC?

5. Which horse won the 1998 Prix de l'Arc de Triomphe?

6. Who succeeded George Graham as manager of Leeds United?

7. Who won the 1998 men's Swiss Indoor tennis singles title?

8. Which golfer won the 1998 World Matchplay title?

9. By what score did the New York Yankees beat the San Diego Padres in the 1998 World Series in baseball?

10. Who did Naseem Hamed outpoint in October, 1998 to retain his WBO featherweight boxing title?

11. Who won the 1994 Boat Race?

12. Which horse won the 1994 William Hill Lincoln Handicap?

13. Who scored Manchester United's goal in the 1994 Coca-Cola Cup Final?

14. Who won the men's 1994 Salem Open tennis title in Osaka?

15. Which Italian world heavyweight boxing champion worked as a strongman in a circus?

ANSWERS 1. Mika Hakkinen **2.** Italy **3.** George Graham **4.** Mike Gatting **5.** Sagamix **6.** David O'Leary **7.** Tim Henman **8.** Mark O'Meara **9.** 4-0 **10.** Wayne McCullogh **11.** Cambridge **12.** Our Rita **13.** Mark Hughes **14.** Pete Sampras **15.** Primo Carnera.

POP MUSIC

1. From which African country does the singer Rozalla come?

2. Which former member of Badfinger committed suicide in 1983?

3. Which group had a Top 20 single in 1993 with *You're in a Bad Way*?

4. In which city were group Balaam and the Angel from?

5. What are rappers Cheryl James & Sandra Denton better known as?

6. What was the debut album of the group Banco De Gaia?

7. Who duetted with Mike Sarne on the 1962 single *Will I What*?

8. Which group's debut L.P. was 1988's *Hope Against Hope*?

9. Which group had a 1997 Top Ten single with *Encore Une Fois*?

10. Who was the singer in the group Bauhaus?

11. Which group had a 1996 Top Ten single with *To Win Just One*?

12. On which studio album by the Beatles does *Norwegian Wood* appear?

13. Which comedian had a 1984 hit with *'Ullo John Got a New Motor*?

14. Which group's debut L.P. in 1990 was *Let Them Eat Bingo*?

15. Which rapper guested on the 1995 single *Hand of the Dead Body* by Scarface?

ANSWERS 1. Zimbabwe 2. Tom Evans 3. St. Etienne 4. Birmingham 5. Salt-n-Pepa 6. Maya 7. Billie Davis 8. The Band of Susans 9. Sash 10. Peter Murphy 11. Saw Doctors 12. Rubber Soul 13. Alexei Sayle 14. Beats International 15. Ice Cube.

ART AND LITERATURE

1. "It is a truth universally acknowledged that a single man in possession of a good fortune, must be in want of a wife". The opening lines of which novel?

2. Whose sculptures include 1946's *Pelagos*?

3. Whose sculptures include 1944's *The Table is Set*?

4. Who wrote *One Hundred Years of Solitude*?

5. Which artist said "Art is only a substitute while the beauty of life is still deficient"?

6. Who wrote *The Levanter*?

7. Who painted 1905's *Women in front of Fireplace*?

8. Who wrote *To Kill a Mockingbird*?

9. Who painted 1920's *Family Picture*?

10. Who wrote *The House of Mirth*?

11. Whose sculptures included 1929's *Reclining Woman*?

12. Who wrote the story *Cannery Row*?

13. Who wrote *The Tenant of Wildfell Hall*?

14. Of what art movement is Gino Severini's painting *Dancer-Helix-Sea* an example?

15. Whose plays include *Ivanov* and *The Seagull*?

ANSWERS 1. Pride and Prejudice, by Jane Austen **2.** Barbara Hepworth **3.** Max Ernst **4.** Gabriel Garcia Marquez **5.** Piet Mondrian **6.** Eric Ambler **7.** André Derain **8.** Harper Lee **9.** Max Beckmann **10.** Edith Wharton **11.** Alberto Giacometti **12.** John Steinbeck **13.** Anne Brontë **14.** Futurism **15.** Anton Chekhov.

GENERAL KNOWLEDGE

1. In which year did the National Coal Board take over the coal-mining industry?

2. Which Irish writer authored *At Swim-Two-Birds*?

3. What is the sweet Rahat Lakhoum better known as?

4. Which film director was born Allen Stewart Konigsberg?

5. Which U.S. president was known as 'Rail Splitter'?

6. What is the Middle Eastern dish of meat and rice known as dolmas wrapped in?

7. Who composed the opera *The Rake's Progress*?

8. What in Scotland is a kaleyard?

9. Who is the hero of the novel *Crime and Punishment*?

10. What was O'Connell Street, Dublin, previously known as?

11. Who composed the *Rasumovsky Quartets*?

12. Blepharitis is inflammation of which part of the face?

13. What did *The Raven* quoth in the poem by Edgar Allan Poe?

14. On what subject are the Reckitt lectures given?

15. Approximately what area, in square miles, is the Portuguese territory of Macao?

ENTERTAINMENT

1. In which European city was film director Mike Nichols born?

2. In which year did Southern Television come into being?

3. Who was *Mr. John Jorrocks* in the 1960s BBC T.V. serial?

4. Who played Len Tollit in the 1994 sitcom *Once Upon A Time In The North*?

5. Who directed the 1995 film *Money Train*?

6. Who starred as a parole officer in the 1949 film *Shockproof*?

7. Who directed the 1970 film *Drive, He Said*?

8. Who wrote the 1999 spoof football T.V. documentary *Bostock's Cup*?

9. Who directed the 1965 film *Never Too Late*?

10. Who plays Mrs. Warboys in the comedy series *One Foot in the Grave*?

11. Who played Lt. Buntz in *Hill Street Blues*?

12. Which detective's housekeeper was Mrs. Bardell in a 1960s T.V. series?

13. Who played Josie Packard in the T.V. drama *Twin Peaks*?

14. Who played Nero in the BBC historical drama *I, Claudius*?

15. Who played Sandy Richardson in the T.V. soap *Crossroads*?

ANSWERS 1. Berlin **2.** 1958 **3.** Jimmy Edwards **4.** Bernard Hill **5.** Joseph Ruben **6.** Cornel Wilde **7.** Jack Nicholson **8.** Chris England **9.** Bud Yorkin **10.** Doreen Mantle **11.** Dennis Franz **12.** Sexton Blake **13.** Joan Chen **14.** Christopher Biggins **15.** Roger Tonge.

SPORT

1. Who was the first Finn to win the World Formula 1 motor racing championship?

2. Who knocked Aston Villa out of the 1998/99 UEFA Cup?

3. Who ceased to be manager of Wolves in November 1998?

4. By what score did England beat the Netherlands in their Rugby World Cup qualifier in November 1998?

5. By what score did England beat the Czech Republic in a 1998 friendly at Wembley?

6. Who won the 1998/99 First Test in cricket between England and Australia?

7. Who knocked Liverpool out of the 1998/99 UEFA Cup?

8. Who did Jane Couch beat in the first official women's professional bout in the U.K.?

9. Who replaced Roy Hodgson as manager of Blackburn Rovers?

10. Which woman won the 1998 European Cross-Country Championships?

11. Who was named BBC Sports Personality of the Year in December 1998?

12. By how many runs did Australia defeat England in the Third Test in December, 1998?

13. Which horse won the 1998 King George VI Chase?

14. Which jockey won the 1953 & '54 Grand National?

15. In which U.S. state was boxer Sonny Liston born?

POP MUSIC

1. Which group had chart success in 1986 with *Rise* and *Home*?

2. How are Tanya Donelly and Kristin Hersh, formerly of Throwing Muses, related?

3. Which duo charted with 1995's *Independent Love Song*?

4. In which year was Chuck Berry born?

5. Who had a 1995 hit single with *Scatman's World*?

6. From which country do the band Bettie Serveert come?

7. Which group's debut chart single in 1997 was *Love is the Law*?

8. Whose 1986 album was *Atomizer*?

9. Which vocalist had a 1997 Top 20 hit with *Fly Like An Angel*?

10. How did Chris Bell, singer with the group Big Star, die?

11. Which group had a Top Ten single in 1997 with *Help the Aged*?

12. To what did Australian group The Boys Next Door change their name in 1978?

13. In which year was singer Neil Sedaka born?

14. On which 1966 studio album by the Beatles did *Yellow Submarine* appear?

15. Which duo had a 1961 hit with *Bangers and Mash*?

GEOGRAPHY

1. Is Airdrie east or west of Glasgow?

2. Which is larger - Alabama or Albania?

3. On which gulf is the Italian seaport of Amalfi?

4. In which South American country is the volcano Antisana?

5. Which strait connects the Mediterranean Sea to the Atlantic?

6. To which island republic does the Mediterranean island of Gozo belong?

7. What is the capital of Nova Scotia, Canada?

8. Which is larger - Lithuania or Latvia?

9. On which river does Leicester stand?

10. As what are the resorts of Paignton, Torquay and Brixham collectively known?

11. The town of Wagga Wagga is in which Australian state?

12. What is the name of the peninsula between Portsmouth and Bognor Regis?

13. What is the name of the group of chalk stacks in the English Channel off the west coast of the Isle of Wight?

14. What is the name of the town in S.E. France famous for nougat manufacture?

15. Which strait separates Sumatra from mainland Malaysia?

ANSWERS 1. East 2. Alabama 3. Gulf of Salerno 4. Ecuador 5. Strait of Gibraltar 6. Malta 7. Halifax 8. Latvia 9. River Soar 10. Torbay 11. New South Wales 12. Selsey Bill 13. The Needles 14. Montélimar 15. Strait of Malacca.

GENERAL KNOWLEDGE

1. Of which country was Sir John Grey Gorton prime minister from 1968 to 1971?

2. Which flag is known as the Red Duster?

3. What type of creature is a chacma?

4. Ragusa was the former Italian name of which port?

5. What type of creature is a kalong?

6. Which Labour M.P. for Jarrow was appointed Minister of Education in 1945?

7. Who wrote the novel *Conducting Bodies*?

8. How many paces to the minute is the double-time march in the U.S. army?

9. Who designed the 14-foot dinghy known as a Redwing?

10. In which year was the Reform Club in London founded?

11. Who authored the short story collection *Dubliners*?

12. Which two places did the bridge over the Rhine at Remagen link?

13. Who wrote the 1920 novel *The Rescue*?

14. Who authored the novel *The Tower of Trebizond*?

15. Which three countries formed the Triple Entente in World War One?

ENTERTAINMENT

1. Which London-born actor's real name was James Stewart?

2. In which city was Cary Grant born?

3. Who played 'the Thief' in the 1989 film *The Cook, the Thief, His Wife and Her Lover*?

4. Which star of the 1941 film *The Maltese Falcon* was born in Sandwich?

5. Which film director died at the Knickerbocker Hotel in Hollywood in 1948?

6. Which actress was given a toy coffin by Alfred Hitchcock containing a doll of her mother?

7. Which historical figure did Sir John Gielgud play in the 1942 film *The Prime Minister*?

8. Which actress wrote the book *The Movies, Mr. Griffith and Me*?

9. Who was married to Charlie Chaplin from 1933 to 1942?

10. Whose novel *Magic* was filmed in 1978?

11. Which actress played Maude in the film *Harold and Maude*?

12. Which actress married her stepson Anthony Ray in 1961?

13. In which Hitchcock film does the character of tennis champion Guy Barnes appear?

14. Whose T.V. plays include *The Insurance Man* and *An Englishman Abroad*?

15. Who was the comedy partner of Lennie Bennett?

ANSWERS 1. Stewart Granger **2.** Bristol **3.** Michael Gambon **4.** Sydney Greenstreet **5.** D.W. Griffith **6.** Melanie Griffith **7.** Disraeli **8.** Lillian Gish **9.** Paulette Goddard **10.** William Goldman **11.** Ruth Gordon **12.** Gloria Grahame **13.** Strangers on a Train **14.** Alan Bennett **15.** Jerry Stevens.

SPORT

1. At what sport is Ross Norman a former world champion?

2. How many fours did Brian Lara hit in his record breaking 375 Test score?

3. How many horses finished in the 1994 Aintree Grand National?

4. Which former Chelsea boss was a coach of the Zambian football team?

5. Who won the 1994 U.S. Masters golf tournament?

6. At what sport did Betty Snowball play for England?

7. Who won cycling's 1994 Grand Prix de L'Escaut?

8. Who rode Miinnehoma in the 1994 Aintree Grand National?

9. Who won the 1994 African Nations Cup in football?

10. Who won the 1994 Japan Open Tennis Tournament?

11. Who won the 1994 British Open snooker tournament?

12. Who won the 1994 Hong Kong Open tennis men's singles title?

13. What is a mashawi?

14. How many times have Liverpool won football's European Champions Cup?

15. In which sport is the Iroquois Cup competed for?

POP MUSIC

1. What was Suzi Quatro's last solo Top Ten hit, in 1978?

2. Under which name did Elvis Costello and T-Bone Burnett release the single *The People's Limousine*?

3. Which group had Top 20 hits in 1992 with *Hold it Down* and *Easy to Smile*?

4. Which punk singer wrote the song *Texas Chainsaw Manicurist*?

5. From which country do the group Sepultra hail?

6. Which singer recorded the 1973 album *Marjory Razorblade*?

7. Who had a Top Ten single in 1997 with *Even After All*?

8. What was the second single of 1960s group The Creation?

9. Which group had a 1975 Top 20 hit with *Let Me Be the One*?

10. Which group recorded the 1993 album *Black Sunday*?

11. Which reggae star had a 1993 hit with *Oh Carolina*?

12. Which band's only album was 1984's *The Waking Hour*?

13. Jeffrey Daniel, Jody Whatley and Howard Hewitt comprised which group?

14. Which group's albums included 1979's *Machine Gun Etiquette*?

15. Which group charted in 1998 with single *Tell Me Ma*?

HISTORY

1. Which island was originally named after a governor-general of the Dutch East India Company?

2. Who was king of France from 1774-92?

3. Of which country was Le Duc Anh president from 1992-97?

4. With whom did Jerry Rubin form the Yippies in 1968?

5. In which year did Margaret Roberts marry Denis Thatcher?

6. Who was president of the Republic of Ireland from 1973-74?

7. Who succeeded Michael Foot as leader of the Labour Party?

8. In which U.S. city did Franklin Pierce live after he left the White House?

9. Who was Chancellor of the Exchequer from 1964-67?

10. Who was prime minister of the Republic of Ireland from 1982-87?

11. Under which U.S. president was Hamilton Fish vice-president from 1869-77?

12. John Grey Gort was prime minister of which country from 1968-71?

13. Who was British Prime Minister from 1970-74?

14. In which year did Hugh Gaitskell become Labour Party leader?

15. In which year did the Soviet *Lunik 1* satellite become the first to escape earth's gravity?

ANSWERS 1. Tasmania **2.** Louis XVI **3.** Vietnam **4.** Abbie Hoffman **5.** 1951 **6.** Erskine Childers **7.** Neil Kinnock **8.** Concord **9.** James Callaghan **10.** Garret FitzGerald **11.** Ulysses S. Grant **12.** Australia **13.** Edward Heath **14.** 1955 **15.** 1959.

GENERAL KNOWLEDGE

1. Who was Conservative prime minister from 1937-40?

2. In which year was the Exxon Valdez oil disaster?

3. What is the standard monetary unit of Uzbekistan?

4. Which place houses the Ulster American Folk Park?

5. What sort of creature is a dowitcher - a fish or a bird?

6. What are the Church of Jesus Christ of Latter-Day Saints also called?

7. John Heathcoat and John Levers designed machinery to manufacture which material?

8. Which city is home to the University of Kentucky?

9. Alcala is the main street of which European capital city?

10. Who is the heroine of the novel *Gone with the Wind*?

11. What type of performer might use a blocked shoe?

12. What is the name of the chief Belgian airline?

13. What was the Roman name for the River Severn?

14. What is the name given to a score of nought in cricket?

15. In which European capital is the Hotel Sacher?

ANSWERS 1. Neville Chamberlain 2. 1989 3. Sum 4. Omagh 5. A bird 6. Mormons 7. Lace 8. Lexington 9. Madrid 10. Scarlett O'Hara 11. A ballet dancer 12. Sabena 13. Sabrina 14. Duck 15. Vienna.

ENTERTAINMENT

1. In which year did the word game *Countdown* start on Channel Four?

2. In which children's show did the quiz *Double or Drop* appear?

3. Which Victorian detective did Alan Dobie play in the early 1980s on T.V.?

4. Which comedian narrated *The Wombles* on T.V. in the 1970s?

5. What was Victor's wife called in the show *One Foot in the Grave*?

6. In which city was comedian Barry Cryer born?

7. Which comedian played Kevin O'Grady in the 1969 sitcom *Curry and Chips*?

8. Who did Colin Bean play in *Dad's Army*?

9. Which actress married director Renny Harlin in 1983?

10. Which writer was played by Daniel Day-Lewis in the film *My Left Foot*?

11. Which actor voiced the cartoon character *Mr. Magoo*?

12. Which actress is the older sister of Joan Fontaine?

13. What does the initial B stand for in the name of director Cecil B. De Mille?

14. *Stop Making Sense* was a film of a concert given by which pop group?

15. In which film did Robert De Niro play Rupert Pupkin?

SPORT

1. Which horse first won two English Classics in the same season?

2. Who was 1993's top earning British sportsman?

3. Which horse won the 1994 Whitbread Gold Cup?

4. Who won the 1994 South Korean Open men's singles tennis tournament?

5. Who won the 1994 Monte Carlo Open men's singles tennis title?

6. Who knocked James Wattana out of the 1994 World professional snooker tournament?

7. Which golfer won the 1988 USPGA title?

8. How many teams comprised the first English football league in 1888?

9. Who won the first British Open golf title in 1860?

10. In which year did Steffi Graf win her first Grand Slam title?

11. Who won snooker's first Pot Black tournament on BBCTV?

12. Who refereed the 1994 F.A. Cup Final at Wembley?

13. Which side won the 1994 Middlesex Sevens competition?

14. Who won the 1994 Tennents Irish Cup in hockey?

15. Who scored twice for Milan in their 1994 European Champions Cup final win?

POP MUSIC

1. In which year did Queen chart with the single *Seven Seas of Rhye*?

2. Who was the drummer in The Spencer Davis Group?

3. Which group had a 1995 hit with *Transamazonia*?

4. Which group recorded the 1990 album *Stay Sick!*?

5. Which duo had a 1996 Top 30 single with *Girl Power*?

6. Whose debut L.P. was 1987's *Introducing the Hardline*?

7. Which singer featured on the 1998 hit *Move Mania* by Sash!?

8. Who was lead singer in the group Curve?

9. In which year was singer Helen Shapiro born?

10. In which city did Southern Death Cult form in 1982?

11. In which year was singer Sandie Shaw born?'

12. Which group recorded the 1971 album *Cosmo's Factory*?

13. Which group's debut chart single was 1994's *Dolphin*?

14. What is drummer Ginger Baker's real first name?

15. Who had a 1998 Top Ten single with *Searchin' my Soul*?

ANSWERS 1. 1974 **2.** Pete York **3.** Shamen **4.** The Cramps **5.** Shampoo **6.** Terence Trent D'Arby **7.** Shannon **8.** Toni Halliday **9.** 1946 **10.** Bradford **11.** 1947 **12.** Creedence Clearwater Revival **13.** Shed Seven **14.** Peter **15.** Vonda Shepard.

WORDS

1. What, politically, does UDI stand for?

2. What would you do with a scrod in the U.S. - cook it or cook with it?

3. What is a gamin?

4. What is mazuma a slang word for?

5. What is hoya - a plant or a bird?

6. What in nautical slang is burgoo?

7. What type of birds' nests are used to make bird's-nest soup?

8. How many strokes under par is a birdie on a golf hole?

9. What does SWALK mean on the back of an envelope?

10. For what is the Australian word 'ocker' slang?

11. What food is also called garbanzo?

12. To which part of the body does the adjective gnathic relate?

13. What would you do with ugali - write with it or eat it?

14. What does 'entre nous' mean?

15. Of which country is ukiyoe a school of painting?

ANSWERS 1. Unilateral declaration of independence 2. Cook it - it's a fish 3. A street urchin or waif 4. Money 5. A plant 6. Porridge 7. Swifts 8. One 9. Sealed with a loving kiss 10. An uncultivated or boorish person 11. Chickpea 12. The jaw 13. Eat it - it's cornmeal and water 14. Between you and me 15. Japan.

GENERAL KNOWLEDGE

1. What acid is also called 2-hydroxypropanoic acid?

2. Yakubu Gowon was head of state of which African country from 1966-75?

3. In which year was the Battle of Leyte Gulf in World War II?

4. What type of farmyard animal is a saddleback?

5. What in Russia were the Okhrana in the late 19th century and early 20th century?

6. In law, what is 'chance-medley'?

7. Which U.S. state is known as the 'Sagebrush State'?

8. In which film is a string quartet by Boccherini used by a group of crooks to provide cover?

9. Which fictional character's symbol is a haloed pin-man?

10. What is the Hungarian name for the River Danube?

11. What does the French firm St-Gobain specialize in making?

12. Over what distance is the Ebor Handicap run at York in August?

13. Who wrote the 1912 play *Hindle Wakes*?

14. Which 1943 musical includes the song *Oh, What a Beautiful Mornin'*?

15. What is the American songbird a crow blackbird also called?

ANSWERS 1. Lactic acid **2.** Nigeria **3.** 1944 **4.** A pig **5.** Russian Imperial secret police **6.** A sudden quarrel in which one party kills another **7.** Nevada **8.** The Ladykillers **9.** The Saint **10.** Duna **11.** Glass **12.** 1 and three-quarter miles **13.** Stanley Houghton **14.** Oklahoma! **15.** Grackle.

ENTERTAINMENT

1. Which actor's 1985 autobiography was called *Blessings in Disguise*?

2. What was Gene Hackman's character name in the film *The French Connection*?

3. Which actor and actress played the leads in the 1986 film *The Money Pit*?

4. Who played *Cromwell* in the 1970 film?

5. Which actor's six wives included Kay Kendall, Rachel Roberts and Lilli Palmer?

6. Who played Joe Lampton in the 1959 film *Room at the Top*?

7. Which actress and ice skater wrote the autobiography *Wings on my Feet*?

8. In which city was Audrey Hepburn born?

9. Who composed the score for the 1976 film *Taxi Driver*?

10. Which actor was born Charles Carter in 1924?

11. On whose stories were Alfred Hitchcock's films *The Birds*, *Jamaica Inn* and *Rebecca* based?

12. The character Joe Gillis narrates which film?

13. Who played Napoleon in the 1981 film *Time Bandits*?

14. Who played Bligh in the 1984 film *The Bounty*?

15. What was Dennis Hopper's character name in the film *Blue Velvet*?

SPORT

1. Who did Everton beat in their last Premier League fixture of 1993/94?

2. For how many years did Bob Beamon's long jump record stand?

3. At what sport was Joe Hagan the first world champion?

4. Who was the 1964 Olympic women's 100m champion?

5. Who was the world amateur snooker champion in 1984 & '85?

6. Who won the 1994 Italian Open men's singles tennis title?

7. Which horse won the 1994 Irish 2,000 Guineas?

8. Which team won the 1994 Welsh Cup Final in football?

9. Who was the 1994 women's USPGA golf champion?

10. In how many Tests did Allan Border captain Australia?

11. Who were the 1993/94 Spanish Football League champions?

12. Which Spanish golf course hosted the 1997 Ryder Cup?

13. Which team were 1993/94 Portuguese Football League champions?

14. Which horse finished second in the 1994 Epsom Derby?

15. Which teams contested the 1994 Stanley Cup Final?

ANSWERS 1. Wimbledon 2. 23 years 3. Croquet 4. Wyomia Tyus 5. Paul Mitsud 6. Pete Sampras 7. Turtle Island 8. Barry Town 9. Laura Davies 10. 93 11. Barcelona 12. Valderrama 13. Benfica 14. King's Theatre 15. New York Rangers and Vancouver Canucks.

POP MUSIC

1. What was Pluto Shervington's 1976 Top 10 single?

2. In which city did The Cowboy Junkies form in 1985?

3. On which record label did Showaddywaddy have a No. 1 single in 1976?

4. Which group's second album was *I-Feel-Like-I'm-Fixin'-To-Die*?

5. Which group had a 1979 No. 2 single with *Some Girls*?

6. In which year was guitarist Elvin Bishop born?

7. In which city did The Dylans form in 1989?

8. Who was the songwriter in the 1980s group Black?

9. Which group recorded the 1974 album *On the Border*?

10. Who was the original bass player in the group Blondie?

11. Which group recorded the 1996 album *Don Solaris*?

12. What is David Bowie's real name?

13. Which Chicago guitarist formed the group the Electric Flag in 1967?

14. In which year was blues singer Bobby Bland born?

15. Which group recorded the 1973 album *Brain Salad Surgery*?

ANSWERS 1. Dat 2. Toronto 3. Bell 4. Country Joe and the Fish 5. Racey 6. 1942 7. Sheffield 8. Colin Vearncombe 9. The Eagles 10. Fred Smith 11. 808 State 12. David Jones 13. Mike Bloomfield 14. 1930 15. E.L.P.

SCIENCE

1. What is the SI unit of magnetic flux?

2. What in meteorology is the name given to the place where a cold front has overtaken a warm front?

3. Which Whitby-born scientist is known as the 'father of genetics'?

4. What in geology is a grike?

5. What do the letters RH stand for in meteorology?

6. How many grams of fibre per 100 grams are there in apples?

7. The element rhodium is named after the Greek word for which flower?

8. What is the name given to the igneous rocks that form on the Earth's surface?

9. Approximately what percentage of the atmosphere is formed by the gas argon?

10. What is the name given to the ratio of power to area in light?

11. What in mathematics do the initials LCM stand for?

12. What are nimbostratus and cirrocumulus?

13. How many arms does a starfish usually have?

14. How many satellites does Venus have?

15. Of what is dendrophobia a fear?

ANSWERS 1. Weber **2.** An occluded front **3.** William Bateson **4.** A cleft in a limestone pavement **5.** Relative humidity **6.** Two **7.** Rose **8.** Extrusive rocks **9.** 1% **10.** Intensity **11.** Lowest common multiple **12.** Cloud types **13.** Five **14.** None **15.** Trees.

GENERAL KNOWLEDGE

1. What is the nickname of Southampton F.C.?

2. What was the pen-name of writer H.H. Munro?

3. In which year was the Battle of Edgehill?

4. In which year did German Protestant theologian Martin Luther die?

5. What sort of creature is a bluetongue?

6. In which month is Bampton Fair, in Devon, usually held?

7. What is the name of the donkey in the *Winnie-the-Pooh* tales?

8. Herm, Jethou and Lihou are part of which island group?

9. Which award given by RIBA did Woodlea Primary School win in 1993?

10. In which year did Wyoming join the Union?

11. Which artist won the 1994 B.P. Portrait Award?

12. Who was Miss United Kingdom in 1992?

13. What is the weedy plant charlock also called?

14. How would you detain someone using jougs?

15. Which was CAMRA's champion beer of Britain in 1993?

ANSWERS 1. The saints 2. Saki 3. 1642 4.1546 5. A lizard 6. October 7. Eeyore 8. The Channel Islands 9. Building of the Year 10. 1908 11. Peter Edwards 12. Claire Smith 13. Wild mustard 14. By the neck - it's an iron ring attached to a wall 15. Adnam's Extra.

ENTERTAINMENT

1. Who played P.C. Nick Rowan in the T.V. show *Heartbeat*?

2. Who played Mo Connell in the cop series *Between the Lines*?

3. Which T.V. show's theme tune was *The Ballad of Jed Clampett*?

4. Who played the character Plaid Shirt in the film *Beat Girl*?

5. Which actor is the father of actress Laura Dern?

6. Which diminutive actor was born in Neptune, New Jersey, in 1944?

7. Who played Feathers in the 1959 film *Rio Bravo*?

8. In which country was Marlene Dietrich born?

9. Chuck Connors appeared as Jason McCord in which T.V. western series?

10. Who did Bryan Murray play in the T.V. comedy *Bread*?

11. Who played Maxim de Winter in the 1979 T.V. adaptation of *Rebecca*?

12. Which comic actor narrated the cartoon *Roobarb and Custard*?

13. Which actor narrated the children's series *Mr. Benn*?

14. Which actor played Pat Hancock in *Brookside*?

15. Who played Jane Maxwell in the 1970s series *The Brothers*?

ANSWERS 1. Nick Berry **2.** Siobhan Redmond **3.** The Beverly Hillbillies **4.** Oliver Reed **5.** Bruce Dern **6.** Danny DeVito **7.** Angie Dickinson **8.** Germany **9.** Branded **10.** Shifty **11.** Jeremy Brett **12.** Richard Briers **13.** Ray Brooks **14.** David Easter **15.** Kate O'Mara.

SPORT

1. What did The Duke win in 1836 & '37?

2. Who won the 1992 Olympic men's 400m title?

3. Who won cycling's 1993 Milk Race?

4. In which year was the Ryder Cup first held in Britain?

5. Which horse won the 1993 Prix de l'Arc de Triomphe?

6. Who was the 1993 world 500c.c. motor cycling champion?

7. Who won the 1994 Spanish Grand Prix in Formula 1?

8. Who won the 1994 women's world snooker championship?

9. Which jockey won the 1994 Oaks?

10. In which year did Hanif Mohammad score his record innings of 499?

11. What nationality is motor racing driver David Coulthard?

12. Which rugby union side are known as 'the Pumas'?

13. What was the name of the mascot in the 1994 Football World Cup?

14. Which golfer won the 1994 Buick Classic in New York?

15. Who were the top male and female seeds in the 1994 Wimbledon tennis tournament?

ANSWERS 1. The Grand National **2.** Quincy Watts **3.** Chris Lillywhite **4.** 1929 **5.** Subotica **6.** Kevin Schwantz **7.** Damon Hill **8.** Allison Fisher **9.** Frankie Dettori **10.** 1958 **11.** Scottish **12.** Argentina **13.** Striker **14.** Lee Janzen **15.** Pete Sampras and Steffi Graf.

POP MUSIC

1. In which year was musician and producer Brian Eno born?

2. What was the debut album by the group The Blue Nile?

3. Which group recorded the 1969 album *What We Did on Our Holidays*?

4. Which songwriter recorded the 1988 album *Worker's Playtime*?

5. On which record label did The Radha Krishna Temple chart in 1970 with *Govinda*?

6. Which band recorded the 1984 album *Ocean Rain*?

7. Which band recorded the 1990 album *Shake Your Money Maker*?

8. In which city were indie group The Blue Aeroplanes formed?

9. In which year did Radiohead have a Top Ten single with *Creep*?

10. In which year was singer Gary 'US' Bonds born?

11. After what is the group Fatima Mansions named?

12. Sam Spoons and Vernon Dudley Bohey-Nowell were members of which 1960s group?

13. Who was lead singer with the group Felt?

14. What was the debut album by the group Boston?

15. In which year did Queen first chart with *Another One Bites the Dust*?

PEOPLE

1. With which T.V. presenter was Sophie Rhys-Jones shown to be frolicking in 1988 in a 1999 newspaper story?

2. Who is Labour leader of the House of Lords?

3. Which circus trainer was convicted of cruelty to a chimpanzee in January 1999?

4. To which D.J. is radio presenter Zoë Ball married?

5. Which celebrity chef was reputedly the first person in Britain to have worn disposable nappies?

6. Which actress, star of the film *Hideous Kinky*, was called 'Blubber' at school?

7. Who wrote the novel *Tara Road*?

8. Which newspaperwoman wrote the novel *Married Alive*?

9. Who played Bianca in *EastEnders*?

10. Who was sacked as England's football coach in February 1999?

11. Which former Conservative M.E.P. was caught bringing drugs and pornography into the U.K. in February 1999?

12. Which comedian wrote the novel *Blast from the Past*?

13. The film *Hilary and Jackie* told the story of which cellist?

14. Jane McDonald was the unlikely star of which T.V. documentary series?

15. Who starred as Alice in a 1998 T.V. version of *Alice Through the Looking-Glass*?

ANSWERS 1. Chris Tarrant **2.** Baroness Jay **3.** Mary Chipperfield **4.** Norman Cook **5.** Antony Worrall Thompson **6.** Kate Winslet **7.** Maeve Binchy **8.** Julie Birchill **9.** Patsy Palmer **10.** Glenn Hoddle **11.** Tom Spencer **12.** Ben Elton **13.** Jacqueline du Pré **14.** The Cruise **15.** Kate Beckinsale.

GENERAL KNOWLEDGE

1. Duroc is an American breed of what animal?

2. What does the abbreviation OPEC stand for?

3. Which artist won the 1991 Turner Prize?

4. Who wrote the novels *The Choir* and *The Rector's Wife*?

5. Which marital award did Kerry Doyland win in 1994?

6. What nutlike seed is produced by the tree *Prunus amygdalus*?

7. Who is Punch's wife in the traditional puppet show?

8. Which athlete was voted world champion budgie breeder in 1993?

9. What was awarded the accolade of 1993 Car of the Year by *What Car?* magazine?

10. What is the oil from the seed of the chaulmoogra tree used to treat?

11. Which TV award did Derek Johns win in 1993?

12. What in South Africa is a jukskei?

13. Which authoress won the 1990 Guardian Children's Fiction Award?

14. In which year did Tchaikovsky write the *1812 Overture*?

15. Which Nobel prize did Gary Becker win in 1992?

ANSWERS 1. Pig **2.** Organization of Petroleum Exporting Countries **3.** Anish Kapoor **4.** Joanna Trollope **5.** Clothes Show Bride of the Year **6.** Almond **7.** Judy **8.** Geoff Capes **9.** Ford Mondeo 1.8 GLX **10.** Leprosy **11.** Masterchef **12.** A game **13.** Anne Fine **14.** 1880 **15.** Economics.

ENTERTAINMENT

1. Which comedy scriptwriting team wrote *Brush Strokes*?

2. What kind of creature was Captain Morgan in the 1950s T.V. series *The Buccaneers*?

3. In which early 1970s drama series did the character Laughing Spam Fritter appear?

4. What was the central character in the ITV drama *Public Eye* called?

5. What was Walt Disney's middle name?

6. In which city was actor Robert Donat born?

7. Which actor was born Issur Danielovich Demsky?

8. Which gangster did Richard Dreyfuss play in the 1973 film *Dillinger*?

9. Which Scottish singer achieved fame after appearing in the BBC show *The Big Time*?

10. Which Hollywood actress played Victoria Barkley in the 1960s western drama series *The Big Valley*?

11. Who played Tosh Lines in *The Bill*?

12. What was the name of the dog in the series *The Bionic Woman*?

13. Which actress was born Hedwig Eva Maria Kiesler in 1913?

14. In which film did Burt Lancaster play H.H. Hunsecker?

15. Which actress starred in the 1976 remake of *King Kong*?

SPORT

1. Who won the 1994 men's French Open tennis singles title?

2. At what sport did Olympic gold medal winner Eric Liddell win seven caps?

3. At what sport was Karl Maier a world champion in the 1980s?

4. What nationality is golfer Vijay Singh?

5. On which course was the 1994 US Open golf tournament held?

6. Which baseball player was known as 'the Yankee Clipper'?

7. Who knocked Zena Garrison-Jackson out of the 1994 Wimbledon women's singles tennis tournament?

8. Who scored five goals for Russia against Cameroon in the 1994 World Cup Finals?

9. When did Martina Navratilova win her first Wimbledon singles title?

10. Where was the 1994 French Grand Prix in Formula 1 held?

11. In which city was Gary Lineker born?

12. Which horse won the 1979 Epsom Derby?

13. Who won Group A in the 1994 World Cup Finals?

14. In motor racing, which is oldest of the Grand Prix races?

15. In which country did real tennis originate?

THE ULTIMATE PUB QUIZ BOOK

POP MUSIC

1. With which song did Caroline Quentin and Leslie Ash chart in 1996?

2. In which year was the group Black Sabbath formed?

3. What was the title of Jesse Rae's only chart single in 1985?

4. John Plain and Jack Black were members of which London punk band?

5. In which year was Bryan Ferry born?

6. Which group recorded the 1994 album *Brother Sister*?

7. Which group recorded the 1984 album *The Works*?

8. What was the debut album of thr group The Breeders?

9. Who recorded the 1986 album *Guitar Town*?

10. In which year did the Chocolate Watch Band form?

11. Who produced the 1995 album *The Bends* by Radiohead?

12. In which city did the group Clock DVA form?

13. What was the second album by The Ramones?

14. In which year did singer Eddie Cochran die?

15. In which city did Red Lorry Yellow Lorry form in 1982?

ART AND LITERATURE

1. Whose sculptures include 1913's *Unique Forms of Continuity in Space*?

2. Which artist painted 1910's *Piano and Lute*?

3. Who wrote the novel *Mary Anne*?

4. Which artist painted 1913's *Violin and Guitar*?

5. Who painted 1912's *Simultaneous Windows*?

6. Whose books include *The Talented Mr. Ripley*?

7. What was the original name of painter Robert Indiana?

8. Who wrote the novel *Carmen* on which Bizet's opera was based?

9. What nationality is the writer Sara Lidman?

10. Who wrote *The Friends of Eddie Coyle*?

11. Whose crime novels include *The Seven Dials Mystery*?

12. In which novel does the character Squire Allworthy appear?

13. Who wrote the children's tale *The Little Prince*?

14. Which 1922 novel by D.H. Lawrence features a flautist as the central character?

15. In which 1742 novel by Henry Fielding do Squire Booby and Mrs. Slipshod feature?

GENERAL KNOWLEDGE

1. What did the initials BOAC stand for in the world of transport?

2. In which year did HMS Lutine sink?

3. How many seats did the Liberal Party get in the 1966 election?

4. Under which party flag did Dick Taverne win a 1973 by-election in Lincoln?

5. Who was British Hairdresser of the Year in 1993?

6. Which London hotel won the Egon Ronay Hotel of the Year award in 1989?

7. Which was found to be most popular hymn in a 1992 survey by BBC's *Songs of Praise*?

8. What sort of creature is a cheese skipper?

9. Gralloch is the name given to the entrails of which animal?

10. What does the abbreviation IQ stand for?

11. What is the standard monetary unit of Thailand?

12. In which year was the Seventh Day Adventist Church founded?

13. Which three metals comprise the alloy alnico?

14. Which king of Poland converted Lithuania to Christianity?

15. What in India is the profession of a durzi?

ANSWERS 1. British Overseas Airways Corporation 2. 1799 3. 12 4. Democratic Labour 5. Andrew Collinge 6. The Savoy 7. Dear Lord and Father of Mankind 8. A fly 9. Deer 10. Intelligence Quotient 11. Baht 12. 1863 13. Aluminium, nickel and cobalt 14. Ladislaus II 15. A tailor.

ENTERTAINMENT

1. Which operatic movie star was born Alfred Arnold Cocozza in 1921?

2. In which town was actor Charles Laughton born?

3. Who played the wife of *Houdini* in the 1953 film?

4. December 10th, 1938, was the first day of shooting of which epic film?

5. Who directed the 1988 film *Rain Man*?

6. Who did Bob Hoskins play in the 1991 film *Hook*?

7. Who played *The Scarlet Pimpernel* in the 1934 film?

8. Who played the lead in the 1980 film *Sir Henry at Rawlinson End*?

9. Which actor was born Roy Harold Scherer Jr.?

10. In which city was Sophia Loren born?

11. During the making of which film did Bela Lugosi die?

12. What object does the camera follow in the title sequence of the film *Forrest Gump*?

13. Who played Mr. Pink in the film *Reservoir Dogs*?

14. What does Sidney Poitier build for a group of nuns in the film *Lilies of the Field*?

15. Who wrote the comedy drama *A Bit of a Do*?

ANSWERS 1. Mario Lanza **2.** Scarborough **3.** Janet Leigh **4.** Gone With the Wind **5.** Barry Levinson **6.** Smee **7.** Leslie Howard **8.** Trevor Howard **9.** Rock Hudson **10.** Rome **11.** Plan 9 from Outer Space **12.** A feather **13.** Steve Buscemi **14.** A chapel **15.** David Nobbs.

SPORT

1. Who was the first Welsh world professional snooker champion?

2. Which horse won the 1994 Irish Derby?

3. Who won the 1994 French Open golf title?

4. Which golfers entered the three-way play-off in the 1994 U.S. Open?

5. Who scored the first goal in the 1994 World Cup Finals?

6. Who won the 1994 Le Mans 24-hour race?

7. Who won the 1994 Stanley Cup?

8. Who did Andre Agassi defeat in the 1994 U.S. Open men's singles tennis final?

9. Who did Linfield play in the first round of the 1994/5 UEFA Cup?

10. Who won the 1994 Minor Counties cricket title?

11. From which country are the football side Bodoe Glimt?

12. Which cyclist won the 1994 Paris-Brussels classic?

13. Who won golf's 1994 European Open?

14. Who won the 1994 Italian Grand Prix in Formula 1?

15. In which year was Ossie Ardiles born?

ANSWERS 1. Ray Reardon 2. Balanchine 3. Mark Roe 4. Colin Montgomerie, Loren Roberts & Ernie Els 5. Jürgen Klinsmann 6. Yannick Dalmas, Hurley Haywood & Mauro Baldi 7. The New York Rangers 8. Michael Stich 9. Odense BK 10. Devon 11. Norway 12. Rolf Sorenson 13. David Gifford 14. Damon Hill 15. 1952.

POP MUSIC

1. In which year was singer Lou Reed born?

2. Who recorded the 1969 album *Songs from a Room*?

3. In which city did the Rezillos form in 1976?

4. In which year was guitarist Ry Cooder born?

5. Who produced the 1976 album *The Modern Lovers*?

6. Which group's 1995 album was called *Showbusiness*?

7. Who is the drummer in The Rolling Stones?

8. Who recorded the 1995 album *20 Mothers*?

9. In which year was David Lee Roth born?

10. In which city were the group The Comsat Angels formed?

11. What was Roxy Music's first single?

12. Which group's debut L.P. was 1985's *Virgins and Philistines*?

13. Which group recorded the 1979 album *The Crack*?

14. In which year was Bootsy Collins born?

15. Which group had a hit in 1977 with the single *Black Betty*?

ANSWERS 1. 1942 **2.** Leonard Cohen **3.** Edinburgh **4.** 1947 **5.** John Cale **6.** Chumbawamba **7.** Charlie Watts **8.** Julian Cope **9.** 1955 **10.** Sheffield **11.** Virginia Plain **12.** The Colourfield **13.** The Ruts **14.** 1951 **15.** Ram Jam.

GEOGRAPHY

1. What is Holy Island, off the coast of Northumberland, also called?

2. Which is the largest island of Japan?

3. Which country was renamed the Democratic Republic of Congo in 1997?

4. Yell is in which Scottish island group?

5. The Welland Ship Canal connects which two of the Great Lakes of North America?

6. Which is the larger island - North Uist or South Uist?

7. Which is the longest river in France?

8. The town of Sault Ste. Marie, Canada is connected by bridge to which town in Michigan?

9. What is the name of the Italian island in the Tyrrhenian Sea made famous in a novel by Dumas?

10. What are Nova Scotia, New Brunswick and Prince Edward Island collectively known as?

11. Which is the largest city in Alaska?

12. In which European country is the province of Albacete?

13. What is the capital of New York state?

14. On which river is the Belgian seaport of Antwerp?

15. On which river does the Devon tourist town of Barnstaple stand?

ANSWERS 1. Lindisfarne 2. Honshu 3. Zaire 4. Shetlands 5. Erie and Ontario 6. North Uist 7. River Loire 8. Sault Ste. Marie 9. Monte Cristo 10. The Maritime Provinces 11. Anchorage 12. Spain 13. Albany 14. River Scheldt 15. River Taw.

GENERAL KNOWLEDGE

1. What is the dominant religion in Liberia?

2. The greenish-blue colour 'Alice blue' takes its name from the daughter of which U.S. president?

3. In which year did 'The El', New York's elevated railway, close down?

4. What sort of creature is a bobolink?

5. What was CAMRA's champion beer of the year in 1982 & 1983?

6. Which author won the 1984 Guardian Children's Fiction Award?

7. From the young of which animal is the leather chevrette made?

8. How many seats did the Liberal Party win in the 1945 election?

9. For which party did Gwynfor Evans win a 1966 by-election in Carmarthen?

10. In which year was the Torrey Canyon oil disaster?

11. Which London hotel won the Egon Ronay Hotel of the Year award in 1992?

12. In which year did Salman Rushdie win the 'Booker of Bookers'?

13. What is the main ingredient of chewing gum?

14. Who did sculptor F.A. Bartholdi use as a model for the Statue of Liberty?

15. In which Canadian province is the village of Grand Pré?

ENTERTAINMENT

1. Who played Dr. Banner in the T.V. drama *The Incredible Hulk*?

2. Who did Tony Robinson play in the T.V. comedy *Blackadder*?

3. In *Blake's 7* what was Blake's forename?

4. Who was the first host of the T.V. quiz *Blankety Blank*?

5. Which comic actor starred in the sitcom *Bless This House*?

6. In which 1935 film does Groucho Marx play Otis B. Driftwood?

7. Which gangster did Faye Dunaway play in a 1967 Arthur Penn film?

8. Who played 'a Girl' in the 1937 film *One Hundred Men and a Girl*?

9. Who played Tom Hagen in the film *The Godfather*?

10. Which cartoon character did Shelley Duvall play in a 1980 Robert Altman film?

11. Which actor is boss of Malpaso Productions?

12. Who directed the 1961 film *Victim*?

13. Who directed the 1995 film *Steal Big, Steal Little*?

14. Who played Kevin McMaxford in the 1997 film *Spice World*?

15. Which 1951 film was based on the novel *Coup de Grace*?

ANSWERS 1. Bill Bixby **2.** Baldrick **3.** Roj **4.** Terry Wogan **5.** Sid James **6.** A Night at the Opera **7.** Bonnie Parker **8.** Deanna Durbin **9.** Robert Duvall **10.** Olive Oyl **11.** Clint Eastwood **12.** Basil Dearden **13.** Andrew Davis **14.** Barry Humphries **15.** Sirocco.

THE ULTIMATE PUB QUIZ BOOK

SPORT

1. Which horse won the British Triple Crown in 1970?

2. Before 1994, when was the last time there was no baseball World Series?

3. What did Indian Joe win in 1980?

4. Who succeeded Allan Border as Australian Test cricket captain?

5. From which club did Aston Villa sign Shaun Teale in 1991?

6. In which Australian state was cricketer Merv Hughes born?

7. What were the forenames of the cricketer C.B. Fry?

8. At what sport did Rollie Fingers achieve prominence?

9. Who won the British Open golf tournament in 1947?

10. In which year was Martina Navratilova born?

11. What nationality was the 1991 British Open golf tournament winner?

12. How many times did Jacky Ickx win the Le Mans 24 hour race?

13. Which baseball player was nicknamed 'Mr. October'?

14. What is Kevin Keegan's first name?

15. In which city was Hana Mandlikova born?

ANSWERS 1. Nijinsky **2.** 1904 **3.** The Greyhound Derby **4.** Mark Taylor **5.** Bournemouth **6.** Victoria **7.** Charles Burgess **8.** Baseball **9.** Fred Daly **10.** 1956 **11.** Australian **12.** Six **13.** Reggie Jackson **14.** Joseph **15.** Prague.

POP MUSIC

1. Which group recorded the 1972 album *Caravanserai*?

2. In which year were the group The Cocteau Twins formed?

3. From which country do the group Shonen Knife come?

4. What was Cockney Rebel's follow-up single to *Judy Teen* in the U.K. charts?

5. What nationality is Jane Siberry?

6. Which singer recorded the 1974 album *I Can Stand a Little Rain*?

7. In which year did Phil Lynott die?

8. What was the second album by The Clash?

9. To whom is singer Siouxsie Sioux married?

10. In which year was Eric Clapton born?

11. What was the title of the debut L.P. by the Slits?

12. Which group recorded the 1979 album *Half Machine Lip Moves*?

13. Which group recorded the 1969 album *Stand!*?

14. What was the Edgar Broughton Band's debut L.P.?

15. Who was bass player in the group The Small Faces?

ANSWERS 1. Santana **2.** 1982 **3.** Japan **4.** Mr. Soft **5.** Canadian **6.** Joe Cocker **7.** 1986 **8.** Give 'Em Enough Rope **9.** Budgie **10.** 1945 **11.** Cut **12.** Chrome **13.** Sly and the Family Stone **14.** Wasa Wasa **15.** Ronnie Lane.

HISTORY

1. In which month of 1963 did Harold Macmillan resign as P.M.?

2. In which month of 1960 did the *Lady Chatterley's Lover* trial begin?

3. What title did Cardinal Albino Luciani take in 1978?

4. Brigadier Murtala Mohammed became head of which African state following a military coup in 1975?

5. Who won the Jamaican general election in December 1976?

6. Austria joined the E.U. on January 1st of which year?

7. How old was Red Rum when he died in 1995?

8. In which year was Yitzhak Rabin assassinated?

9. How did Louis XVI of France die?

10. In which year did Beethoven die?

11. In which year did Chaucer die?

12. In which century did the Venerable Bede die?

13. Who was deselected as Tory M.P. for Reigate in January 1997?

14. How many seats did the Liberal Democrats win at the 1997 election?

15. Which Tory M.P. for Beaconsfield resigned in 1997 over the cash-for-questions affair?

ANSWERS 1. October **2.** October **3.** Pope John Paul I **4.** Nigeria **5.** Michael Manley **6.** 1995 **7.** 30 **8.** 1995 **9.** He was beheaded **10.** 1827 **11.** 1100 **12.** 8th **13.** Sir George Gardiner **14.** 46 **15.** Tim Smith.

GENERAL KNOWLEDGE

1. What nationality was novelist Pär Lagerkvist?

2. In which year was the first by-election victory for the S.D.P.?

3. Of which country was Joseph Chifley prime minister from 1945-49?

4. Who wrote the science fiction novel *Ringpull*?

5. To whom did the Crime Writers' Association award the Diamond Dagger in 1993?

6. Which book won the William Hill Sports Book of the Year award in 1992?

7. What do you do if you grangerize a book?

8. Which entertainer was voted Young Magician of the Year 1981 by the Magic Circle?

9. What is the name given to the world memory championships organized by the Brains Trust?

10. Which national award did Irene Hall of Blackburn win in 1993?

11. What was awarded the Museum of the Year title in 1974?

12. Which writer coined the word 'chortle'?

13. Who directed the film *Star Wars*?

14. In which year was the Ballet Rambert founded?

15. What type of fruit is named after Maria Ann Smith?

ANSWERS 1. Swedish **2.** 1981 **3.** Australia **4.** Jeff Noon **5.** Ellis Peters **6.** Fever Pitch by Nick Hornby **7.** Illustrate it by inserting drawings taken from other works **8.** Andrew O'Connor **9.** Memoriad **10.** Milkwoman of the Year **11.** National Motor Museum in Beaulieu **12.** Lewis Carroll **13.** George Lucas **14.** 1930 **15.** An apple (Granny Smith).

ENTERTAINMENT

1. Who did Dan Blocker play in the T.V. show *Bonanza*?

2. *Barnacle Bill* is the theme music of which children's show?

3. Who played *Andy Capp* in the T.V. version of the comic strip?

4. Who played Rocky Holeczek in the 1995 film *Roommates*?

5. Who played the title role in the 1975 film *Rooster Cogburn*?

6. Who directed the film *Rosencrantz and Guildenstern are Dead* from his own play?

7. Who directed the 1965 film comedy *Rotten to the Core*?

8. Who directed the 1989 film *She-Devil*?

9. Which actor is conned into becoming *The Sheriff of Fractured Jaw* in the 1958 film?

10. Who directed and starred in the 1924 film *Sherlock, Jr.*?

11. Who directed the 1997 film *Scream 2*?

12. Which 1955 film tells the tale of the ship *Ergenstrasse*?

13. Who played Peter Loew in the 1988 film *Vampire's Kiss*?

14. Who directed the 1996 film *The Van*?

15. Who did Jonathan Rhys Meyers play in the 1998 film *Velvet Goldmine*?

SPORT

1. What relationship is Christy O'Connor Jr. to Christy O'Connor?

2. Who was world archery champion in 1979?

3. Who was the first Spaniard to win a tennis Grand Slam singles title?

4. In which county was snooker player Dennis Taylor born?

5. With whom did Marco van Basten begin his soccer career?

6. Who was men's Olympic 100m champion in 1980?

7. Where were the first 12 British Open golf tournaments held?

8. How many times have Ipswich Town won the F.A. Cup?

9. What nationality was the first individual speedway world champion?

10. For which Japanese football team did Gary Lineker play?

11. Who did Yorkshire sign as their overseas player in the 1995 cricket season?

12. Which man won the 1994 Berlin marathon?

13. Who won snooker's 1994 Regal Masters title?

14. Which golfer won the 1994 Lancôme Trophy?

15. Who was the 1980 Olympic men's 800m champion?

ANSWERS 1. Nephew **2.** Darrell Pace **3.** Manuel Santana **4.** County Tyrone **5.** Ajax **6.** Allan Wells **7.** Prestwick **8.** Once **9.** Australian **10.** Nagoya Grampus Eight **11.** Michael Bevan **12.** Antonio Pinto **13.** Ken Doherty **14.** Vijay Singh **15.** Steve Ovett.

POP MUSIC

1. In which year was singer Patti Smith born?

2. Who recorded the 1976 album *Troubadour*?

3. In which year did The Smiths disband?

4. About which musician was the 1976 play *The Stars That Play With Laughing Sam's Dice*?

5. Which group recorded the 1988 album *Daydream Nation*?

6. What was Bill Harkleroad called in Captain Beefheart's Magic Band?

7. Which group recorded the 1988 album *A Little Man And a House And the Whole World Window*?

8. Which group recorded the 1980 album *Underwater Moonlight*?

9. In which city were the Soup Dragons formed?

10. What was the debut album of Nick Cave and the Bad Seeds?

11. What is guitarist Pete Kember better known as?

12. Bob 'the Bear' Hite and Al 'Blind Owl' Wilson formed which group in 1966?

13. Who recorded the album *Journeys to Glory*?

14. Which German group recorded the 1971 album *Tago Mago*?

15. Which group recorded the 1974 album *Kimono My House*?

ANSWERS 1. 1946 2. J.J. Cale 3. 1987 4. Jimi Hendrix 5. Sonic Youth 6. Zoot Horn Rollo 7. The Cardiacs 8. The Soft Boys 9. Glasgow 10. From Her to Eternity 11. Sonic Boom 12. Canned Heat 13. Spandau Ballet 14. Can 15. Sparks.

WORDS

1. What in New Zealand is a kumera?

2. Why might you cook using 'garam masala'?

3. What is the name of the mass of cartilage beneath the tongue in a dog?

4. What is a hornbeam - a bird or a tree?

5. What in printing does the abbreviation oct. mean?

6. The pub sign 'Goat and Compasses' is a corruption of what phrase?

7. What would you do with a 'lyra viol'?

8. Which saint is sometimes known as the Bishop of Hippo?

9. What is geoponics?

10. How many sides does an octagon have?

11. What sort of creature is a godwit?

12. What in the textile industry is a swatch?

13. What were fuggers?

14. What is the Latin word for vinegar?

15. What creature is known in Scottish dialect as clipshears?

1. A sweet potato 2. It is a mixture of spices 3. Lytta 4. A tree 5. Octavo 6. God en-compasses (us) 7. Play it - it is a musical instrument 8. St. Augustine 9. The science of agriculture 10. Eight 11. A bird 12. A sample of cloth, or book containing same 13. German merchants 14. Acetum 15. Earwig.

GENERAL KNOWLEDGE

1. How many seats did the Liberals get in the 1979 election?

2. Which artist won the Melody Maker Jazz Musician of the Year award 1949-52?

3. Henri Christophe was king of which country from 1811-20?

4. What, in Australian slang, is a 'John Hop'?

5. Who won the Member to Watch award at the 1984 Parliamentarian of the Year luncheon?

6. What was awarded the Museum of the Year accolade in 1977?

7. Which world title did Magnus Ver Magnusson win in 1991?

8. Who won Pipe Smoker of the Year award in 1993?

9. What type of fruit is an amarelle?

10. Which award did Graeme Witty win from 1988-92?

11. In which century did lexicographer Dr. Johnson live?

12. Which bird's Latin name is *Bubo bubo*?

13. Who won the 1974 Queen's Gold Medal for Poetry?

14. To whom did the Crime Writer's Association award the Diamond Dagger in 1992?

15. What would you do with a bobotie?

ANSWERS 1. 11 **2.** Johnny Dankworth **3.** Haiti **4.** A policeman **5.** Malcolm Rifkind **6.** The Ironbridge Gorge Museum in Telford **7.** World's Strongest Man **8.** Rod Hull **9.** Cherry **10.** British National Champion Ploughman (Conventional Ploughing) **11.** 18th **12.** Eagle owl **13.** Ted Hughes **14.** Leslie Charteris **15.** Eat it - it's a dish of curried mincemeat.

ENTERTAINMENT

1. Which actress is the second wife of film director Blake Edwards?

2. Which Shakespearean character did Douglas Fairbanks play in his first talking picture?

3. Which actress played the mother of *Forrest Gump*?

4. Who played W.C. Fields in the 1976 film *W.C. Fields and Me*?

5. The 1980s drama *By the Sword Divided* centred on which war?

6. Who did Freddie Jones play in the 1960 drama series *The Caesars*?

7. Who played Cagney in the pilot for the T.V. show *Cagney and Lacey*?

8. Who was the first chairman of the T.V. show *Call My Bluff*?

9. Who was the fishmonger in the children's T.V. series *Camberwick Green*?

10. Who was the first presenter of ITV's *Candid Camera*?

11. Who directed the 1935 film *The Skin Game*?

12. Who played underground cartoonist C.C. Drood in the 1987 film *Slam Dance*?

13. Who directed and starred in the 1973 comedy film *Sleeper*?

14. Who directed the 1989 film *Soursweet*?

15. Who played Nellie Forbush in the 1958 film *South Pacific*?

ANSWERS 1. Julie Andrews **2.** Petruchio **3.** Sally Field **4.** Rod Steiger **5.** The English Civil War **6.** Claudius **7.** Loretta Swit **8.** Robin Ray **9.** Mr. Carraway **10.** Bob Monkhouse **11.** Alfred Hitchcock **12.** Tom Hulce **13.** Woody Allen **14.** Timothy Mo **15.** Mitzi Gaynor.

SPORT

1. Which baseball team won the 1990 World Series?

2. When was cricket's Benson and Hedges Cup first held?

3. In which year was the Tour de France first won by a non-Frenchman?

4. For which Premier League club did footballer Karl-Heinz Riedle play in the 1998/9 season?

5. Who did Great Britain play in the 1995 Davis Cup first round?

6. From which club did Wimbledon sign Efan Ekoku?

7. Who finished in the top 15 of both the 1994 bowling and batting averages?

8. Which horse won the 1994 Cesarewitch?

9. Which horse won the 1994 Prix de l'Arc de Triomphe?

10. Which horse won the 1990 St. Leger?

11. From what country do the team Trabzonspor hail?

12. Where were the 25th Summer Olympics held?

13. Who were the last British winners of the UEFA Cup?

14. What did *Reliance*, in 1903 and *Weatherly*, in 1962, win?

15. Who was women's World Cup Alpine skiing champion from 1971-75?

ANSWERS 1. Cincinnati Reds **2.** 1972 **3.** 1909 **4.** Liverpool **5.** Slovakia **6.** Norwich **7.** Chris Lewis **8.** Captain's Guest **9.** Carnegie **10.** Snurge **11.** Turkey **12.** Barcelona **13.** Tottenham Hotspur **14.** The America's Cup **15.** Annemarie Moser-Pröll.

POP MUSIC

1. In which city did The Specials form in 1977?

2. Which funk group's debut single was *Rigor Mortis*?

3. In which year was Phil Spector born?

4. In which city did Cabaret Voltaire form?

5. In which year did Squeeze form?

6. Which two members of the Byrds left to form the Flying Burrito Brothers?

7. Who recorded the 1971 album *Please to See the King*?

8. Which punk group recorded the single *Orgasm Addict*?

9. Who recorded the 1970 album *Gasoline Alley*?

10. On which studio album does Kate Bush's song *Breathing* appear?

11. What is singer Gordon Sumner better known as?

12. What was the title of Buffalo Tom's debut album in 1989?

13. Which songwriter had a Top 40 hit in 1992 with *God's Great Banana Skin*?

14. In which country was Jackson Browne born?

15. In which year was Bruce Springsteen born?

ANSWERS 1. Coventry **2.** Cameo **3.** 1940 **4.** Sheffield **5.** 1974 **6.** Chris Hillman and Gram Parsons **7.** Steeleye Span **8.** The Buzzcocks **9.** Rod Stewart **10.** Never Forever **11.** Sting **12.** Buffalo Tom **13.** Chris Rea **14.** Germany **15.** 1949.

SCIENCE

1. How many light years from Earth are the Pleiades?

2. What is the most common sedimentary rock?

3. The rudimentary classification of particles is divided into four groups:- gauge bosons, baryons, leptons and which other?

4. Does a tapeworm have a gut?

5. In which year was the Omega Particle discovered?

6. During which period of geological time was the Pliocene epoch?

7. To which phylum do sponges belong?

8. Which element's symbol is W?

9. How many grains are there in a pennyweight?

10. What measurement is equal to 7.92 inches?

11. What is a rognon?

12. How many grams of fibre per 100 grams are there in butter beans?

13. Of what is pteronophobia a fear?

14. Which vitamin is also called pyridoxine?

15. Of what is emerald a green transparent variety?

GENERAL KNOWLEDGE

1. Who won Melody Maker British Male Jazz Vocalist of the Year award 1962-65?

2. What nationality was the actress Eleonora Duse?

3. Who won the Pipe Smoker of the Year award in 1992?

4. The name of which island in the Bristol Channel derives from the Norse 'Puffin Island'?

5. Who became Great Britain's Prime Minister in 1979?

6. What was awarded the Museum of the Year title in 1991?

7. Who won 1972's *Mastermind* title?

8. What type of bird is a chukar?

9. In what year did pianist Scott Joplin die?

10. Who won the Member to Watch award at the 1985 Parliamentarian of the Year luncheon?

11. Who authored *The Lady of Shalott*?

12. Which river in England is known locally as the Granta?

13. What is the Indo-European language of modern Iran?

14. Who invented the saxophone?

15. Who won the 1965 Queen's Gold Medal for Poetry?

ANSWERS 1. Matt Monroe **2.** Italian **3.** Tony Benn **4.** Lundy **5.** Margaret Thatcher **6.** The National Railway Museum, York **7.** Nancy Wilkinson **8.** A partridge **9.** 1917 **10.** Simon Hughes **11.** Tennyson **12.** Cam **13.** Farsi **14.** Adolphe Sax **15.** Philip Larkin.

ENTERTAINMENT

1. Cut Throat Jake appeared in which animated children's T.V. series?

2. What did SPV stand for in *Captain Scarlet and the Mysterons*?

3. Who played Bertie Wooster in the 1965 T.V. series *The World of Wooster*?

4. Who played Mr. Waverly in *The Man from UNCLE* on T.V.?

5. Which former Miss USA was T.V.'s *Wonder Woman*?

6. Who played *Casanova* in the 1971 BBC2 series?

7. Who played Dr. Watson to Peter Cushing's Sherlock Holmes in a 1968 BBC drama series?

8. Who does George C. Scott think he is in the film *They Might Be Giants*?

9. Who plays a washed up horror film star in the 1968 film *Targets*?

10. Who directed the 1993 film *Super Mario Brothers*?

11. Who starred in the 1971 film *Support Your Local Gunfighter*?

12. What was the subtitle of the film *Star Trek III*?

13. Who directed the 1977 Bond film *The Spy Who Loved Me*?

14. Who directed the 1939 film *Stagecoach*?

15. Which comedian starred in the 1994 film *The Santa Clause*?

ANSWERS 1. Captain Pugwash 2. Spectrum Pursuit Vehicle 3. Ian Carmichael 4. Leo G. Carroll 5. Lynda Carter 6. Frank Finlay 7. Nigel Stock 8. Sherlock Holmes 9. Boris Karloff 10. Rocky Morton and Annabel Jankel 11. James Garner 12. The Search for Spock 13. Lewis Gilbert 14. John Ford 15. Tim Allen.

SPORT

1. Who won golf's 1994 Solheim Cup?

2. Who won the 1994 Skoda Grand Prix in snooker?

3. Who won the 1974 World Cup in football?

4. Which golfer won the 1994 Volvo Masters?

5. Which aborigine won a world boxing title in 1968?

6. Which U.S. basketball player was known as 'Dr. J'?

7. Which jockey's first classic ride was on High Top in 1972?

8. Which Olympic showjumper was arrested for drug smuggling in 1972?

9. How many metres wide is a basketball court?

10. Which American boxer was known as 'the Toy Bulldog'?

11. From what does the game 'pelota' take its name?

12. In which year were the first table tennis world championships held?

13. Who was the first American Professional Football Association president?

14. What is the less familiar name of the Davis Cup?

15. What were the names of the five losing yachts in the Americas Cup from 1899 to 1930?

ANSWERS 1. United States 2. John Higgins 3. West Germany 4. Bernhard Langer 5. Lionel Rose 6. Julius Erving 7. Willie Carson 8. Humberto Mariles 9. 15 10. Mickey Walker 11. The Spanish word for ball 12. 1927 13. Jim Thorpe 14. The International Lawn Tennis Challenge Trophy 15. Shamrock I, Shamrock II, Shamrock III, Shamrock IV and Shamrock V.

POP MUSIC

1. Which Jamaican singer featured on the 1991 single *She's a Woman* by Scritti Politti?

2. In which year was singer Arthur Brown of *Fire* fame born?

3. Who was the drummer with the group The Stone Roses?

4. Who was the vocalist in the Manchester band The Chameleons?

5. Who is the drummer in the Stranglers?

6. In which year was singer Tracy Chapman born?

7. Who was keyboard player in The Style Council?

8. What was the debut album of the group Cheap Trick?

9. In which city did Super Furry Animals form in 1993?

10. Which songwriter recorded the 1995 album *Is the Actor Happy*?

11. Who is the drummer in the group Supergrass?

12. From which country did the group The Chills come?

13. Which group recorded the 1987 album *Children of God*?

14. What is Big Star's *Third Album* also called?

15. Which group recorded the 1973 album *Bursting at the Seams*?

PEOPLE

1. What was French murderer Henri Desire Landru better known as?

2. What was the maiden name of show-jumper Lucinda Green?

3. What were the forenames of the Kray Brothers?

4. Who first drew the strip cartoon *Jane* in 1932?

5. What was the stage name of actress Gertrude Klasen?

6. Who played Ricky in *EastEnders*?

7. What was the middle name of painter L.S. Lowry?

8. Which cartoonist created the syndicated comic strip *Archie*?

9. Which T.V. cook is associated with Norwich City F.C.?

10. Which cartoonist created the comic book hero *Captain America*?

11. What was the name of the wife of radio quiz show host Wilfred Pickles?

12. What was the middle name of author J.B. Priestley?

13. Keith Cooper was the unlikely star of which T.V. documentary series?

14. Which feminist wrote the book *The Whole Woman*?

15. Who was the male star of the film *You've Got Mail*?

ANSWERS 1. Bluebeard 2. Lucinda Prior-Palmer 3. Ronnie and Reggie 4. Norman Pett 5. Gertrude Lawrence 6. Sid Owen 7. Stephen 8. Bob Montana 9. Delia Smith 10. Jack Kirby 11. Mabel 12. Boynton 13. The House 14. Germaine Greer 15. Tom Hanks.

GENERAL KNOWLEDGE

1. In which novel does the character Yossarian appear?

2. What would you do with a hanepoot in South Africa?

3. What is the largest of all living arthropods?

4. Which horse won the 1943 Epsom Derby?

5. What nationality was author André Malraux?

6. Who is the patron saint of Portugal?

7. Which jazz musician was nicknamed 'Prez'?

8. In which European country is the resort of Bergenz?

9. Who wrote the novel *I, Robot*?

10. What type of creature was captured by Hercules as his fourth labour?

11. In which U.S. state is the city of Akron?

12. In which year did Jack the Ripper kill seven prostitutes?

13. Who was British prime minister 1970-74?

14. What is the major religion of Malta?

15. With which woodwind instrument is Evelyn Rothwell associated?

ANSWERS 1. Catch-22 **2.** Make wine - it's a grape **3.** Lobster **4.** Straight Deal **5.** French **6.** St. George **7.** Lester Young **8.** Austria **9.** Isaac Asimov **10.** Boar **11.** Ohio **12.** 1888 **13.** Edward Heath **14.** Roman Catholic **15.** Oboe.